Dragon Eye
Volume 3

Kairi Fujiyama

Translated and adapted by Mari Morimoto

Lettered by North Market Street Graphics

DEL REY

Ballantine Books · New York

Dragon Eye volume 3 is a work of fiction. Names, characters, places, and incidents are the products of the author's imagination or are used fictitiously. Any resemblance to actual events, locales, or persons, living or dead, is entirely coincidental.

A Del Rey Books Trade Paperback Original

Published in the United States by Del Rey Books, an imprint of The Random House Publishing Group, a division of Random House, Inc., New York.

Publication rights arranged through Kodansha Ltd.

First published in Japan in 2006 by Kodansha Ltd., Tokyo

ISBN 978-0-345-49884-7

Printed in the United States of America

www.delreymanga.com

98765432

Translator/Adaptor: Mari Morimoto
Lettering: NMSG

Contents

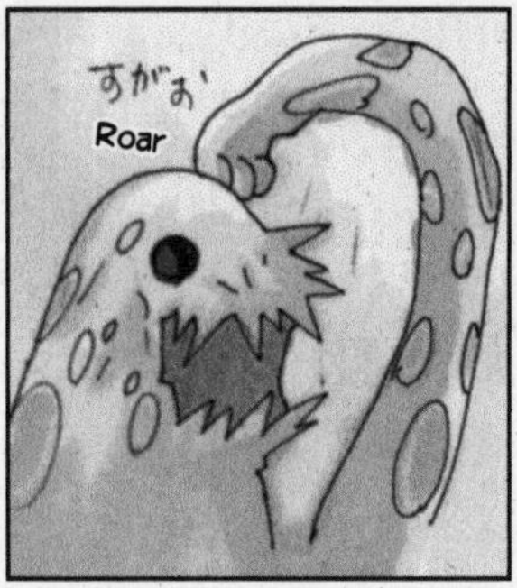
すがぉ
Roar

In the eighth tale, there appears a Dracule sprouting nameko mushrooms. The mushrooms are growing on it and are alive—so even if the Dracule is destroyed, they will not disappear. Thus, there are probably nameko mushrooms scattered all over the battlefield. The above picture is completely unrelated.

—Kairi Fujiyama

Honorifics Explained

Throughout the Del Rey Manga books, you will find Japanese honorifics left intact in the translations. For those not familiar with how the Japanese use honorifics and, more important, how they differ from American honorifics, we present this brief overview.

Politeness has always been a critical facet of Japanese culture. Ever since the feudal era, when Japan was a highly stratified society, use of honorifics—which can be defined as polite speech that indicates relationship or status—has played an essential role in the Japanese language. When you address someone in Japanese, an honorific usually takes the form of a suffix attached to one's name (example: "Asuna-san"), is used as a title at the end of one's name, or appears in place of the name itself (example: "Negi-sensei," or simply "Sensei!").

Honorifics can be expressions of respect or endearment. In the context of manga and anime, honorifics give insight into the nature of the relationship between characters. Many English translations leave out these important honorifics and therefore distort the feel of the original Japanese. Because Japanese honorifics contain nuances that English honorifics lack, it is our policy at Del Rey not to translate them. Here, instead, is a guide to some of the honorifics you may encounter in Del Rey Manga.

-*san:*   This is the most common honorific and is equivalent to Mr., Miss, Ms., or Mrs. It is the all-purpose honorific and can be used in any situation where politeness is required.

-*sama:*   This is one level higher than "-san." It is used to confer great respect.

-*dono:*   This comes from the word "tono," which means "lord." It is an even higher level than "-sama" and confers utmost respect.

-kun: This suffix is used at the end of boys' names to express familiarity or endearment. It is also sometimes used by men among friends, or when addressing someone younger or of a lower station.

-chan: This is used to express endearment, mostly toward girls. It is also used for little boys, pets, and even among lovers. It gives a sense of childish cuteness.

Bozu: This is an informal way to refer to a boy, similar to the English terms "kid" and "squirt."

Sempai/Senpai: This title suggests that the addressee is one's senior in a group or organization. It is most often used in a school setting, where underclassmen refer to their upperclassmen as "sempai." It can also be used in the workplace, such as when a newer employee addresses an employee who has seniority in the company.

Kohai: This is the opposite of "sempai" and is used toward underclassmen in school or newcomers in the workplace. It connotes that the addressee is of a lower station.

Sensei: Literally meaning "one who has come before," this title is used for teachers, doctors, or masters of any profession or art.

-[blank]: This is usually forgotten in these lists, but it is perhaps the most significant difference between Japanese and English. The lack of honorific means that the speaker has permission to address the person in a very intimate way. Usually, only family, spouses, or very close friends have this kind of permission. Known as *yobisute*, it can be gratifying when someone who has earned the intimacy starts to call one by one's name without an honorific. But when that intimacy hasn't been earned, it can be very insulting.

Dragon Eye

Kairi Fujiyama

3

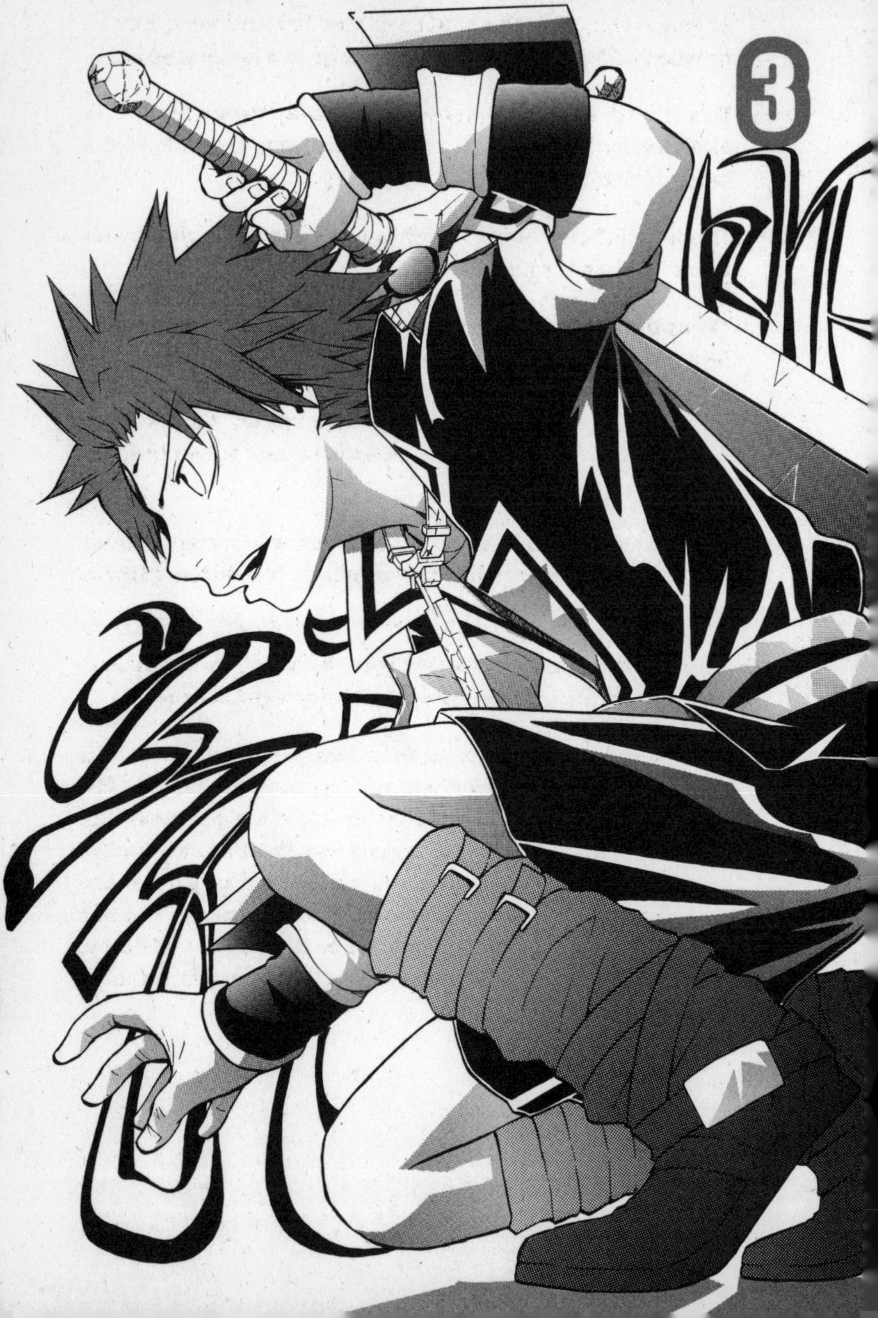

The Story of DRAGON EYE

龍眼物語

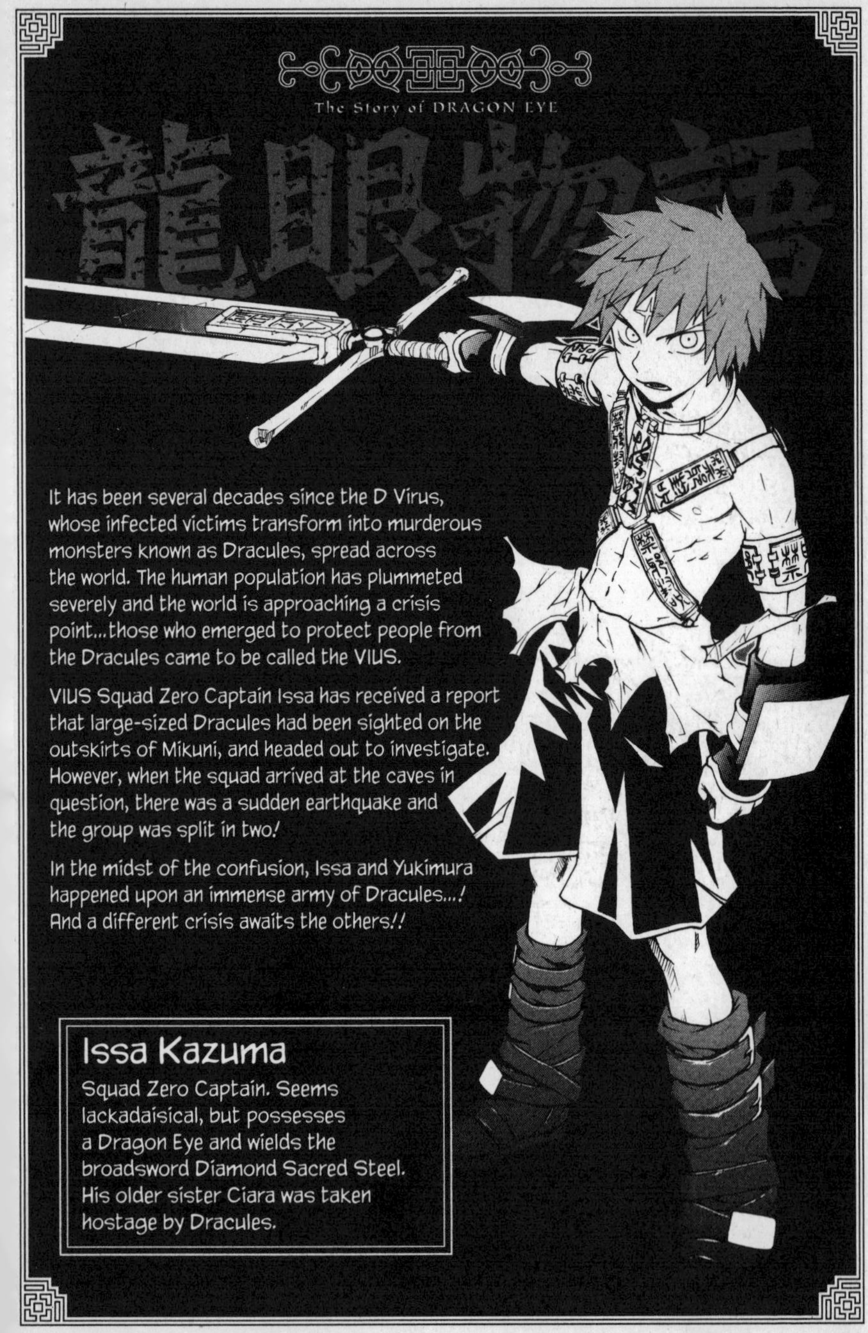

It has been several decades since the D Virus, whose infected victims transform into murderous monsters known as Dracules, spread across the world. The human population has plummeted severely and the world is approaching a crisis point...those who emerged to protect people from the Dracules came to be called the VIUS.

VIUS Squad Zero Captain Issa has received a report that large-sized Dracules had been sighted on the outskirts of Mikuni, and headed out to investigate. However, when the squad arrived at the caves in question, there was a sudden earthquake and the group was split in two!

In the midst of the confusion, Issa and Yukimura happened upon an immense army of Dracules...! And a different crisis awaits the others!!

Issa Kazuma

Squad Zero Captain. Seems lackadaisical, but possesses a Dragon Eye and wields the broadsword Diamond Sacred Steel. His older sister Ciara was taken hostage by Dracules.

Sōsei Yukimura

A former Squad Five member currently on tempo-
rary reassignment to Squad Zero. Believes Issa
killed his twin sister—and so he wields twin blades
in her memory and secretly plots for vengeance.

Leila Mikami

Newly inducted VIUS member. When she was
little both her parents were killed by Dracules,
but she alone survived. Her weapon of choice is
the katana blade.

Kajiyama

Volunteer helper on loan from Squad Two. Uses
rigged shells he invented himself that he fires
from his bazooka. Has served on a mission with
Issa once before.

Hibiki Masamune

Squad Six member. Volunteers as a helper on
missions of the short-handed Squad Zero.
Simultaneously wields the two giant blades he
carries on his back in two-sword style.

Nanbu

Volunteer helper on loan from Squad Seven.
Expert at unarmed combat, but can cast certain
spells as well. His short staff can serve to
enhance his spell power.

Sazanami

Volunteer helper on loan from Squad Three.
Wields a waistband whip containing spell power.

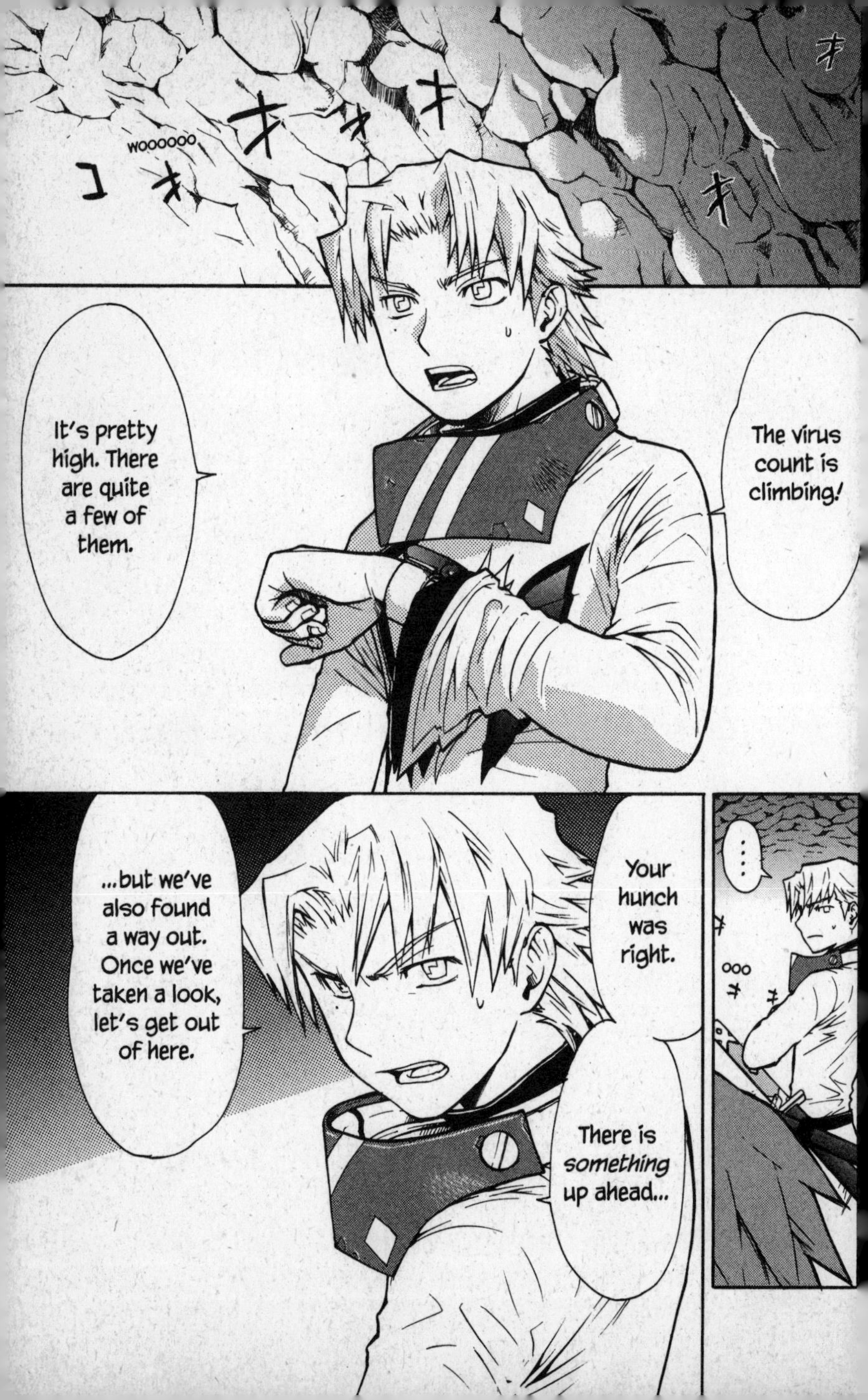
WOOOOOO
The virus count is climbing!
It's pretty high. There are quite a few of them.
....
OOO
Your hunch was right.
There is *something* up ahead...
...but we've also found a way out. Once we've taken a look, let's get out of here.

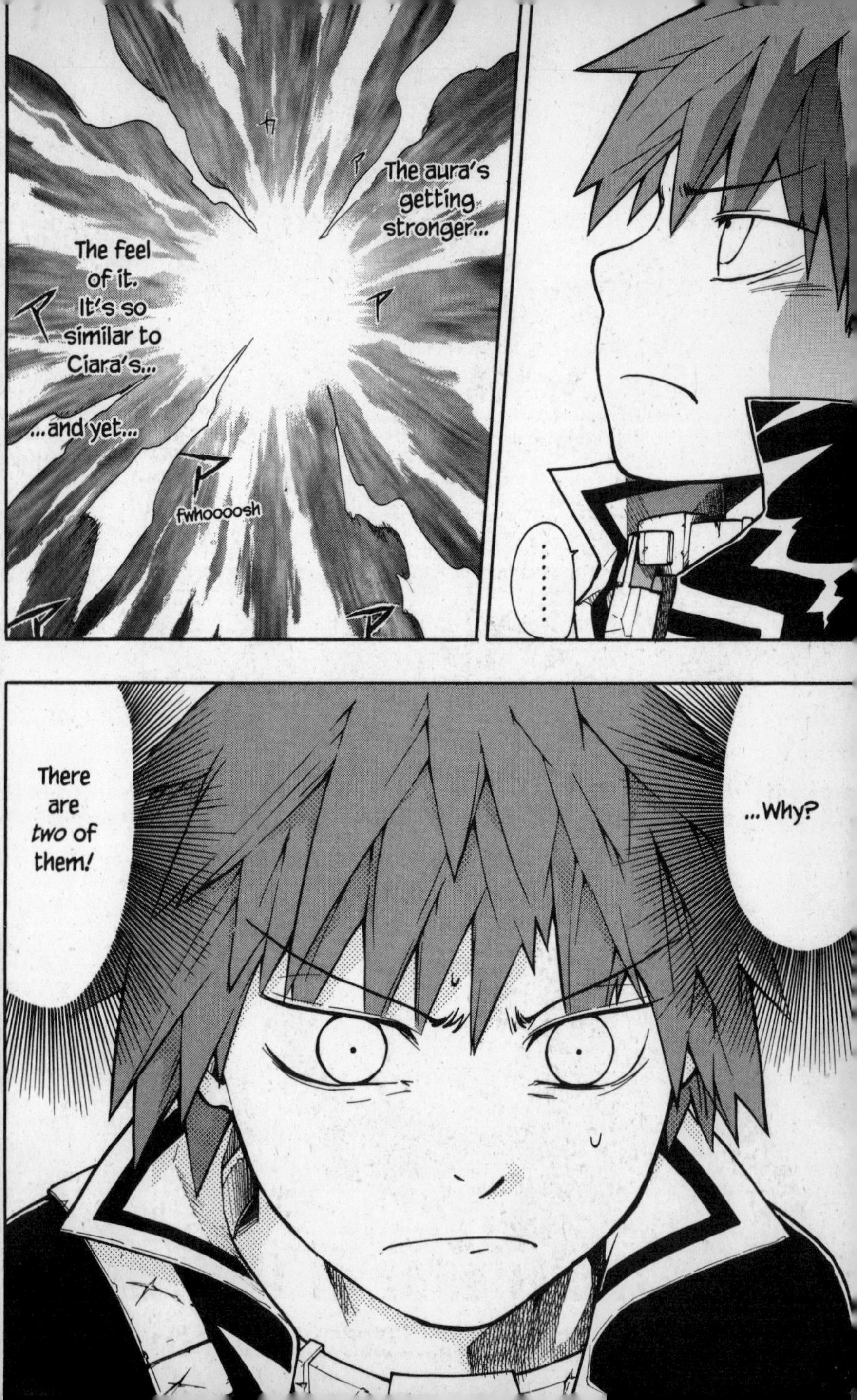
......
The aura's getting stronger...
The feel of it. It's so similar to Ciara's...
...and yet...
fwhoooosh
...Why?
There are *two* of them!

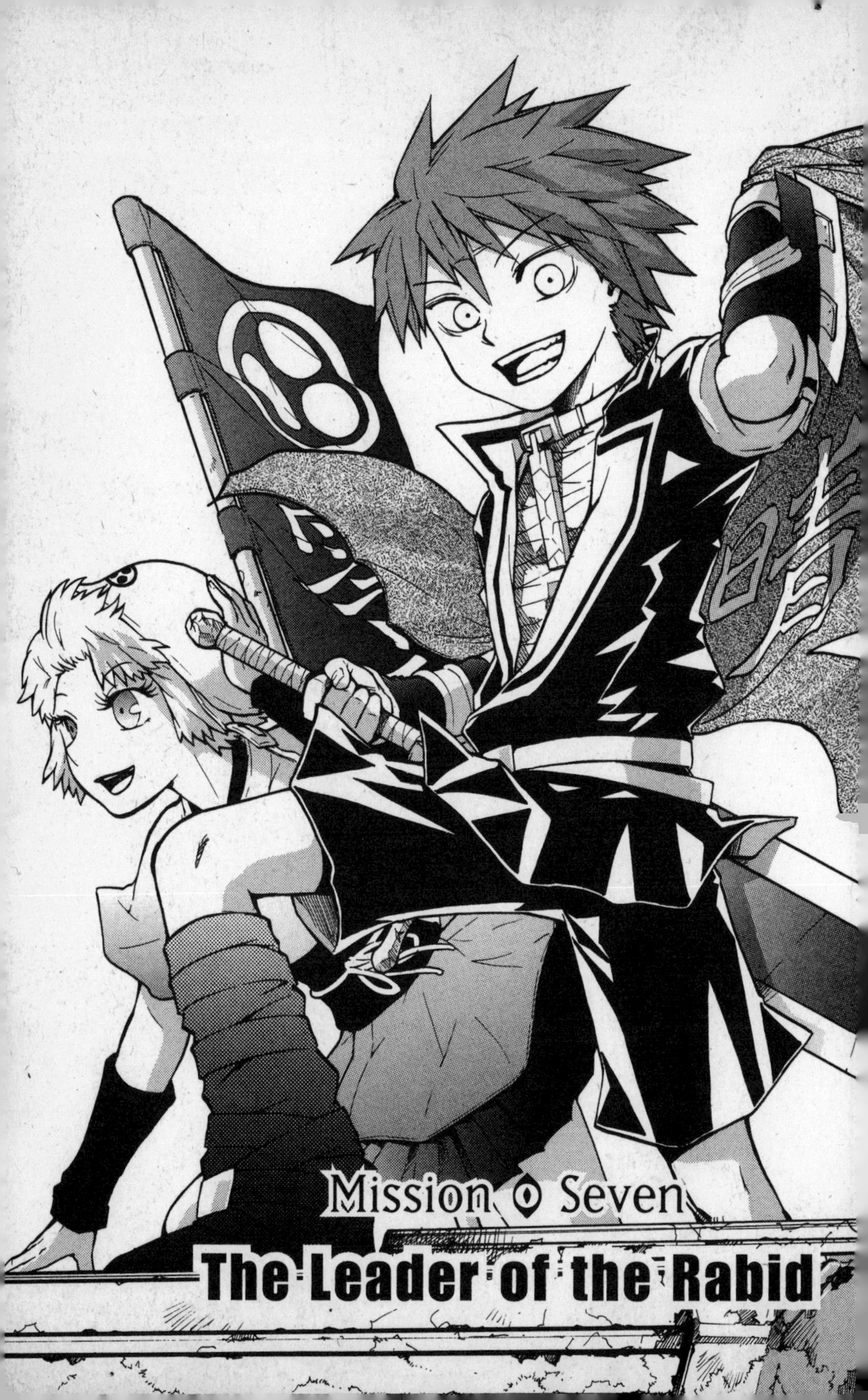
Mission Seven
The Leader of the Rabid

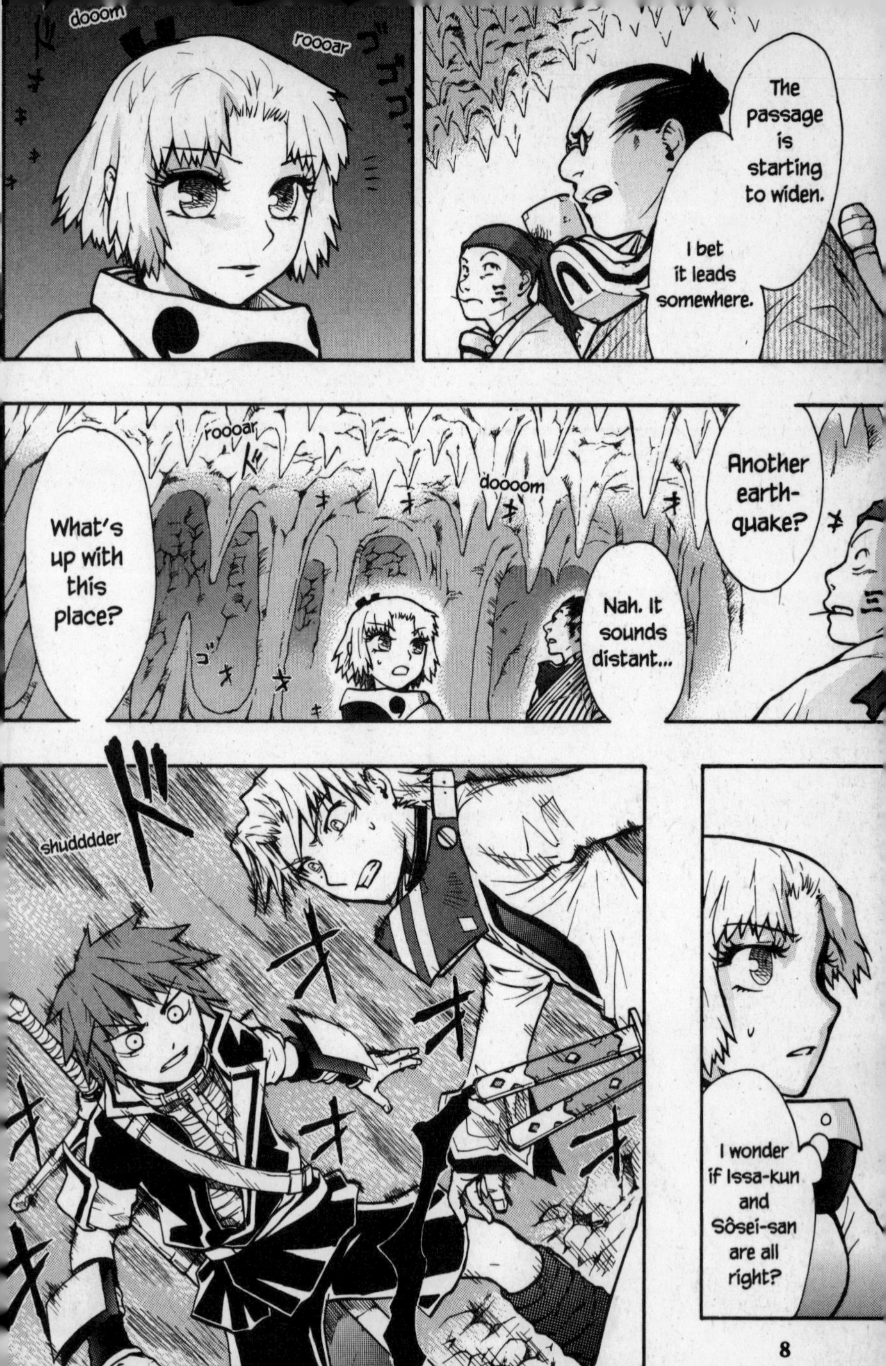
The passage is starting to widen.
I bet it leads somewhere.
dooom
roooar
Another earthquake?
Nah. It sounds distant...
roooar
doooom
What's up with this place?
I wonder if Issa-kun and Sôsei-san are all right?
shudddder

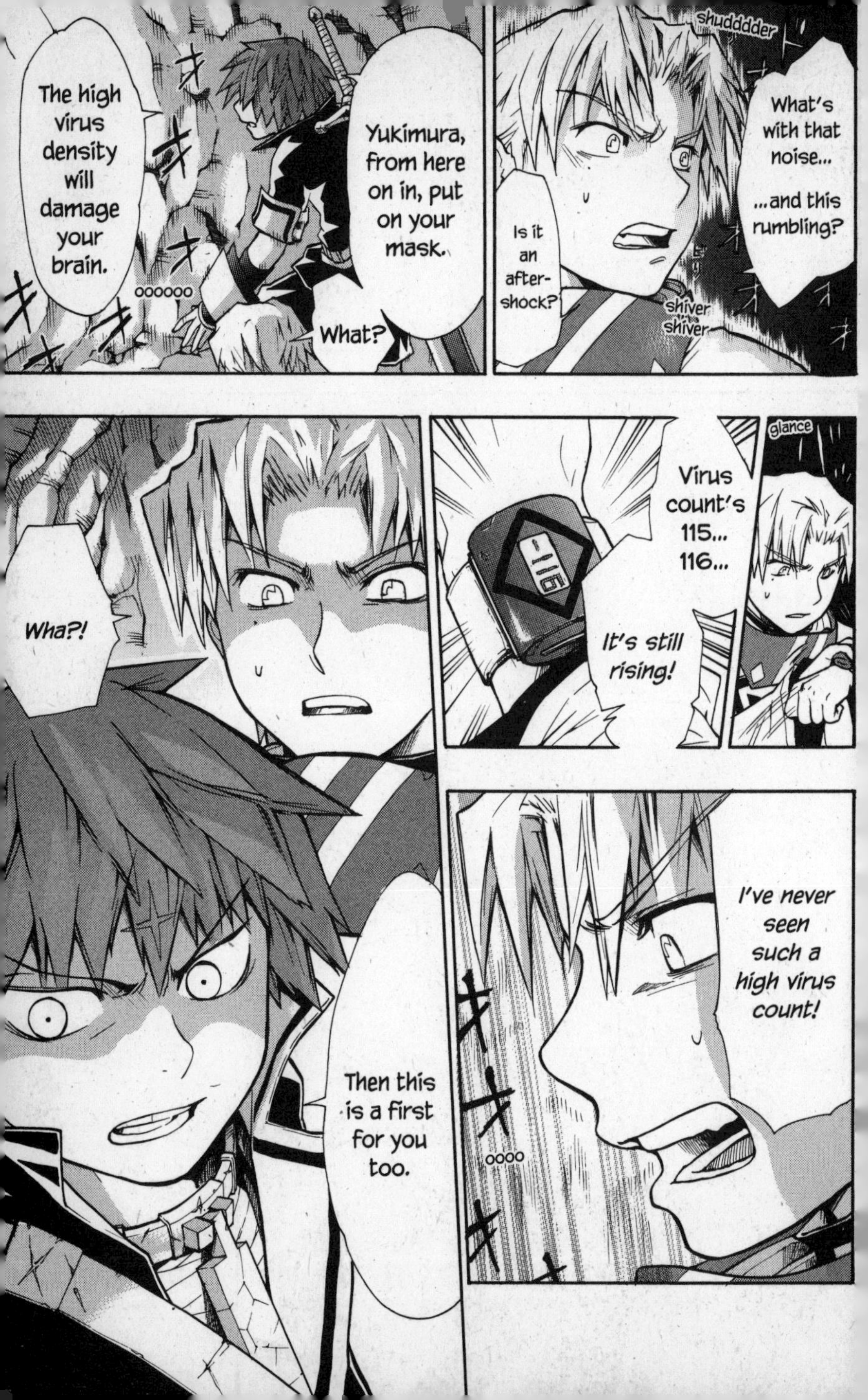
shudddder
What's with that noise...
...and this rumbling?
Is it an after-shock?
shiver shiver
Yukimura, from here on in, put on your mask.
The high virus density will damage your brain.
oooooo
What?
glance
Virus count's 115... 116...
It's still rising!
I've never seen such a high virus count!
oooo
Wha?!
Then this is a first for you too.

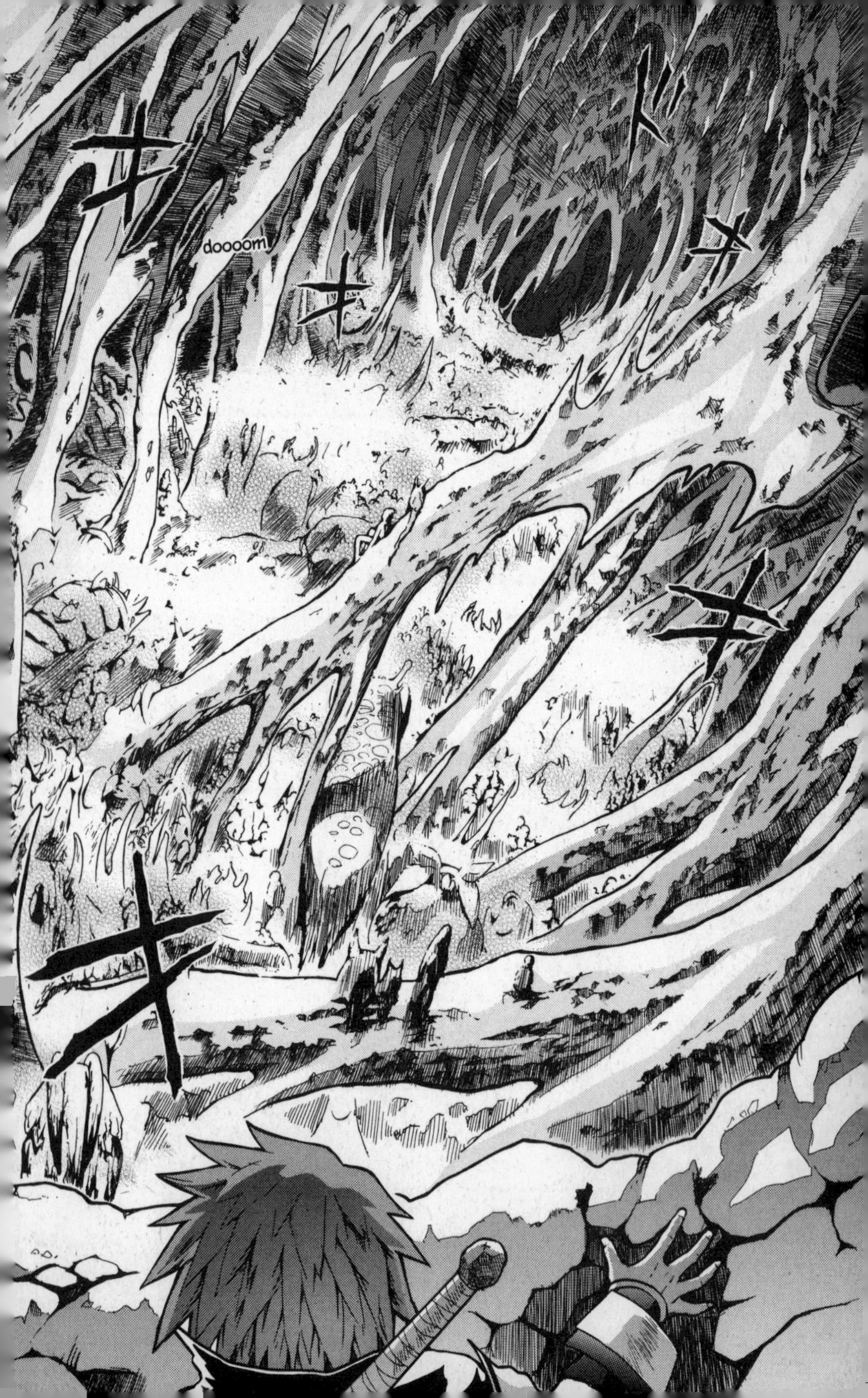
doooom

dooooooom

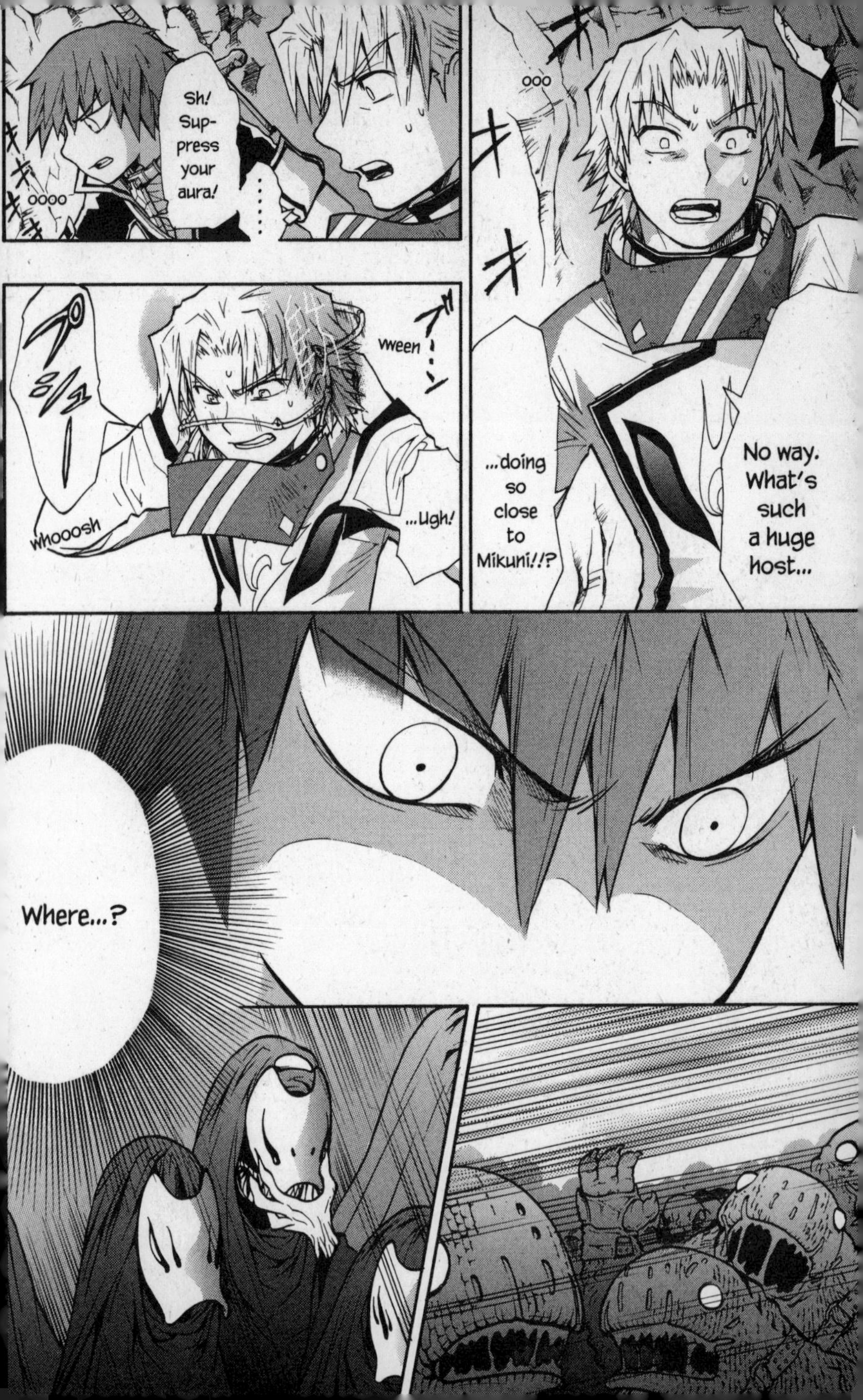
ooo
No way. What's such a huge host...
...doing so close to Mikuni!!?
Sh! Sup-press your aura!
oooo
......
vween
...Ugh!
whooosh
Where...?

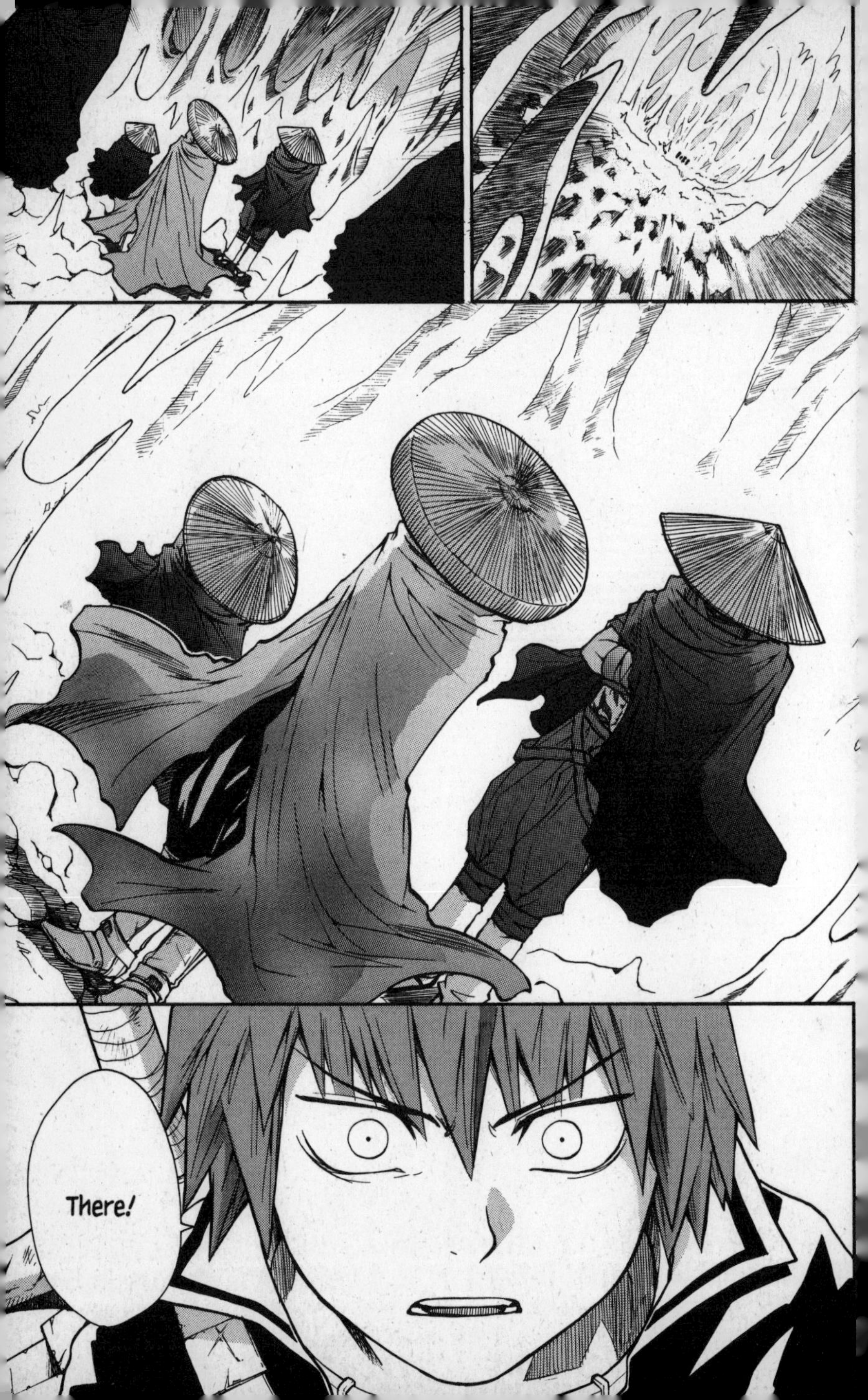
There!

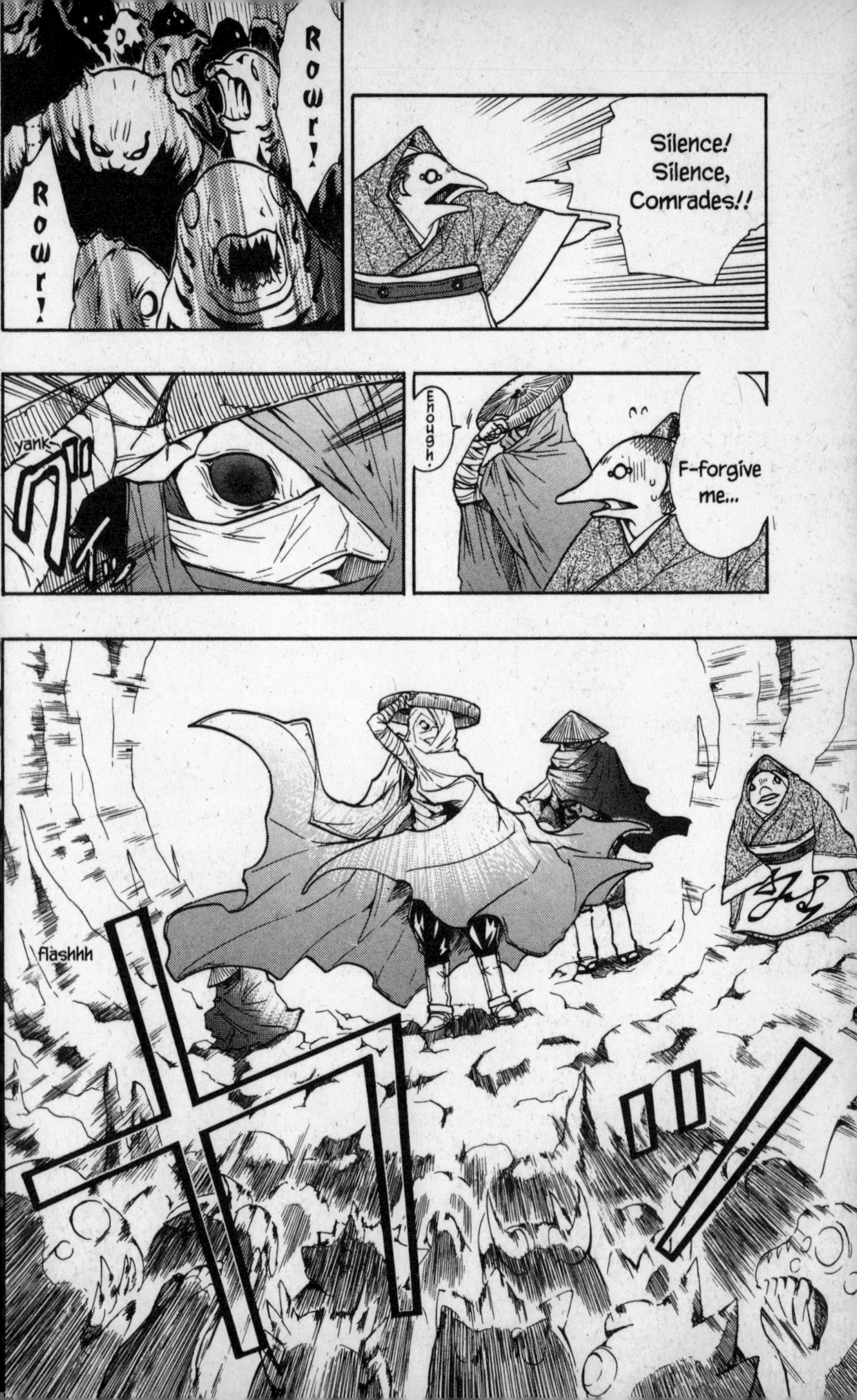
Silence! Silence, Comrades!!
Rowr!
Rowr!
Enough.
F-forgive me...
yank
flashhh

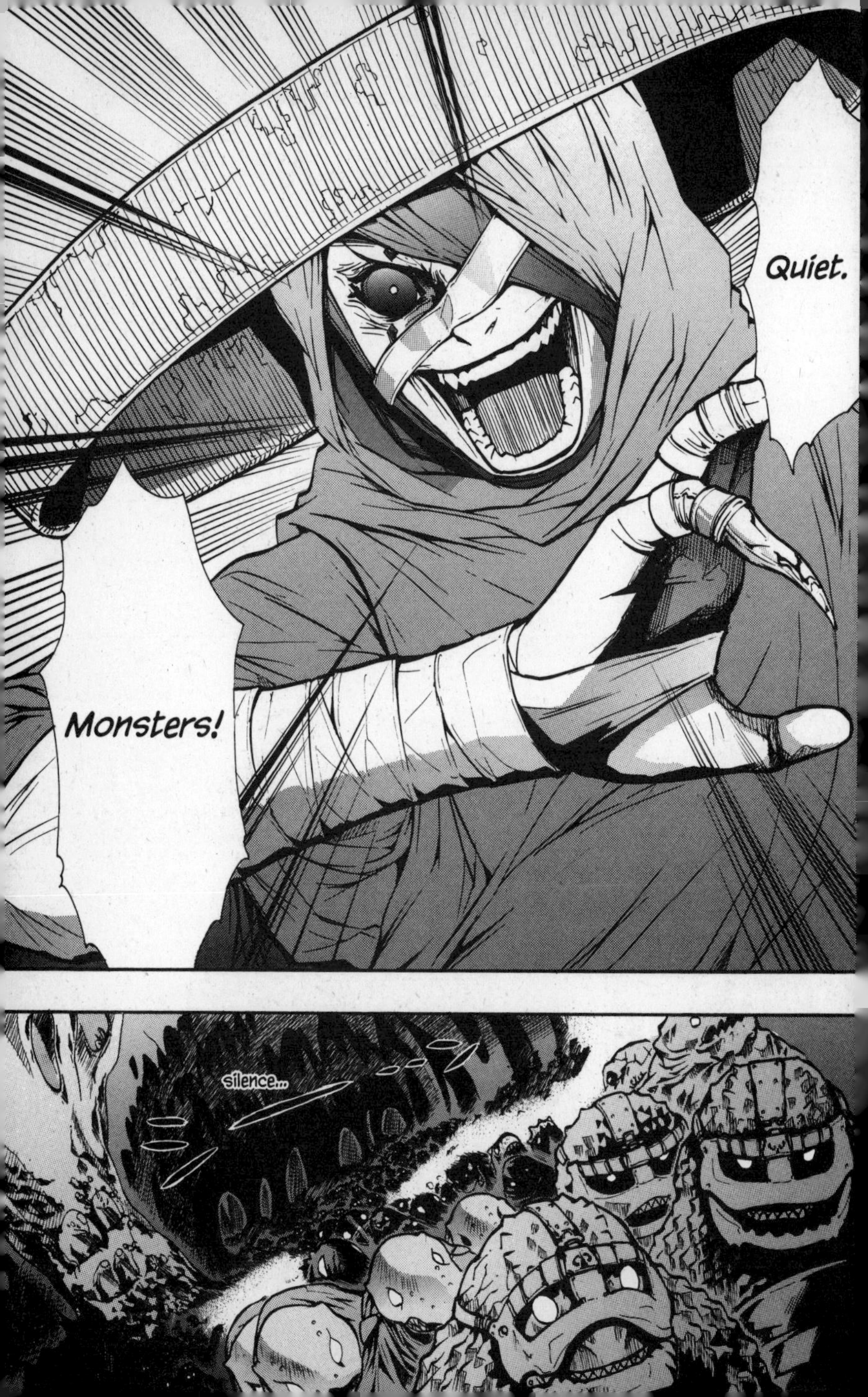
Quiet.
Monsters!
silence...

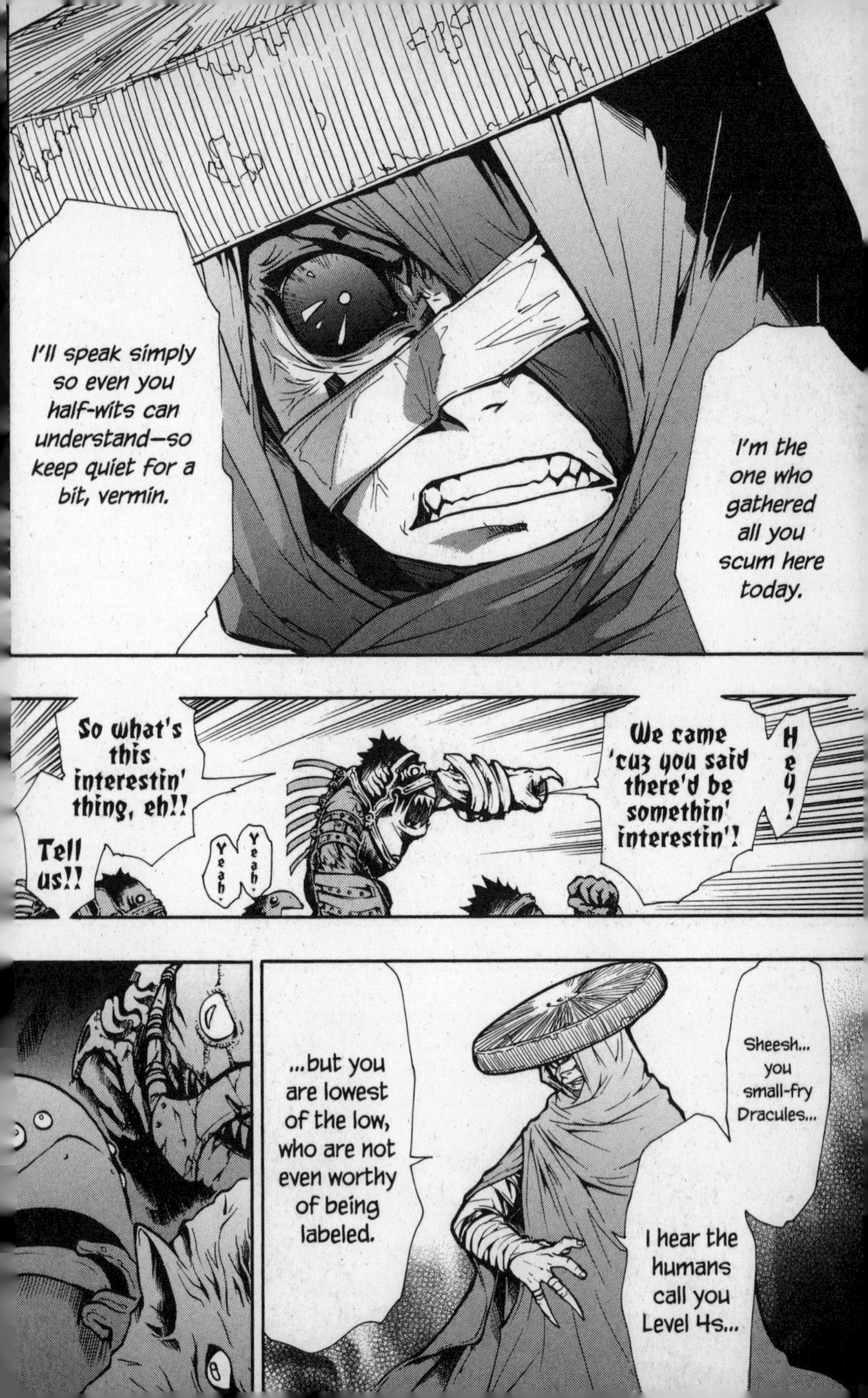
I'm the one who gathered all you scum here today.
I'll speak simply so even you half-wits can understand—so keep quiet for a bit, vermin.
Hey!
We came 'cuz you said there'd be somethin' interestin'!
Yeah.
Yeah.
So what's this interestin' thing, eh!!
Tell us!!
Sheesh... you small-fry Dracules...
I hear the humans call you Level 4s...
...but you are lowest of the low, who are not even worthy of being labeled.

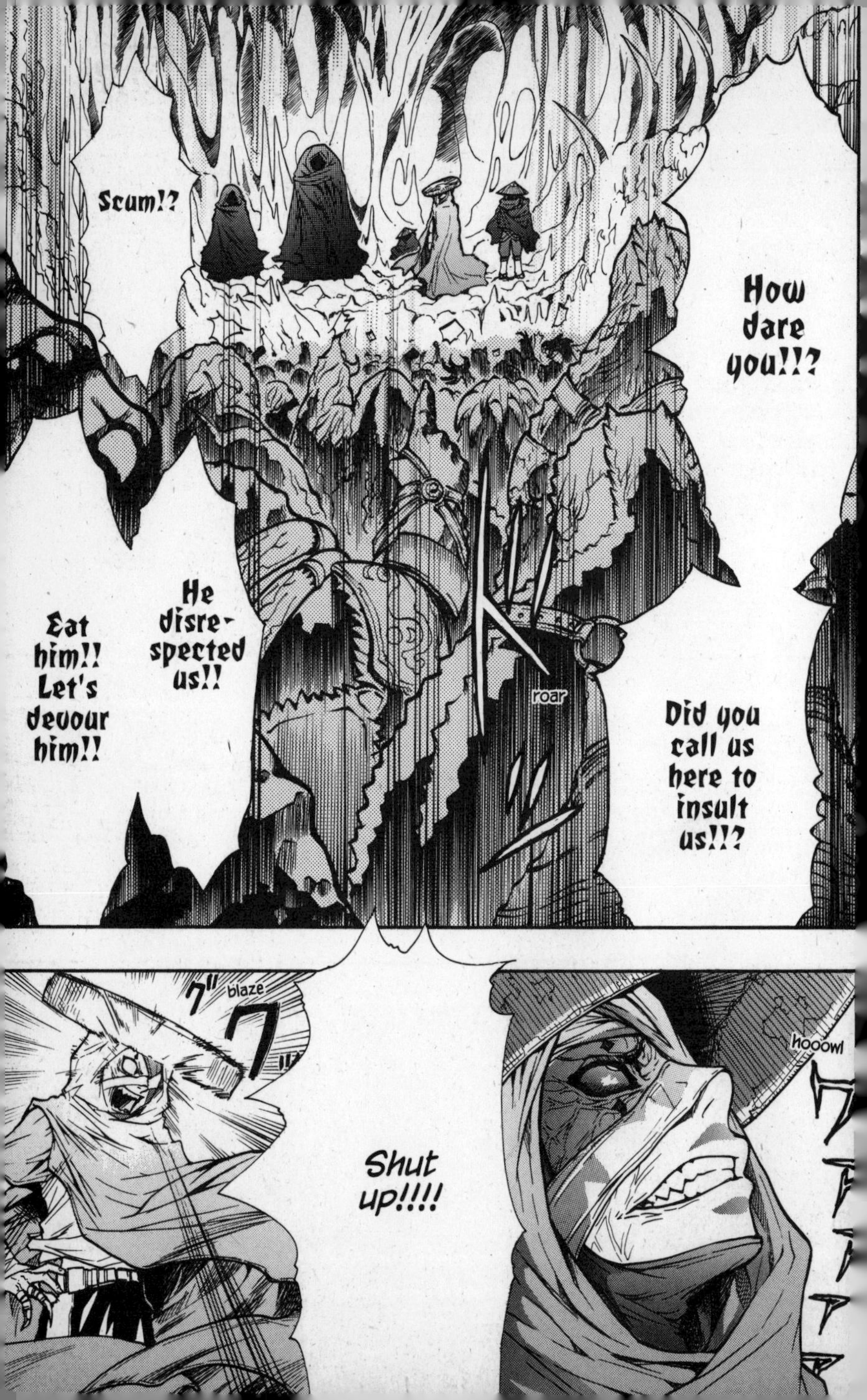
How dare you!!?
Scum!?
Did you call us here to insult us!!?
roar
He disre-spected us!!
Eat him!! Let's devour him!!
hooowl
Shut up!!!!
blaze

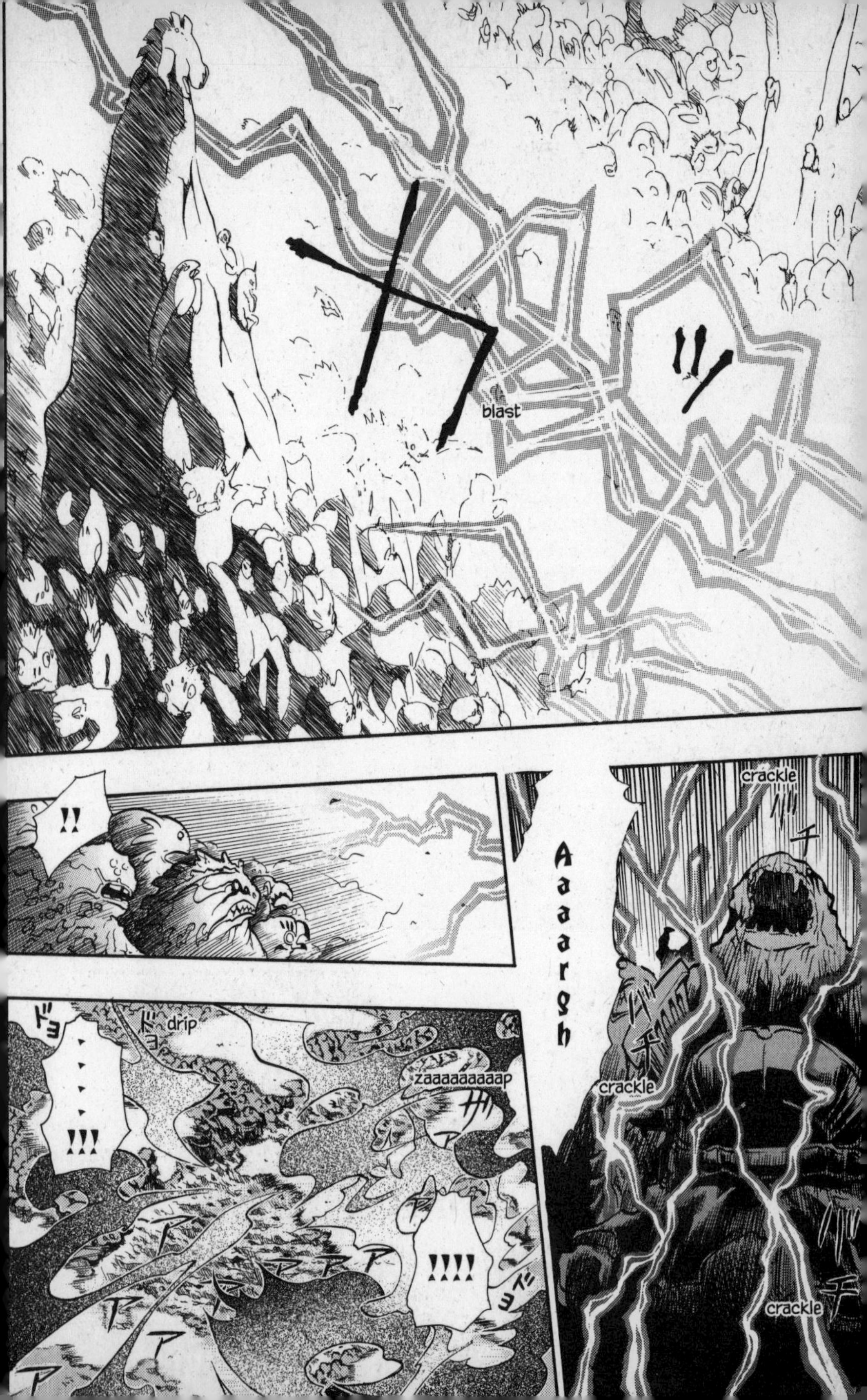
blast
crackle
Aaaargh
crackle
crackle
!!
drip
zaaaaaaaaap
......!!!
!!!!

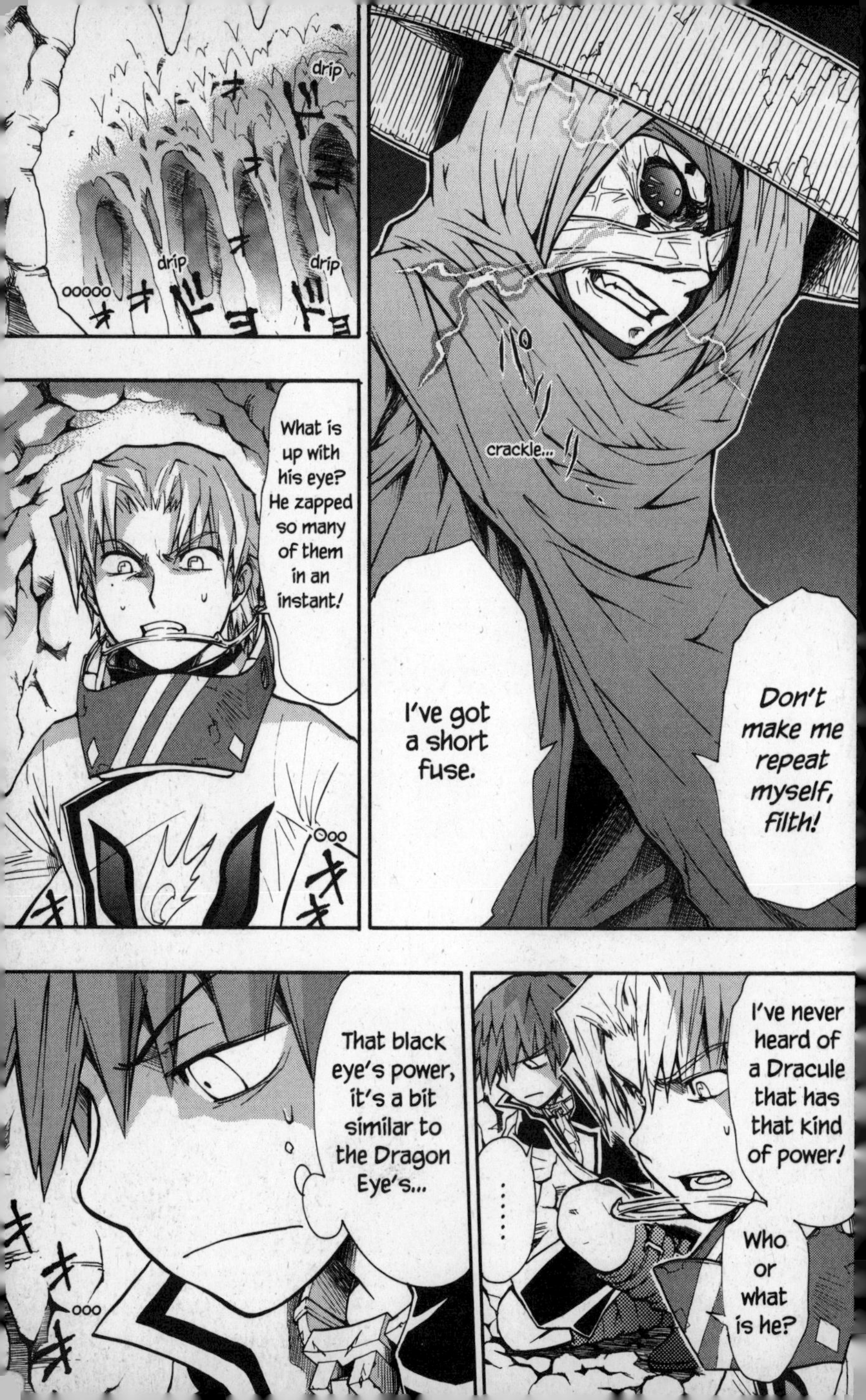

crackle...
Don't make me repeat myself, filth!
I've got a short fuse.
drip
drip
drip
ooooo
What is up with his eye? He zapped so many of them in an instant!
Ooo
I've never heard of a Dracule that has that kind of power!
Who or what is he?
......
That black eye's power, it's a bit similar to the Dragon Eye's...
ooo

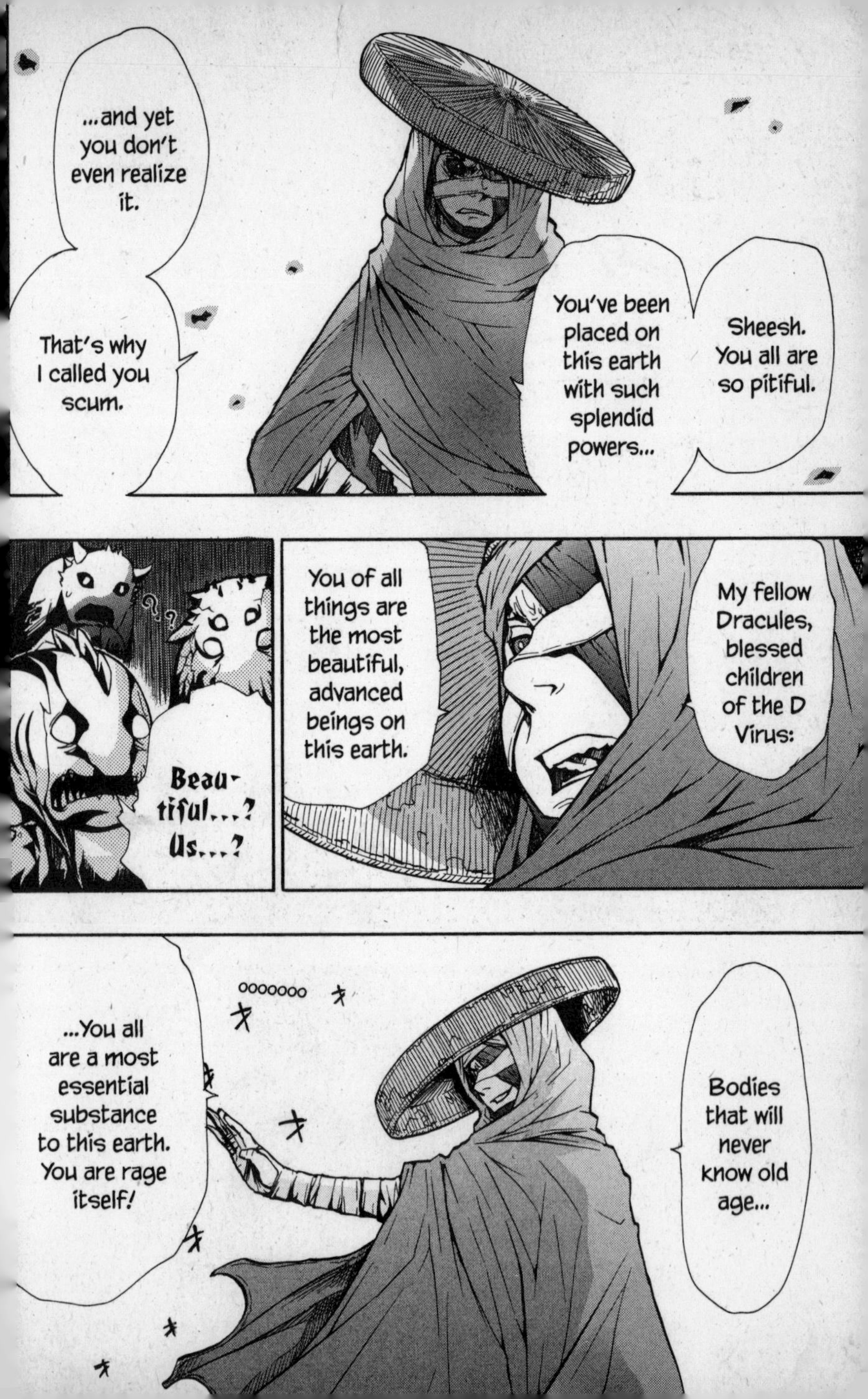
Sheesh. You all are so pitiful.
You've been placed on this earth with such splendid powers...
...and yet you don't even realize it.
That's why I called you scum.
My fellow Dracules, blessed children of the D Virus:
You of all things are the most beautiful, advanced beings on this earth.
Beau-tiful...? Us...?
Bodies that will never know old age...
...You all are a most essential substance to this earth. You are rage itself!
ooooooo

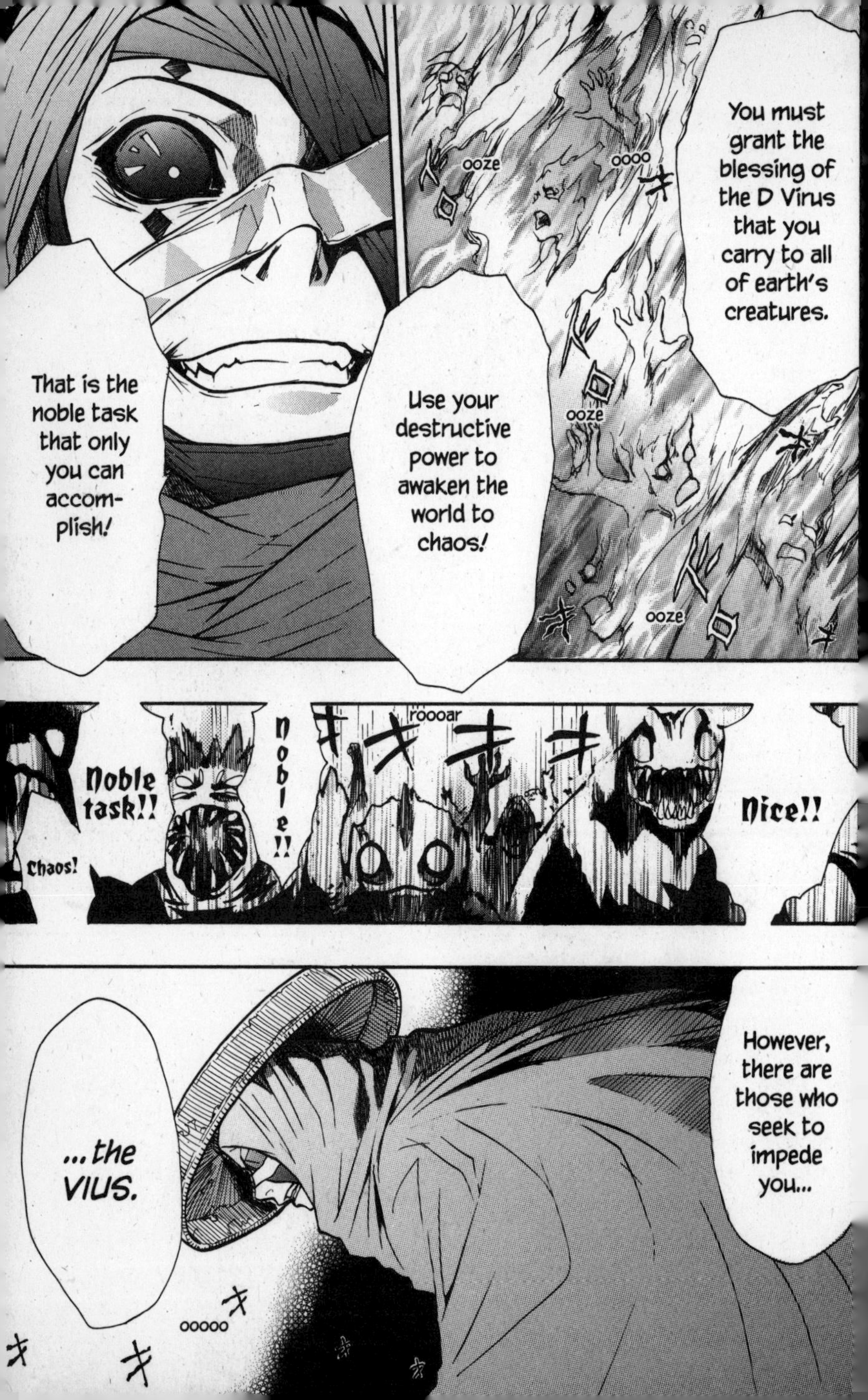
You must grant the blessing of the D Virus that you carry to all of earth's creatures.
oooo
ooze
ooze
ooze
Use your destructive power to awaken the world to chaos!
That is the noble task that only you can accom-plish!
Nice!!
roooar
noble!!
Noble task!!
Chaos!
However, there are those who seek to impede you...
...the VIUS.
ooooo

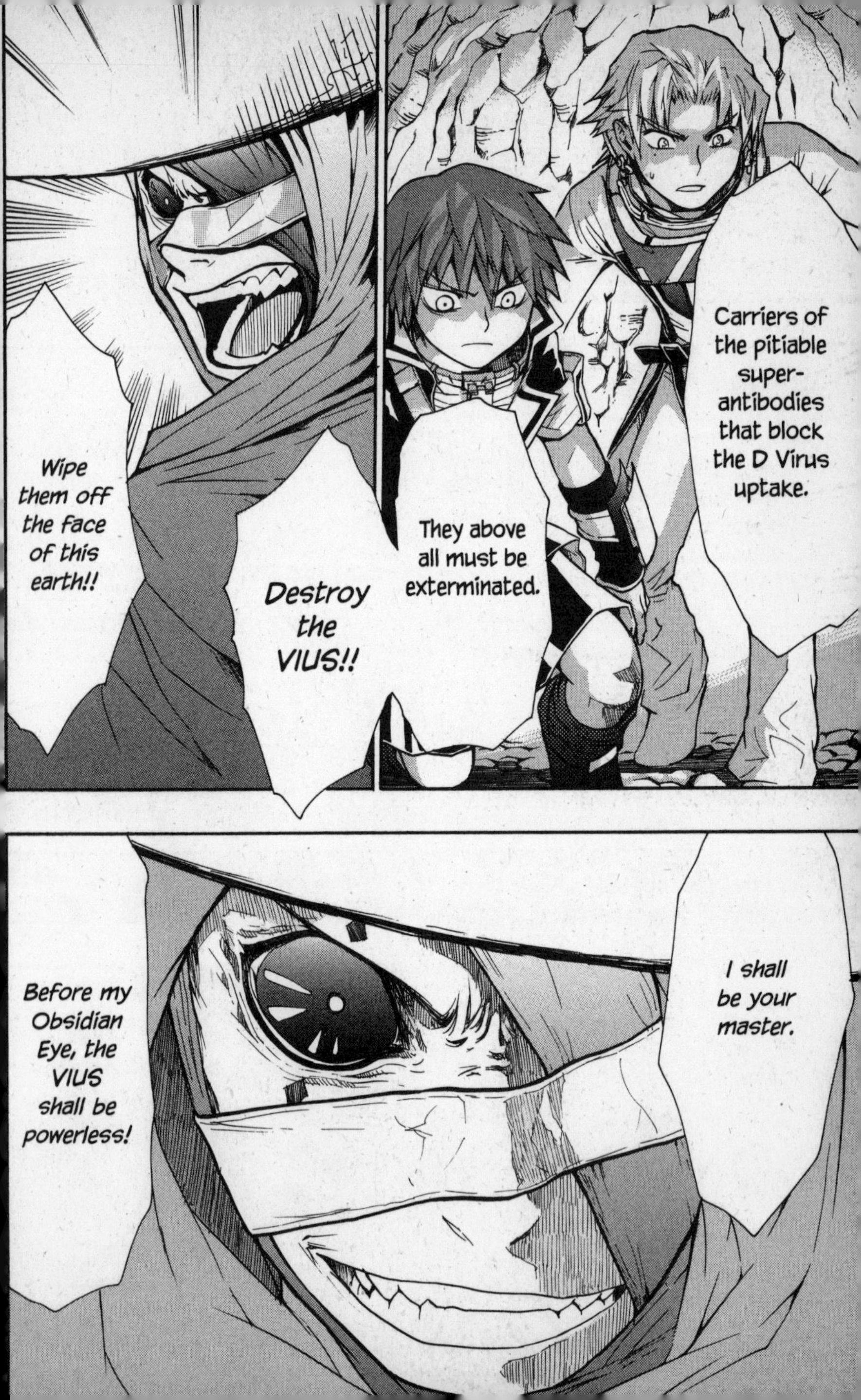
Carriers of the pitiable super-antibodies that block the D Virus uptake.
They above all must be exterminated.
Destroy the VIUS!!
Wipe them off the face of this earth!!
I shall be your master.
Before my Obsidian Eye, the VIUS shall be powerless!

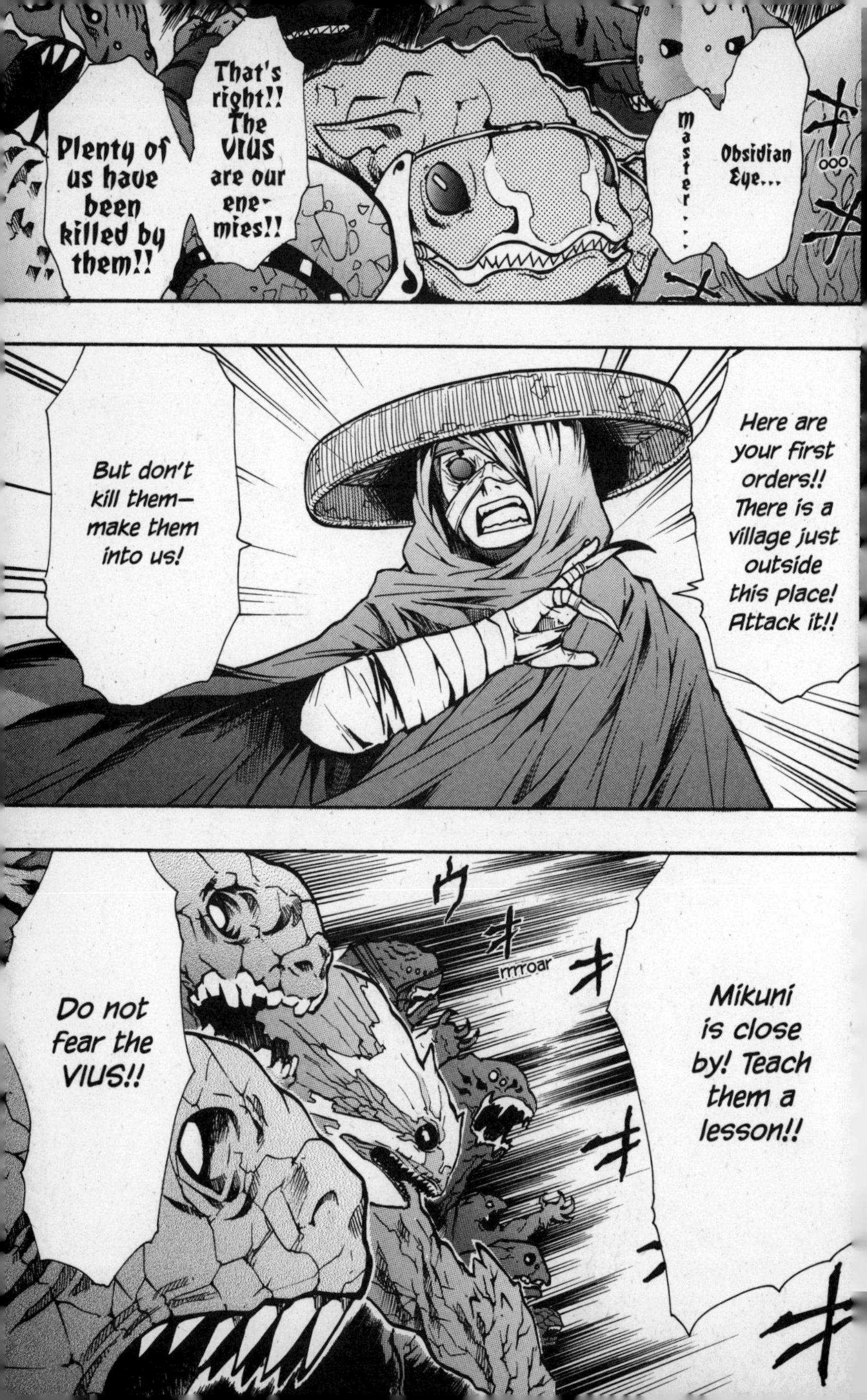
Obsidian Eye...
Master...
That's right!! The VIUS are our enemies!!
Plenty of us have been killed by them!!
Here are your first orders!! There is a village just outside this place! Attack it!!
But don't kill them—make them into us!
rrrroar
Mikuni is close by! Teach them a lesson!!
Do not fear the VIUS!!

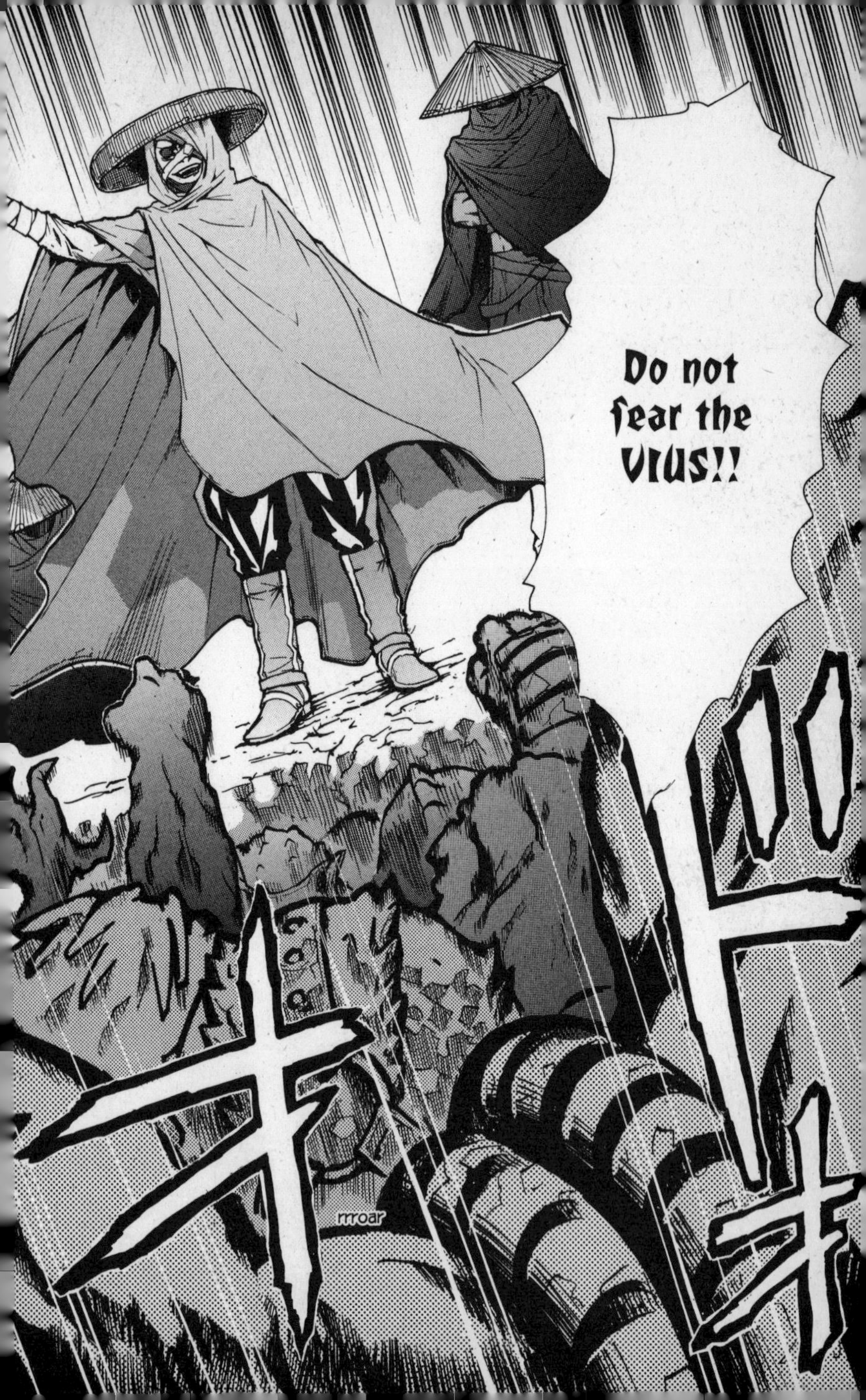
Do not fear the VIUS!!
rrroar

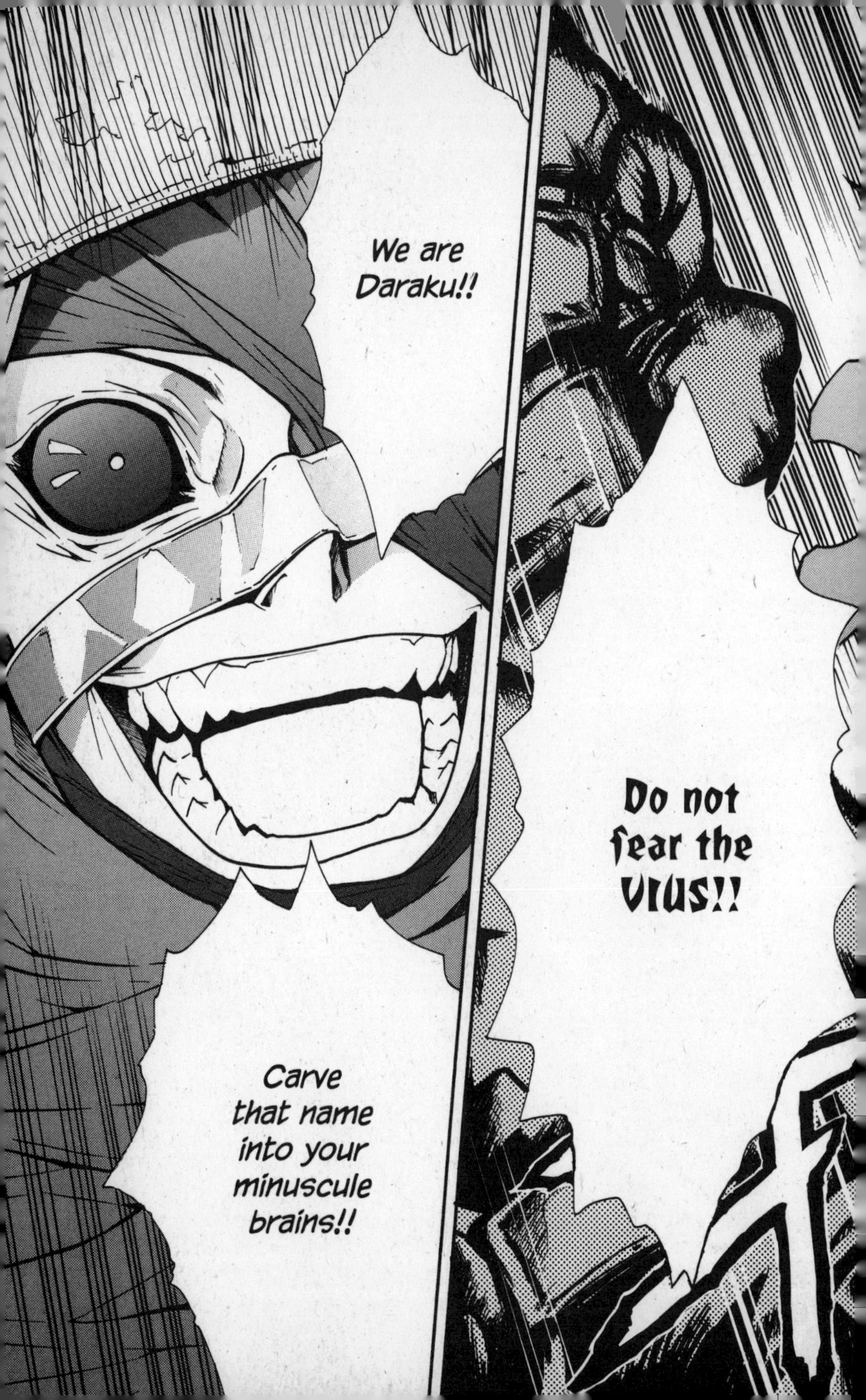
Do not fear the VIUS!!
We are Daraku!!
Carve that name into your minuscule brains!!

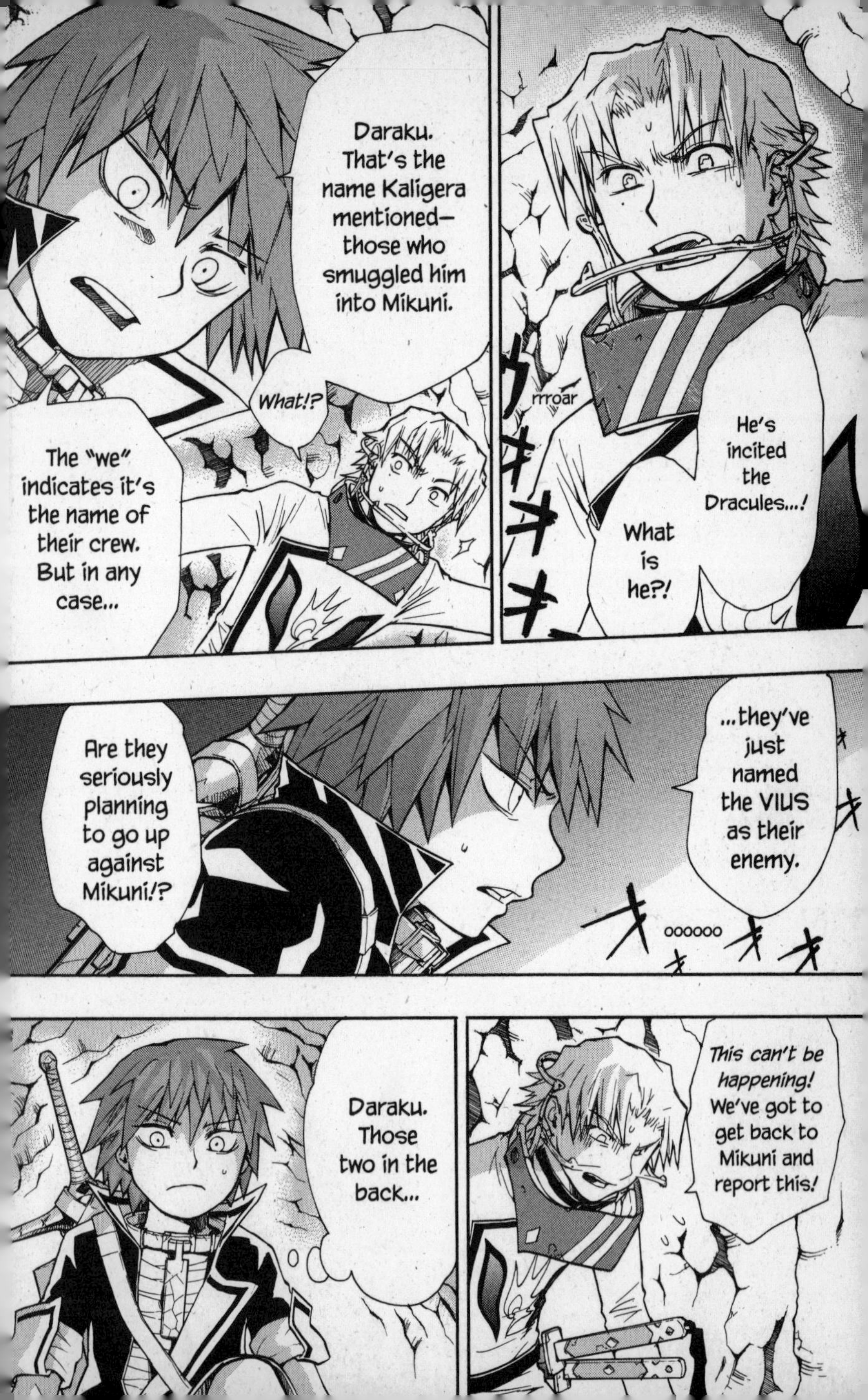
He's incited the Dracules...!
rrroar
What is he?!
Daraku. That's the name Kaligera mentioned— those who smuggled him into Mikuni.
What!?
The "we" indicates it's the name of their crew. But in any case...
...they've just named the VIUS as their enemy.
oooooo
Are they seriously planning to go up against Mikuni!?
This can't be happening! We've got to get back to Mikuni and report this!
Daraku. Those two in the back...

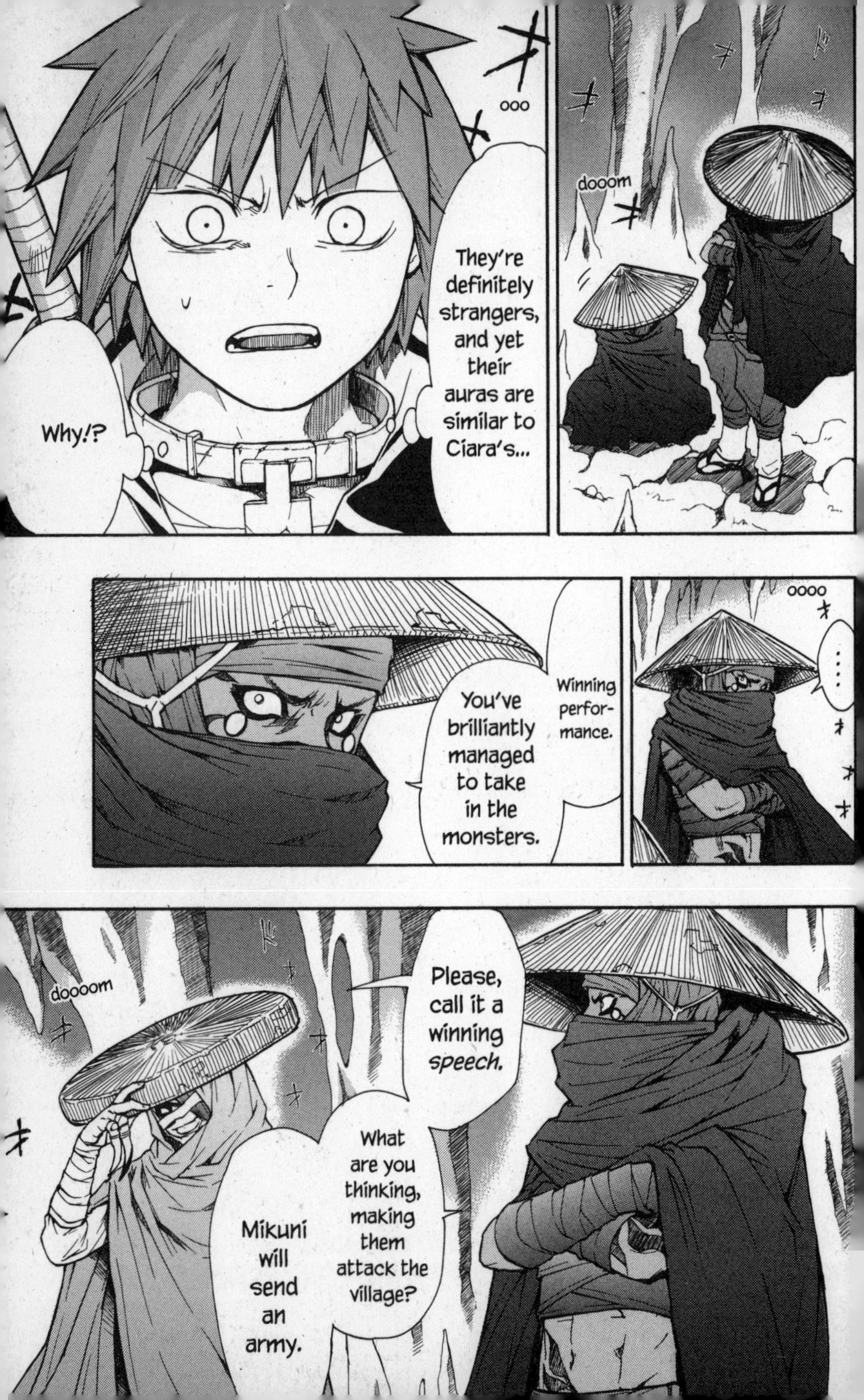
dooom
ooo
They're definitely strangers, and yet their auras are similar to Ciara's...
Why!?
oooo
....
Winning performance.
You've brilliantly managed to take in the monsters.
doooom
Please, call it a winning *speech.*
What are you thinking, making them attack the village?
Mikuni will send an army.

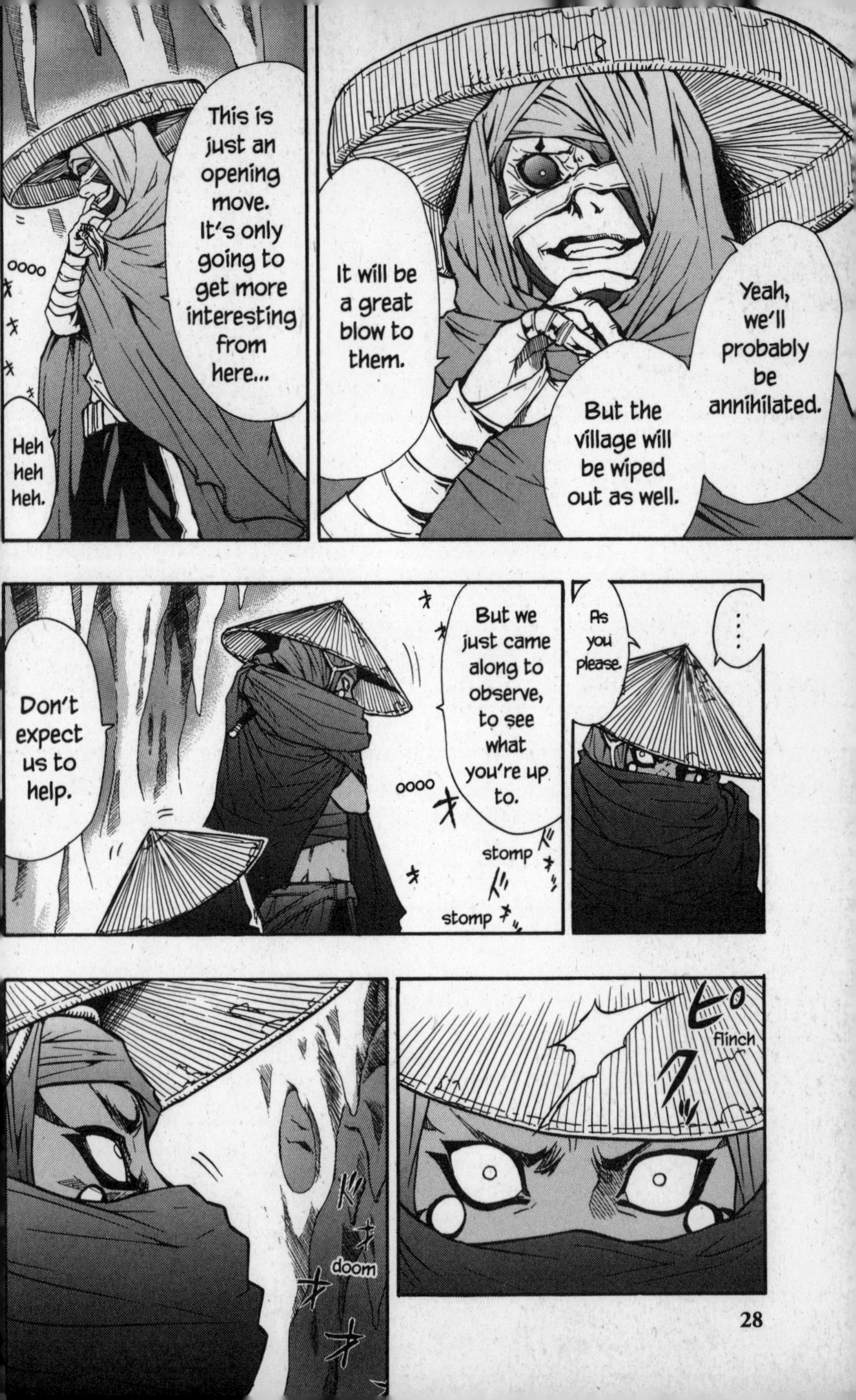
It will be a great blow to them.
Yeah, we'll probably be annihilated.
But the village will be wiped out as well.
This is just an opening move. It's only going to get more interesting from here...
oooo
Heh heh heh.
....
As you please.
But we just came along to observe, to see what you're up to.
oooo
stomp
stomp
Don't expect us to help.
Flinch
doom

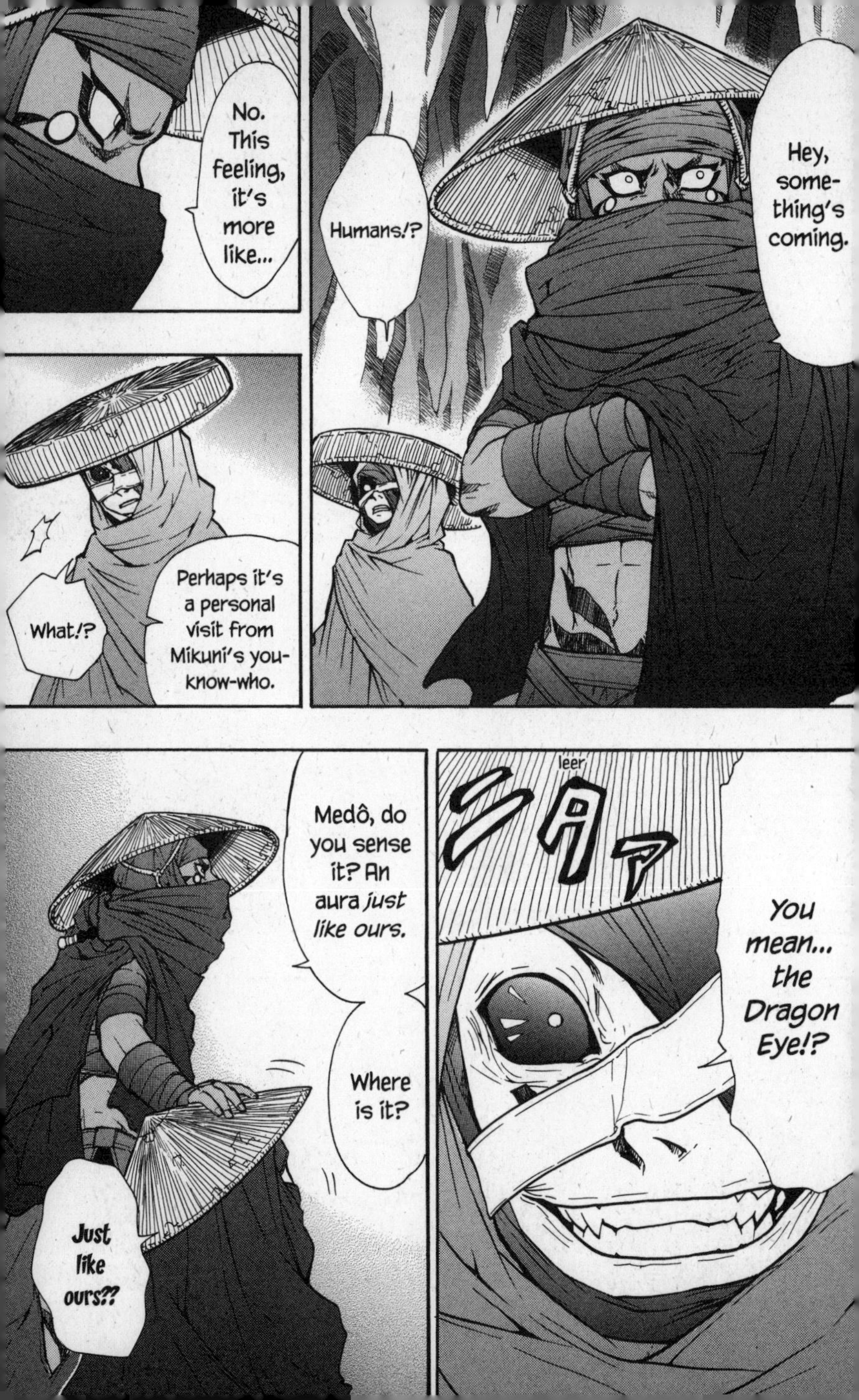
Hey, something's coming.
Humans!?
No. This feeling, it's more like...
Perhaps it's a personal visit from Mikuni's you-know-who.
What!?
leer
ニタァ
You mean... the Dragon Eye!?
Medô, do you sense it? An aura *just like ours.*
Where is it?
Just like ours??

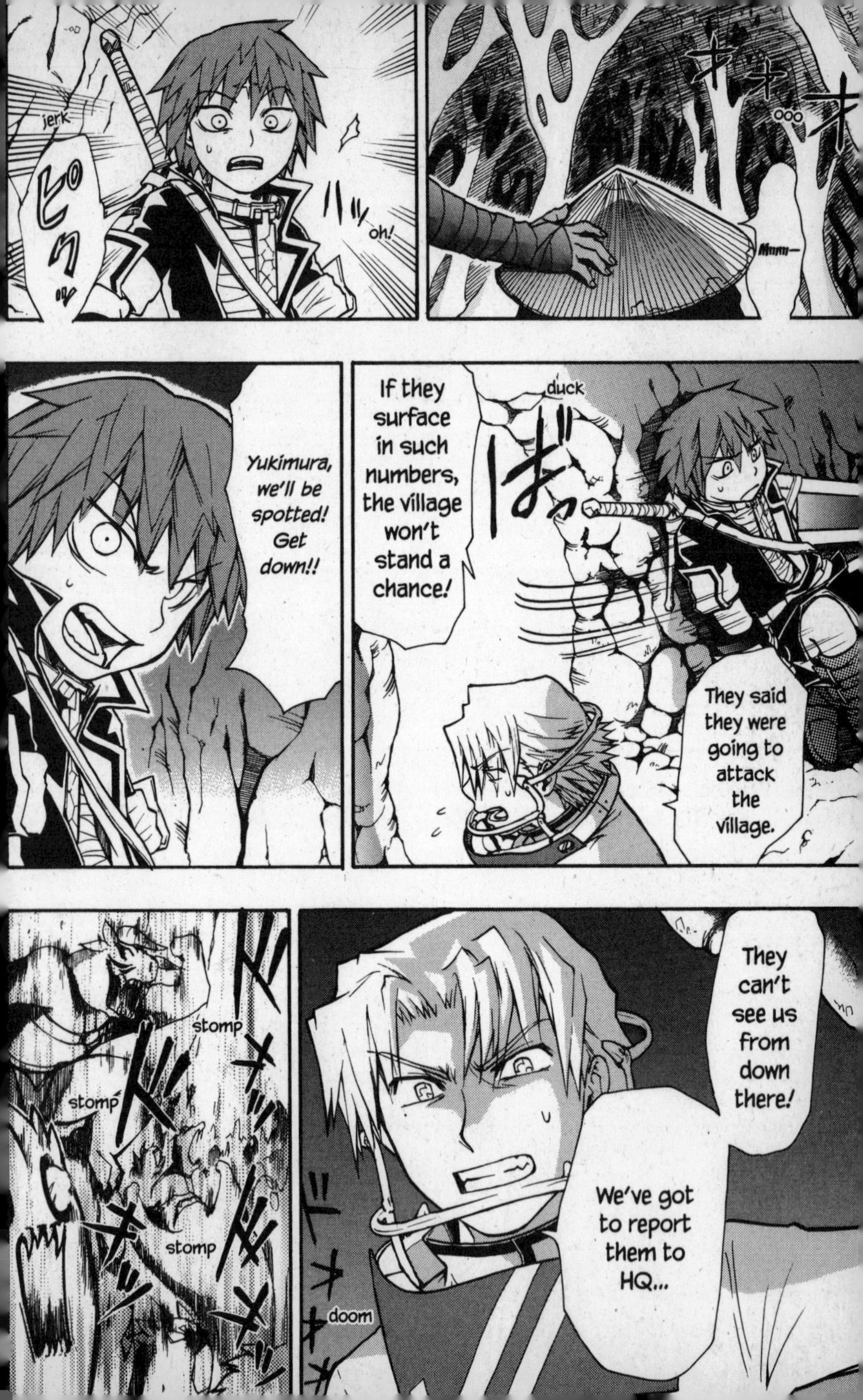
ooo
Mmm—
jerk
oh!
duck
If they surface in such numbers, the village won't stand a chance!
They said they were going to attack the village.
Yukimura, we'll be spotted! Get down!!
They can't see us from down there!
We've got to report them to HQ...
doom
stomp
stomp
stomp

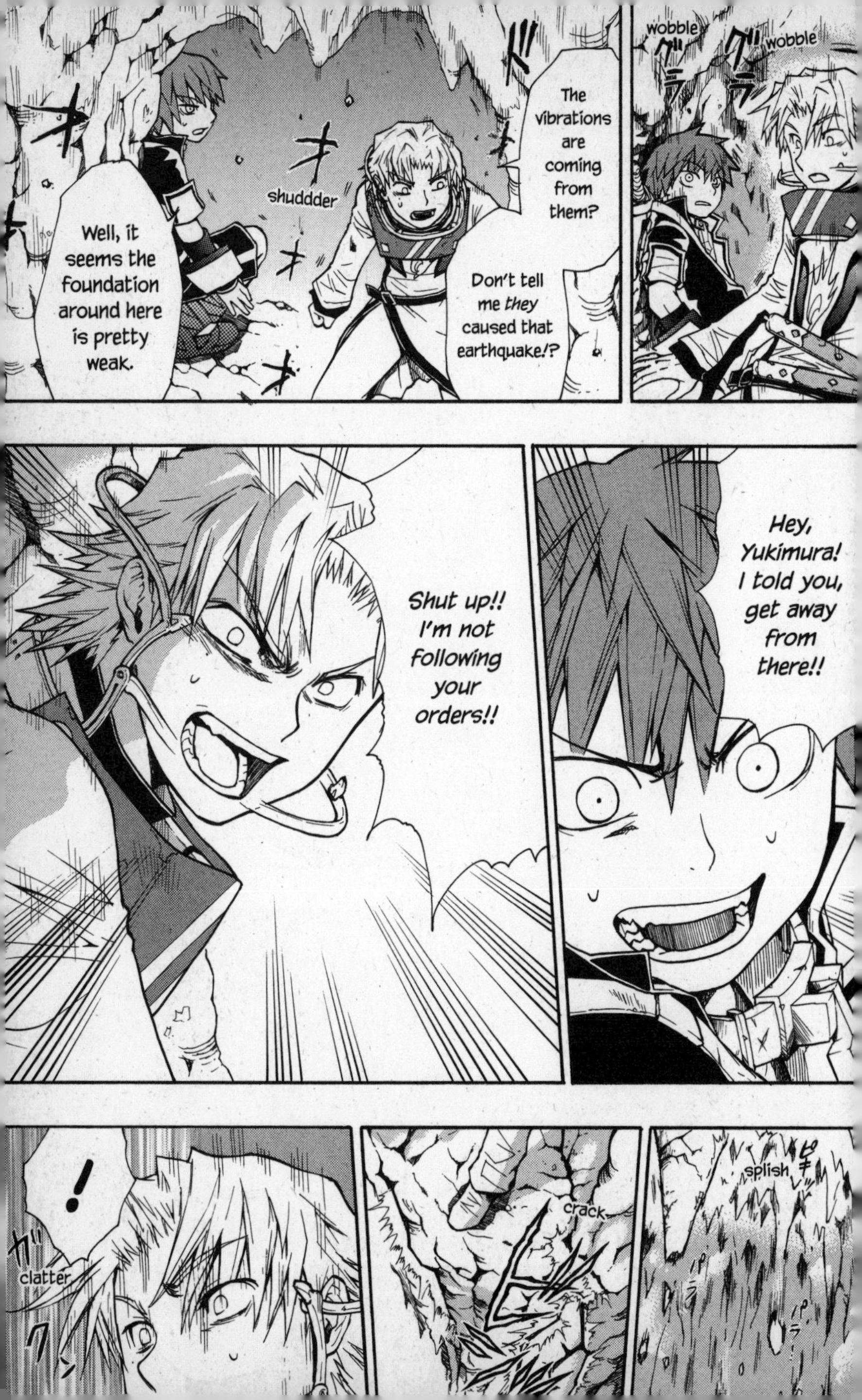
wobble
wobble
The vibrations are coming from them?
Don't tell me *they* caused that earthquake!?
shuddder
Well, it seems the foundation around here is pretty weak.
Hey, Yukimura! I told you, get away from there!!
Shut up!! I'm not following your orders!!
splish
crack
!
clatter

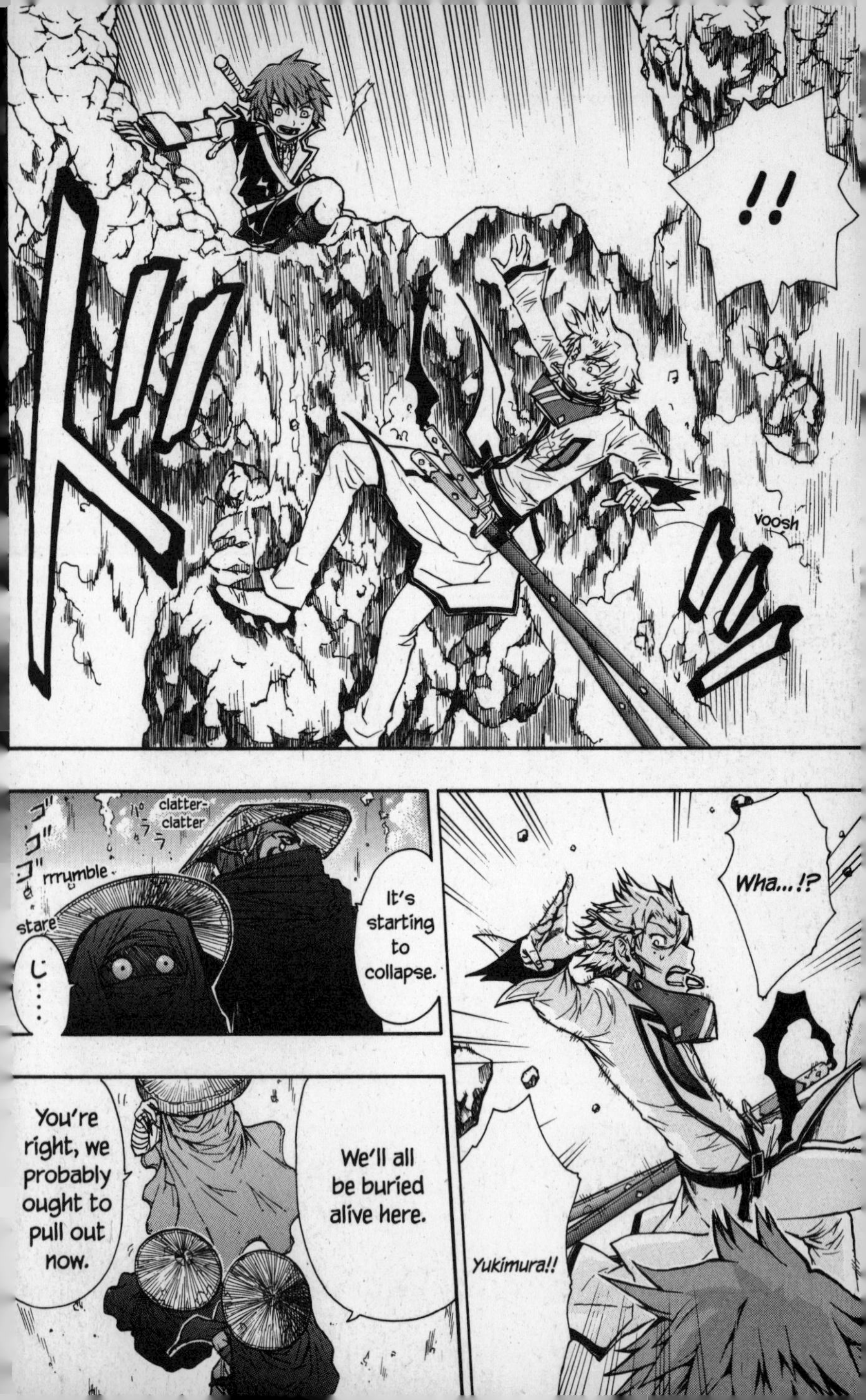
!!
voosh
Wha...!?
Yukimura!!
clatter-clatter
It's starting to collapse.
rrrumble
stare
We'll all be buried alive here.
You're right, we probably ought to pull out now.

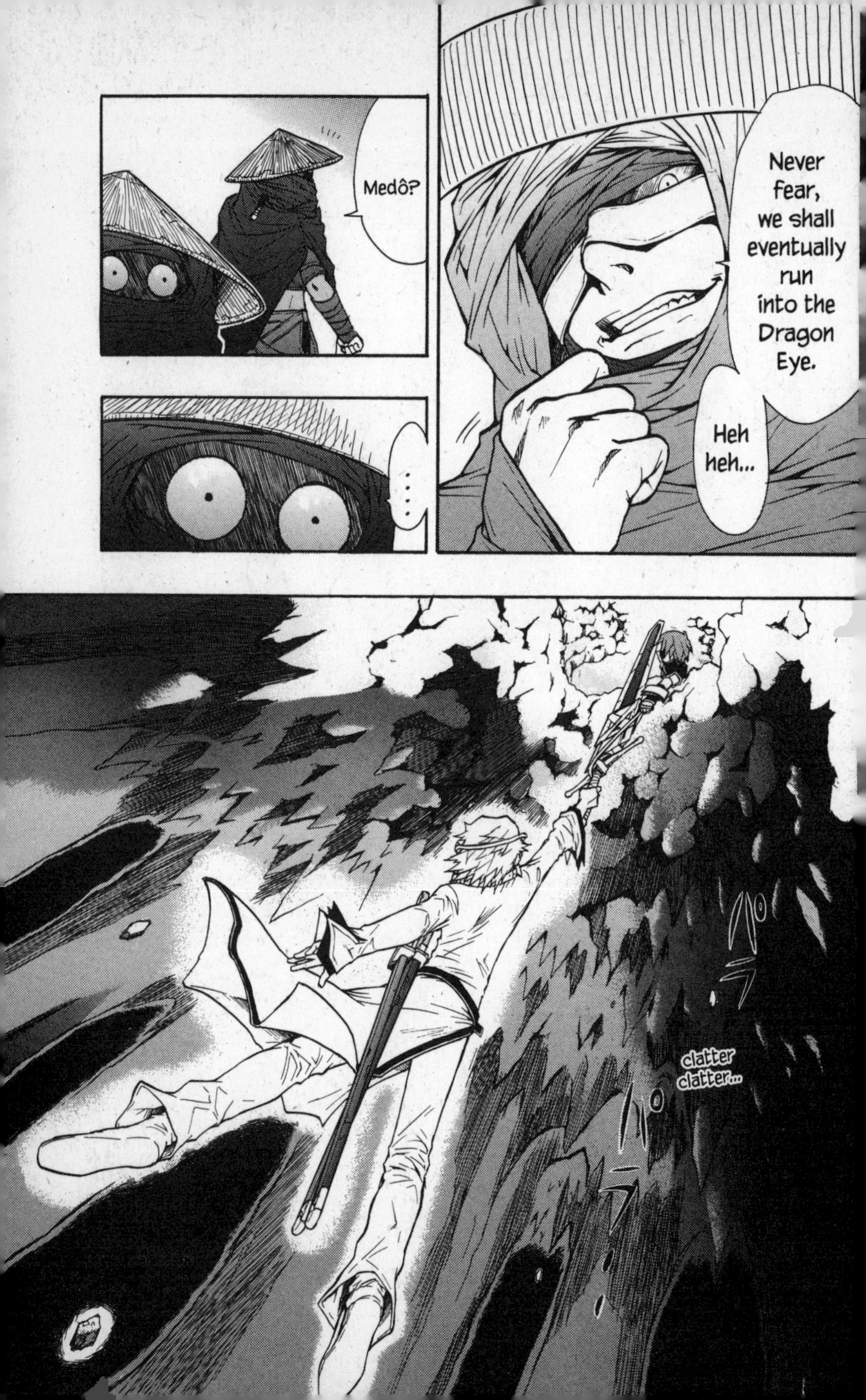
Never fear, we shall eventually run into the Dragon Eye.
Heh heh...
Medô?
...
clatter clatter...

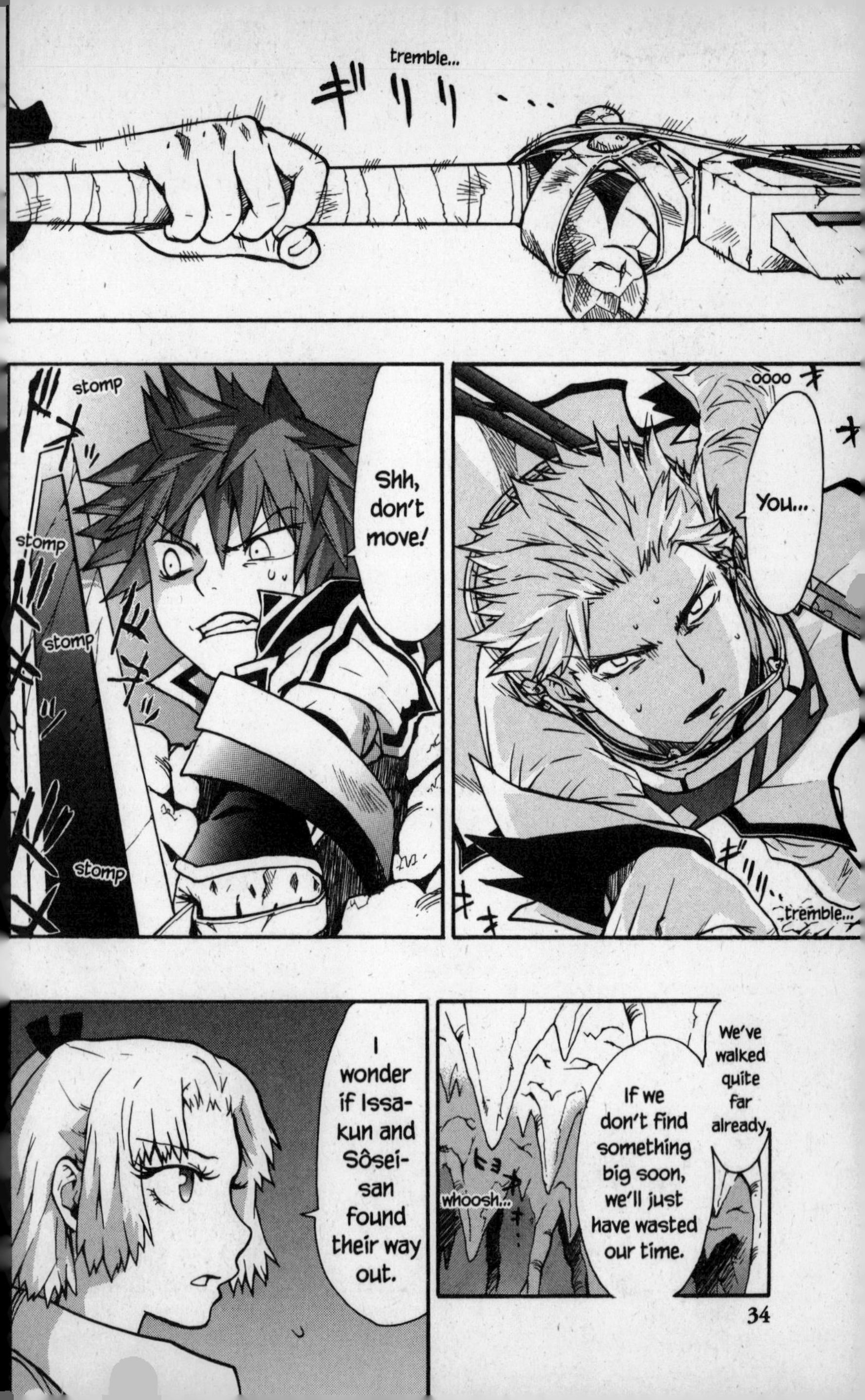
tremble...
ギリリ…
oooo
You...
tremble...
stomp
stomp
stomp
stomp
Shh, don't move!
We've walked quite far already.
If we don't find something big soon, we'll just have wasted our time.
whoosh...
I wonder if Issa-kun and Sôsei-san found their way out.

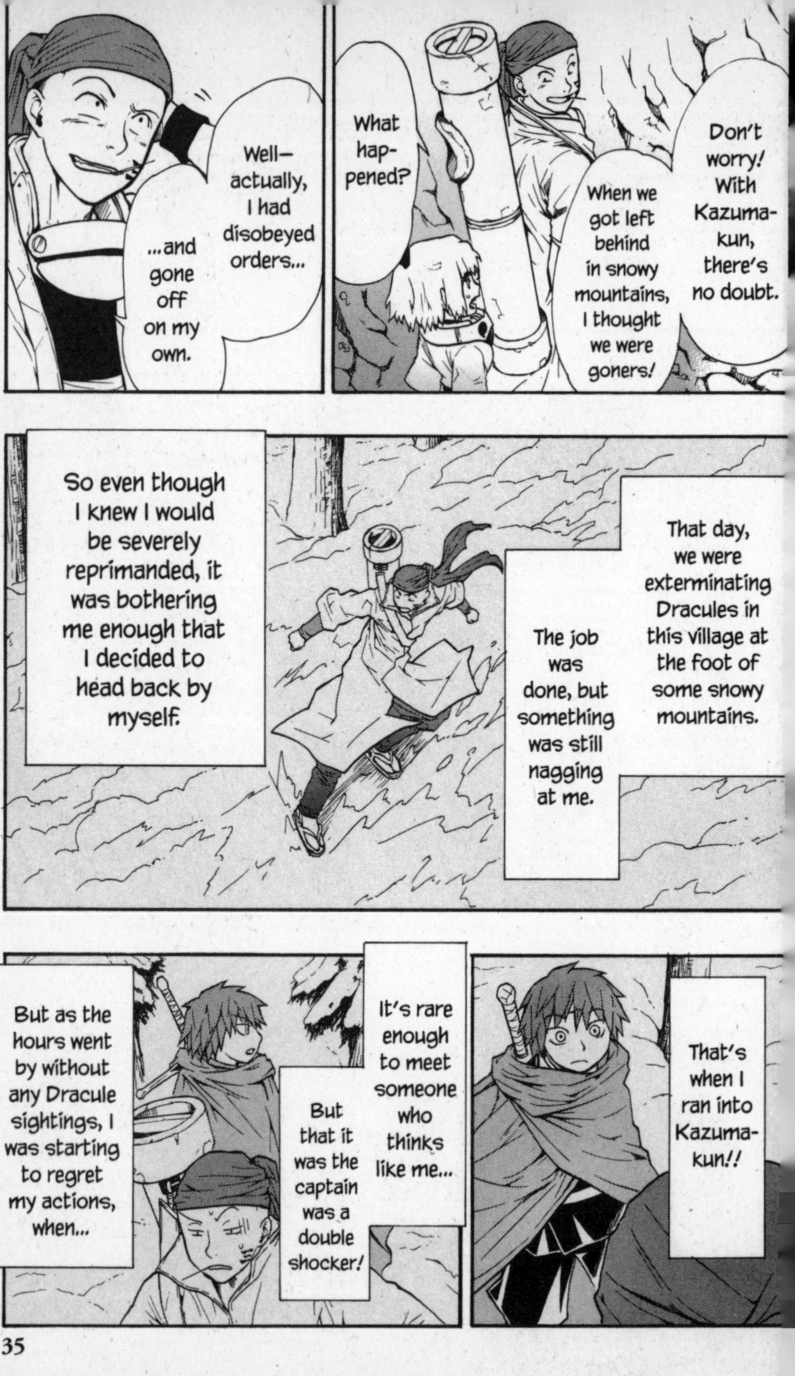
Don't worry! With Kazuma-kun, there's no doubt.
When we got left behind in snowy mountains, I thought we were goners!
What hap-pened?
Well— actually, I had disobeyed orders...
...and gone off on my own.
That day, we were exterminating Dracules in this village at the foot of some snowy mountains.
The job was done, but something was still nagging at me.
So even though I knew I would be severely reprimanded, it was bothering me enough that I decided to head back by myself.
That's when I ran into Kazuma-kun!!
It's rare enough to meet someone who thinks like me...
But that it was the captain was a double shocker!
But as the hours went by without any Dracule sightings, I was starting to regret my actions, when...

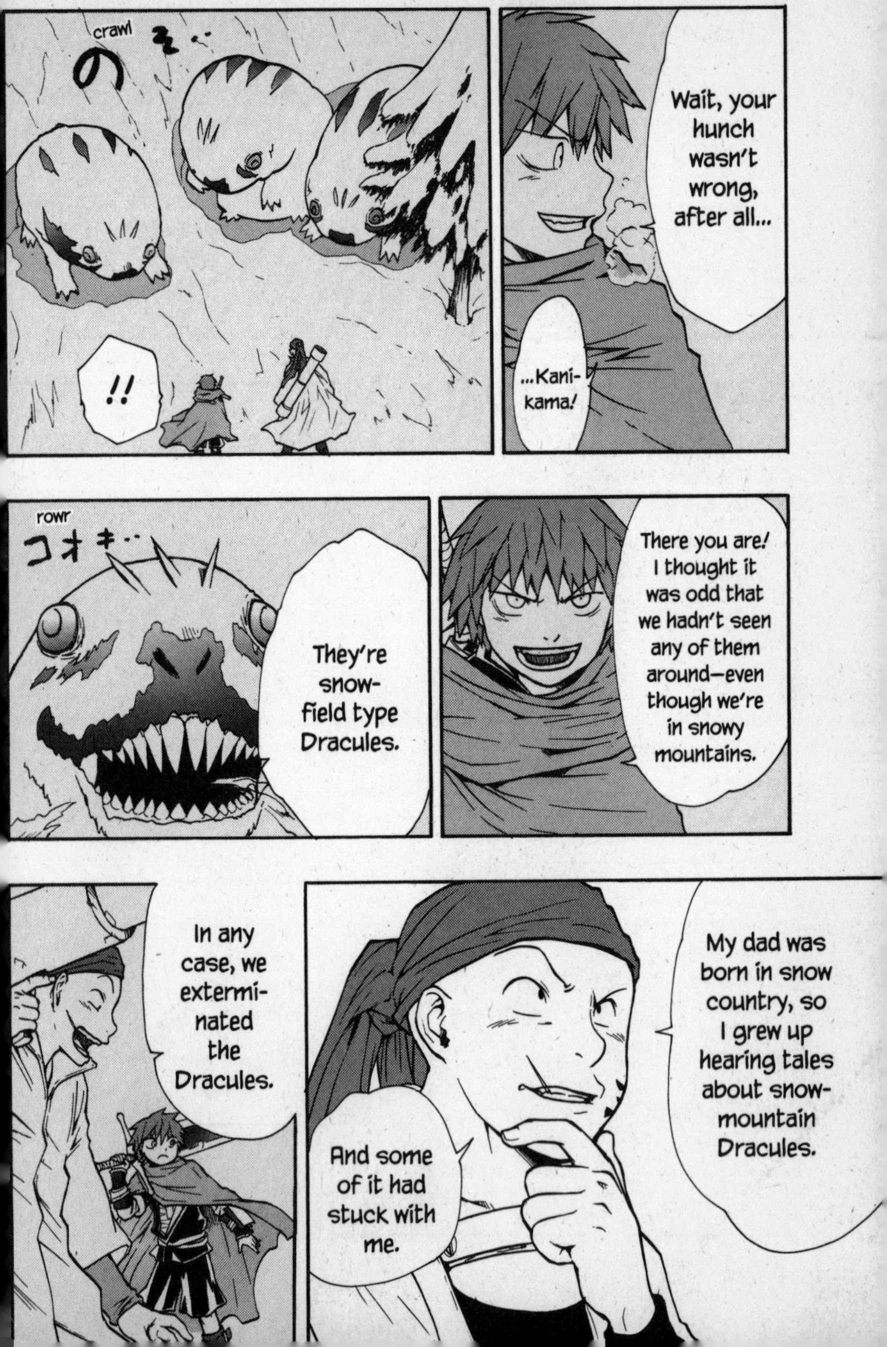
Wait, your hunch wasn't wrong, after all...
...Kani-kama!
crawl
!!
There you are! I thought it was odd that we hadn't seen any of them around—even though we're in snowy mountains.
rowr
They're snow-field type Dracules.
My dad was born in snow country, so I grew up hearing tales about snow-mountain Dracules.
And some of it had stuck with me.
In any case, we extermi-nated the Dracules.

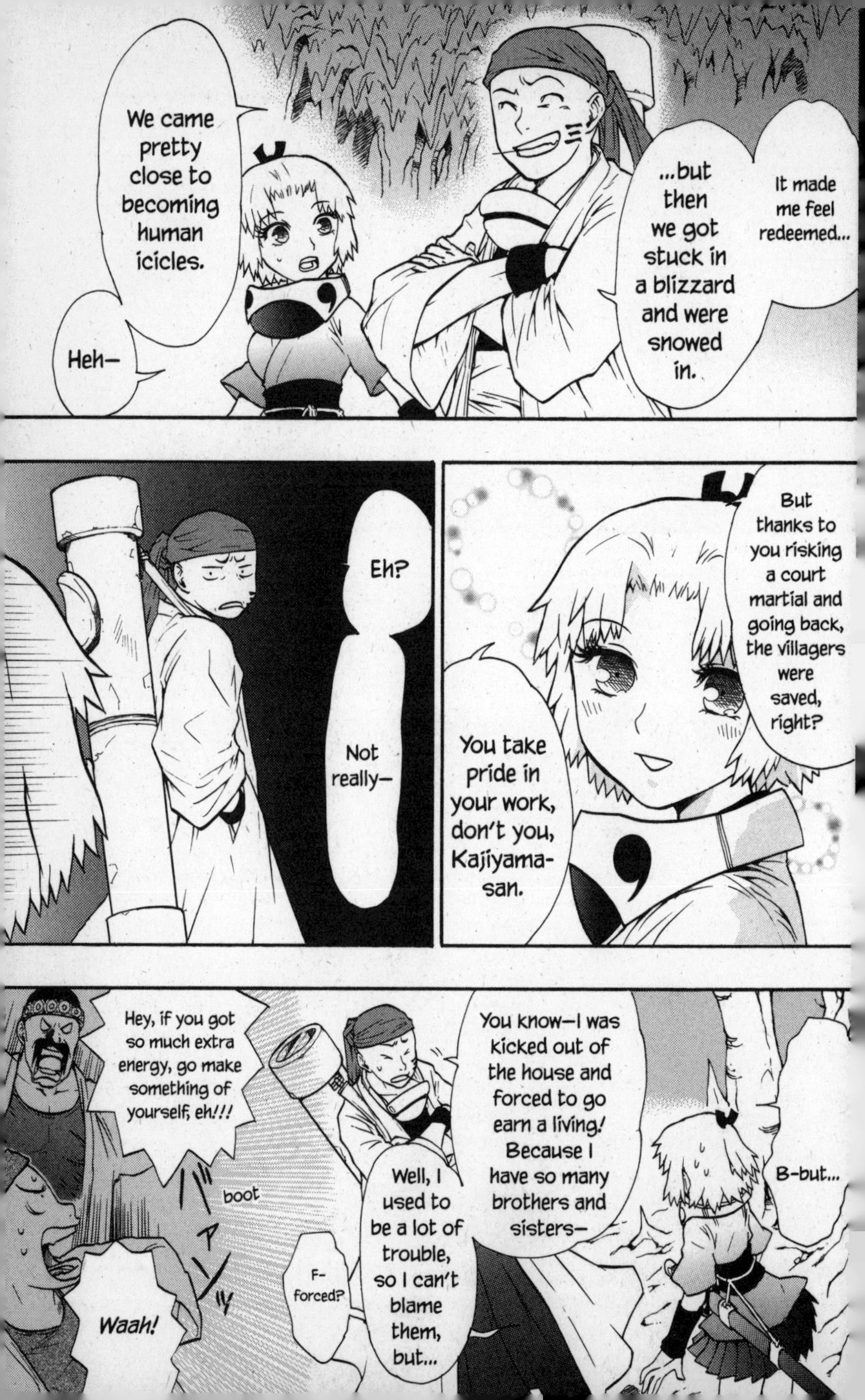
It made me feel redeemed...
...but then we got stuck in a blizzard and were snowed in.
We came pretty close to becoming human icicles.
Heh—
But thanks to you risking a court martial and going back, the villagers were saved, right?
You take pride in your work, don't you, Kajiyama-san.
Eh?
Not really—
B-but...
You know—I was kicked out of the house and forced to go earn a living! Because I have so many brothers and sisters—
Well, I used to be a lot of trouble, so I can't blame them, but...
F-forced?
Hey, if you got so much extra energy, go make something of yourself, eh!!!
boot
Waah!

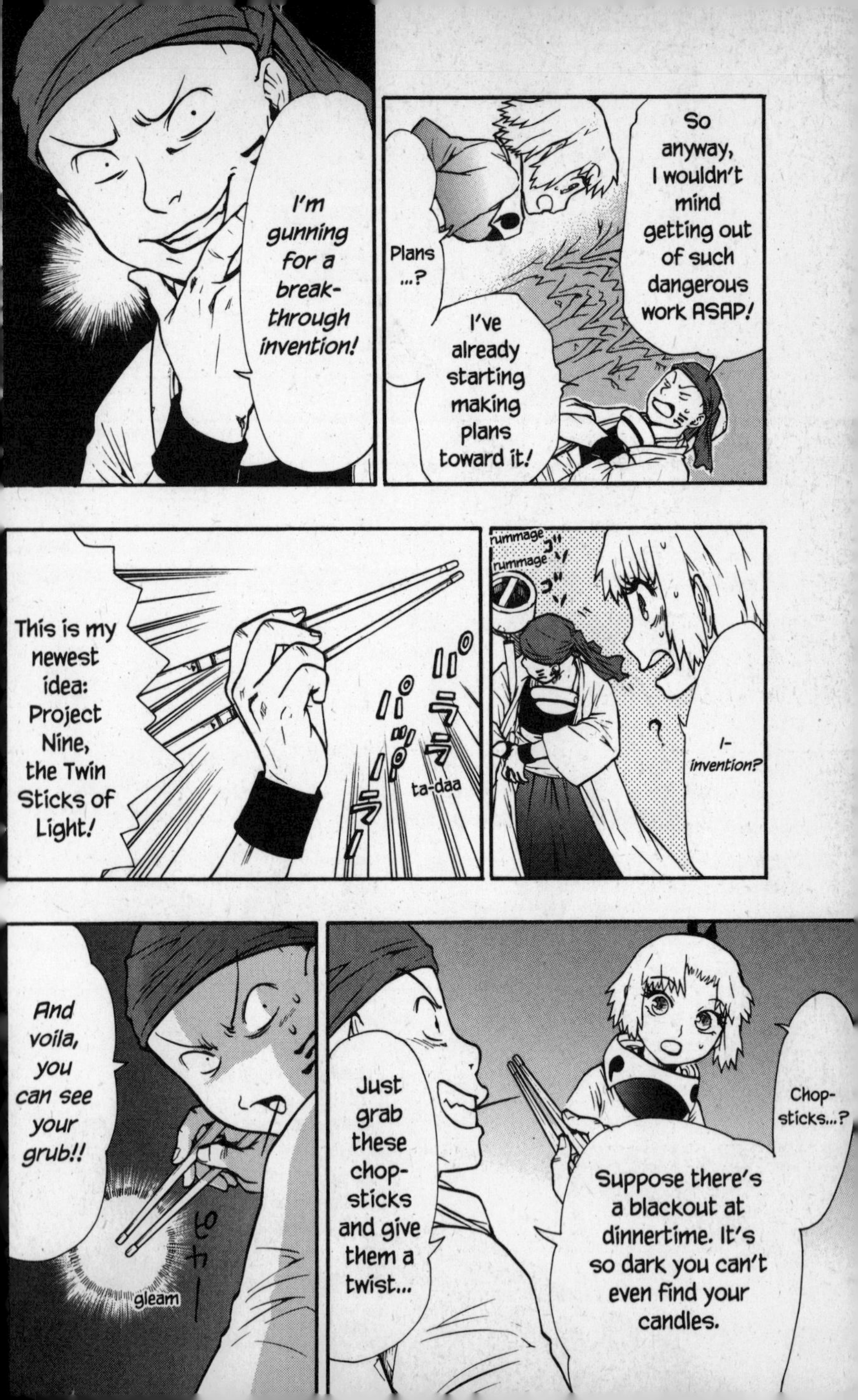
So anyway, I wouldn't mind getting out of such dangerous work ASAP!
Plans ...?
I've already starting making plans toward it!
I'm gunning for a break-through invention!
rummage
rummage
I-invention?
This is my newest idea: Project Nine, the Twin Sticks of Light!
ta-daa
Chop-sticks...?
Suppose there's a blackout at dinnertime. It's so dark you can't even find your candles.
Just grab these chop-sticks and give them a twist...
And voila, you can see your grub!!
gleam

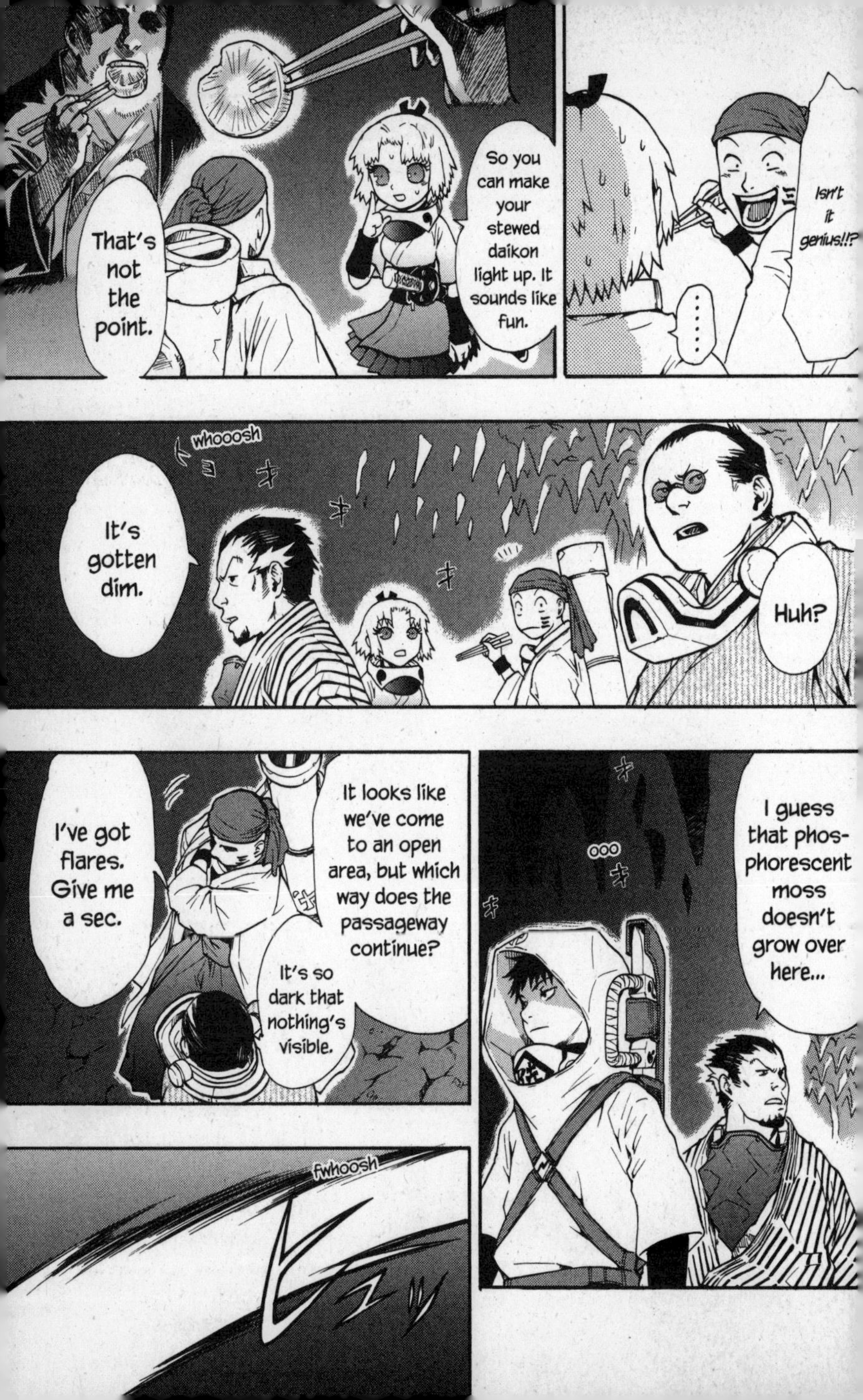
Isn't it genius!!?
......
So you can make your stewed daikon light up. It sounds like fun.
That's not the point.
whooosh
It's gotten dim.
Huh?
I guess that phos-phorescent moss doesn't grow over here...
ooo
It looks like we've come to an open area, but which way does the passageway continue?
It's so dark that nothing's visible.
I've got flares. Give me a sec.
fwhoosh

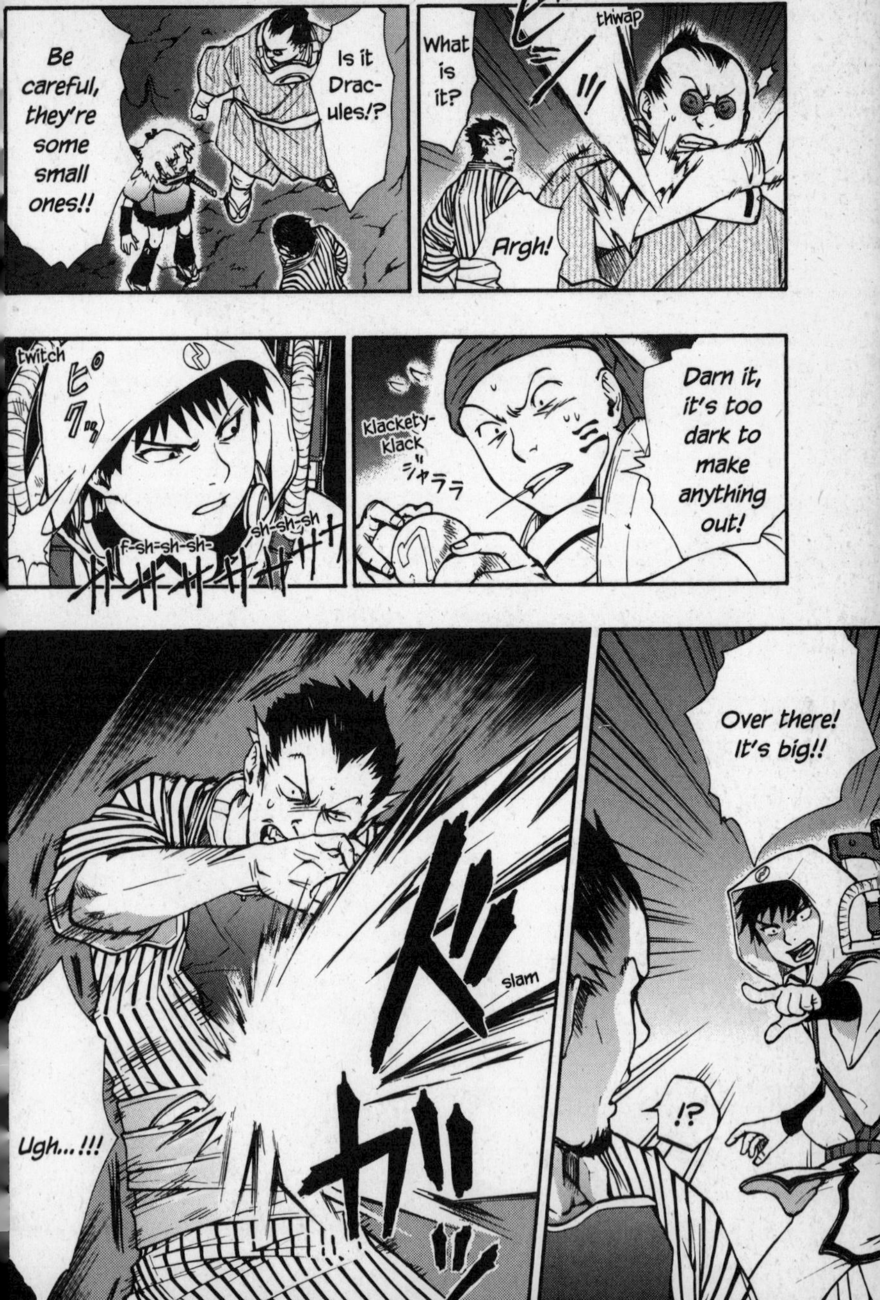
thwap
What is it?
Argh!
Is it Dracules!?
Be careful, they're some small ones!!
Darn it, it's too dark to make anything out!
klackety-klack
twitch
sh-sh-sh
f-sh-sh-sh
Over there! It's big!!
!?
slam
Ugh...!!!

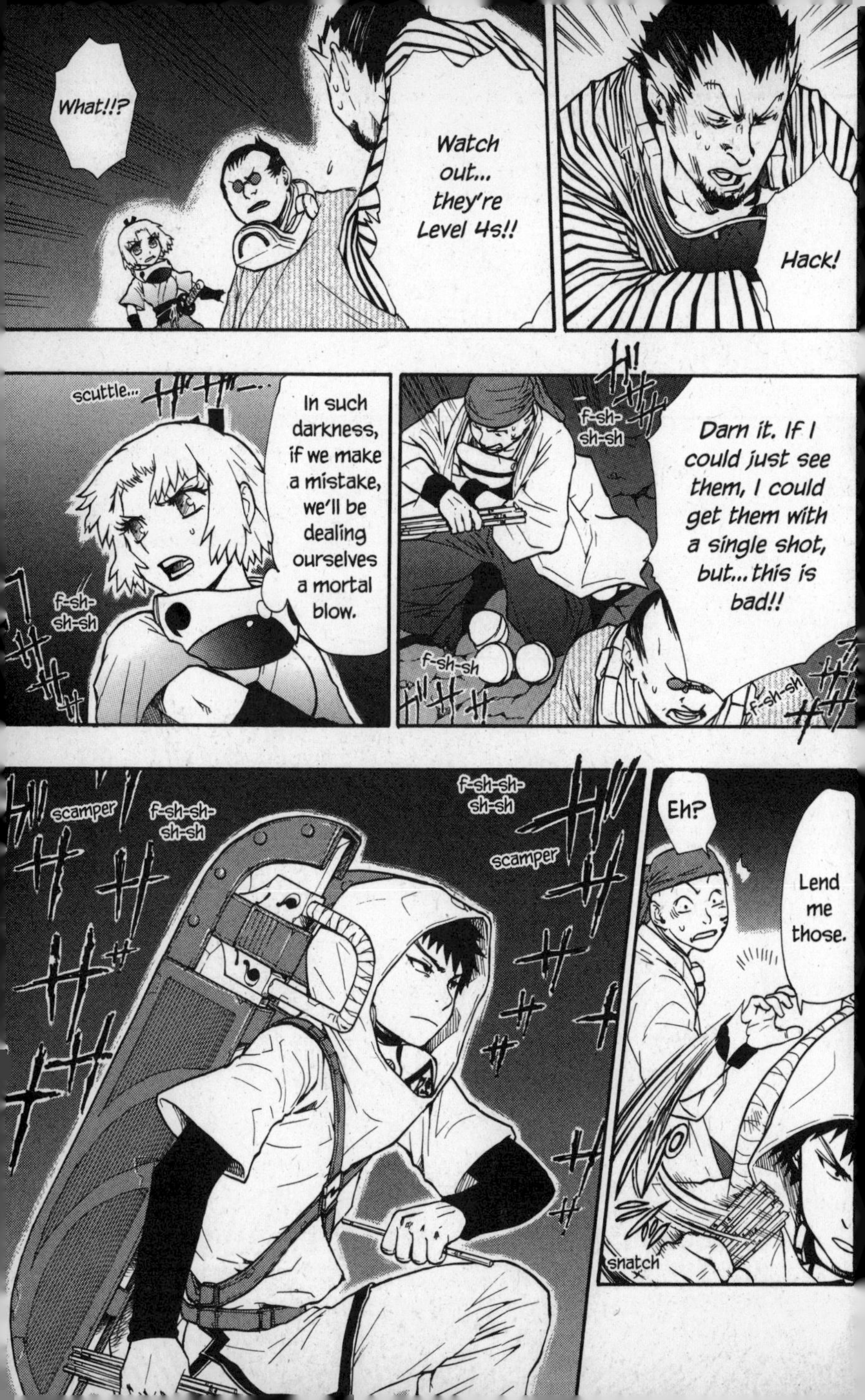
Hack!
Watch out... they're Level 4s!!
What!!?
Darn it. If I could just see them, I could get them with a single shot, but...this is bad!!
f-sh-sh-sh
f-sh-sh
f-sh-sh
In such darkness, if we make a mistake, we'll be dealing ourselves a mortal blow.
scuttle...
f-sh-sh-sh
Eh?
Lend me those.
snatch
f-sh-sh-sh-sh-sh
scamper
scamper
f-sh-sh-sh-sh

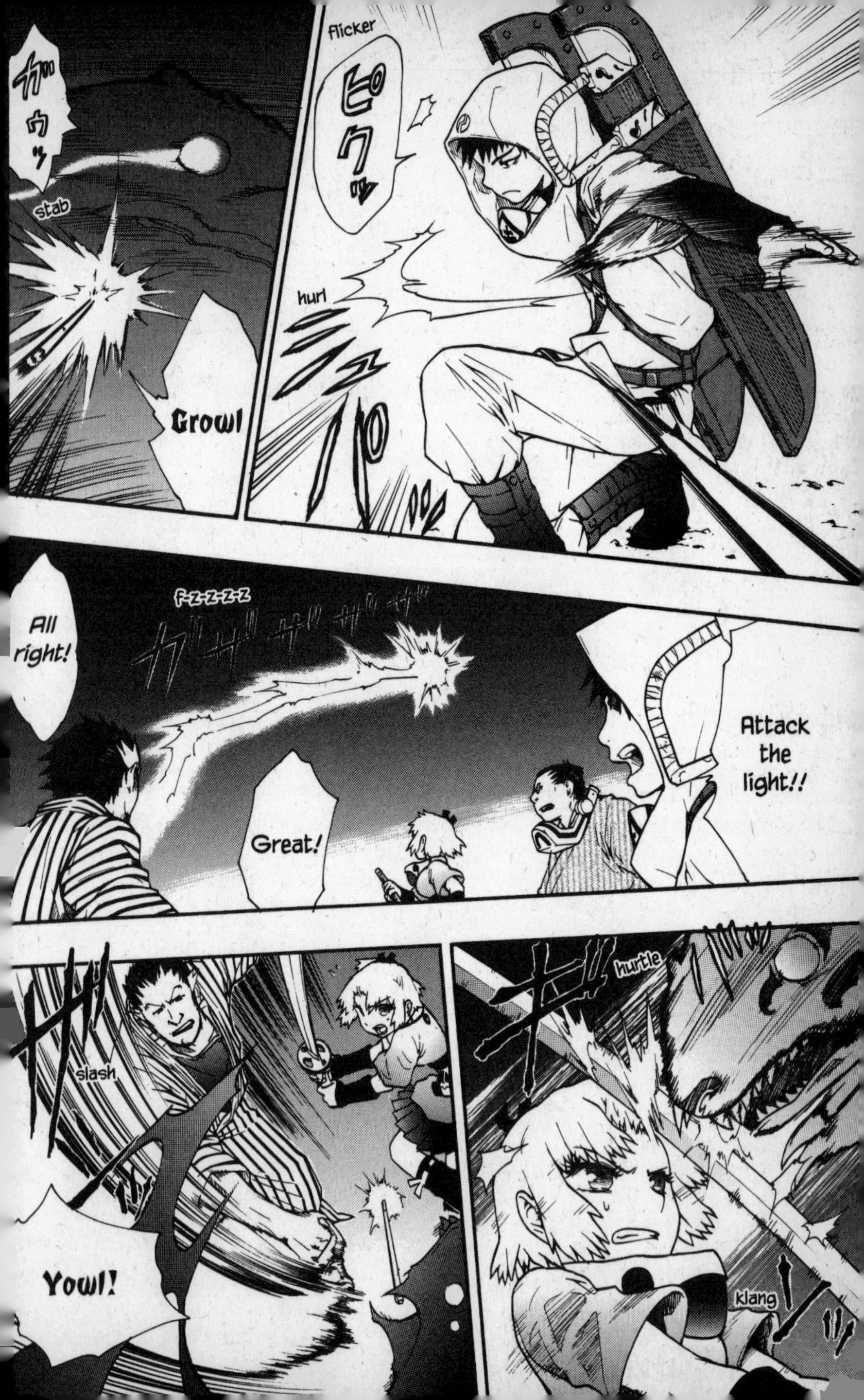
flicker
ピクッ
hurl
stab
ガウッ
Growl
Attack the light!!
Great!
All right!
f-z-z-z-z
hurtle
klang
slash
Yowl!

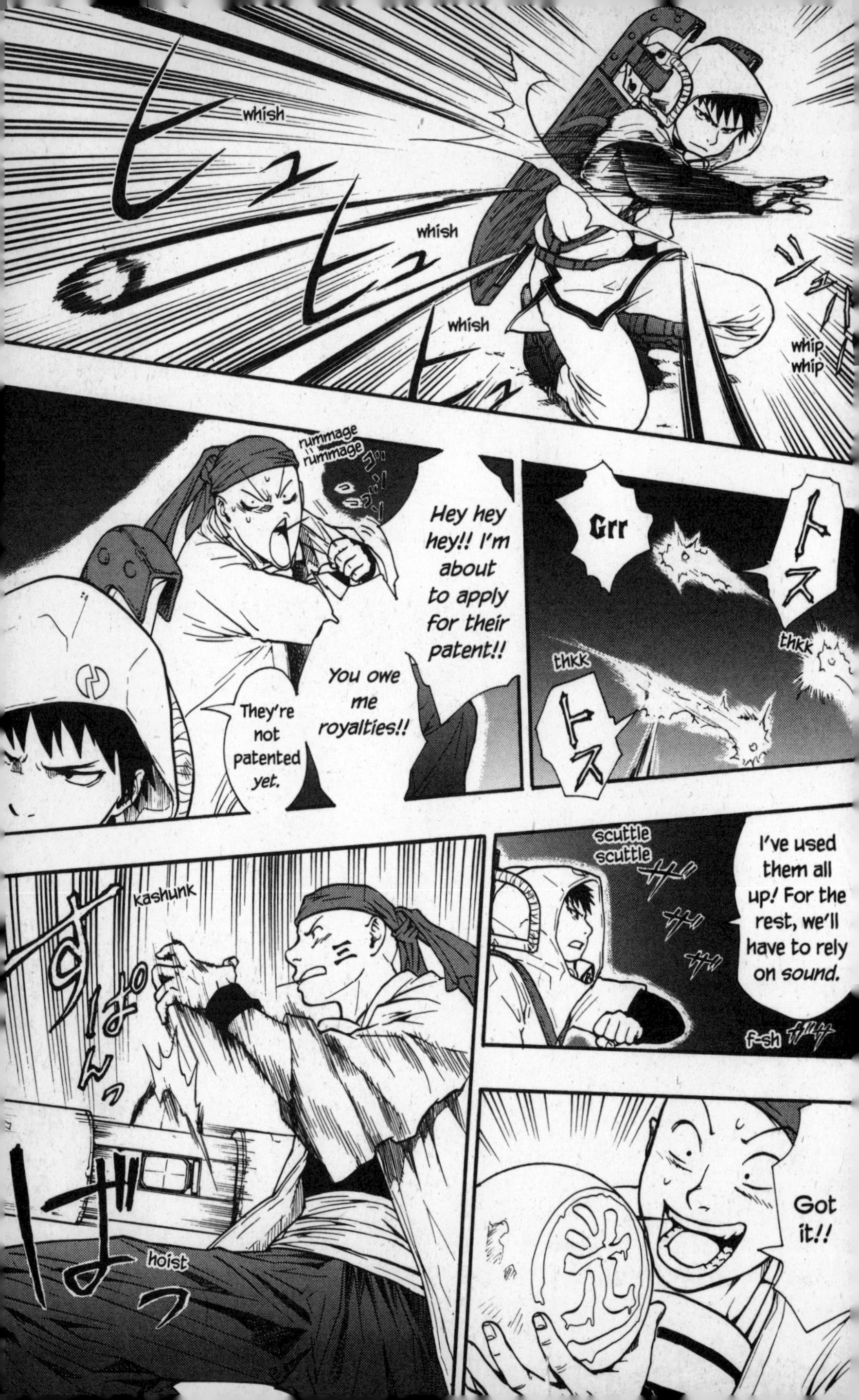
whip whip
whish
whish
whish
Grr
thkk
thkk
rummage rummage
Hey hey hey!! I'm about to apply for their patent!!
You owe me royalties!!
They're not patented yet.
scuttle scuttle
I've used them all up! For the rest, we'll have to rely on sound.
f-sh
kashunk
hoist
Got it!!

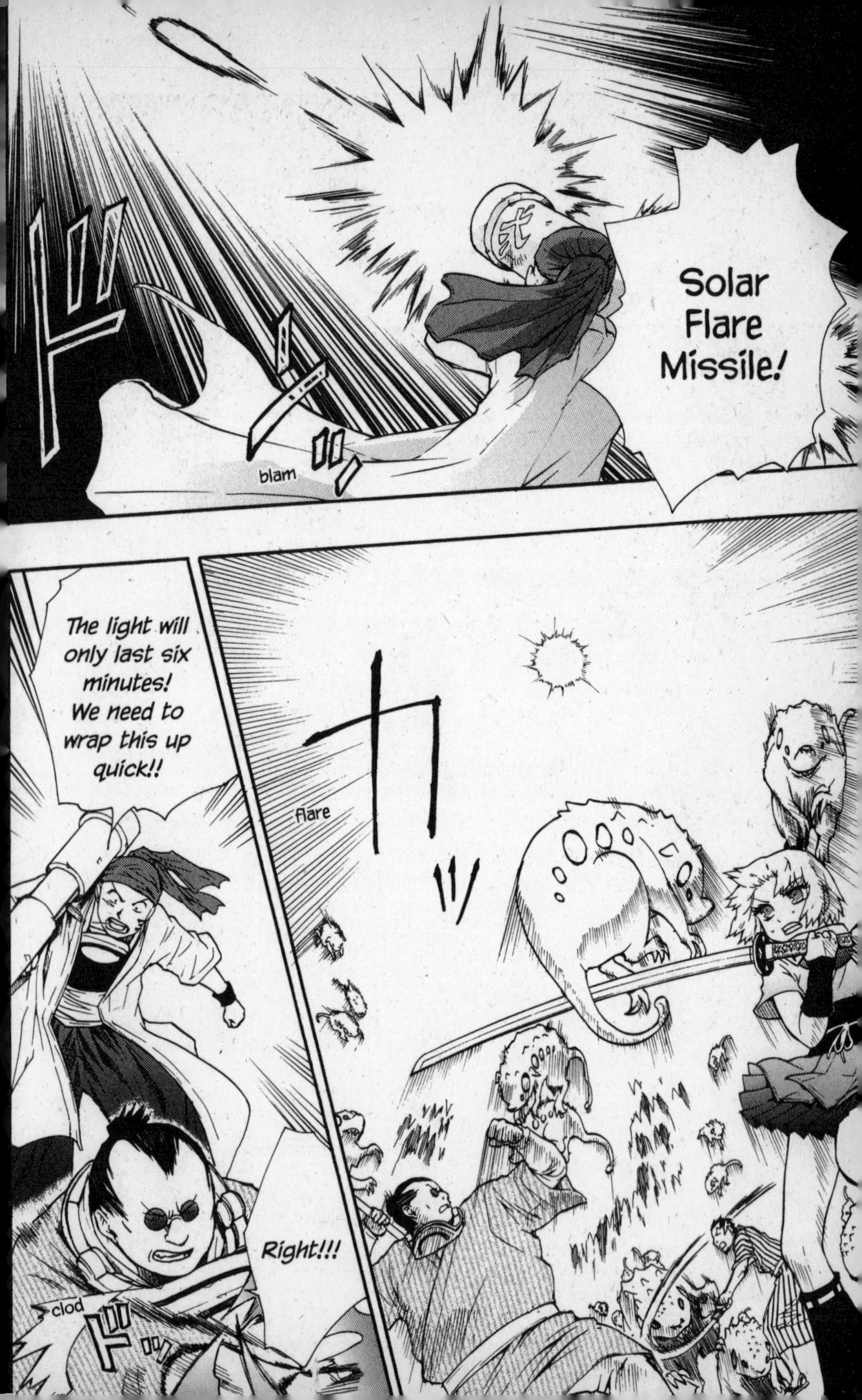
Solar Flare Missile!
blam
flare
The light will only last six minutes! We need to wrap this up quick!!
Right!!!
clod

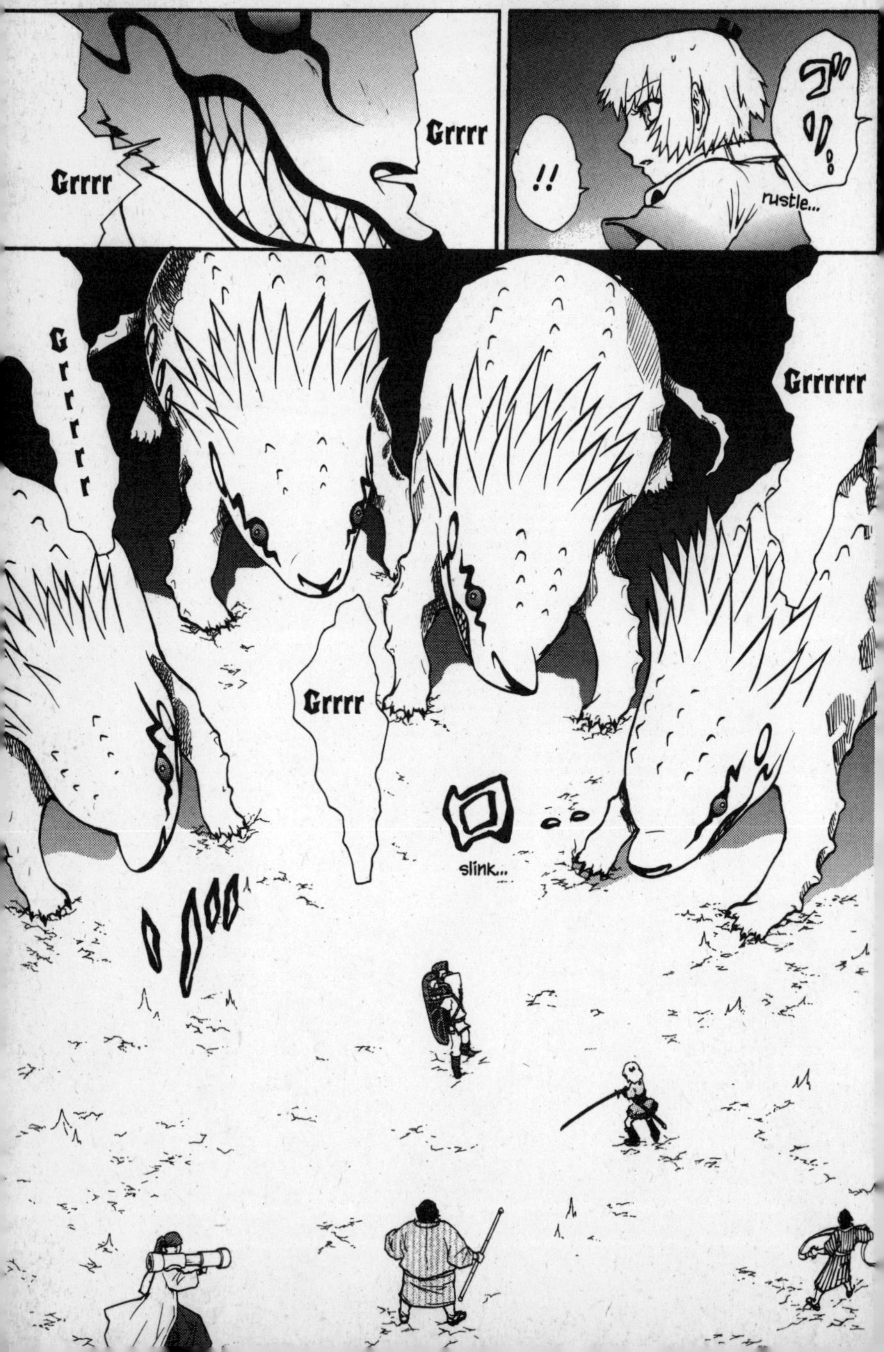
!!
rustle...
Grrrr
Grrrr
Grrrrrr
Grrrrrr
Grrrr
slink...

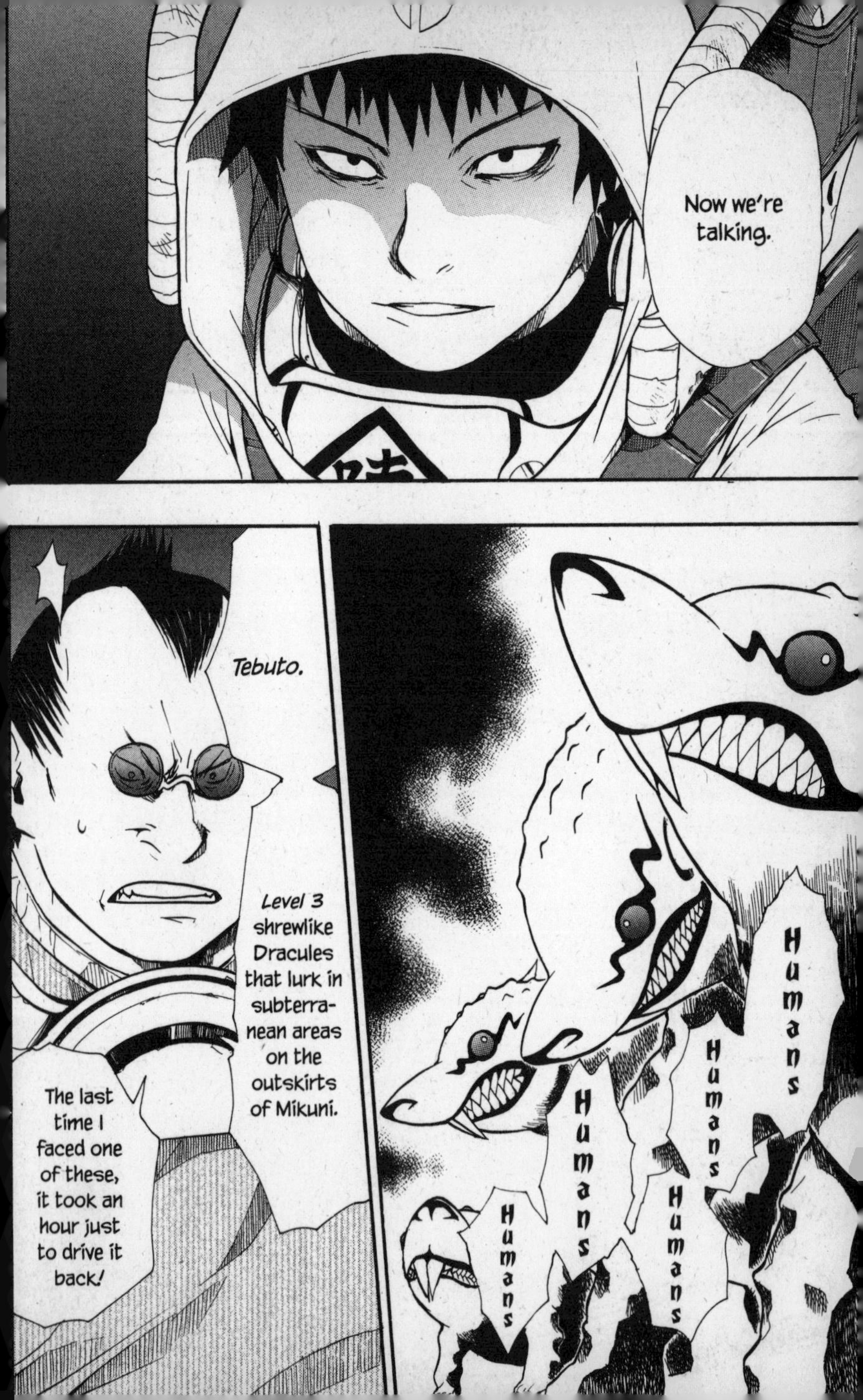

Now we're talking.
Humans
Humans
Humans
Humans
Humans
Tebuto.
Level 3 shrewlike Dracules that lurk in subterranean areas on the outskirts of Mikuni.
The last time I faced one of these, it took an hour just to drive it back!

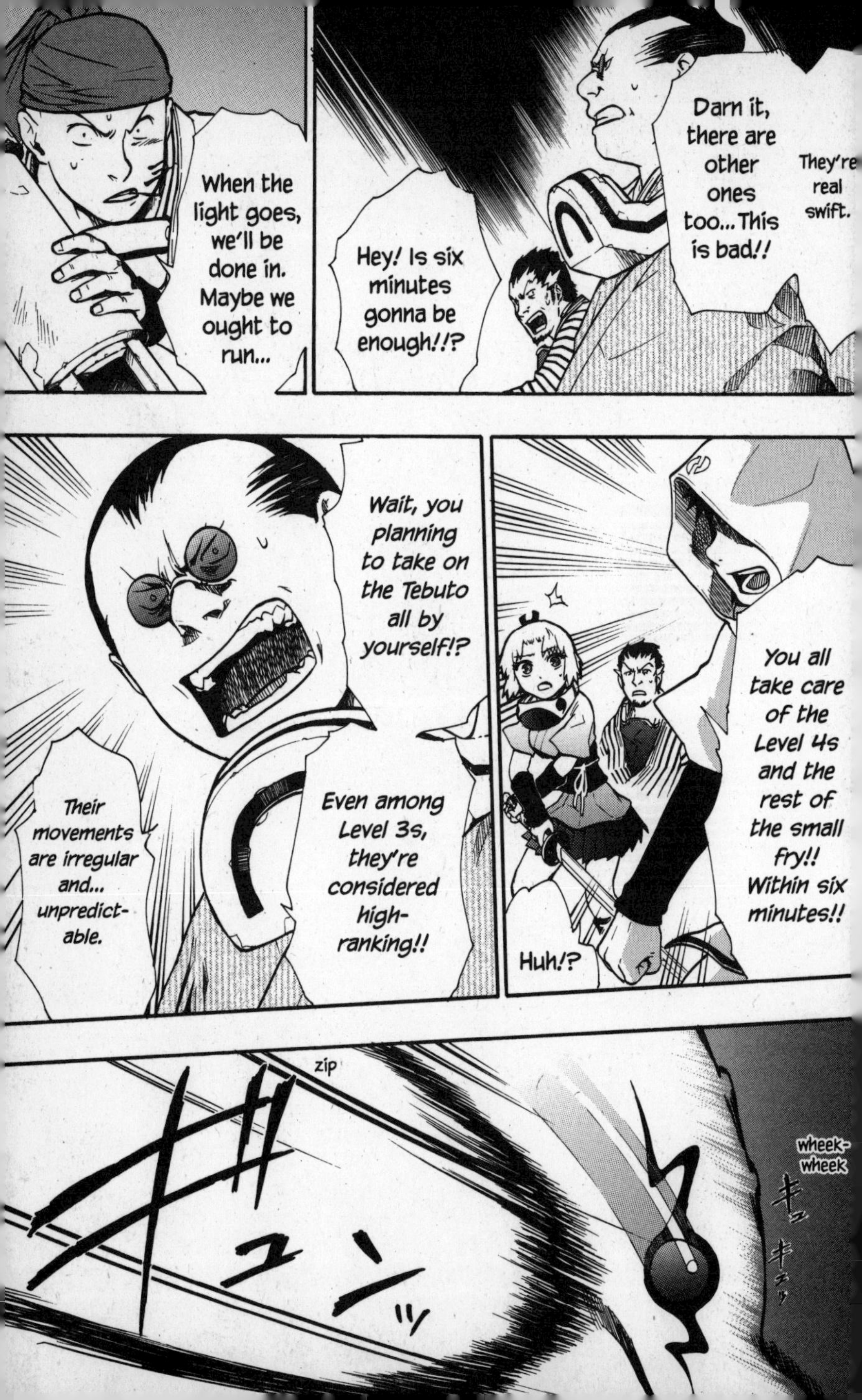
Darn it, there are other ones too... This is bad!!
They're real swift.
Hey! Is six minutes gonna be enough!!?
When the light goes, we'll be done in. Maybe we ought to run...
You all take care of the Level 4s and the rest of the small fry!! Within six minutes!!
Huh!?
Wait, you planning to take on the Tebuto all by yourself!?
Even among Level 3s, they're considered high-ranking!!
Their movements are irregular and... unpredict-able.
wheek-wheek
zip

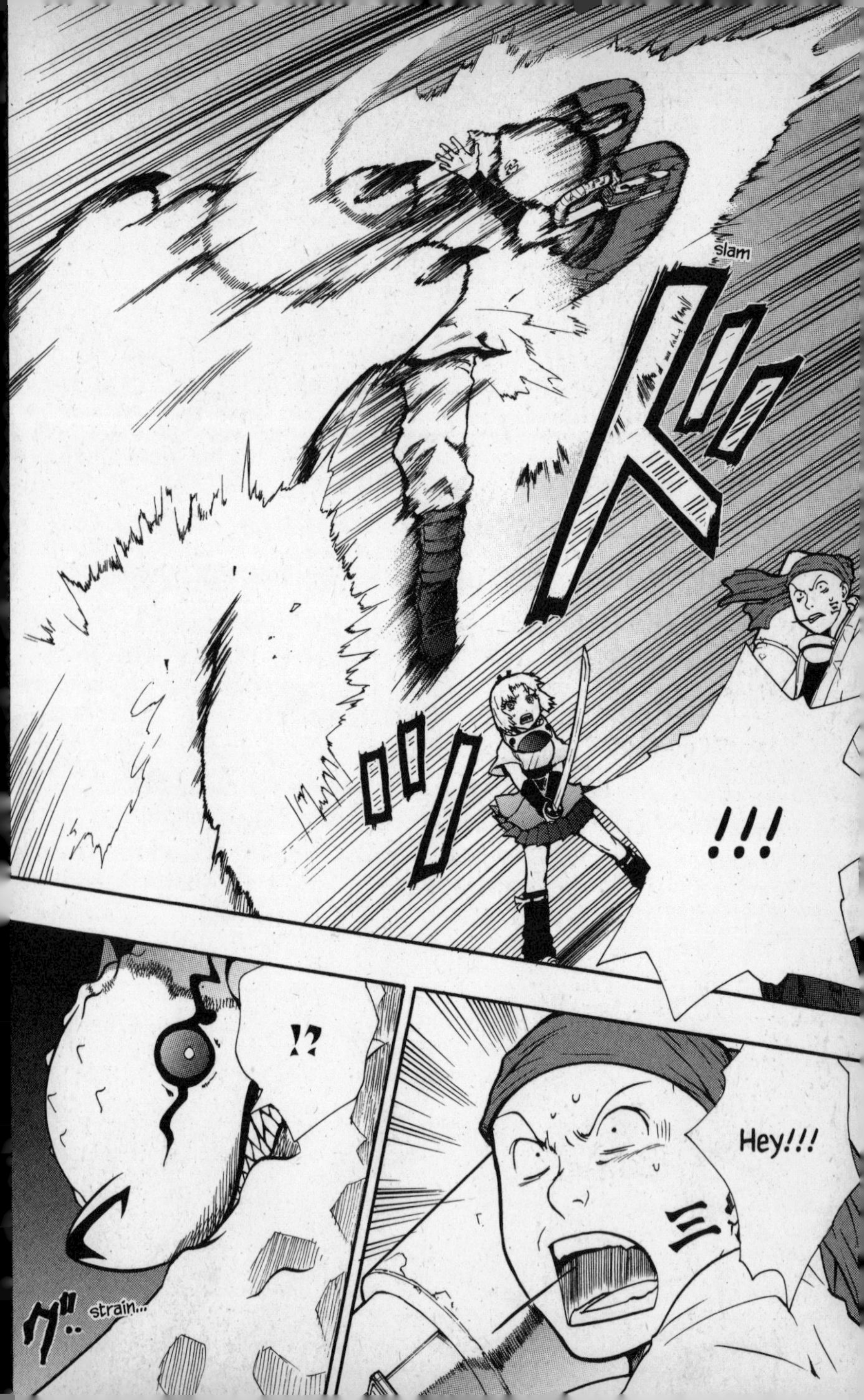
slam
!!!
Hey!!!
!?
strain...

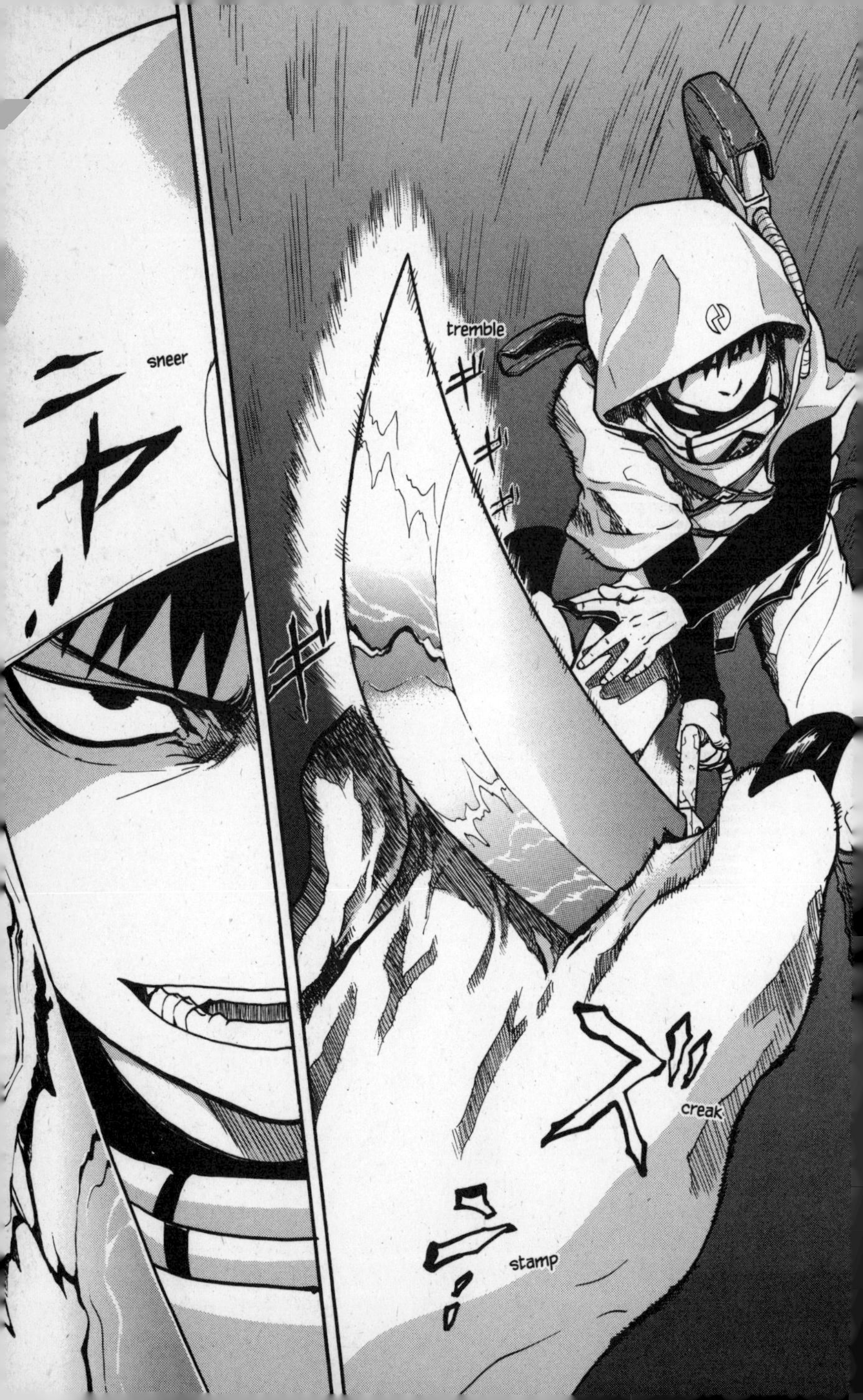
tremble
creak
stamp
sneer

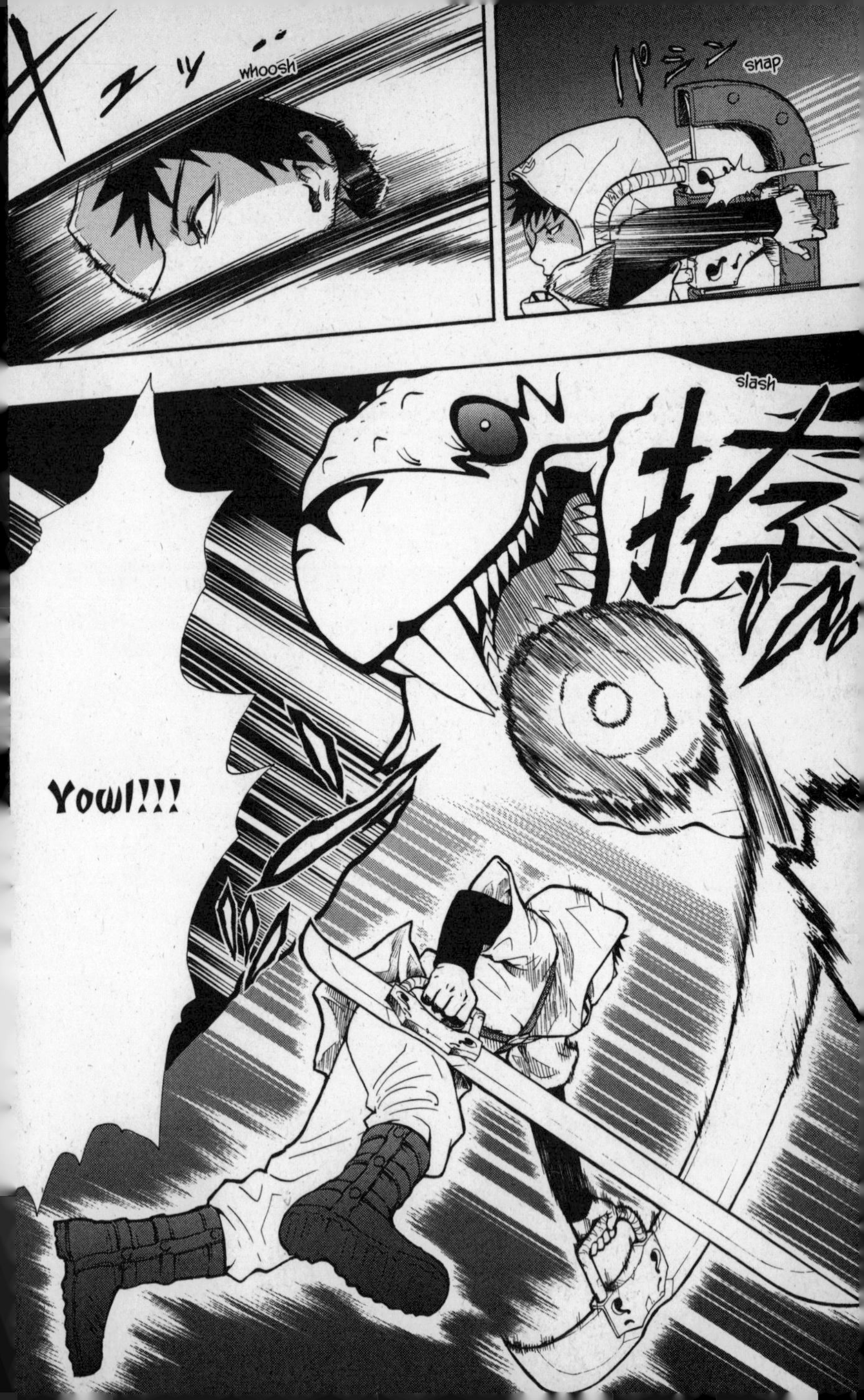
snap
whoosh
slash
Yowl!!!

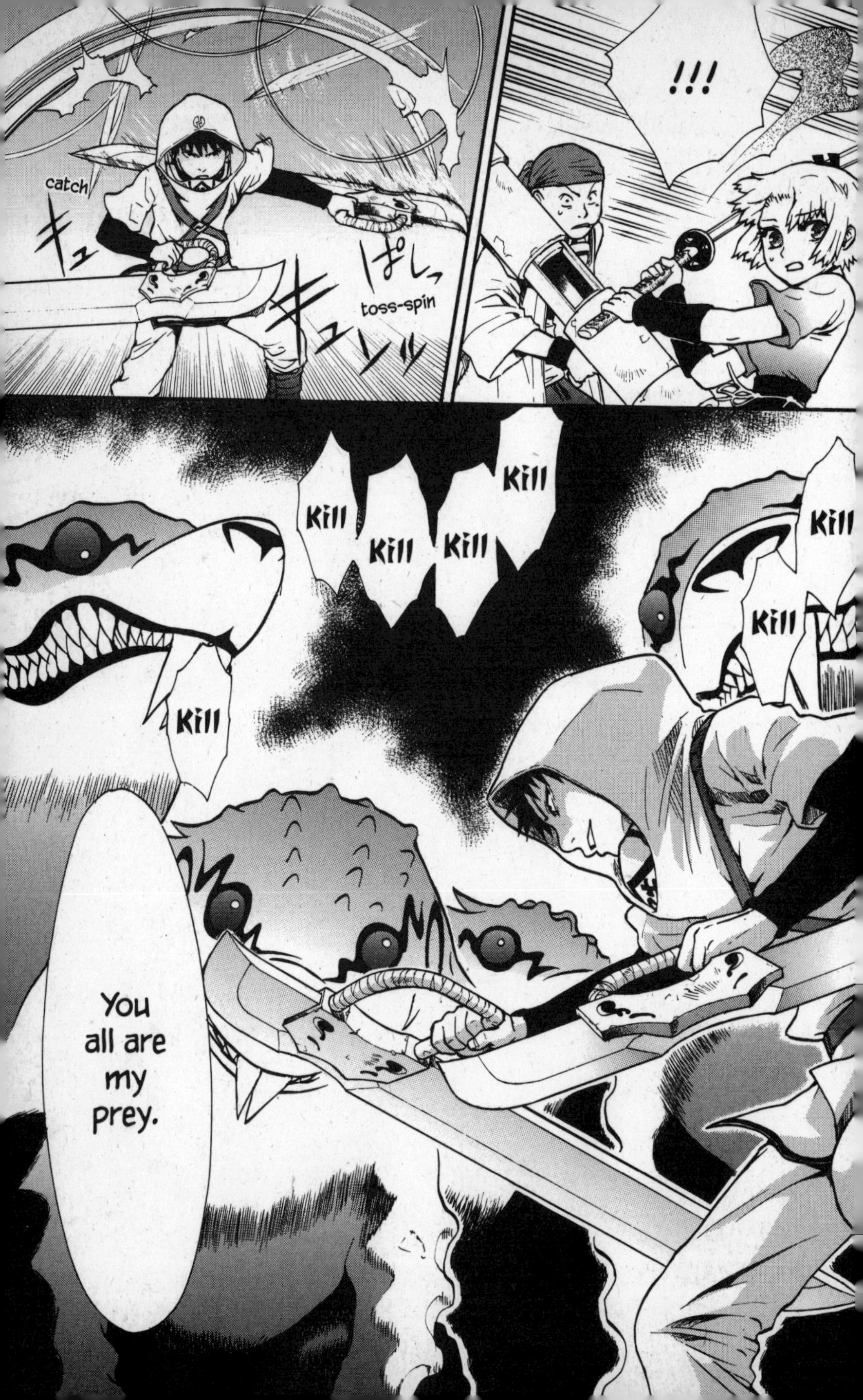
!!!
catch
キュ
ぱしっ
toss-spin
キュンッ
Kill
Kill
Kill
Kill
Kill
Kill
Kill
You all are my prey.

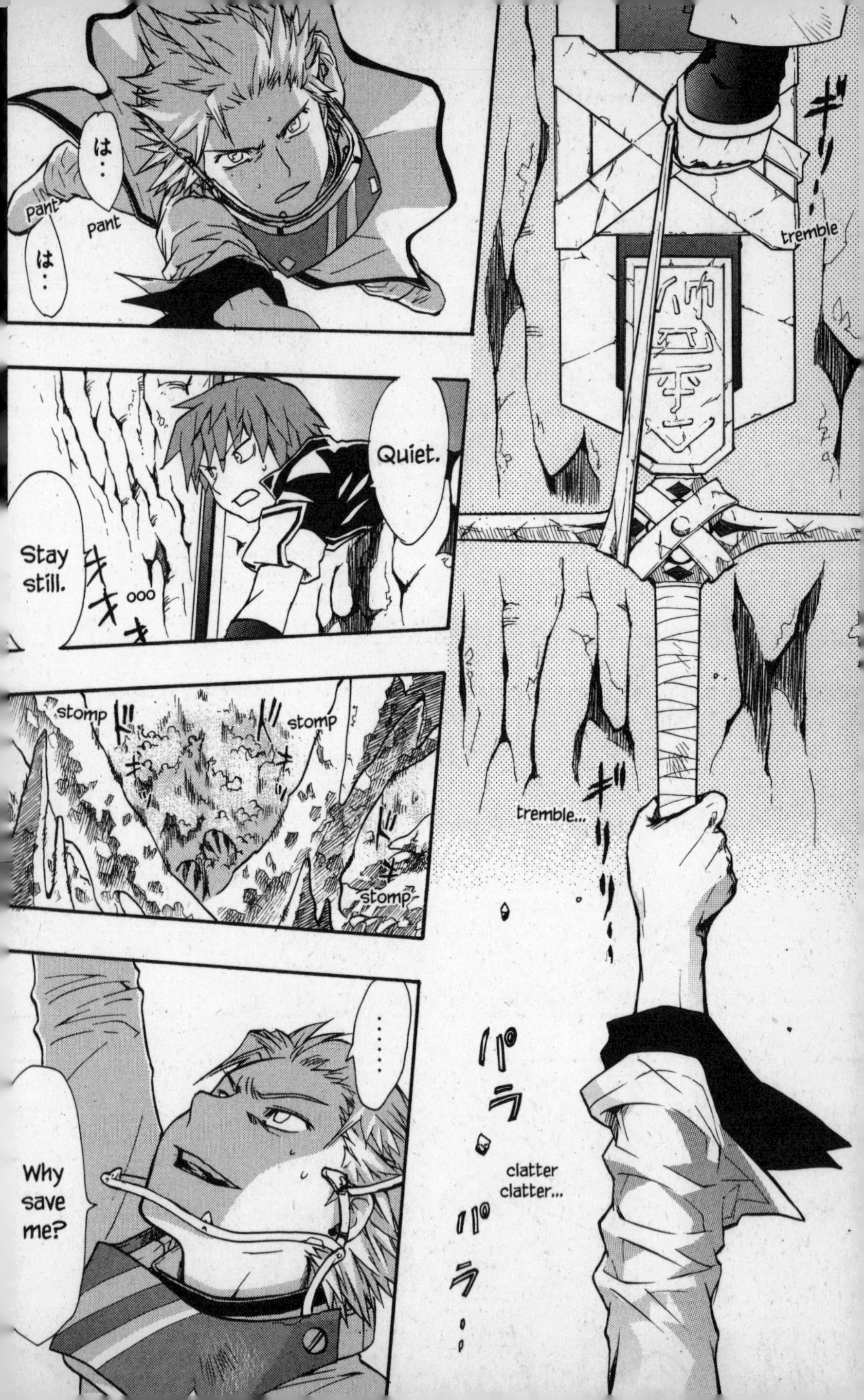

tremble
tremble...
clatter clatter...
は・・
pant
pant
は・・
Quiet.
Stay still.
ooo
stomp
stomp
stomp
......
Why save me?

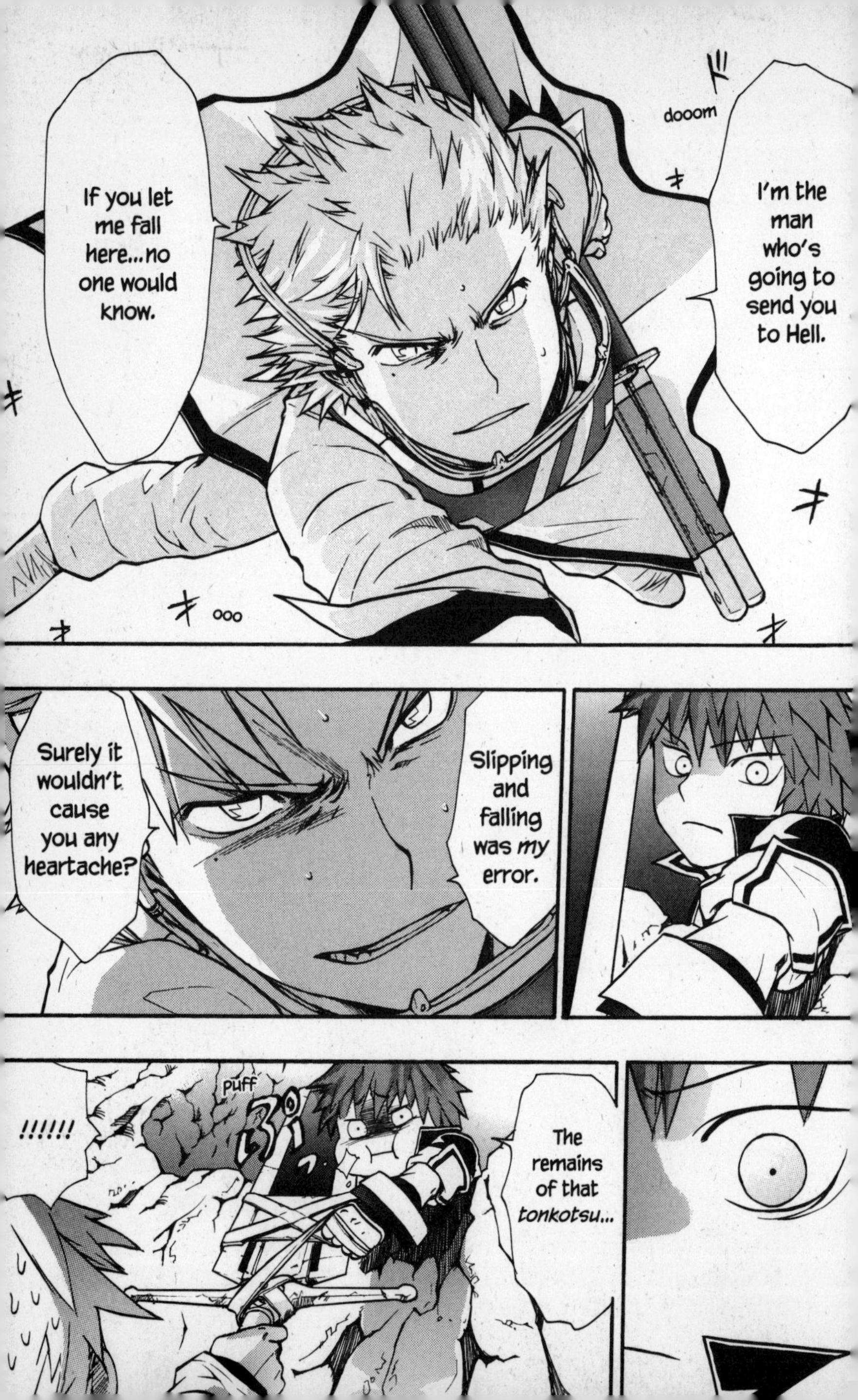
dooom
I'm the man who's going to send you to Hell.
If you let me fall here...no one would know.
ooo
Slipping and falling was *my* error.
Surely it wouldn't cause you any heartache?
The remains of that *tonkotsu*...
puff
!!!!!!

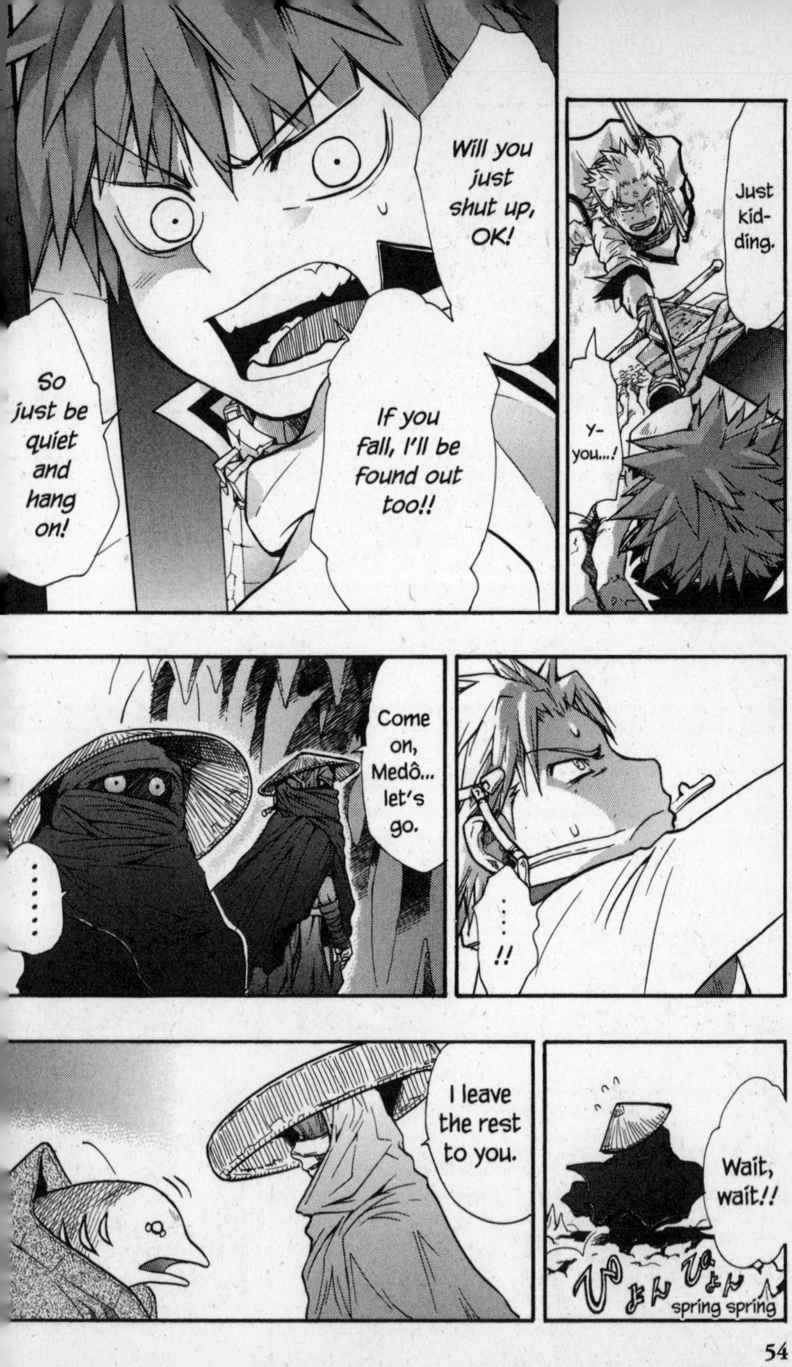
Just kid-ding.
Y-you...!
Will you just shut up, OK!
If you fall, I'll be found out too!!
So just be quiet and hang on!
....!!
Come on, Medô... let's go.
......
Wait, wait!!
spring spring
I leave the rest to you.

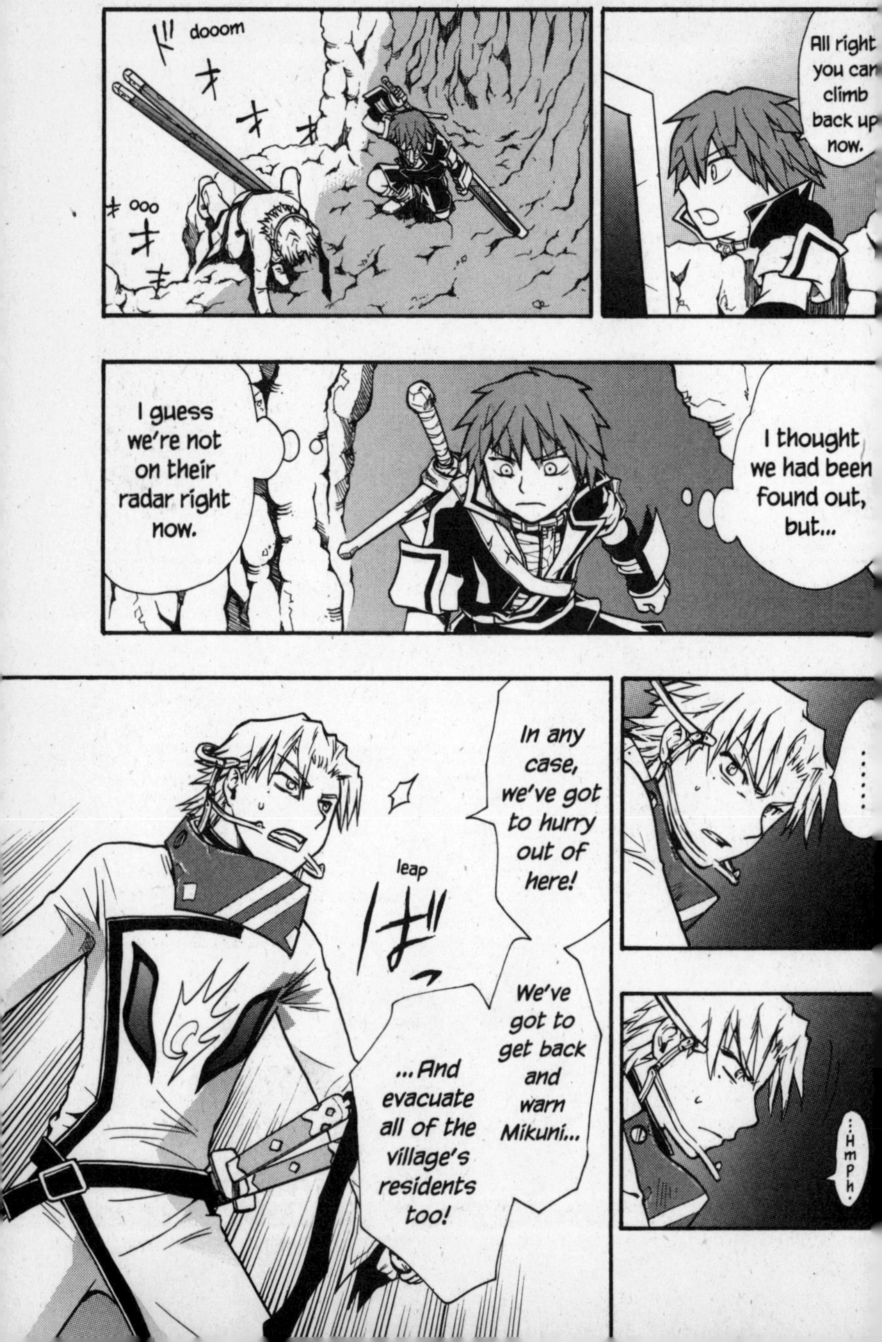

All right you can climb back up now.
dooom
ooo
I thought we had been found out, but...
I guess we're not on their radar right now.
......
...Hmph.
In any case, we've got to hurry out of here!
leap
We've got to get back and warn Mikuni...
...And evacuate all of the village's residents too!

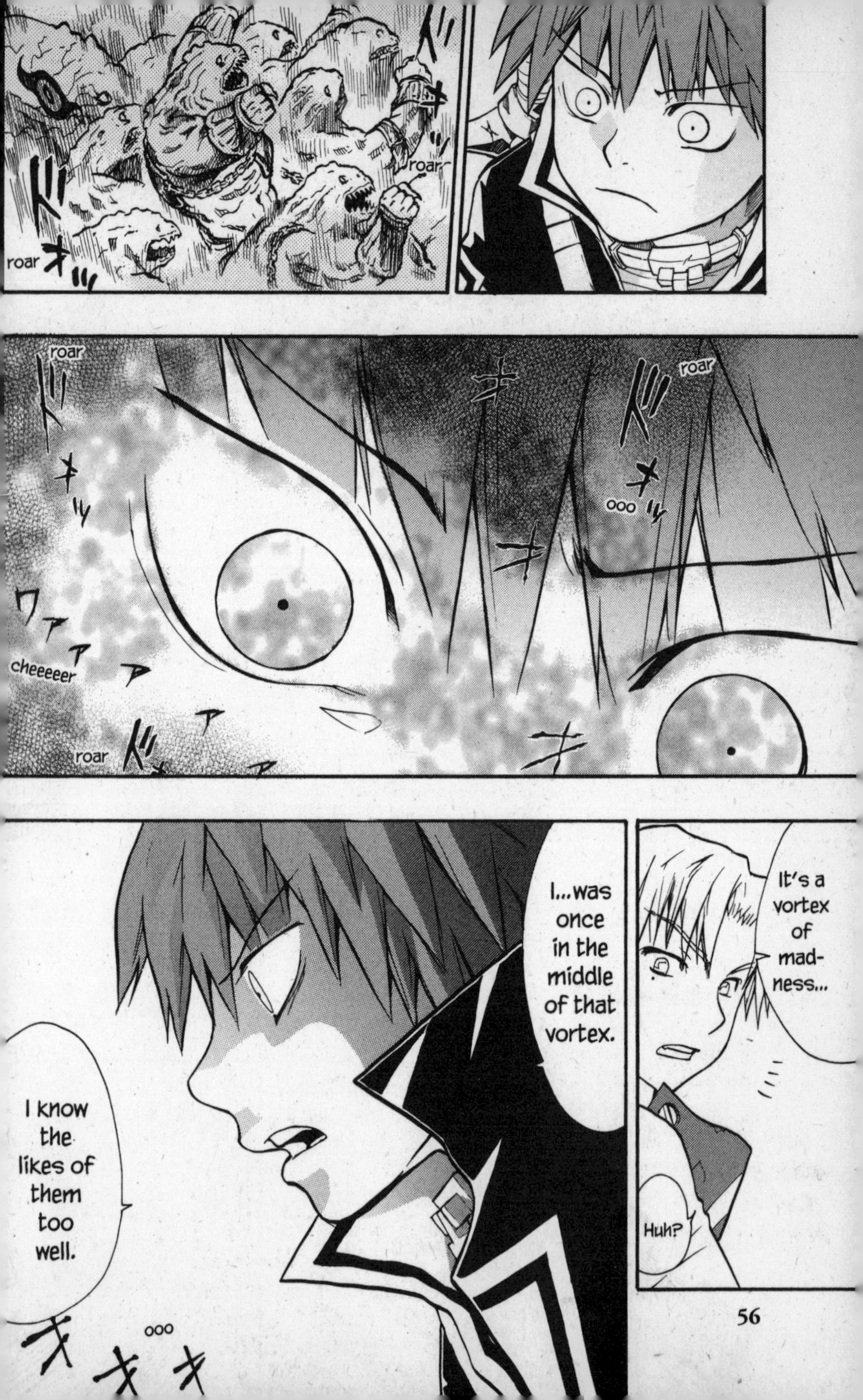
roar
roar
roar
roar
ooo
cheeeeer
roar
It's a vortex of mad-ness...
Huh?
I...was once in the middle of that vortex.
I know the likes of them too well.
ooo

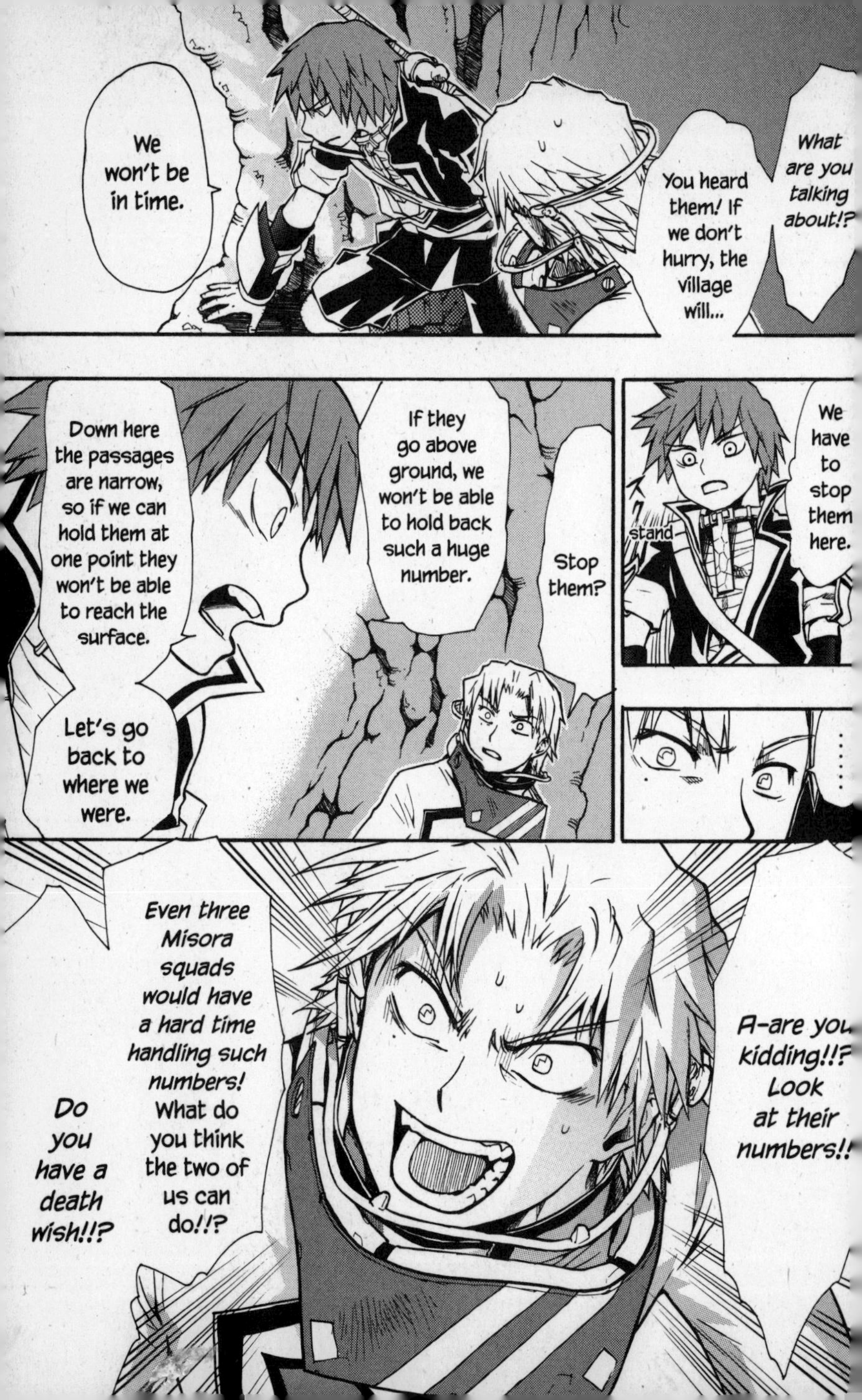
What are you talking about!?
You heard them! If we don't hurry, the village will...
We won't be in time.
stand
We have to stop them here.
......
Stop them?
If they go above ground, we won't be able to hold back such a huge number.
Down here the passages are narrow, so if we can hold them at one point they won't be able to reach the surface.
Let's go back to where we were.
A-are you kidding!!? Look at their numbers!!
Even three Misora squads would have a hard time handling such numbers! What do you think the two of us can do!!?
Do you have a death wish!!?

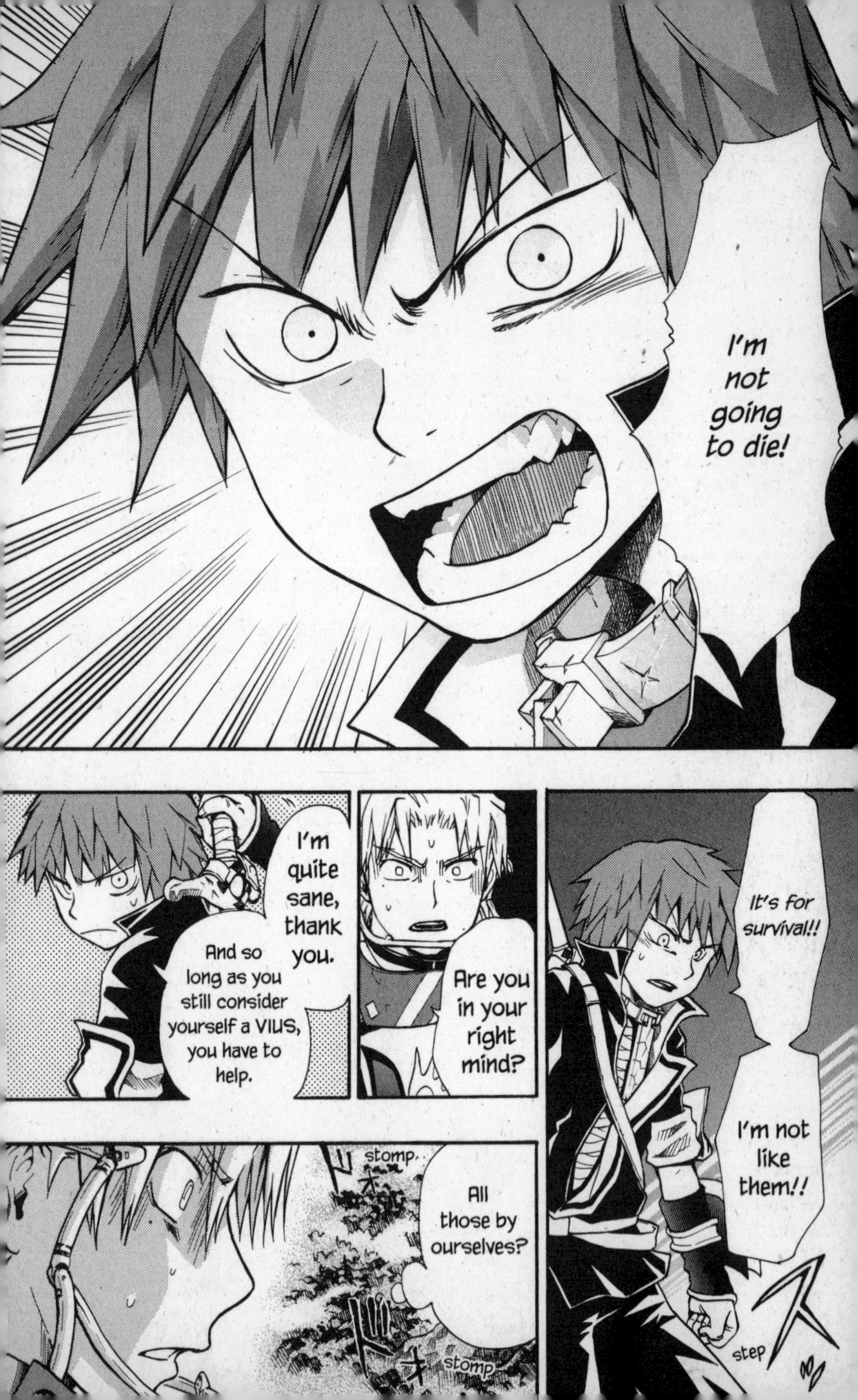
I'm not going to die!
It's for survival!!
I'm not like them!!
step
Are you in your right mind?
I'm quite sane, thank you.
And so long as you still consider yourself a VIUS, you have to help.
stomp
All those by ourselves?
stomp

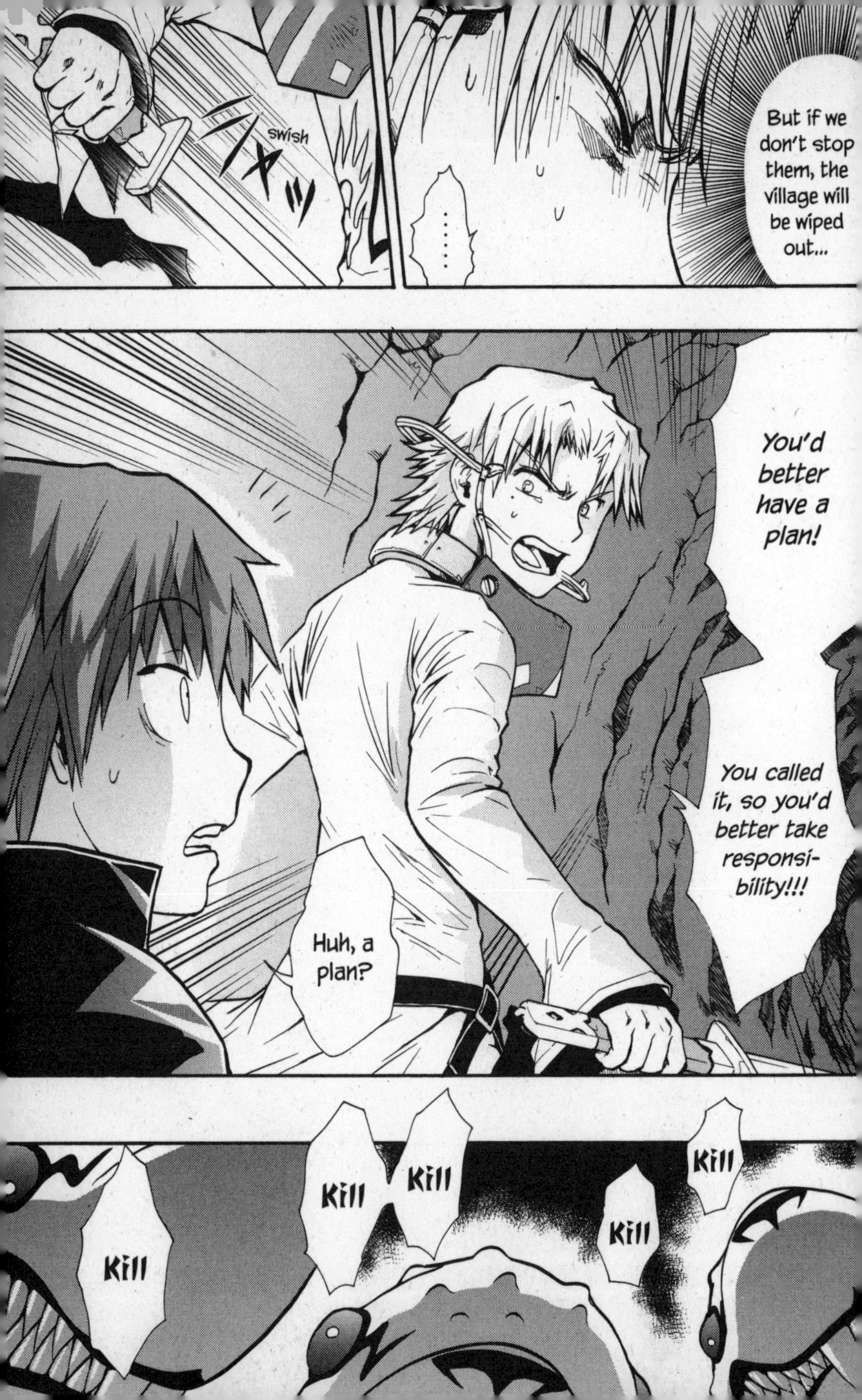
But if we don't stop them, the village will be wiped out...
......
swish
You'd better have a plan!
You called it, so you'd better take responsi-bility!!!
Huh, a plan?
Kill
Kill
Kill
Kill
Kill

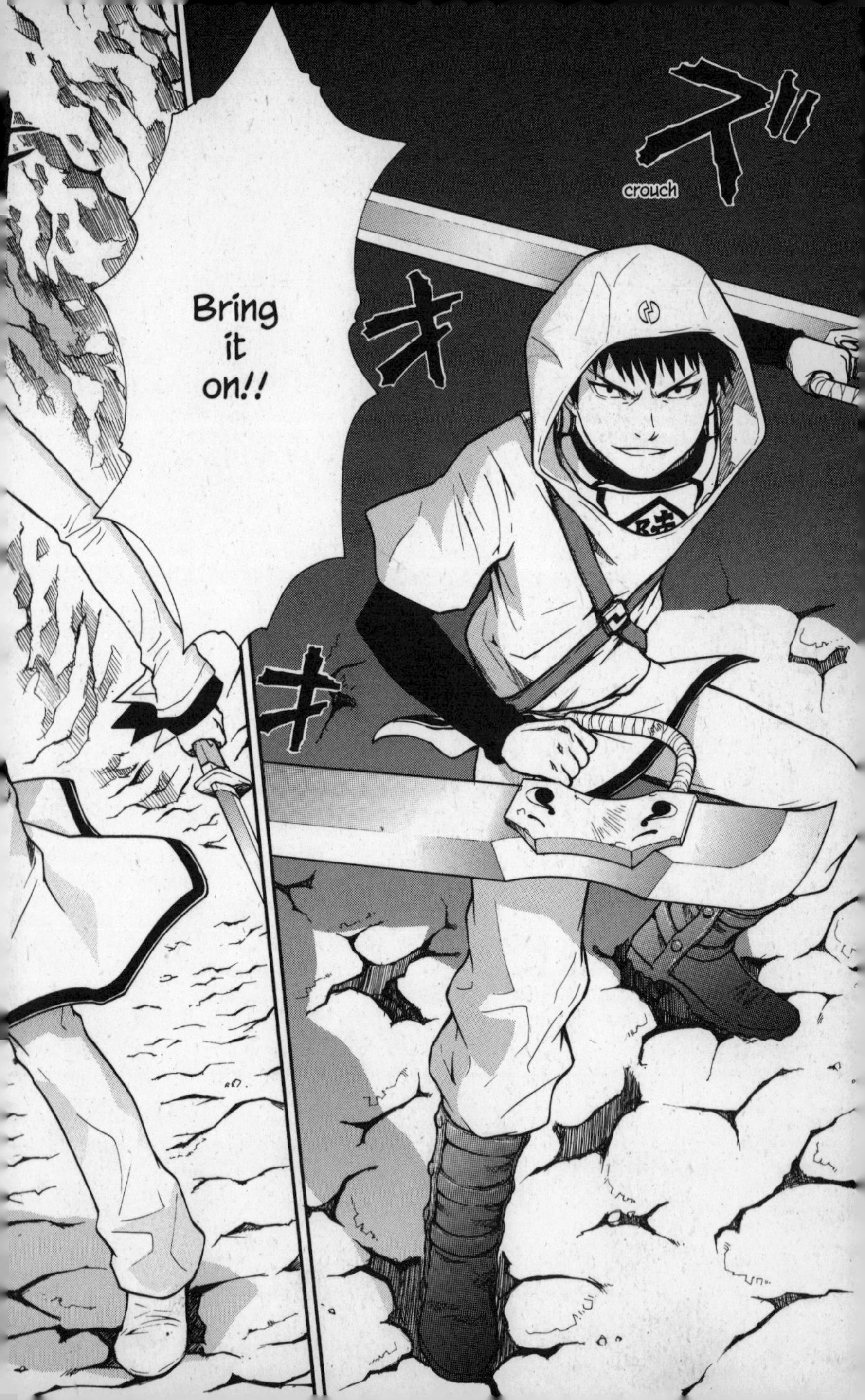
crouch
Bring it on!!

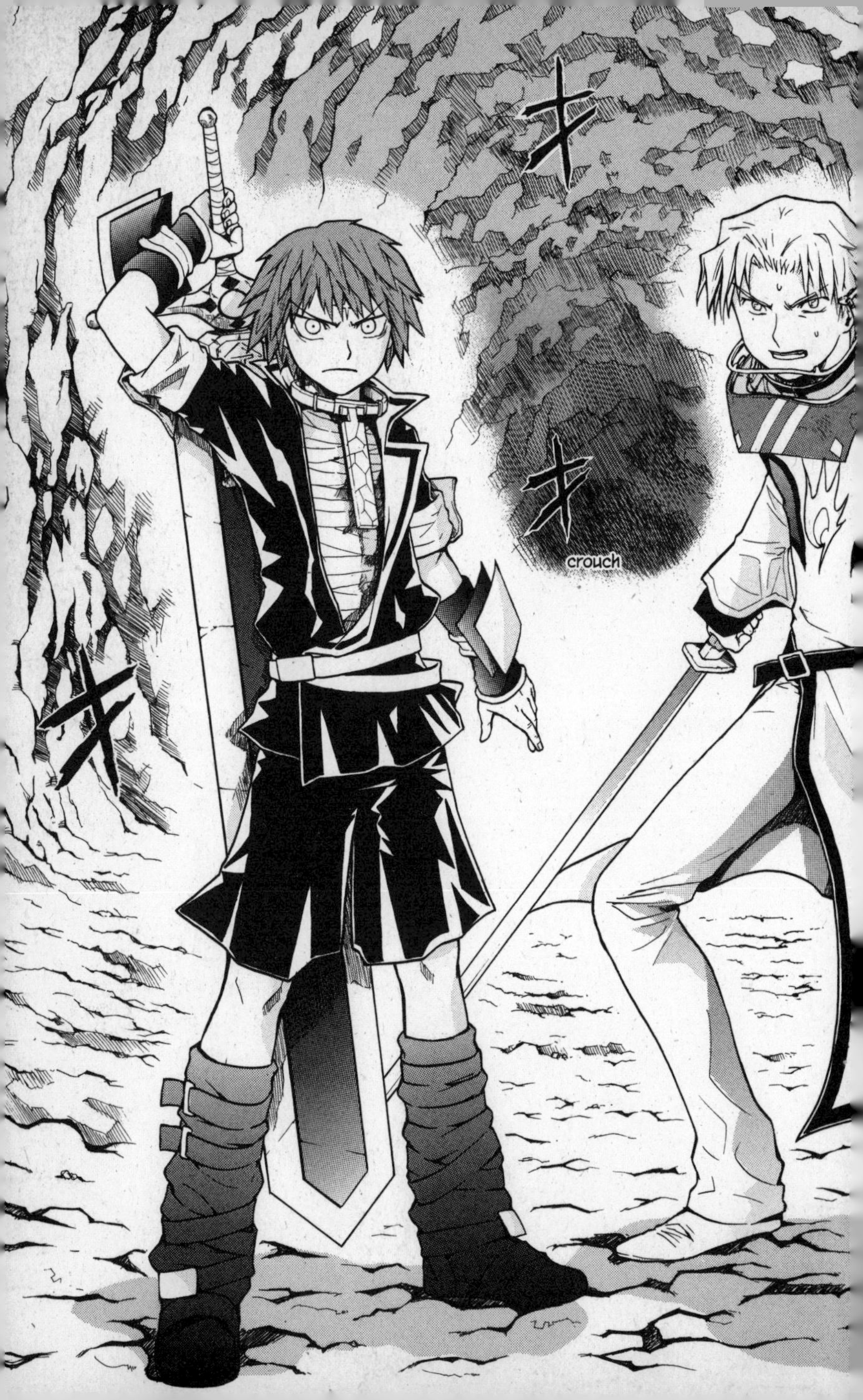
crouch

One
bowl
of rice
a day

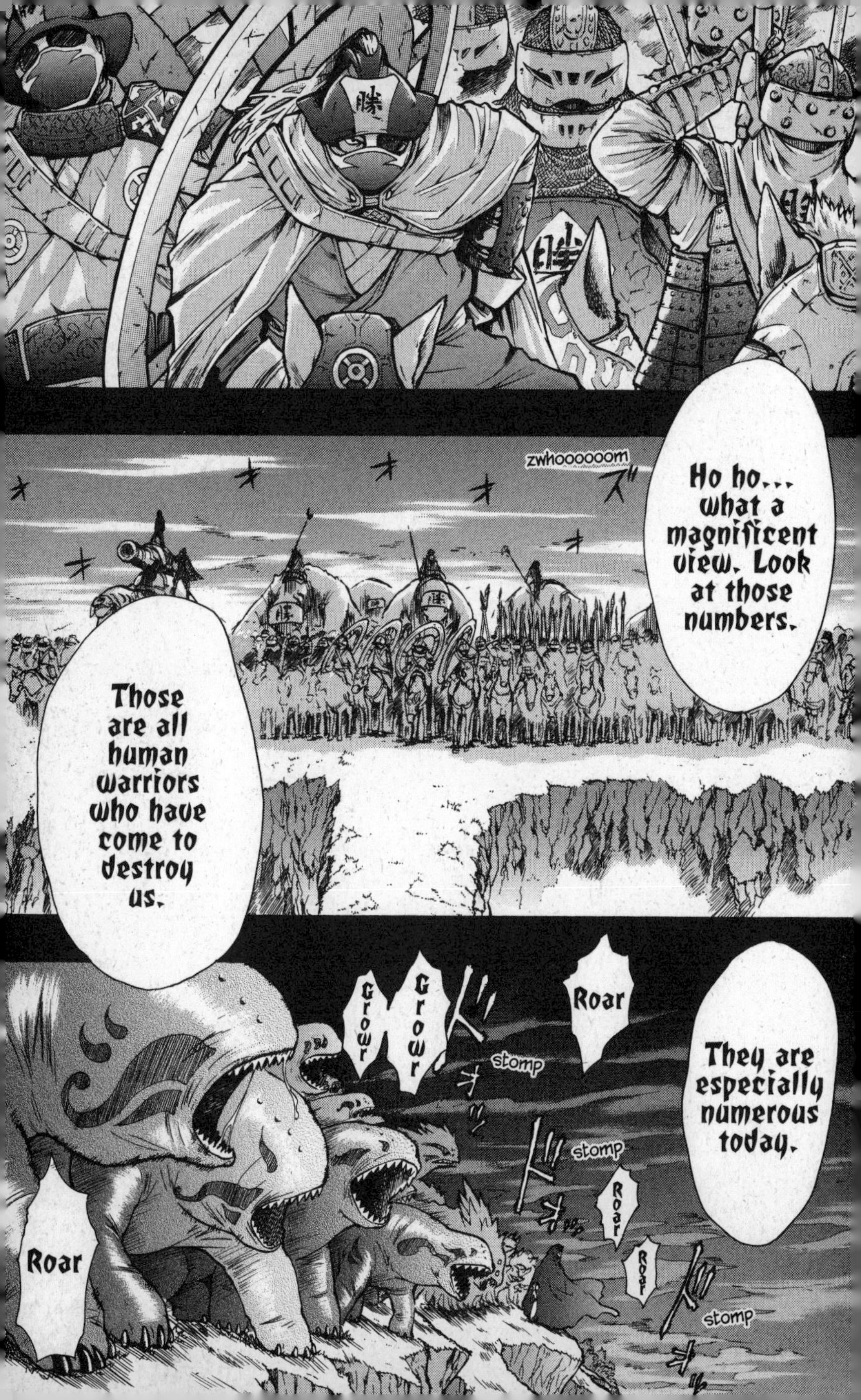
zwhooooom
Ho ho... what a magnificent view. Look at those numbers.
Those are all human warriors who have come to destroy us.
Roar
They are especially numerous today.
Growr
Growr
stomp
stomp
Roar
Roar
stomp
Roar

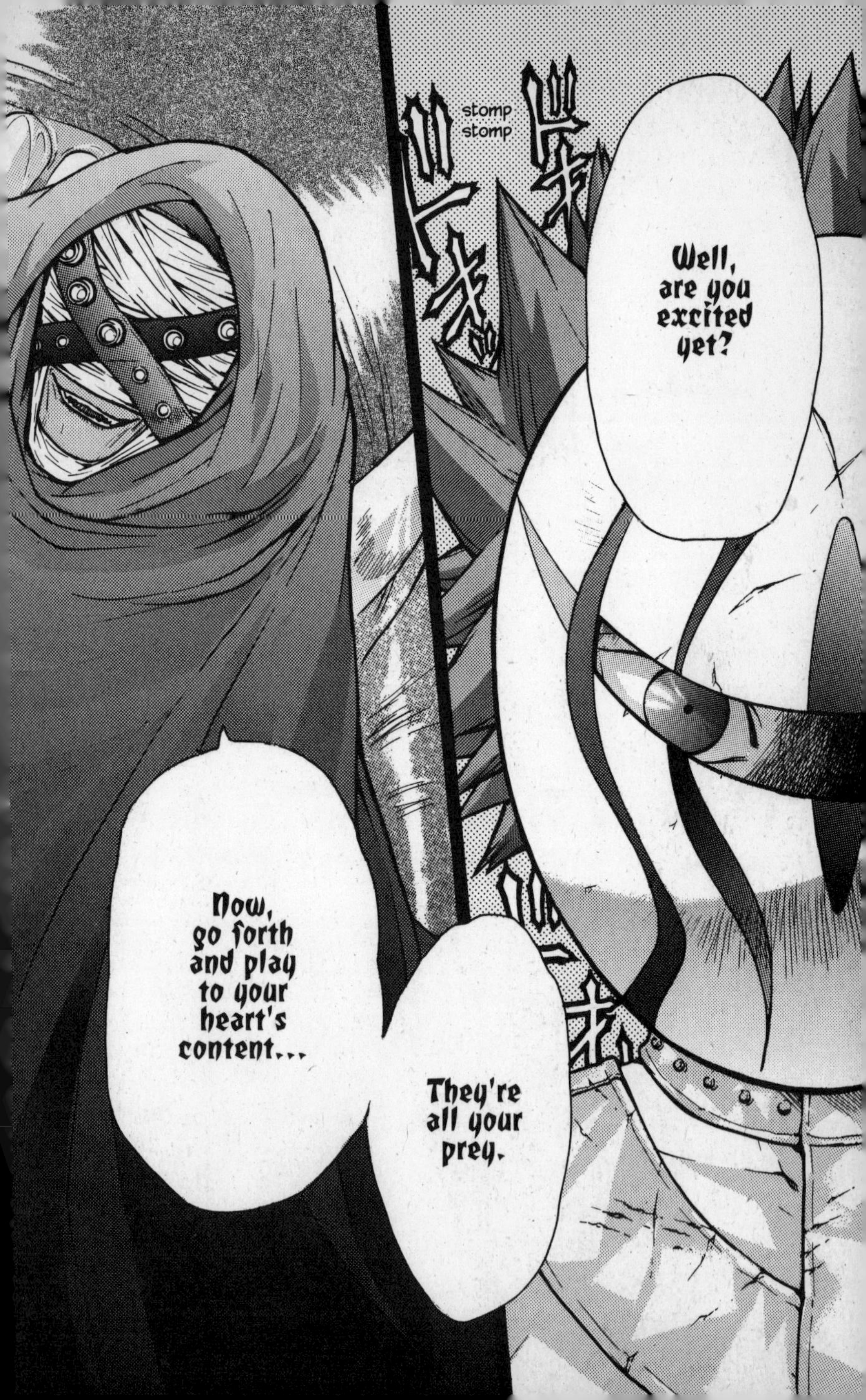
stomp stomp
Well, are you excited yet?
Now, go forth and play to your heart's content...
They're all your prey.

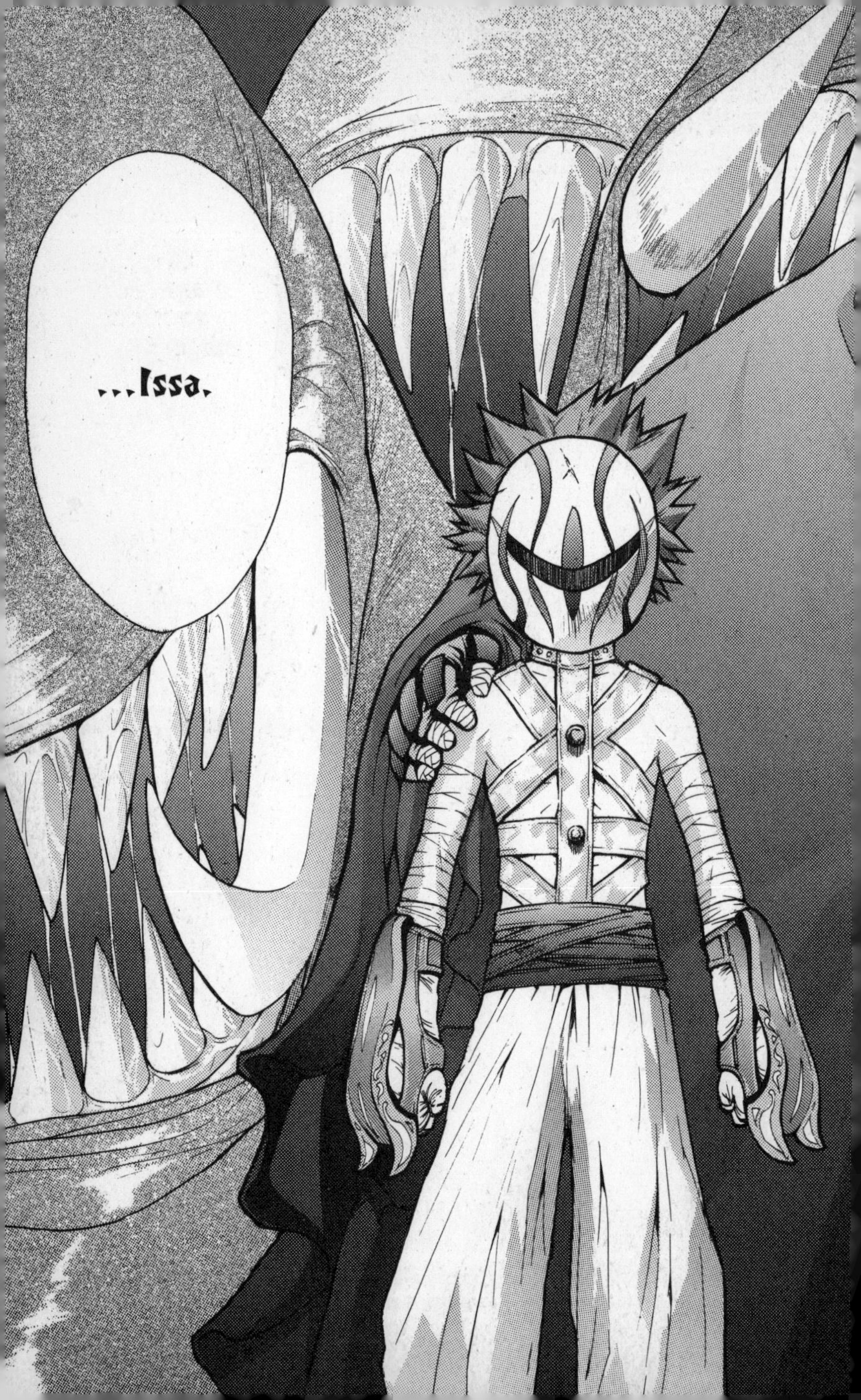
...Issa.

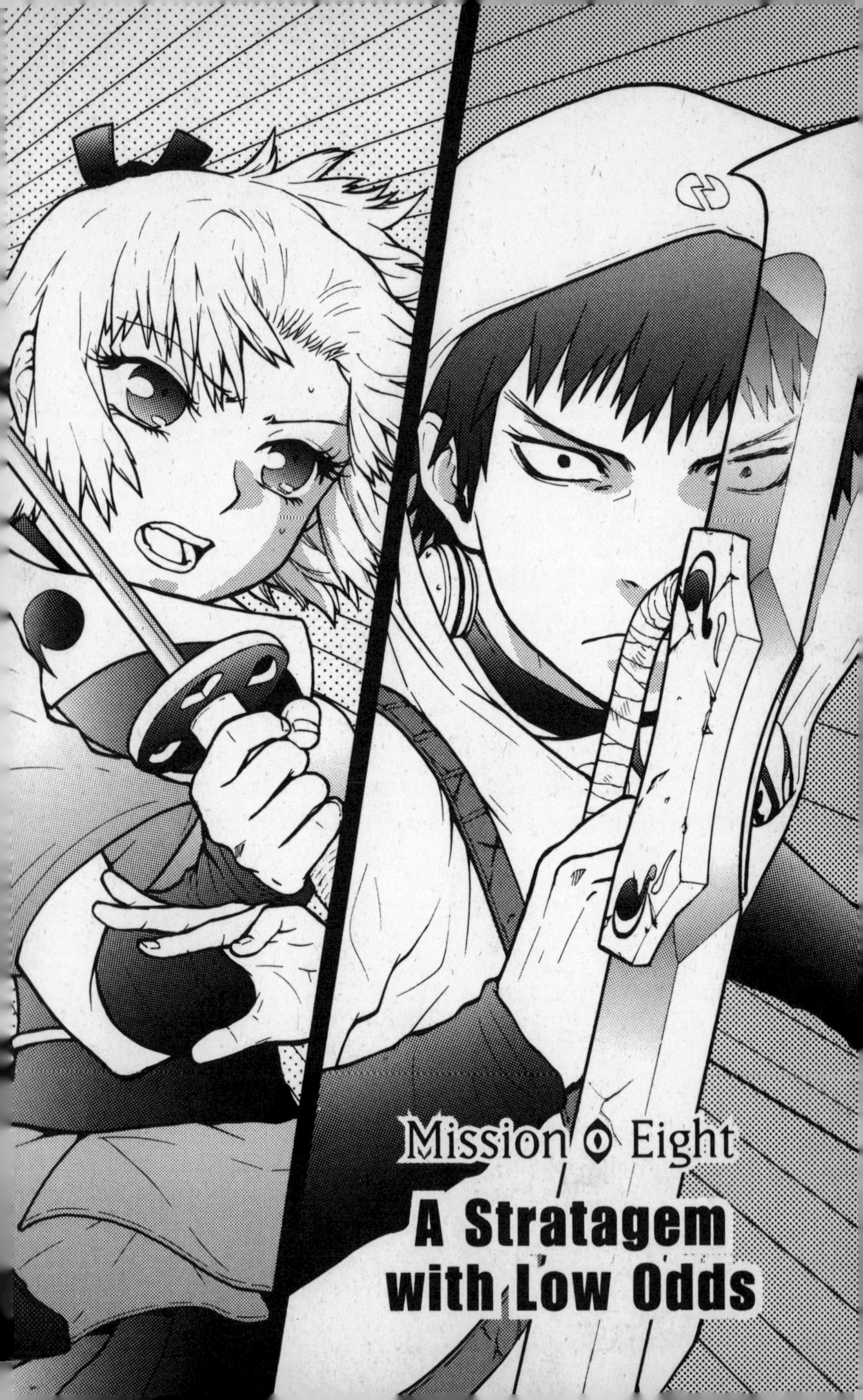
Mission Eight
A Stratagem with Low Odds

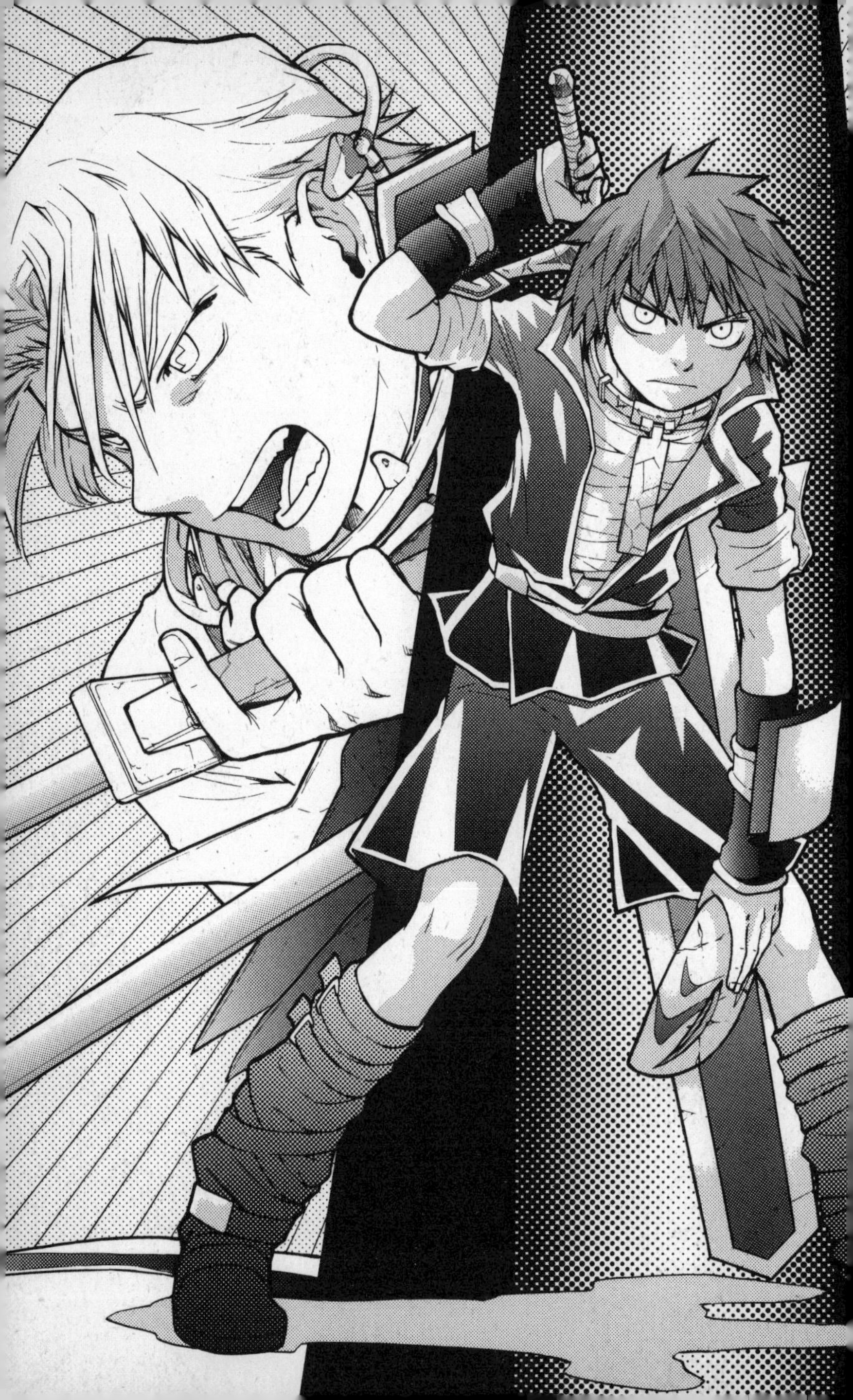

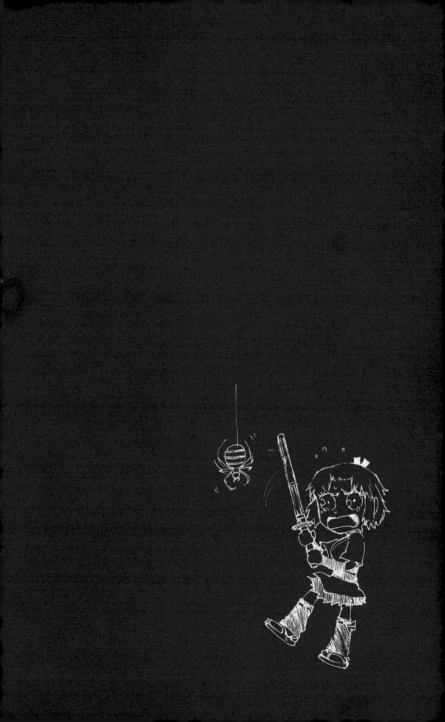

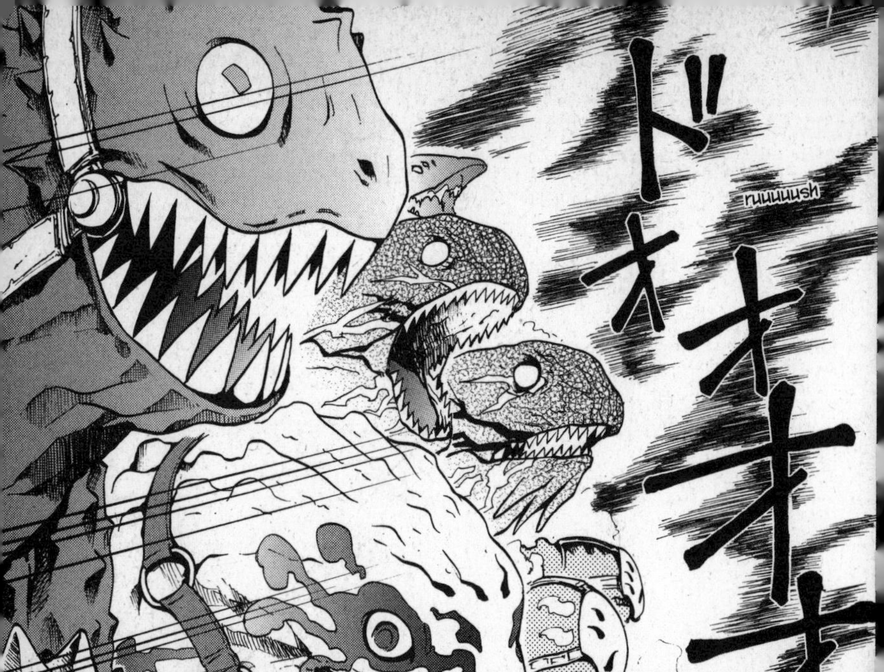
ドオオオオオ
ruuuuuush

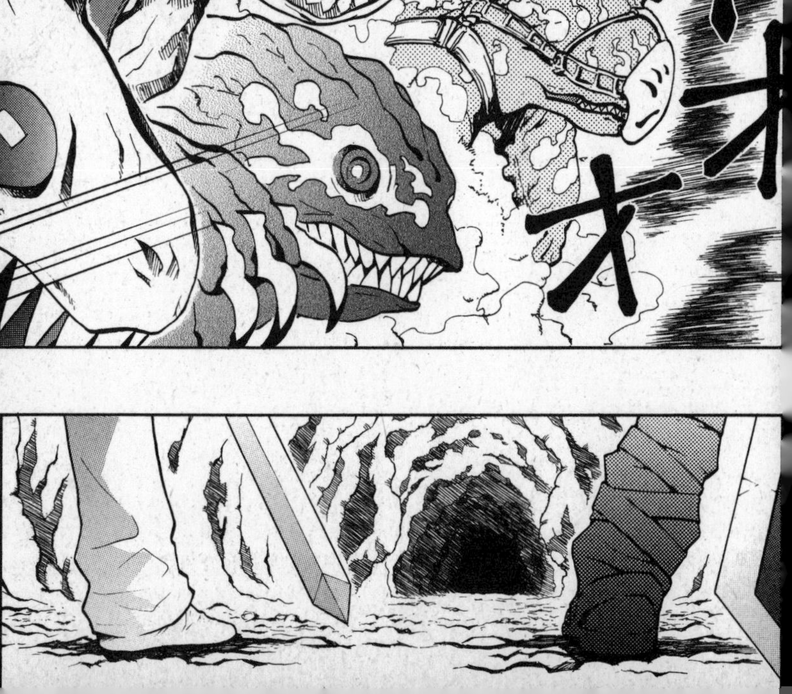

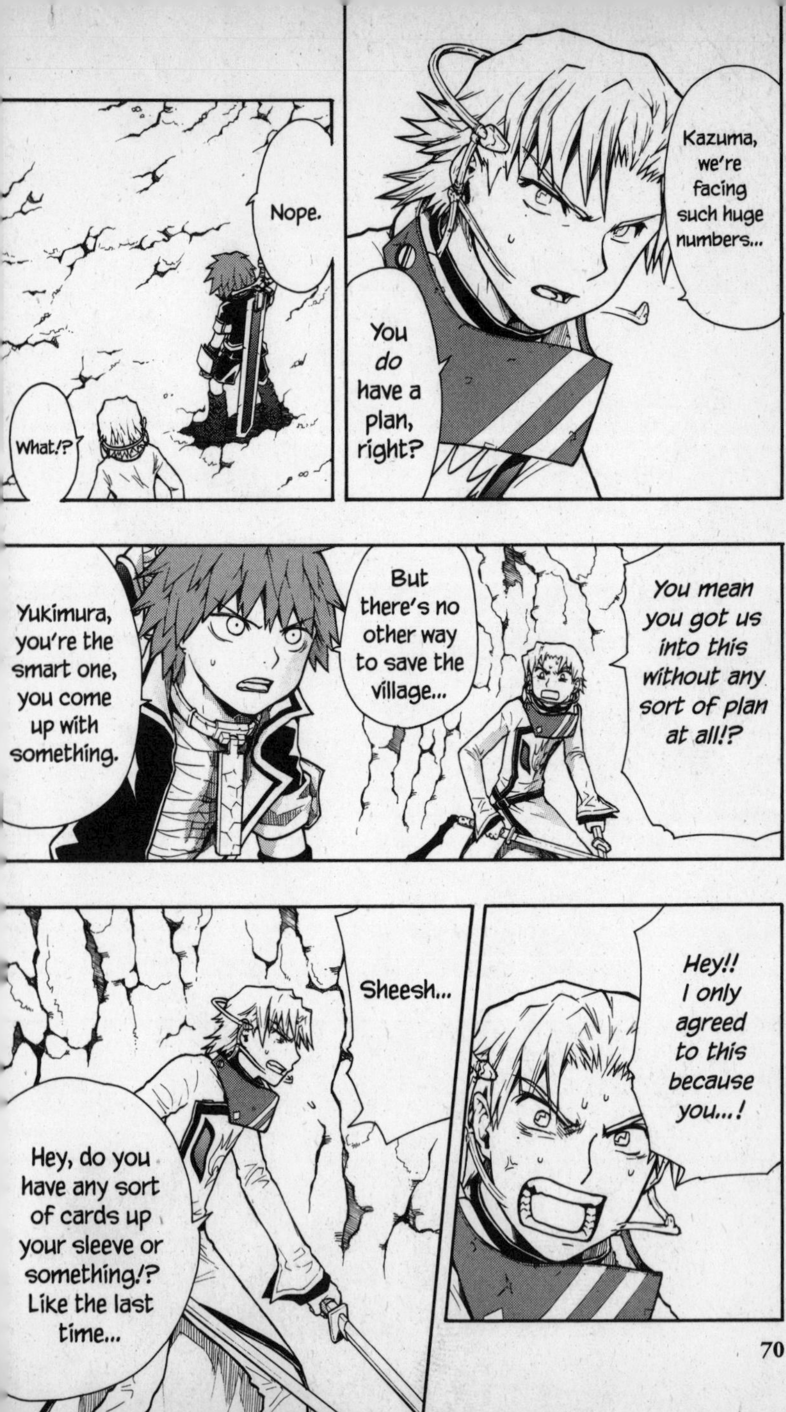
Kazuma, we're facing such huge numbers...
You do have a plan, right?
Nope.
What!?
You mean you got us into this without any sort of plan at all!?
But there's no other way to save the village...
Yukimura, you're the smart one, you come up with something.
Hey!! I only agreed to this because you...!
Sheesh...
Hey, do you have any sort of cards up your sleeve or something!? Like the last time...

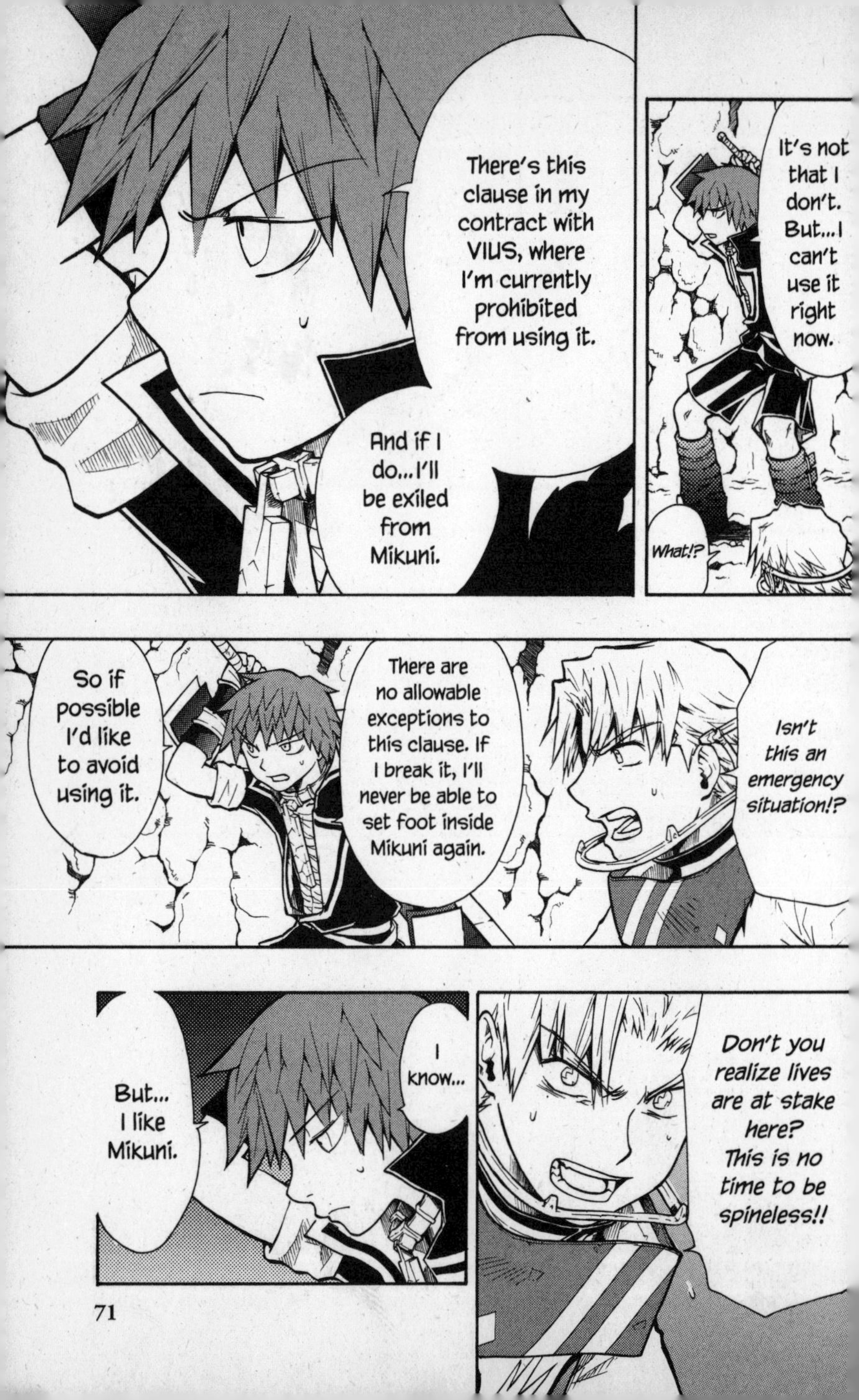
It's not that I don't. But...I can't use it right now.
What!?
There's this clause in my contract with VIUS, where I'm currently prohibited from using it.
And if I do...I'll be exiled from Mikuni.
Isn't this an emergency situation!?
There are no allowable exceptions to this clause. If I break it, I'll never be able to set foot inside Mikuni again.
So if possible I'd like to avoid using it.
Don't you realize lives are at stake here? This is no time to be spineless!!
I know...
But... I like Mikuni.

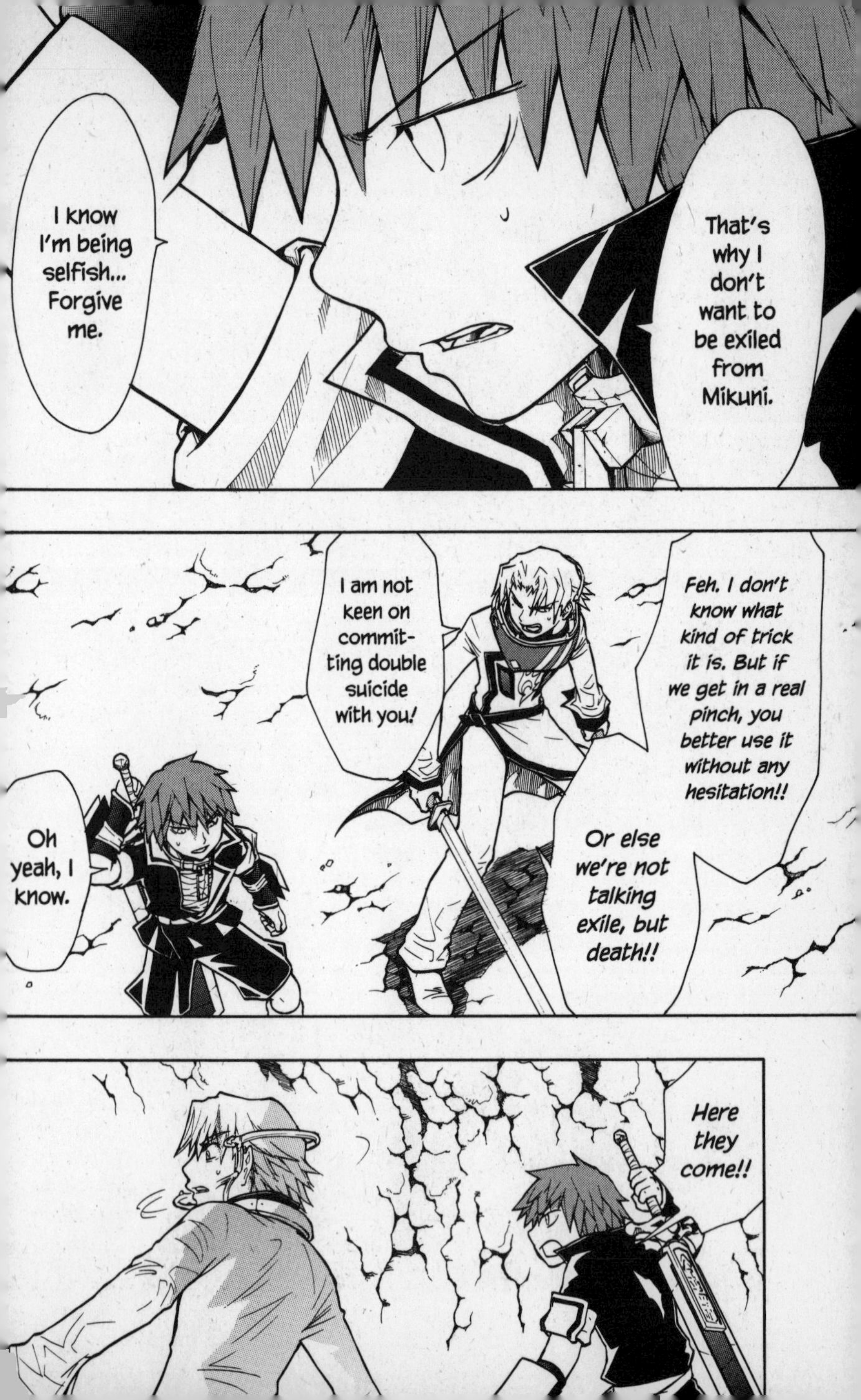
That's why I don't want to be exiled from Mikuni.
I know I'm being selfish... Forgive me.
Feh. I don't know what kind of trick it is. But if we get in a real pinch, you better use it without any hesitation!!
Or else we're not talking exile, but death!!
I am not keen on commit-ting double suicide with you!
Oh yeah, I know.
Here they come!!

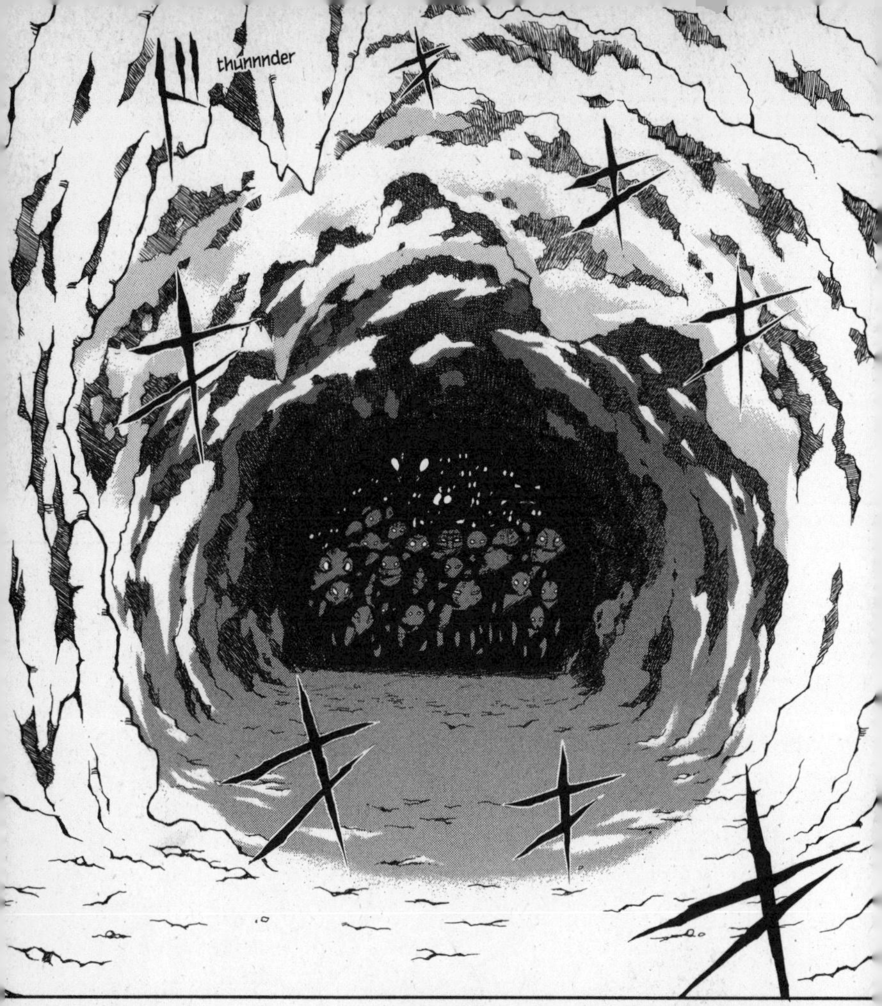
thunnnder

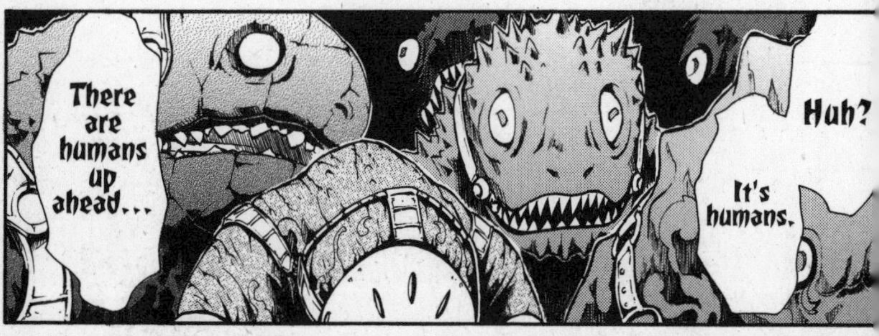
Huh?
It's humans.
There are humans up ahead...

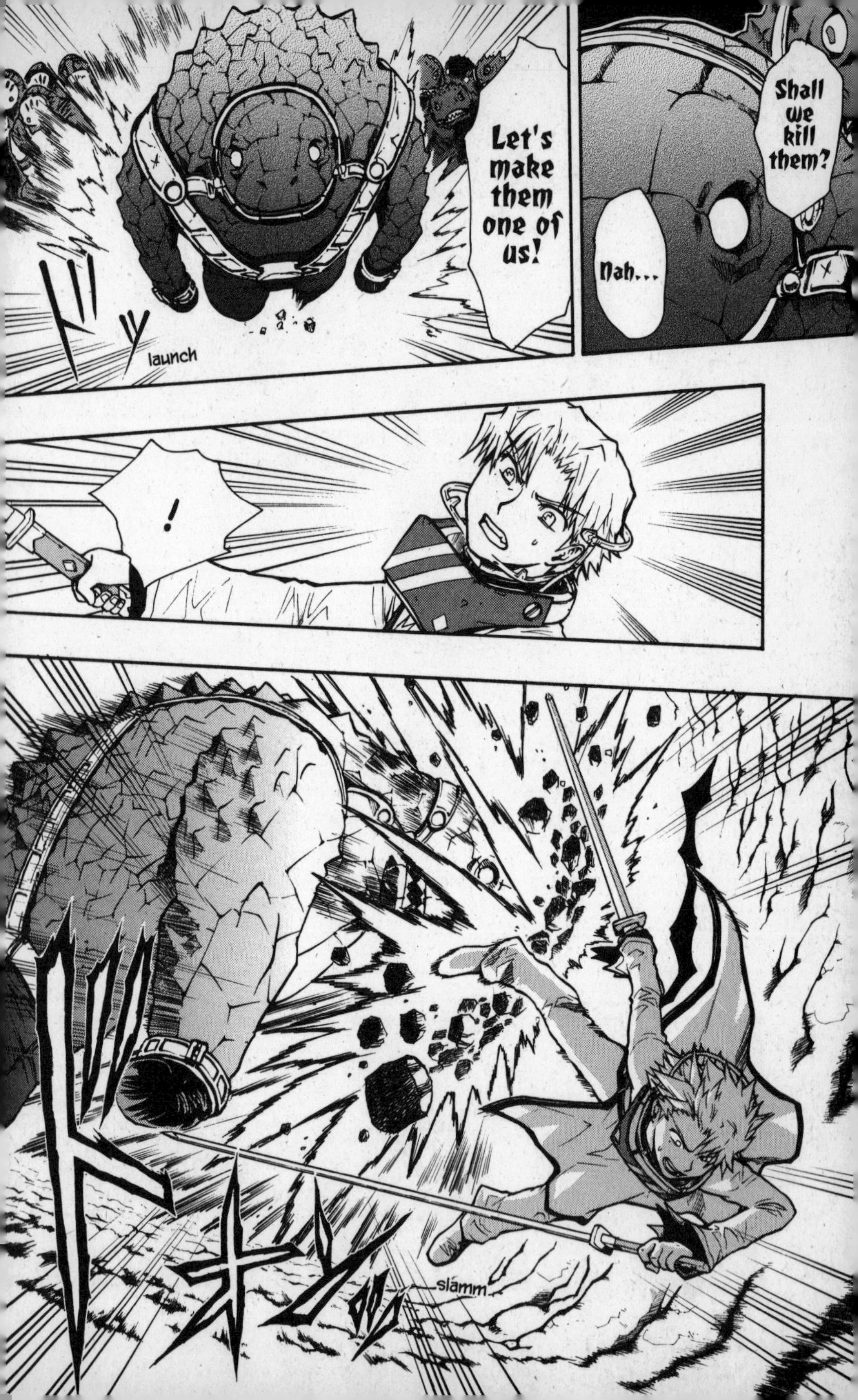
Shall we kill them?
Nah...
Let's make them one of us!
launch
!
slamm

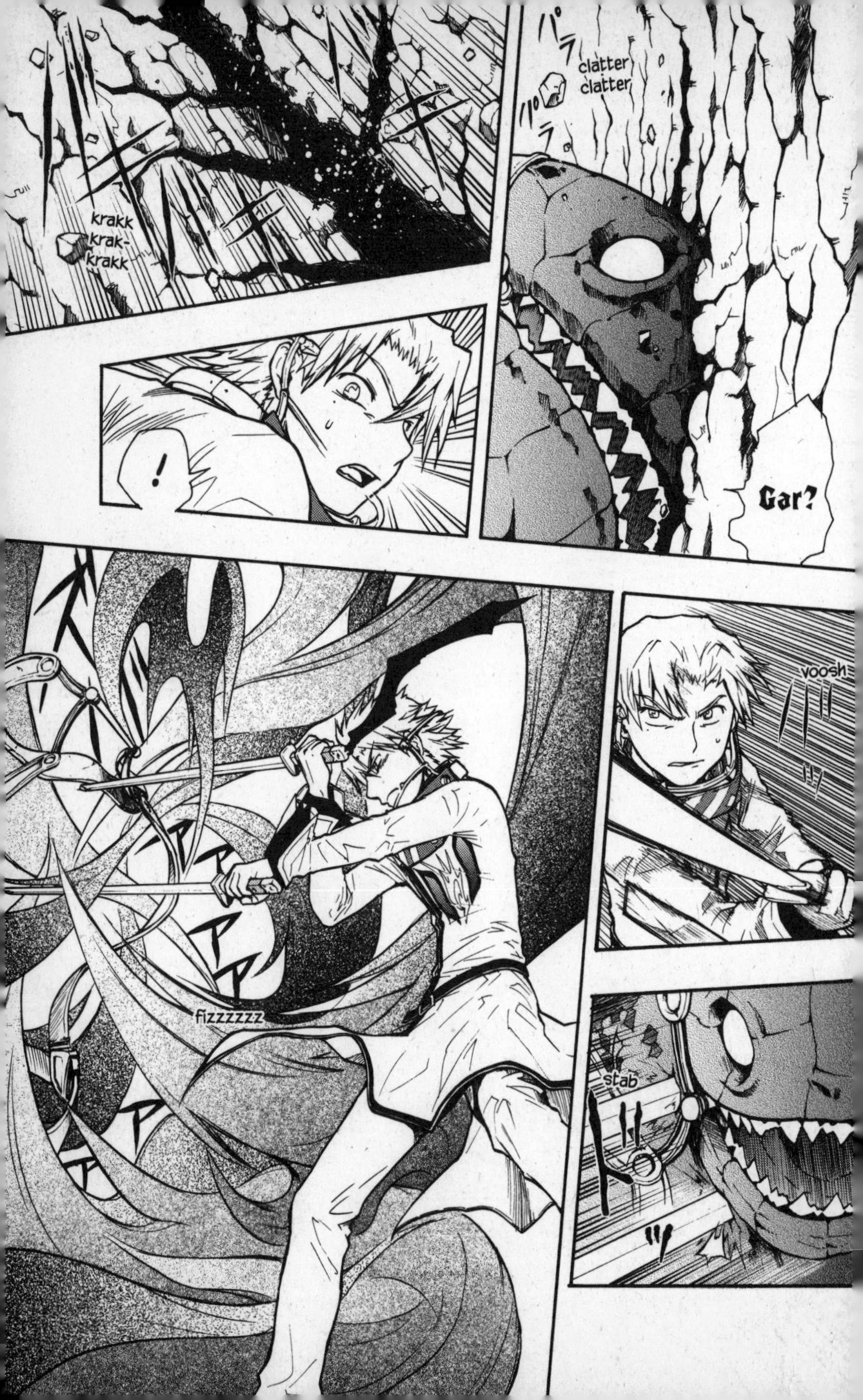
clatter
clatter
Gar?
krakk
krak-
krakk
!
voosh
stab
fizzzzzz

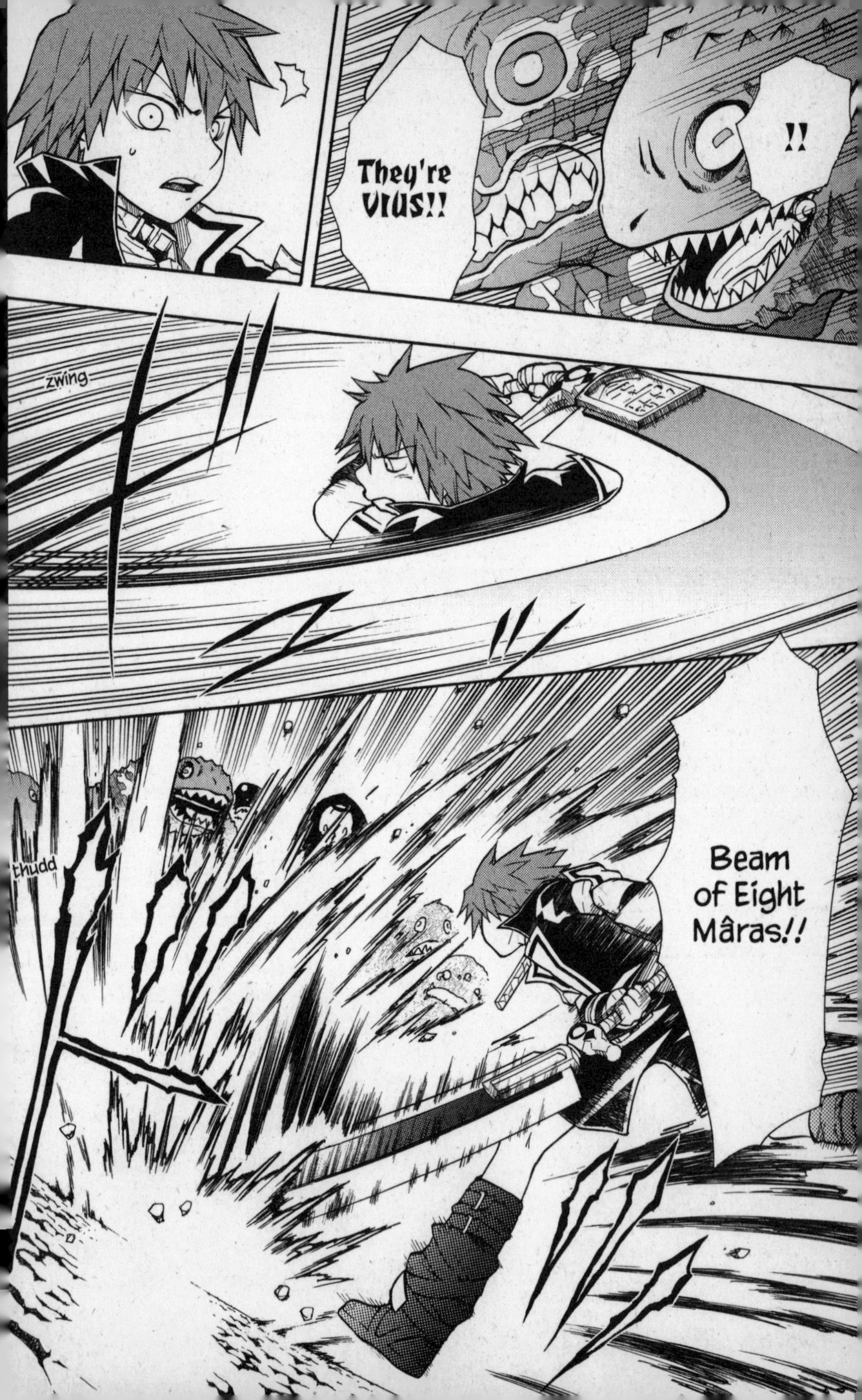
!!
They're VIUS!!
zwing
Beam of Eight Mâras!!
thudd

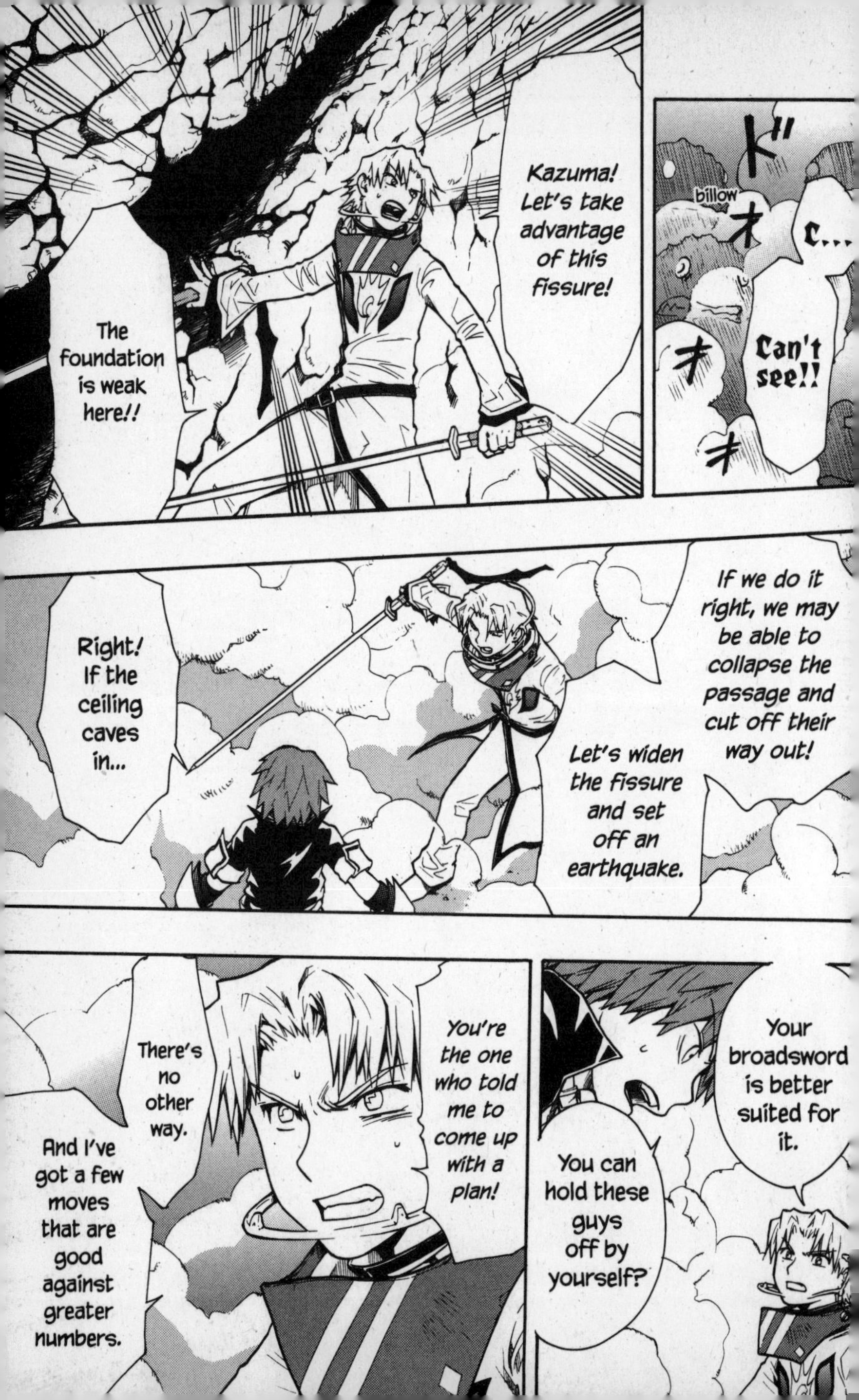
ド
billow
オ
C...
Can't see!!
オ
オ
Kazuma! Let's take advantage of this fissure!
The foundation is weak here!!
If we do it right, we may be able to collapse the passage and cut off their way out!
Let's widen the fissure and set off an earthquake.
Right! If the ceiling caves in...
Your broadsword is better suited for it.
You can hold these guys off by yourself?
You're the one who told me to come up with a plan!
There's no other way.
And I've got a few moves that are good against greater numbers.

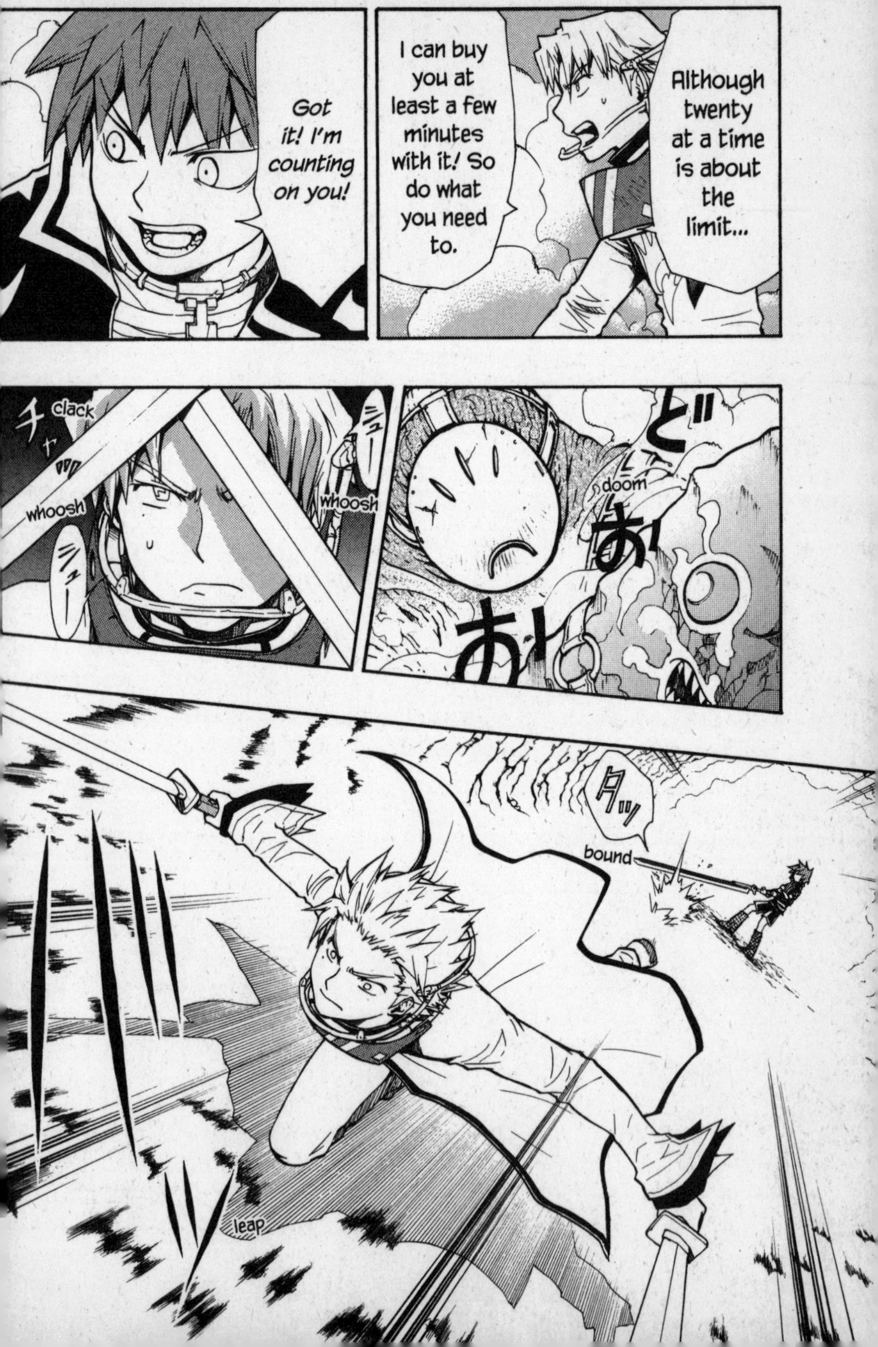
Although twenty at a time is about the limit...
I can buy you at least a few minutes with it! So do what you need to.
Got it! I'm counting on you!
doom
whoosh
clack
whoosh
bound
leap

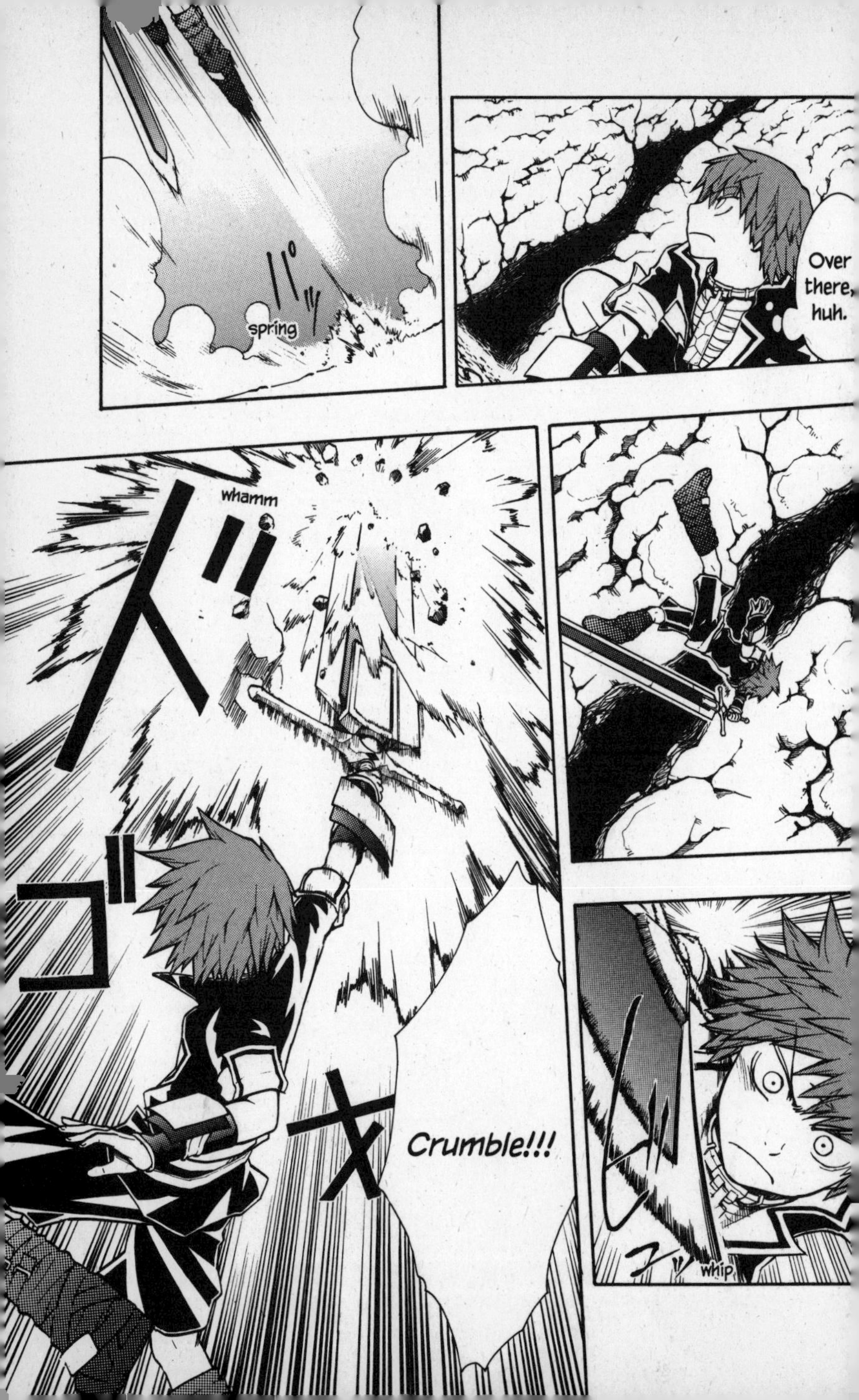
Over there, huh.
spring
whip
whamm
Crumble!!!

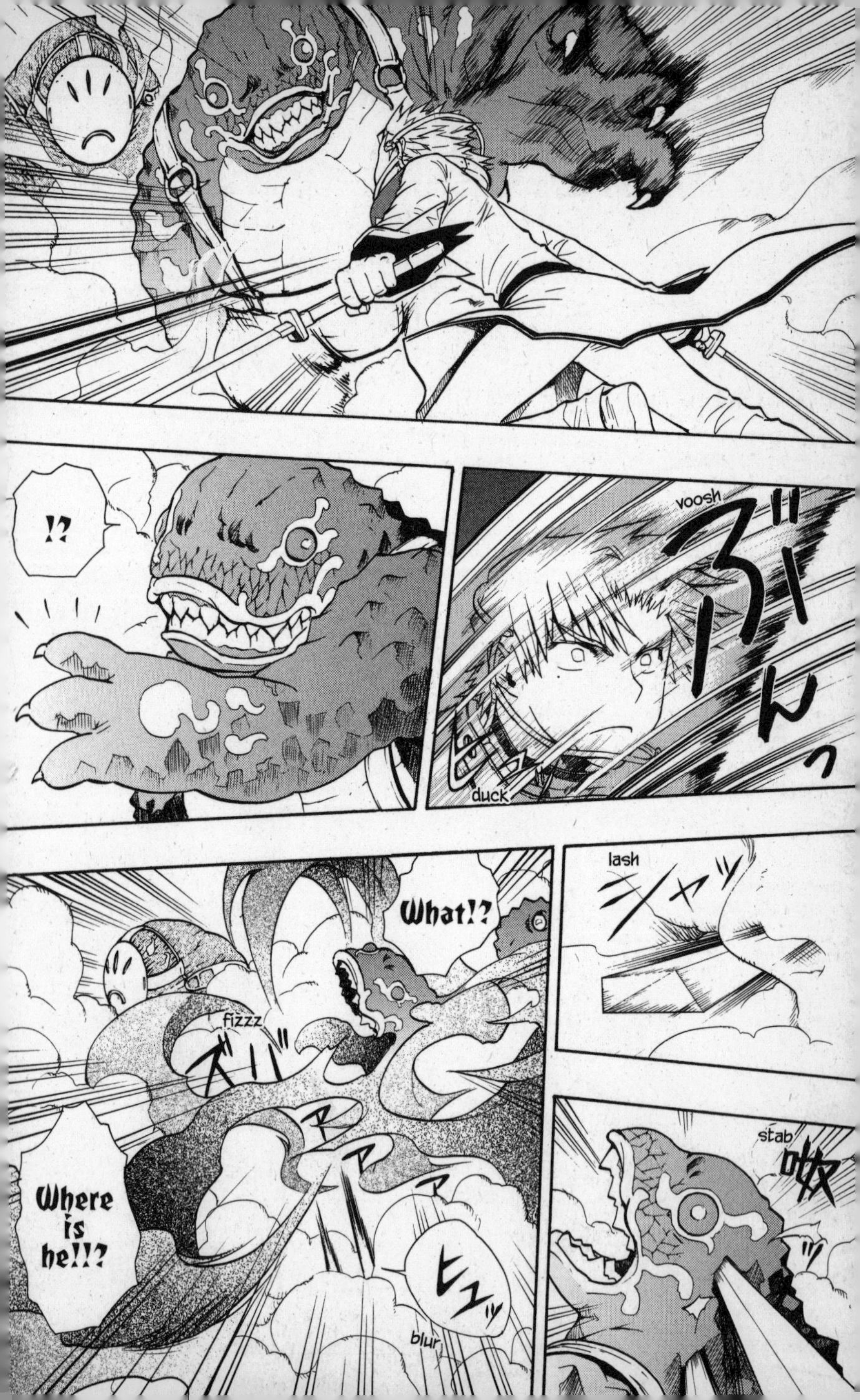

voosh
duck
!?
lash
stab
What!?
fizzz
Where is he!!?
blur

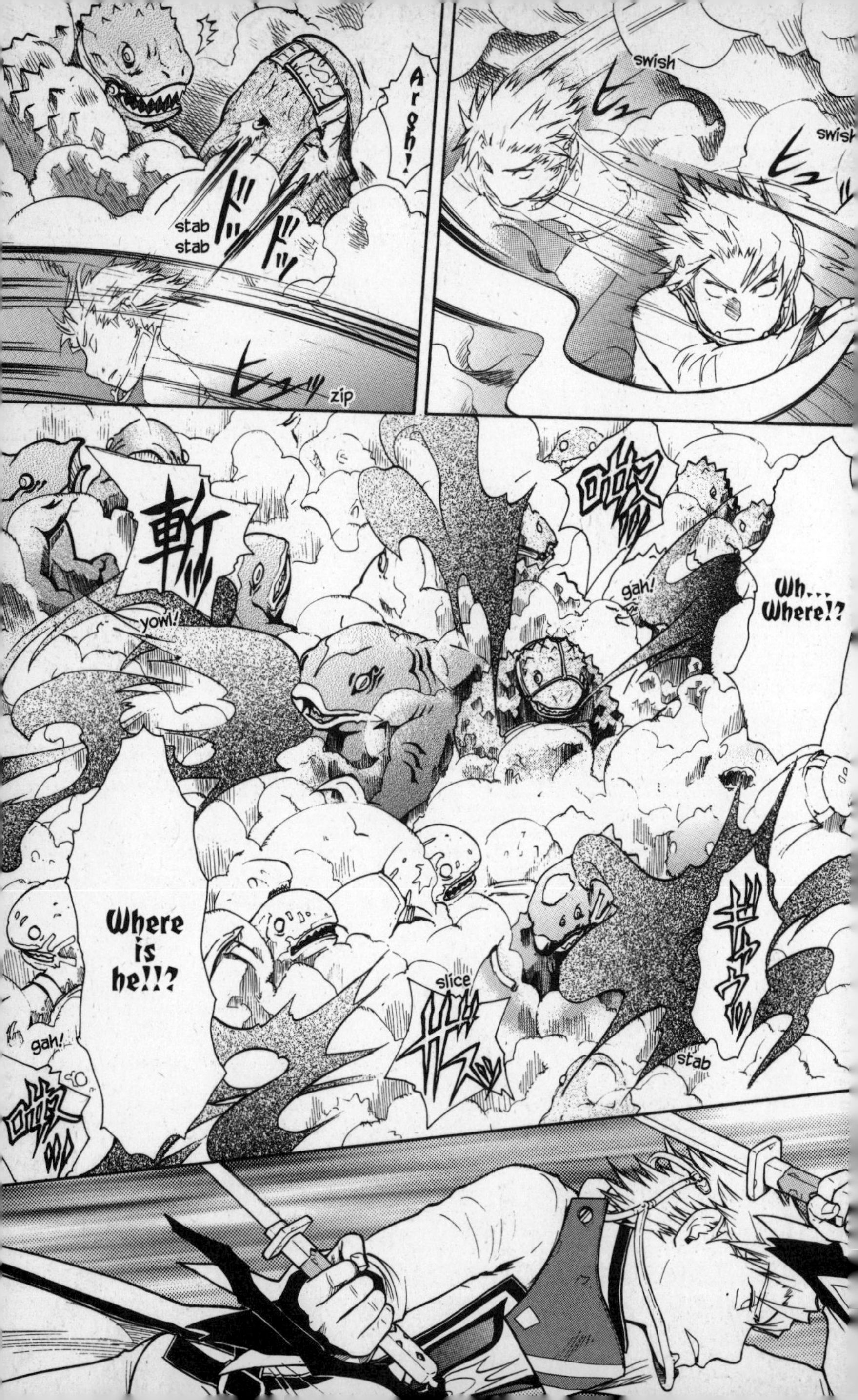
swish
swish
Argh!
stab
stab
zip
Wh... Where!?
gah!
yowl!
stab
slice
Where is he!!?
gah!

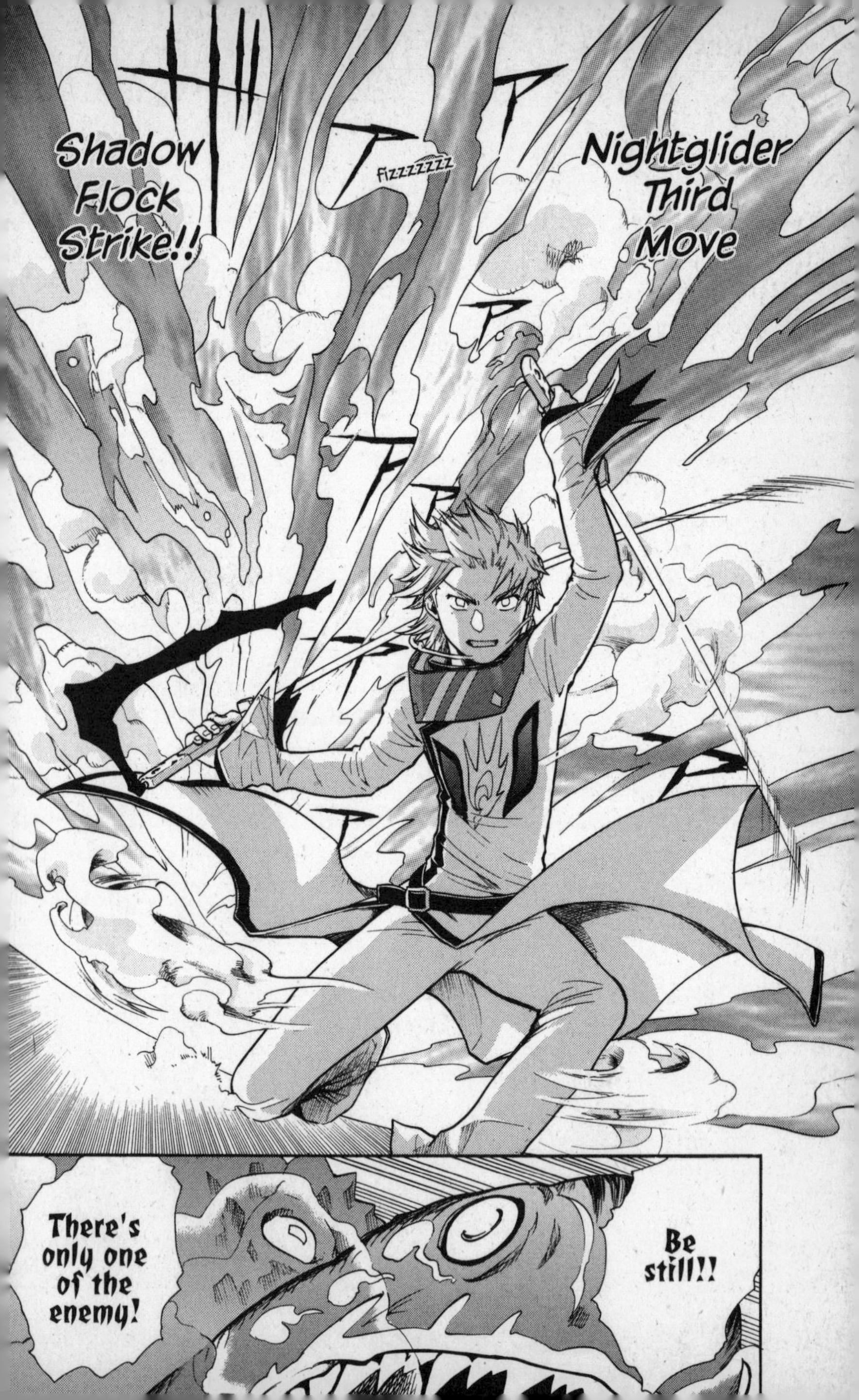
Nightglider Third Move
Fizzzzzzzz
Shadow Flock Strike!!
Be still!!
There's only one of the enemy!

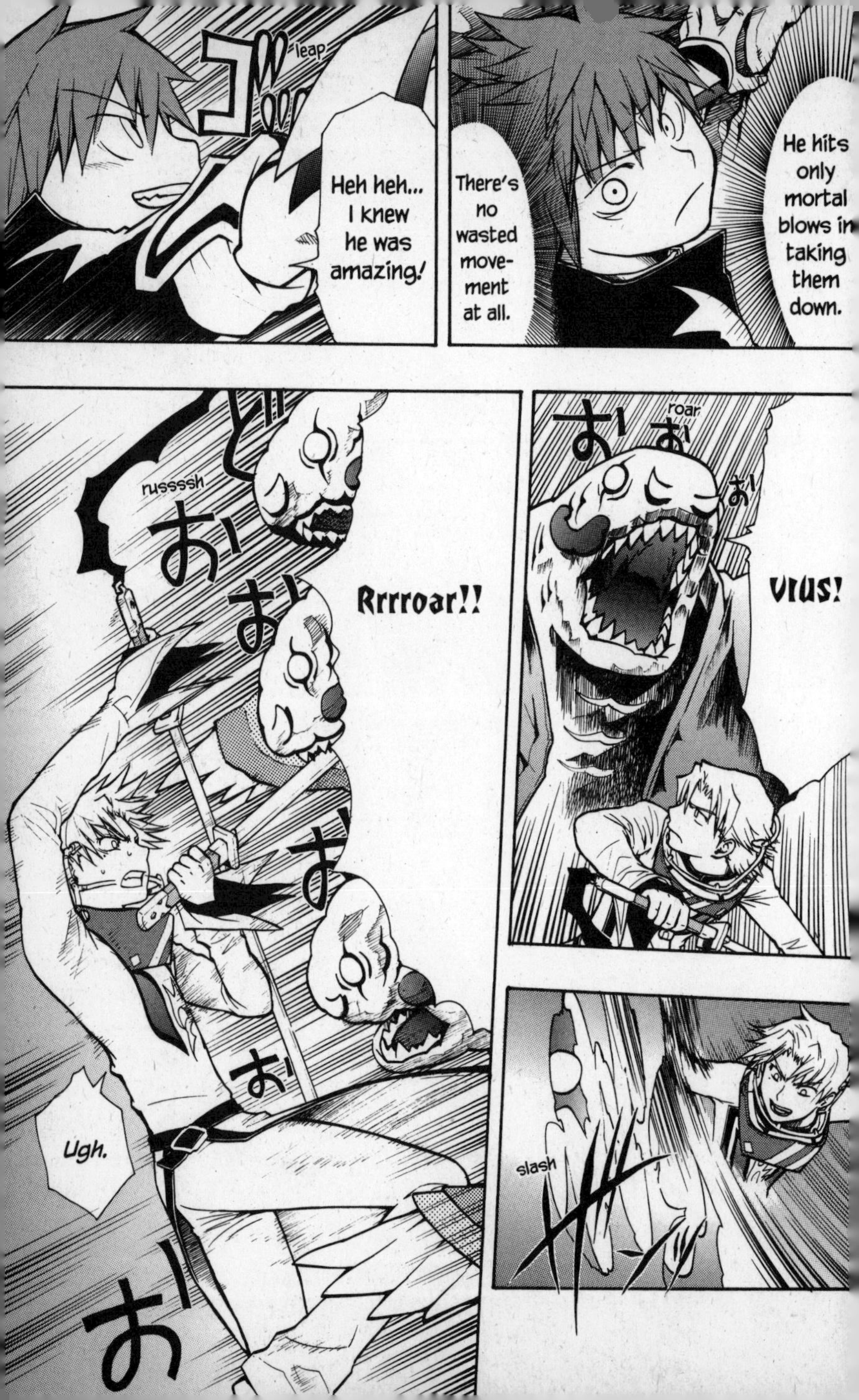
He hits only mortal blows in taking them down.
There's no wasted move-ment at all.
leap
Heh heh... I knew he was amazing!
roar
VIUS!
slash
russssh
Rrrroar!!
Ugh.

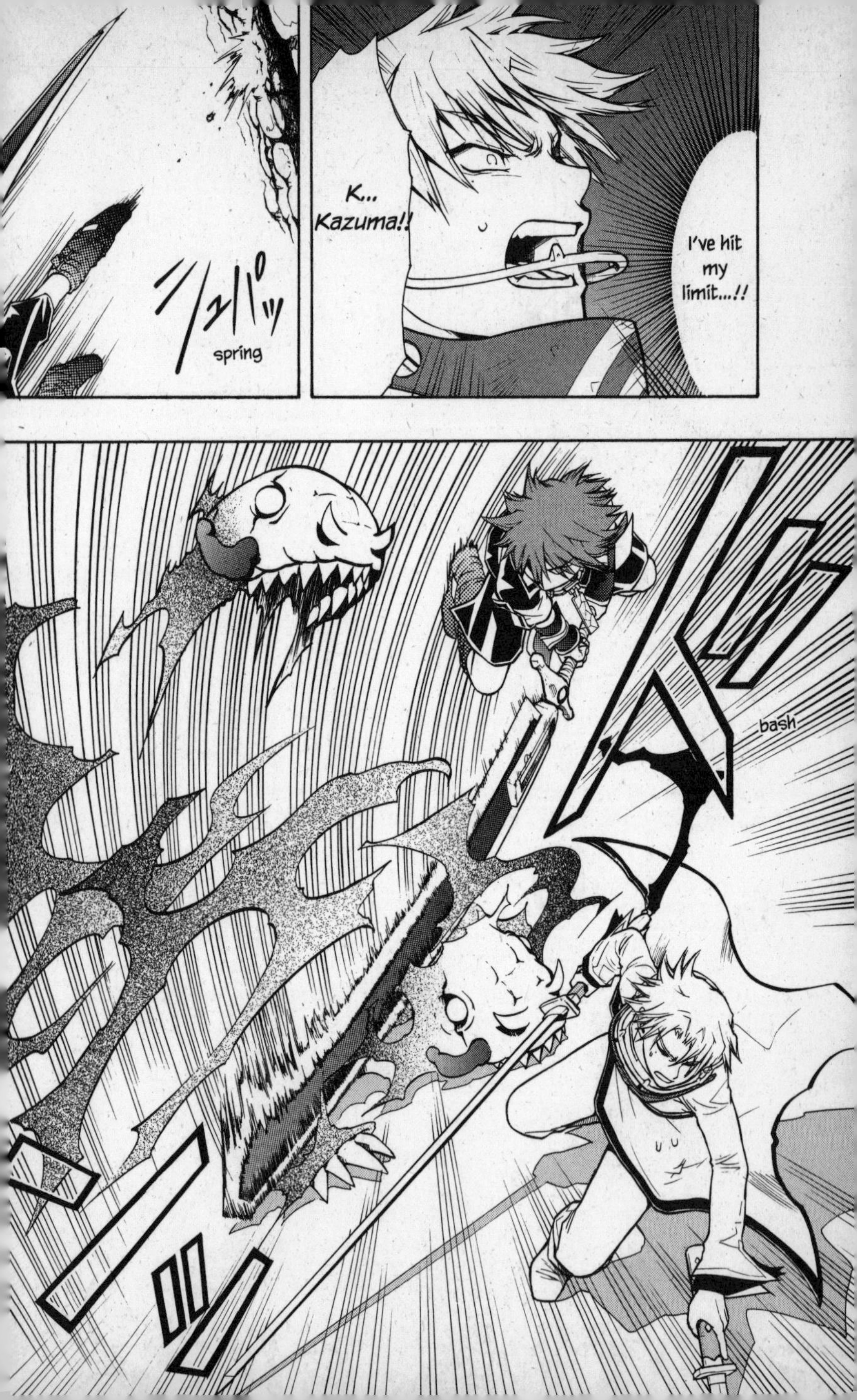
I've hit my limit...!!
K... Kazuma!!
シュパッ
spring
bash

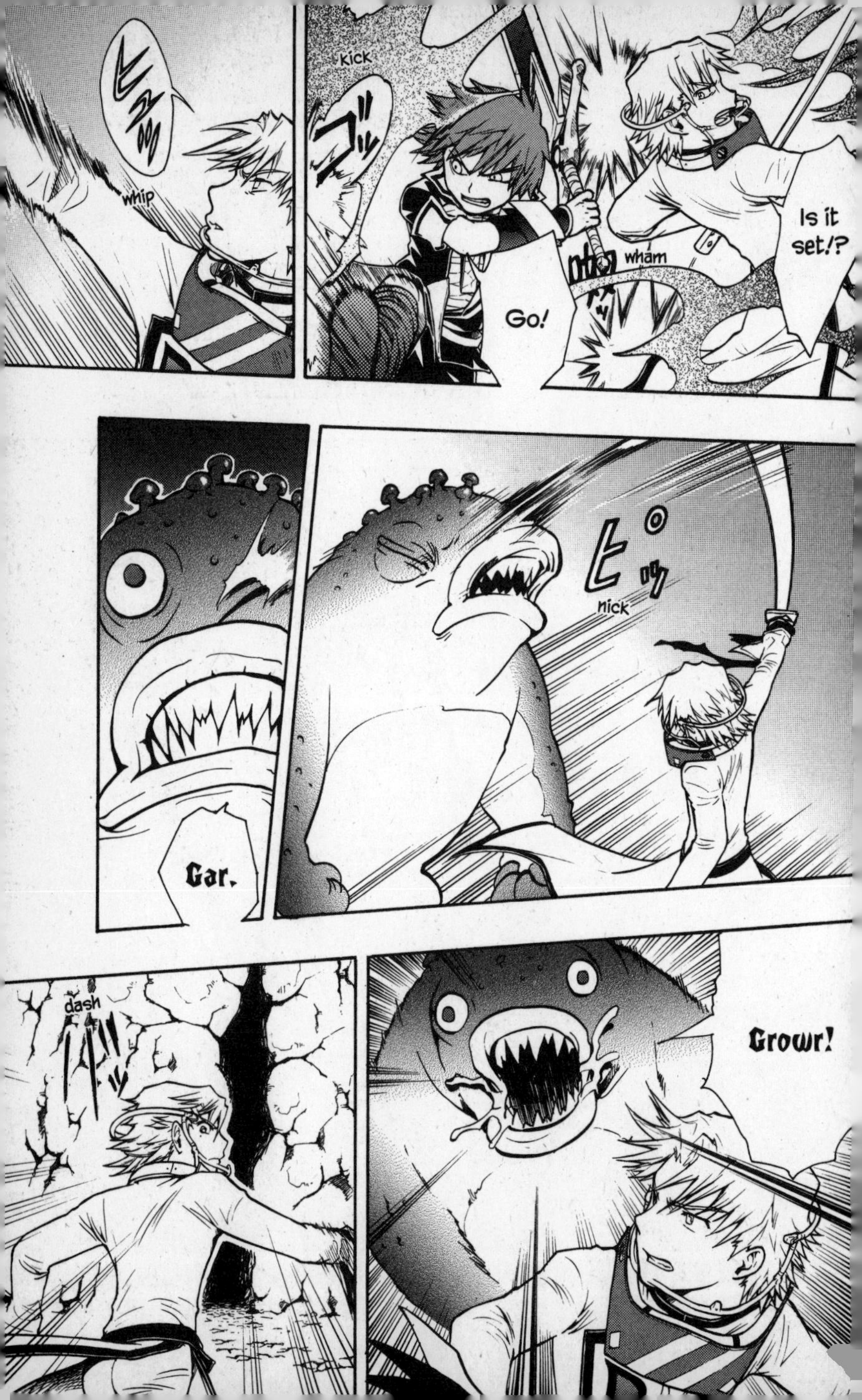
Is it set!?
wham
Go!
kick
whip
nick
Gar.
Growr!
dash

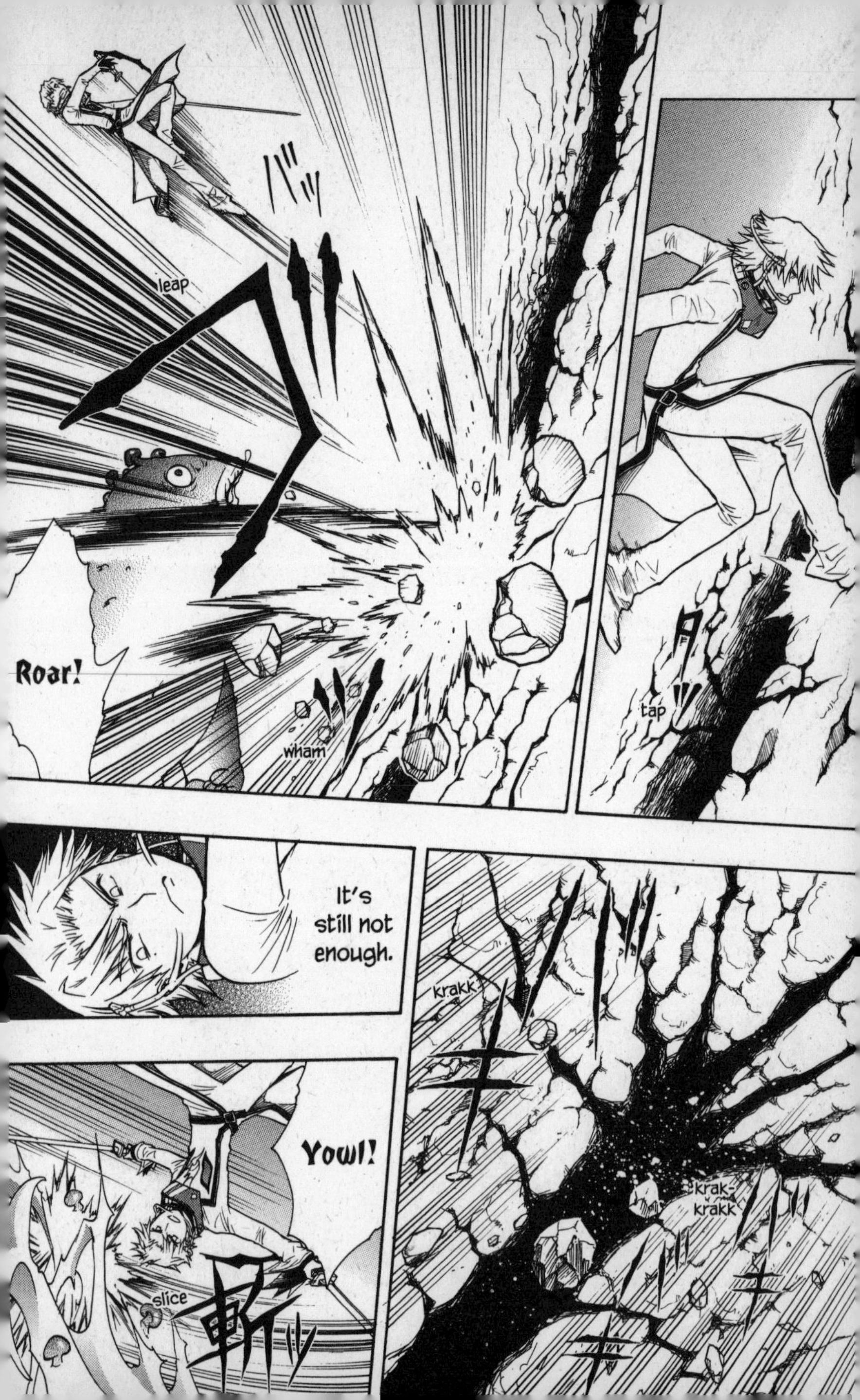
tap
バッ
leap
Roar!
wham
krakk
krak-krakk
It's still not enough.
Yowl!
slice

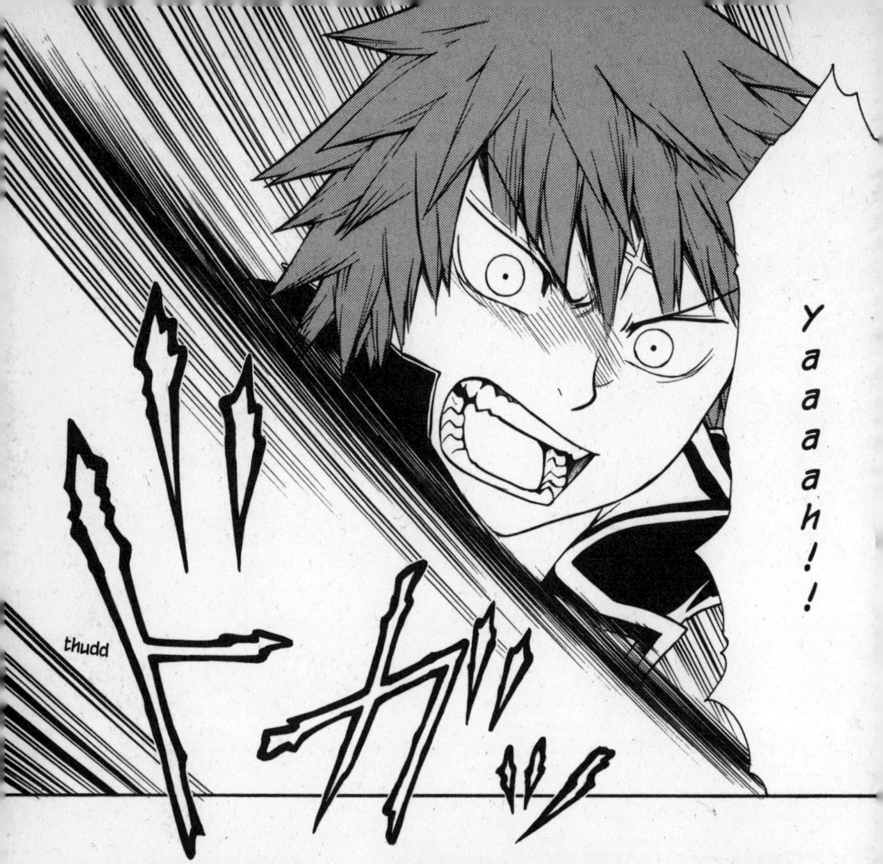
Yaaaaah!!
thudd
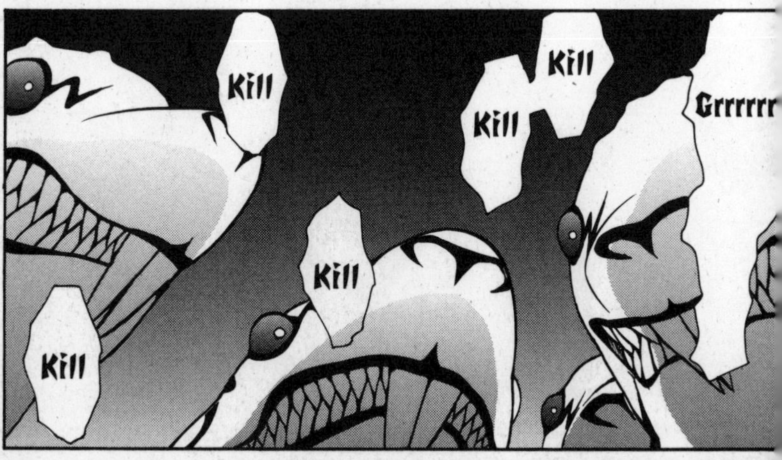
Grrrrrr
Kill
Kill
Kill
Kill
Kill

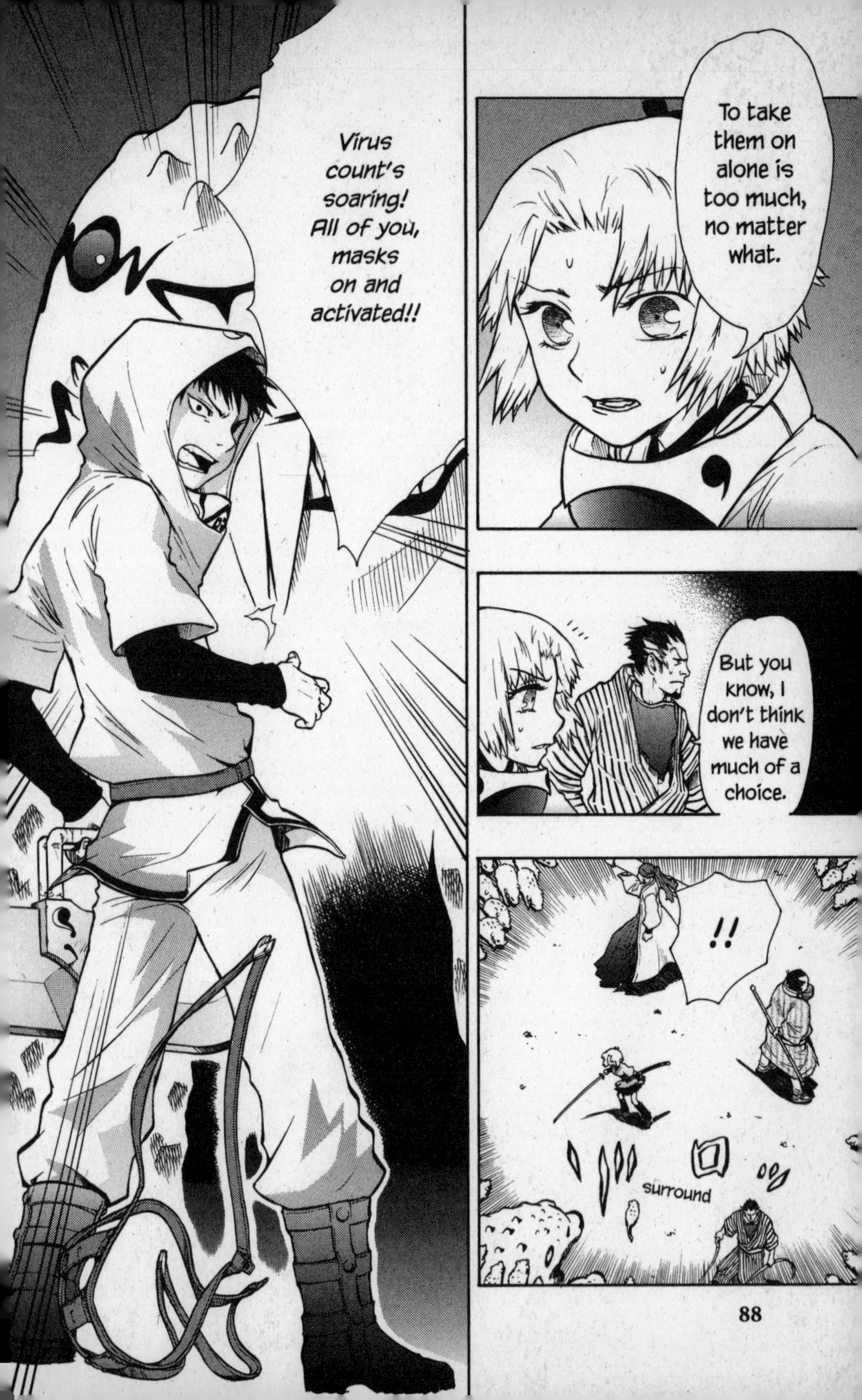

To take them on alone is too much, no matter what.
But you know, I don't think we have much of a choice.
!!
surround
Virus count's soaring! All of you, masks on and activated!!

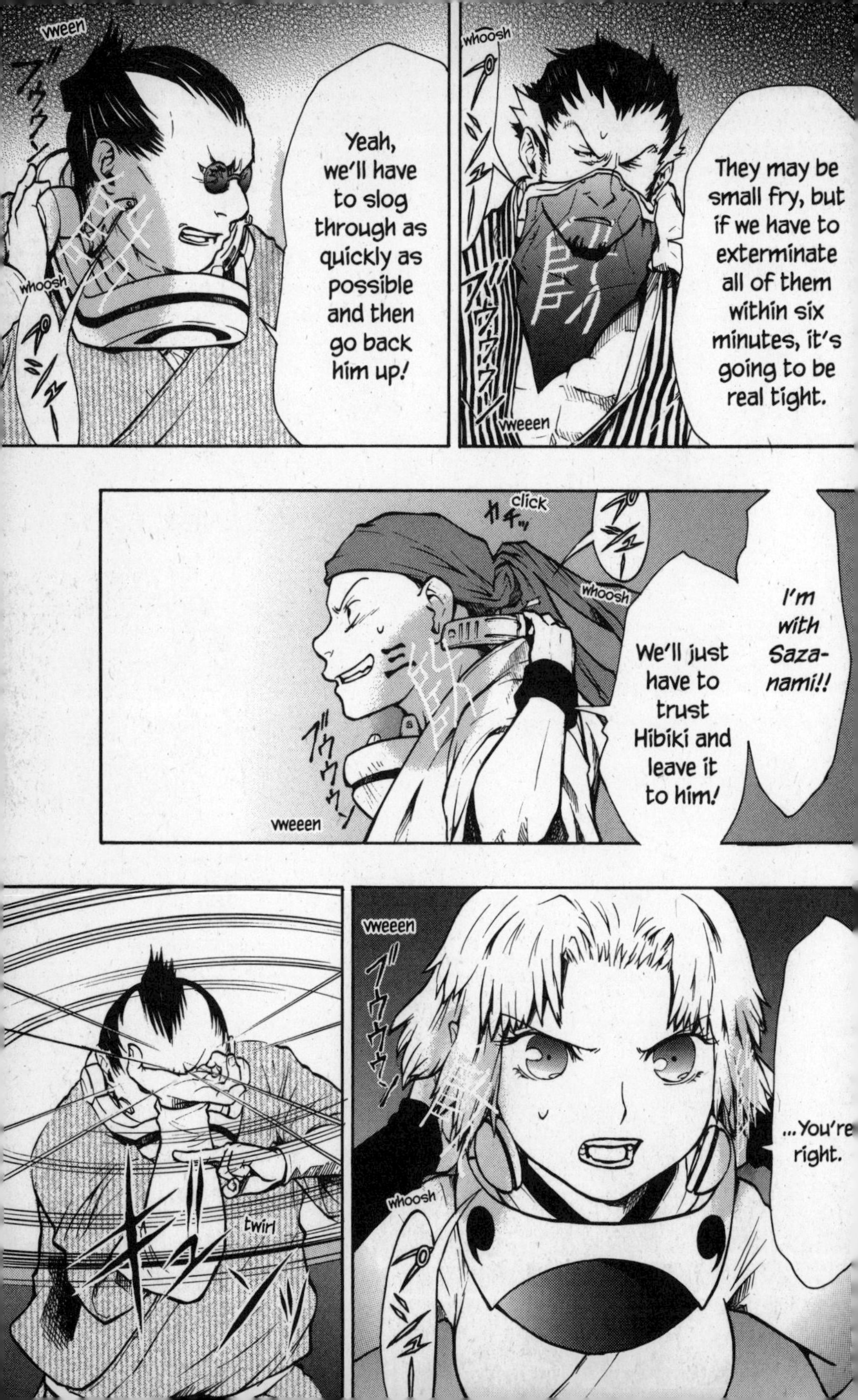
whoosh
They may be small fry, but if we have to exterminate all of them within six minutes, it's going to be real tight.
vweeen
vween
Yeah, we'll have to slog through as quickly as possible and then go back him up!
whoosh
click
whoosh
I'm with Saza-nami!!
We'll just have to trust Hibiki and leave it to him!
vweeen
vweeen
...You're right.
whoosh
twirl

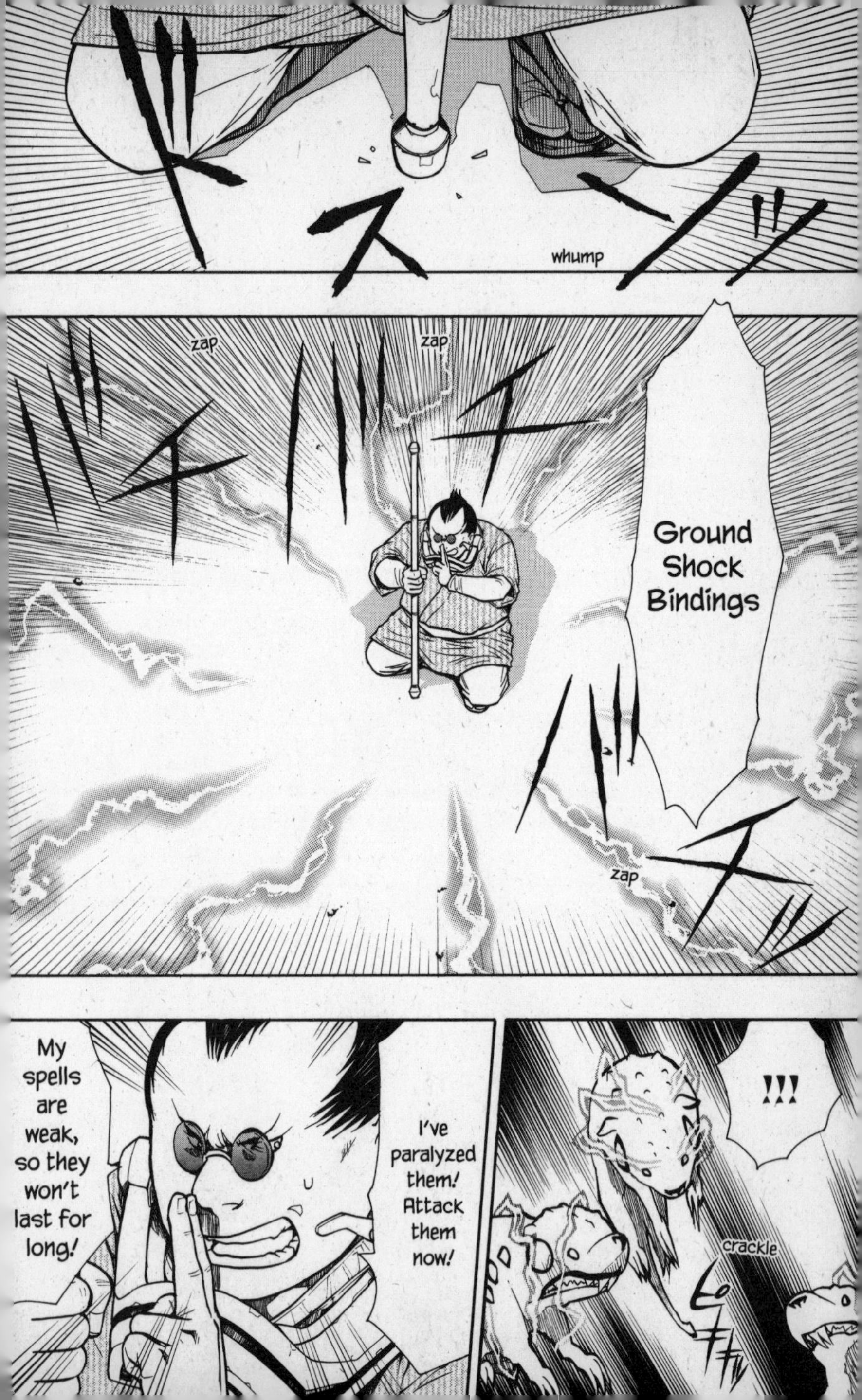
whump
zap
zap
Ground Shock Bindings
zap
!!!
crackle
I've paralyzed them! Attack them now!
My spells are weak, so they won't last for long!

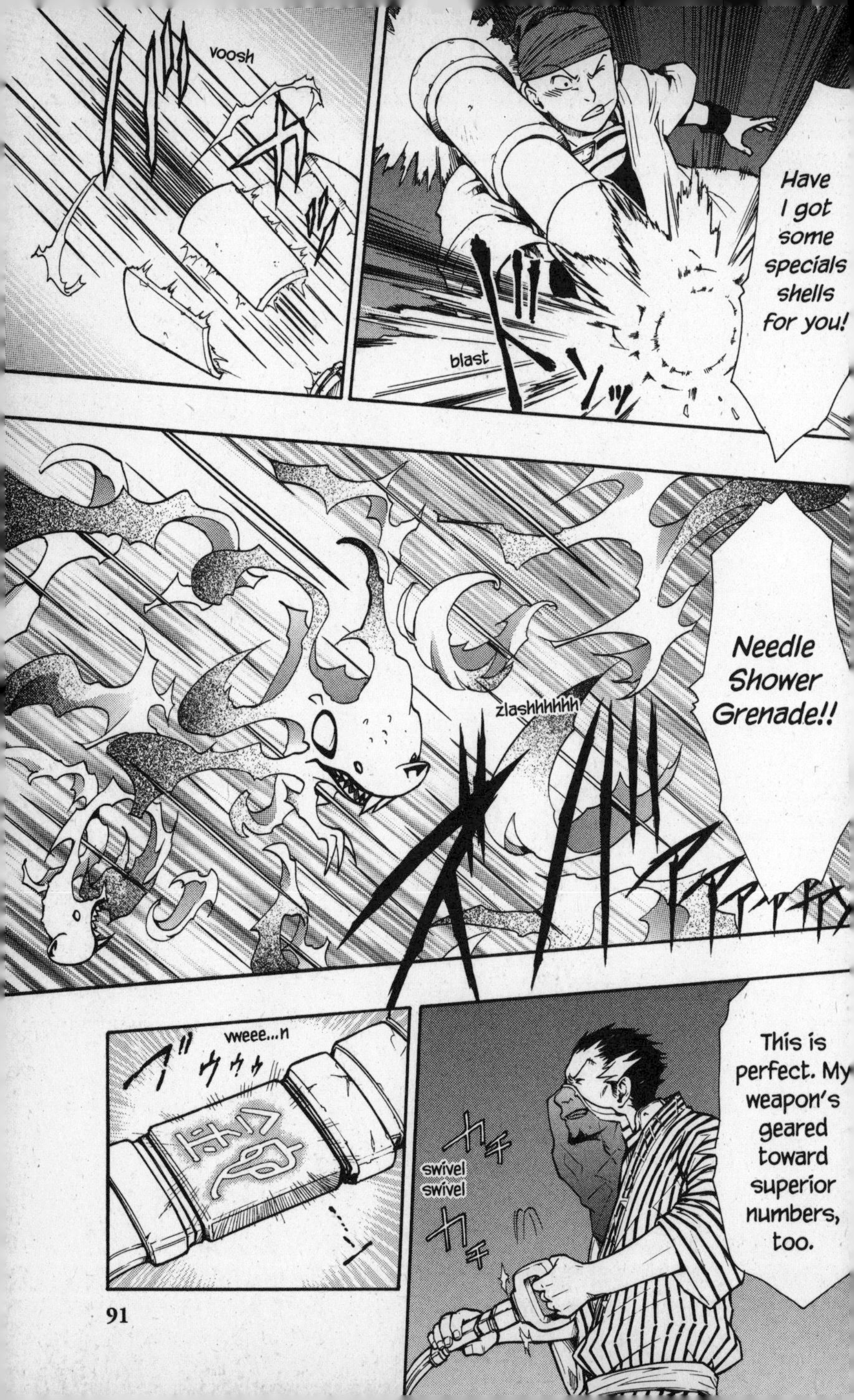
Have I got some specials shells for you!
blast
voosh
Needle Shower Grenade!!
zlashhhhhh
This is perfect. My weapon's geared toward superior numbers, too.
swivel swivel
vweee...n

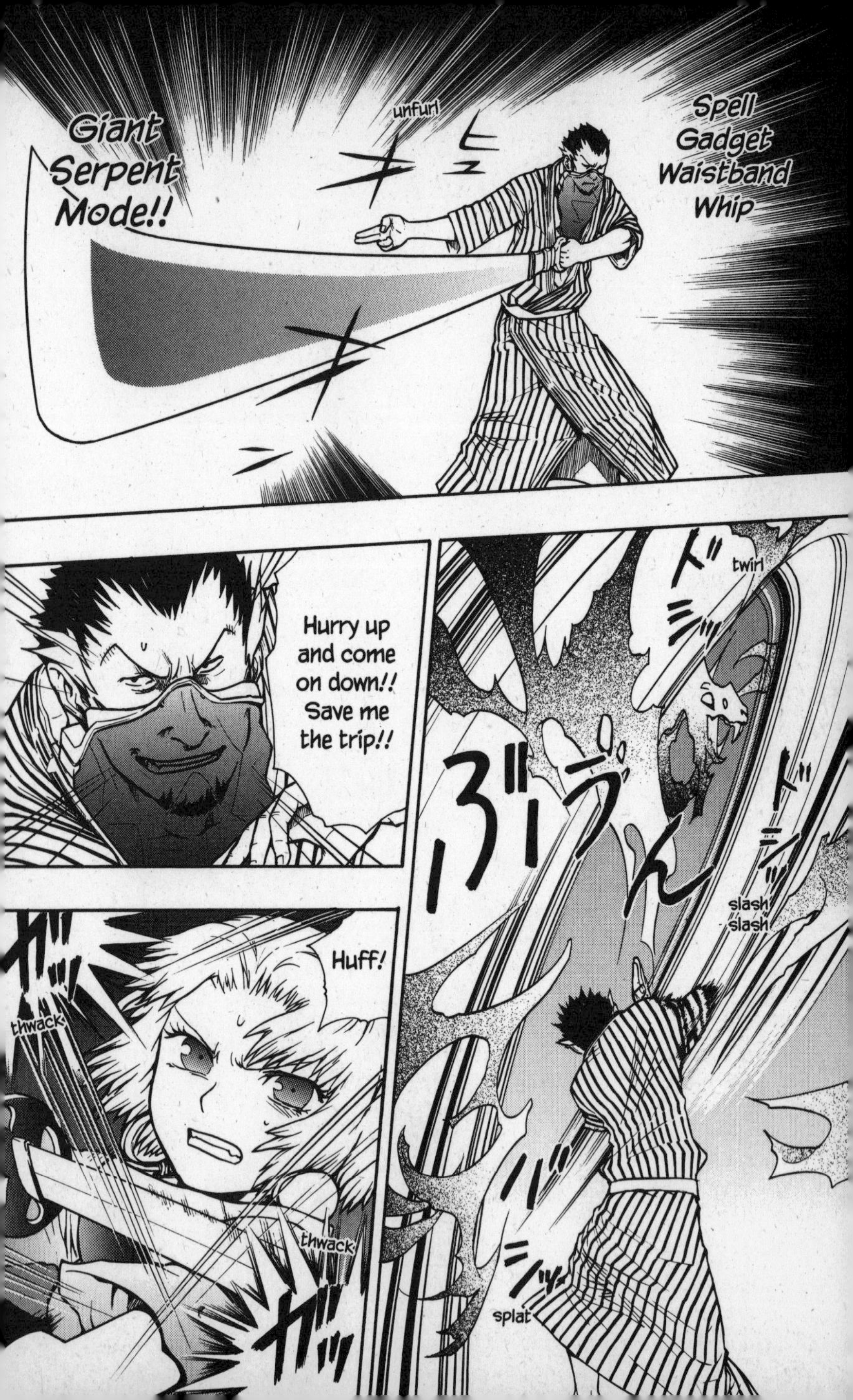
Spell Gadget Waistband Whip
unfurl
Giant Serpent Mode!!
twirl
slash slash
splat
Hurry up and come on down!! Save me the trip!!
Huff!
thwack
thwack

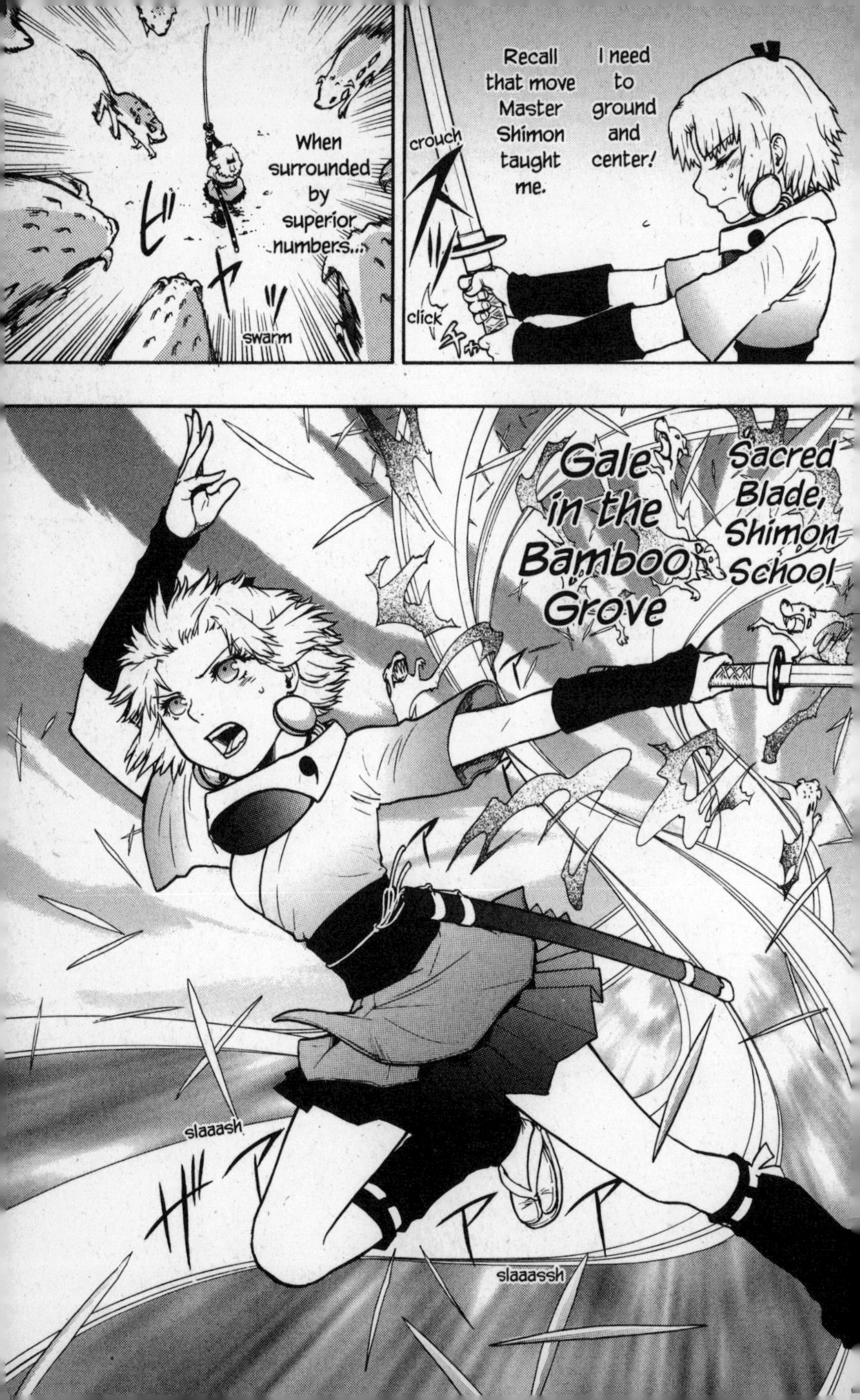
I need to ground and center!
Recall that move Master Shimon taught me.
crouch
click
When surrounded by superior numbers...
swarm
Sacred Blade, Shimon School
Gale in the Bamboo Grove
slaaassh
slaaash

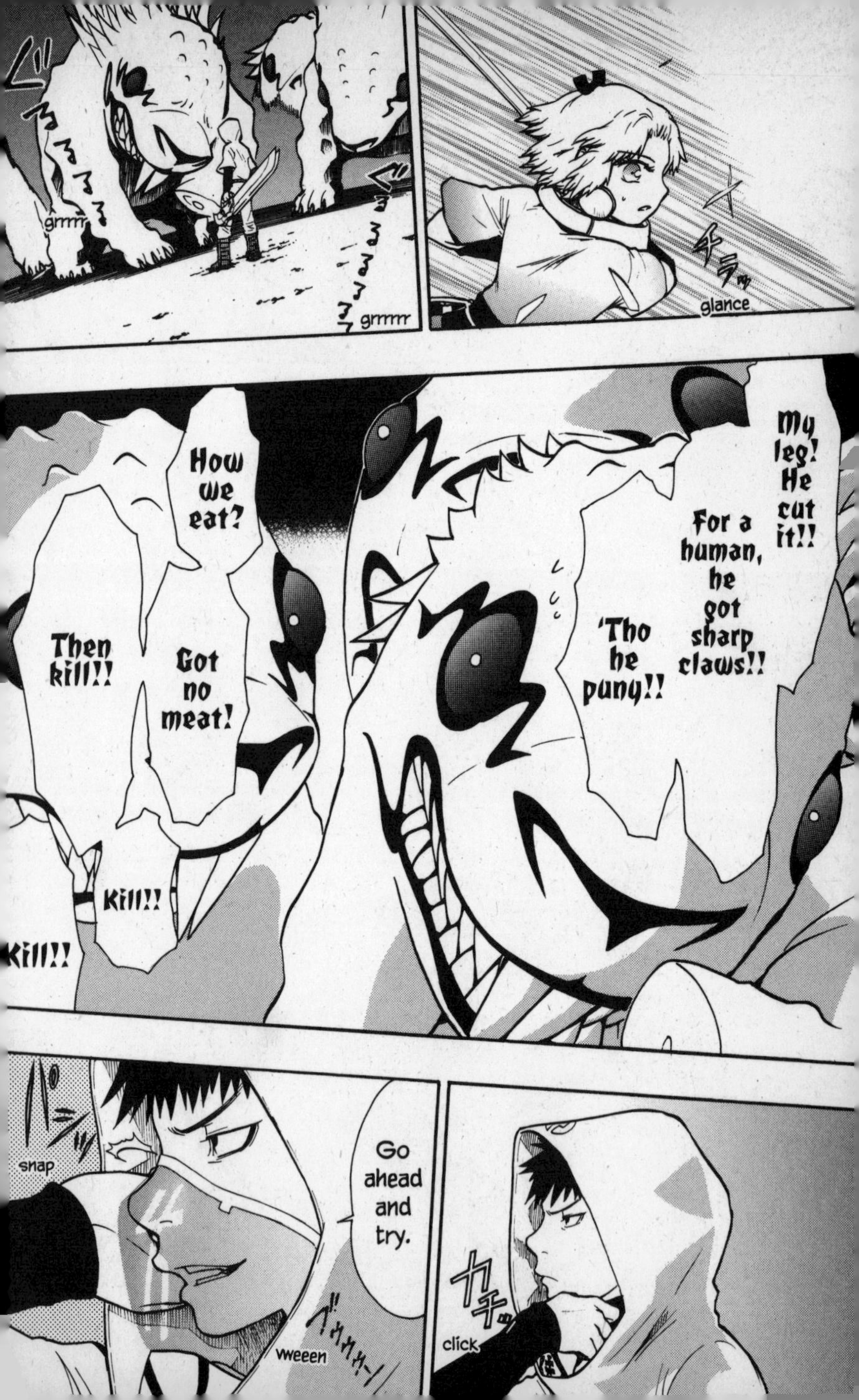
glance
grrrrr
grrrrr
My leg! He cut it!!
For a human, he got sharp claws!!
'Tho he puny!!
How we eat?
Got no meat!
Then kill!!
Kill!!
Kill!!
click
Go ahead and try.
snap
vweeen

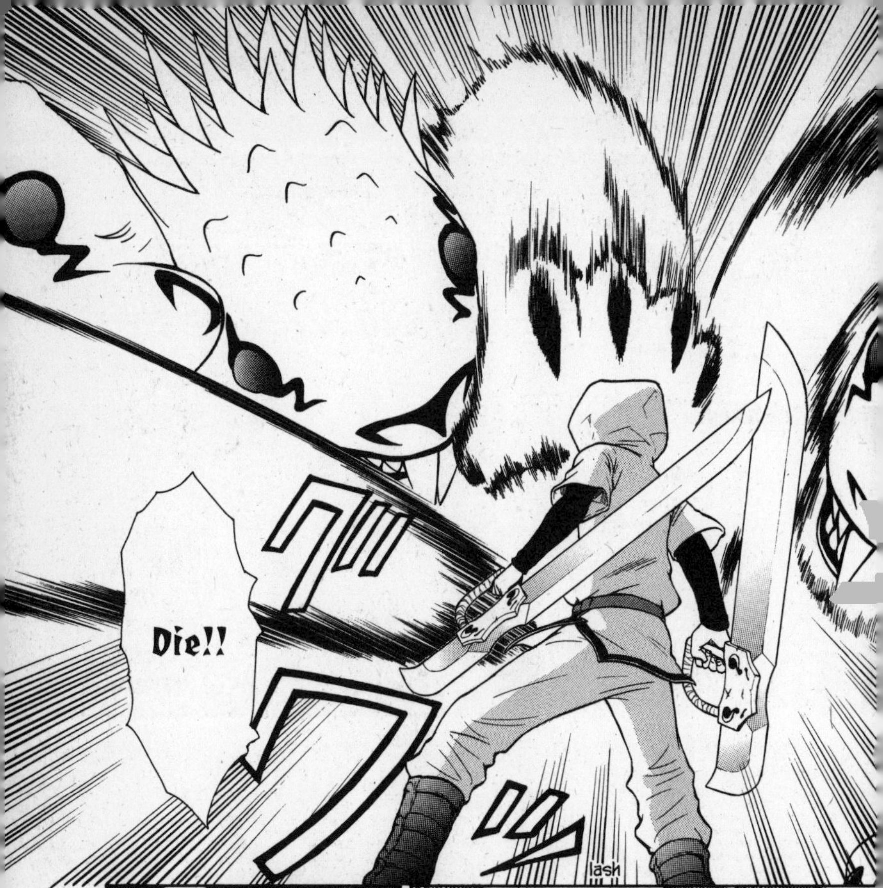
Die!!
lash
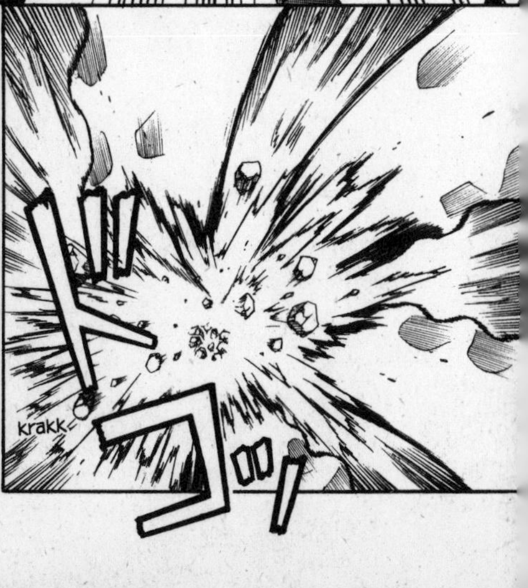
krakk
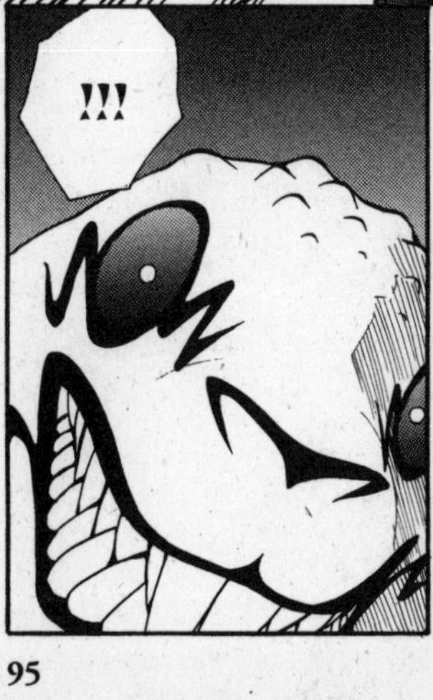
!!!

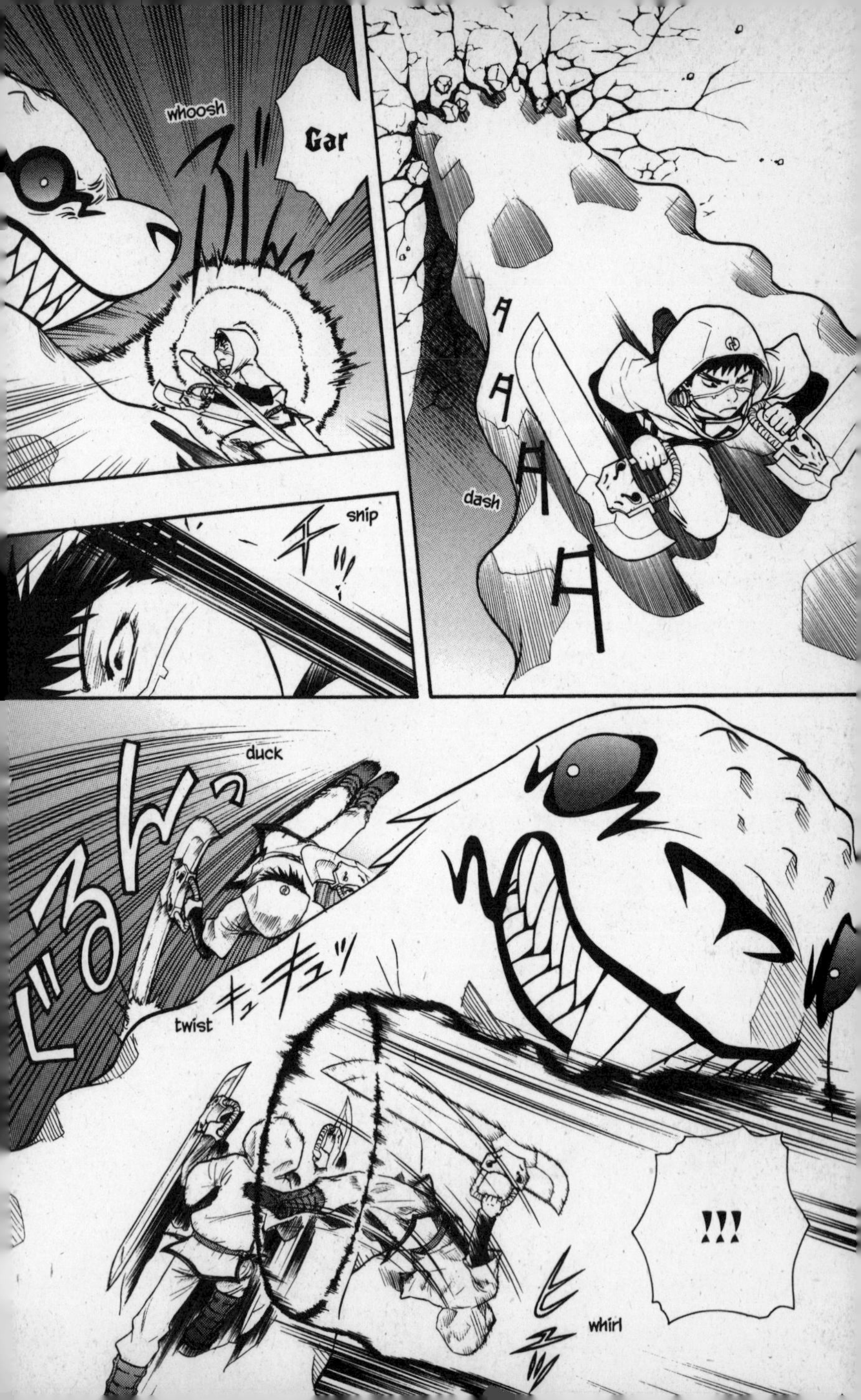
dash
whoosh
Gar
snip
duck
twist
!!!
whirl

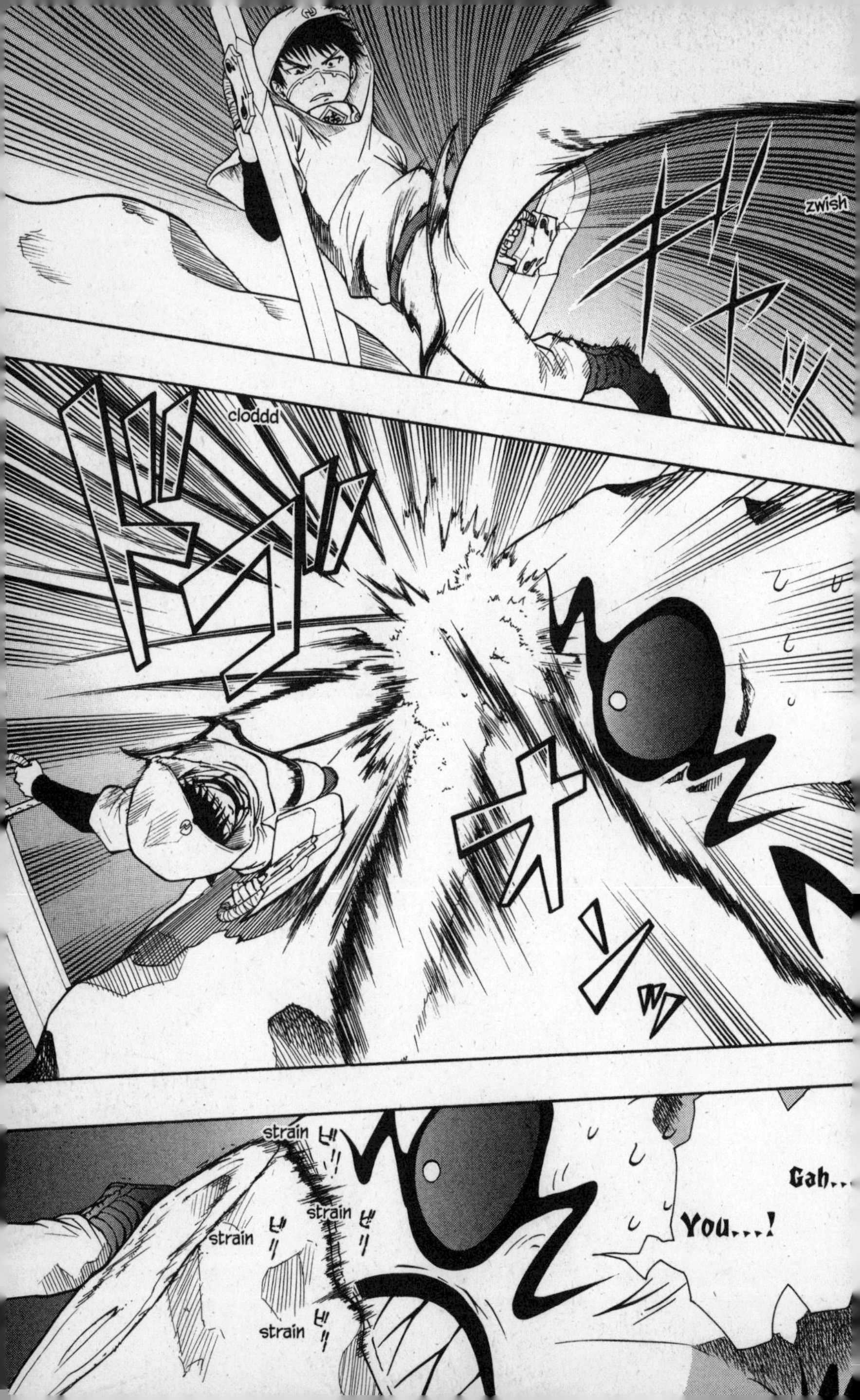
zwish
cloddd
Gah...
You...!
strain
strain
strain
strain

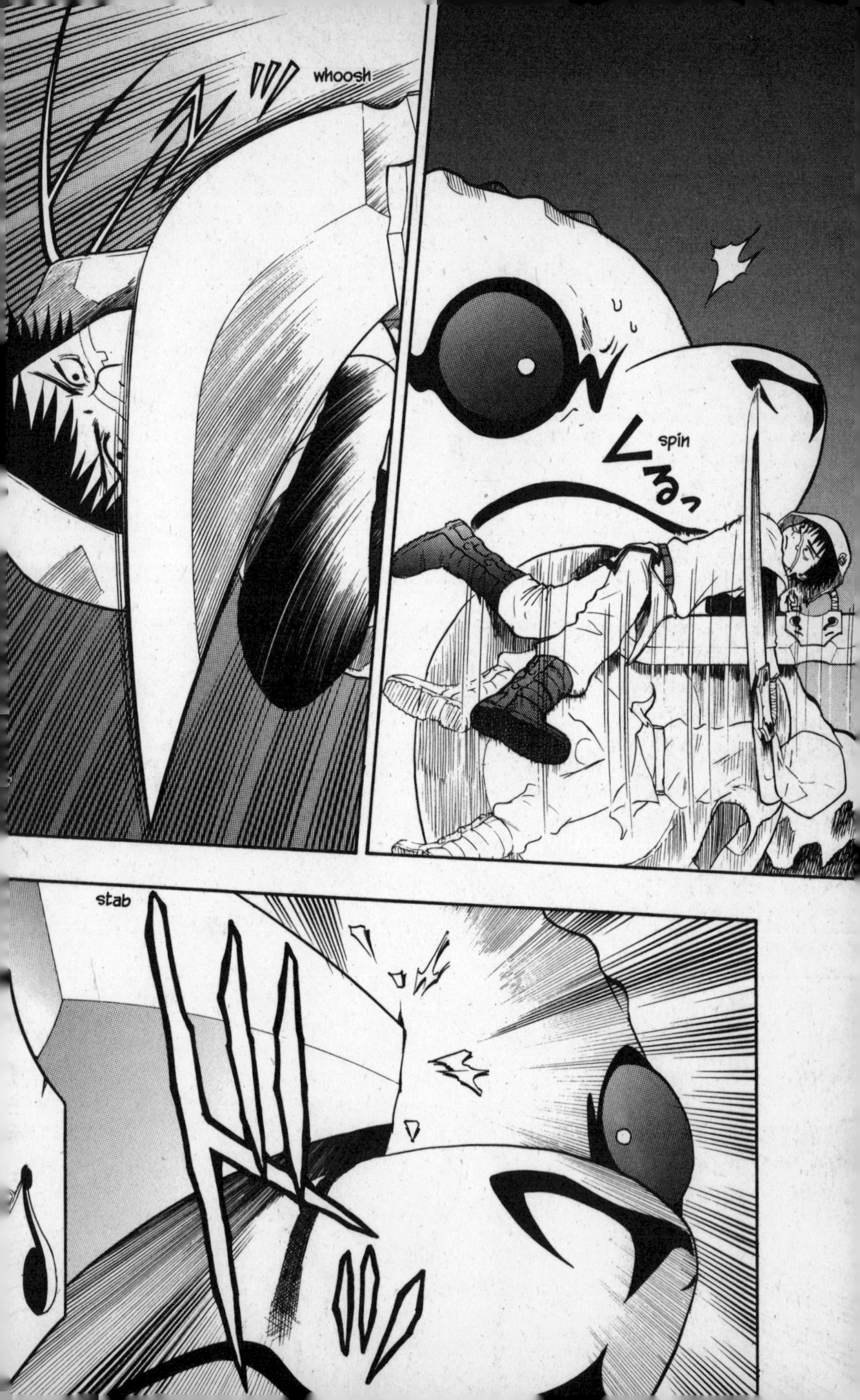

spin
くるっ
whoosh
stab

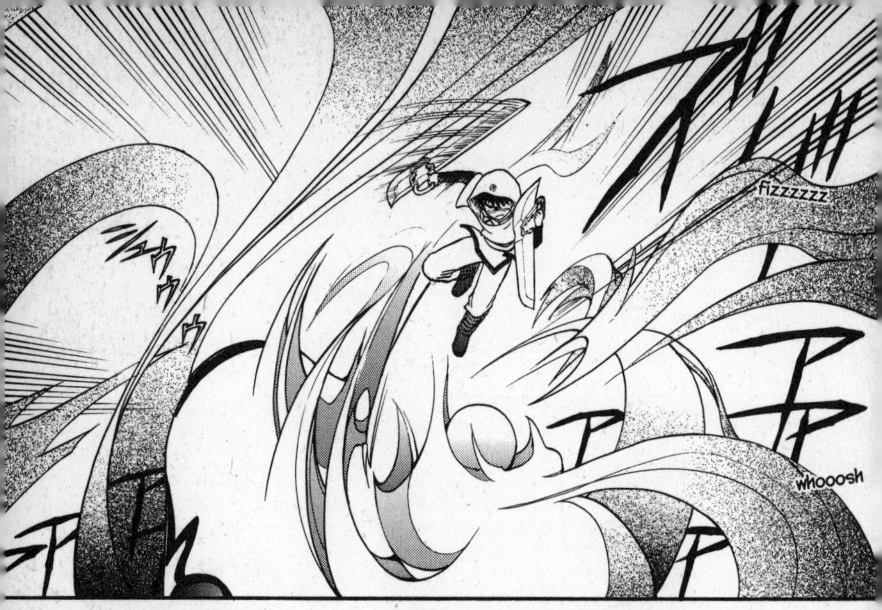
fizzzzzz
whooosh

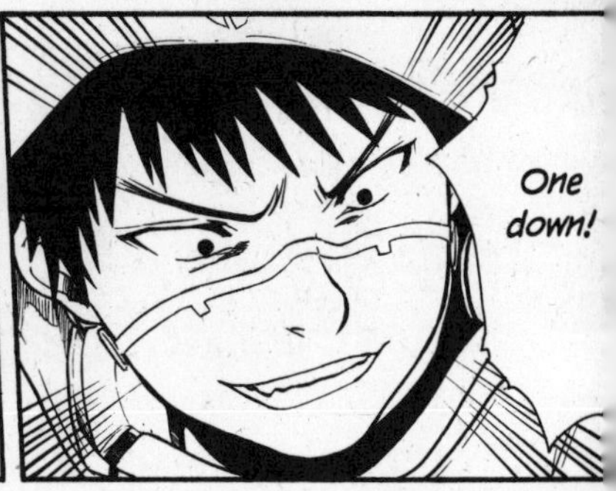
One down!

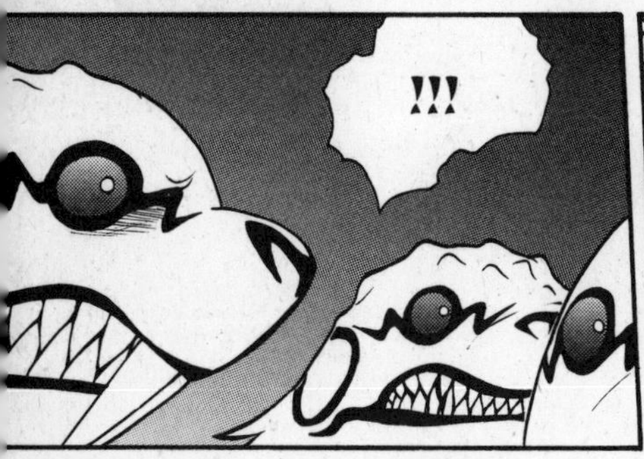
!!!

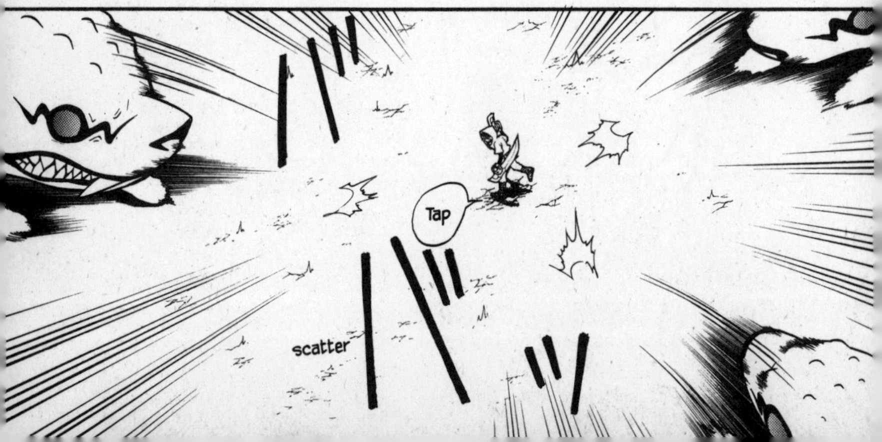
Tap
scatter

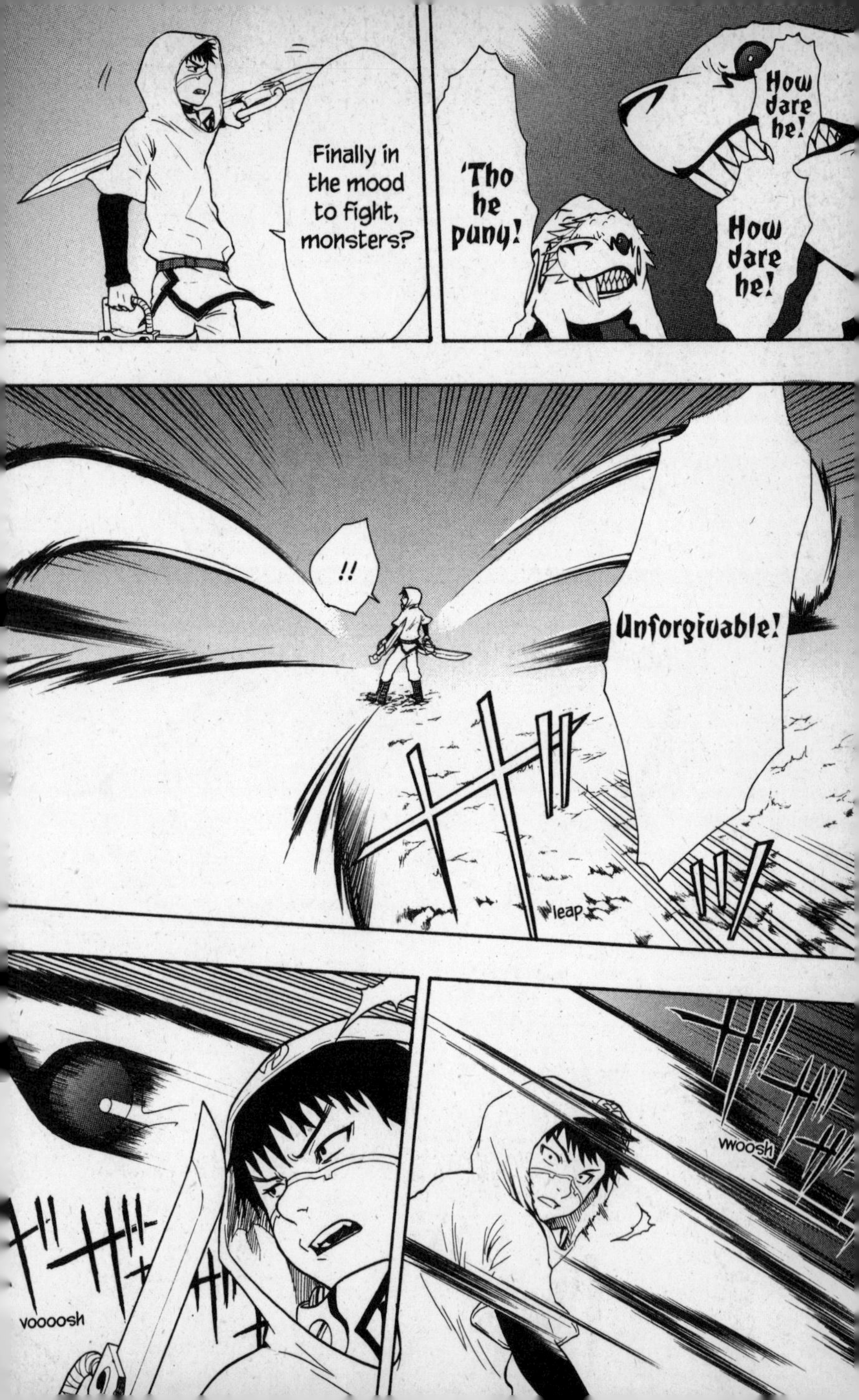
How dare he!
How dare he!
'Tho he puny!
Finally in the mood to fight, monsters?
Unforgivable!
!!
leap
vwoosh
voooosh

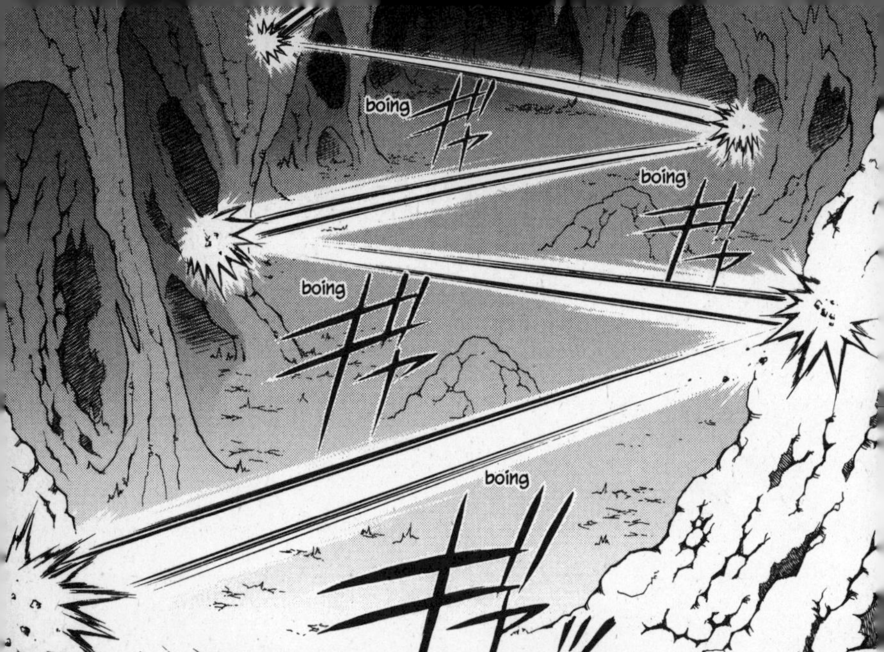
boing
boing
boing
boing
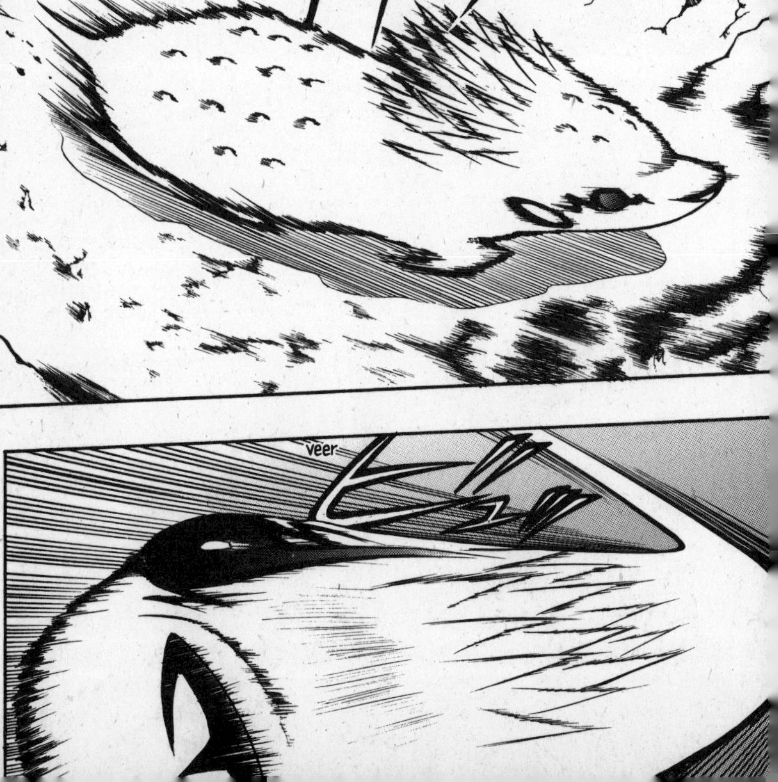
veer

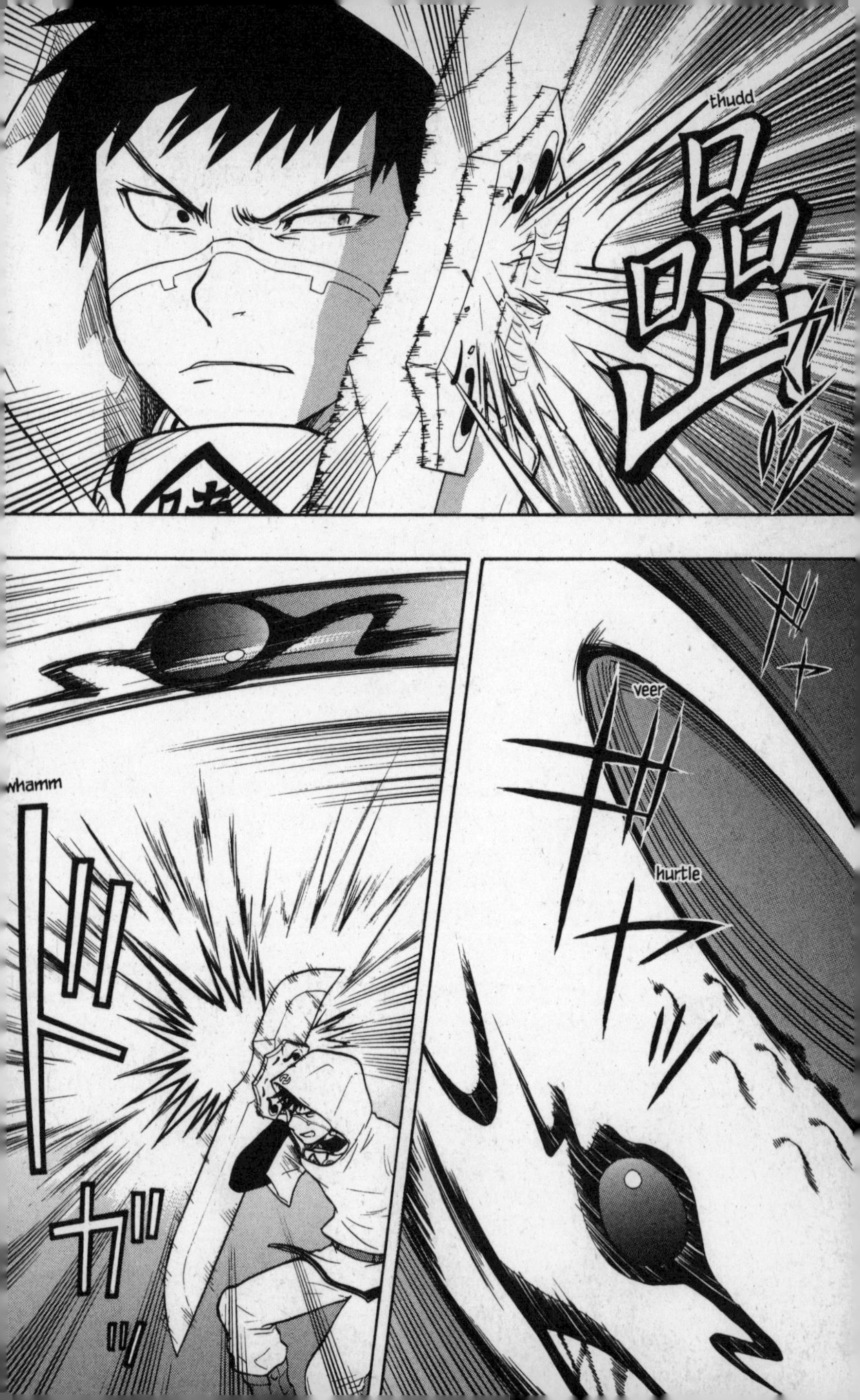
thudd
veer
hurtle
whamm

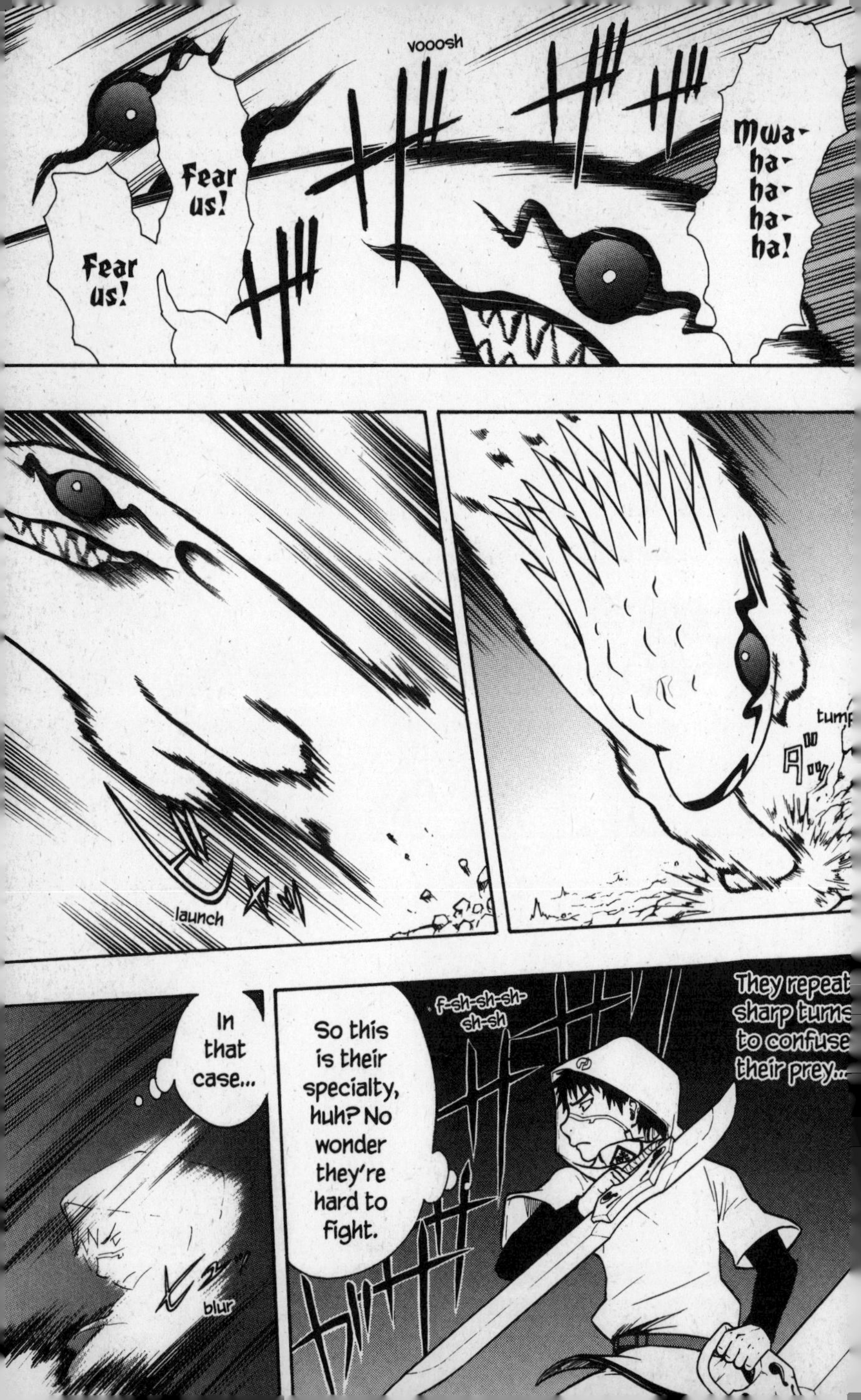
Mwa-ha-ha-ha-ha!
vooosh
Fear us!
Fear us!
tump
launch
They repeat sharp turns to confuse their prey...
f-sh-sh-sh-sh-sh
So this is their specialty, huh? No wonder they're hard to fight.
In that case...
blur

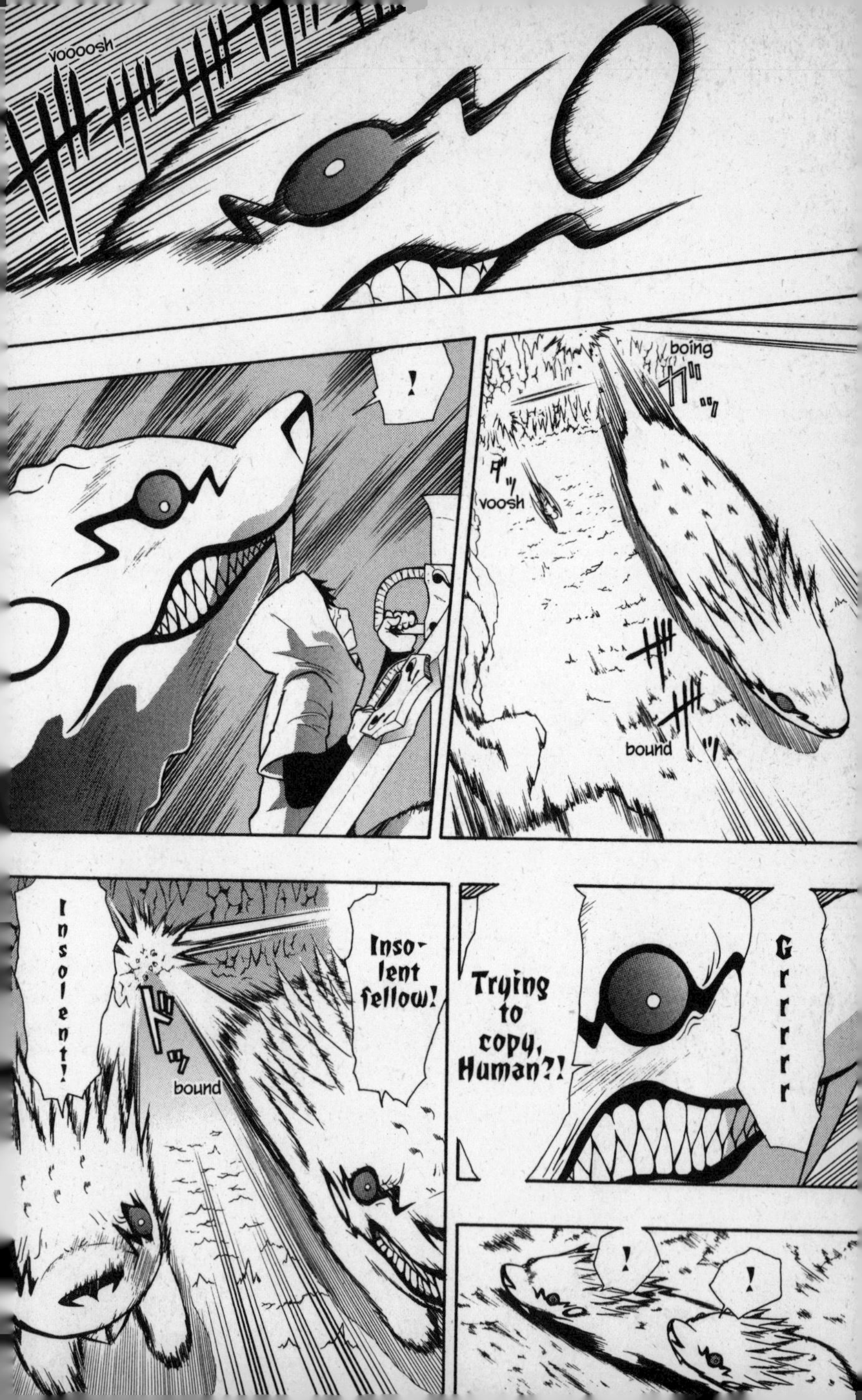
vooooosh
boing
voosh
bound
!
Grrrrr
Trying to copy, Human?!
!
!
Insolent fellow!
Insolent!
bound

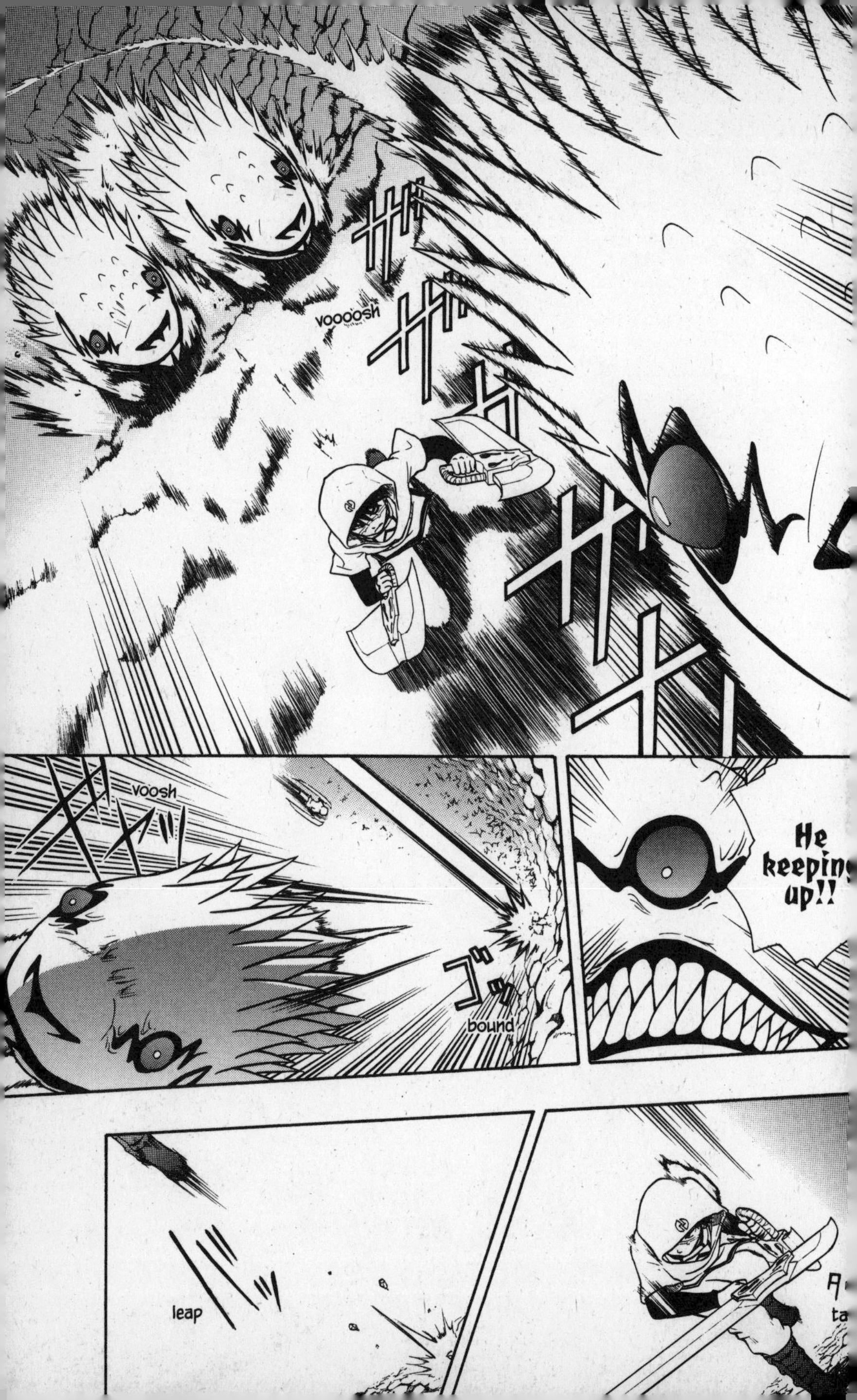
voooosh
He
keeping
up!!
voosh
bound
leap

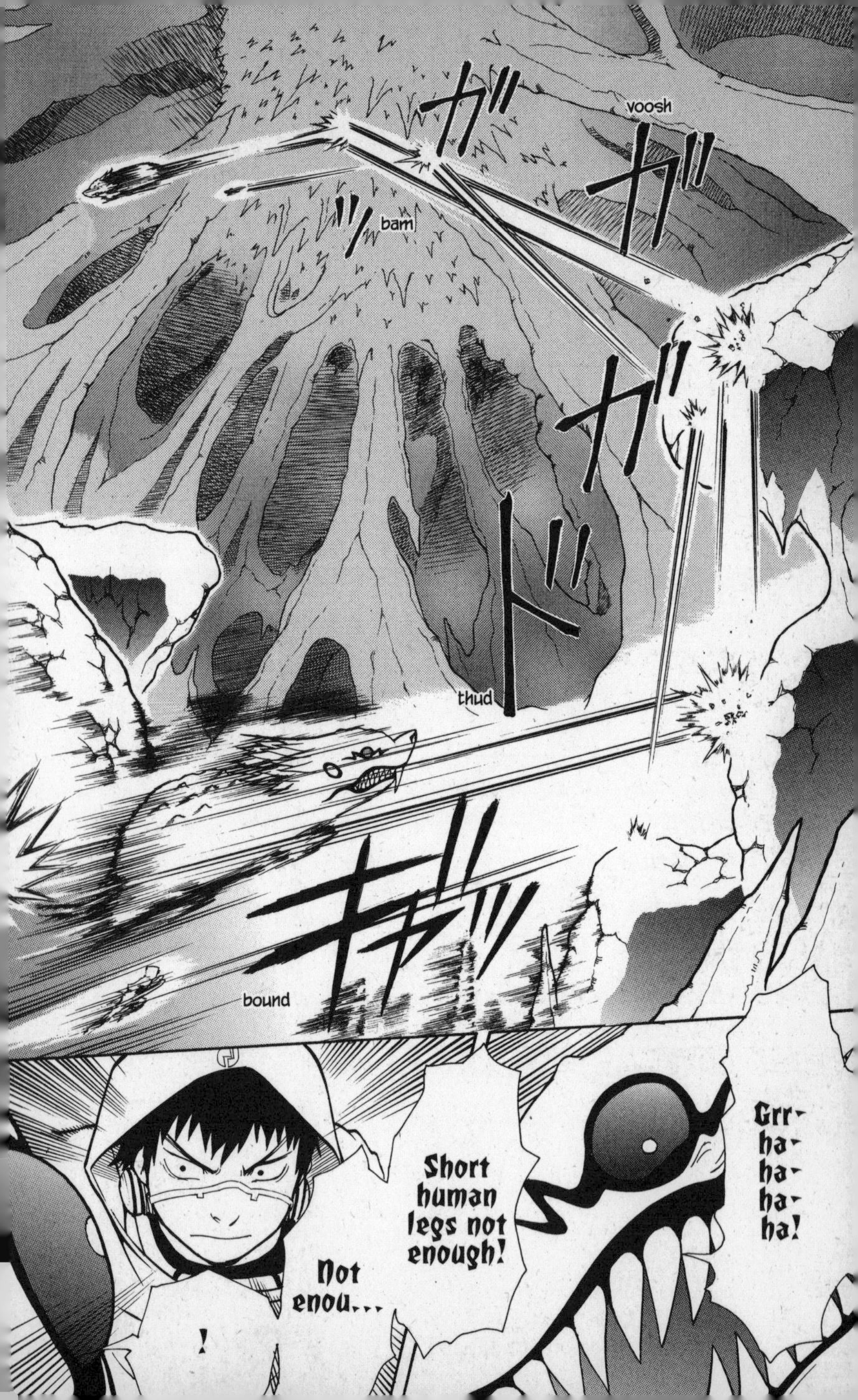
voosh
bam
thud
bound
Grr-ha-ha-ha-ha!
Short human legs not enough!
Not enou...
!

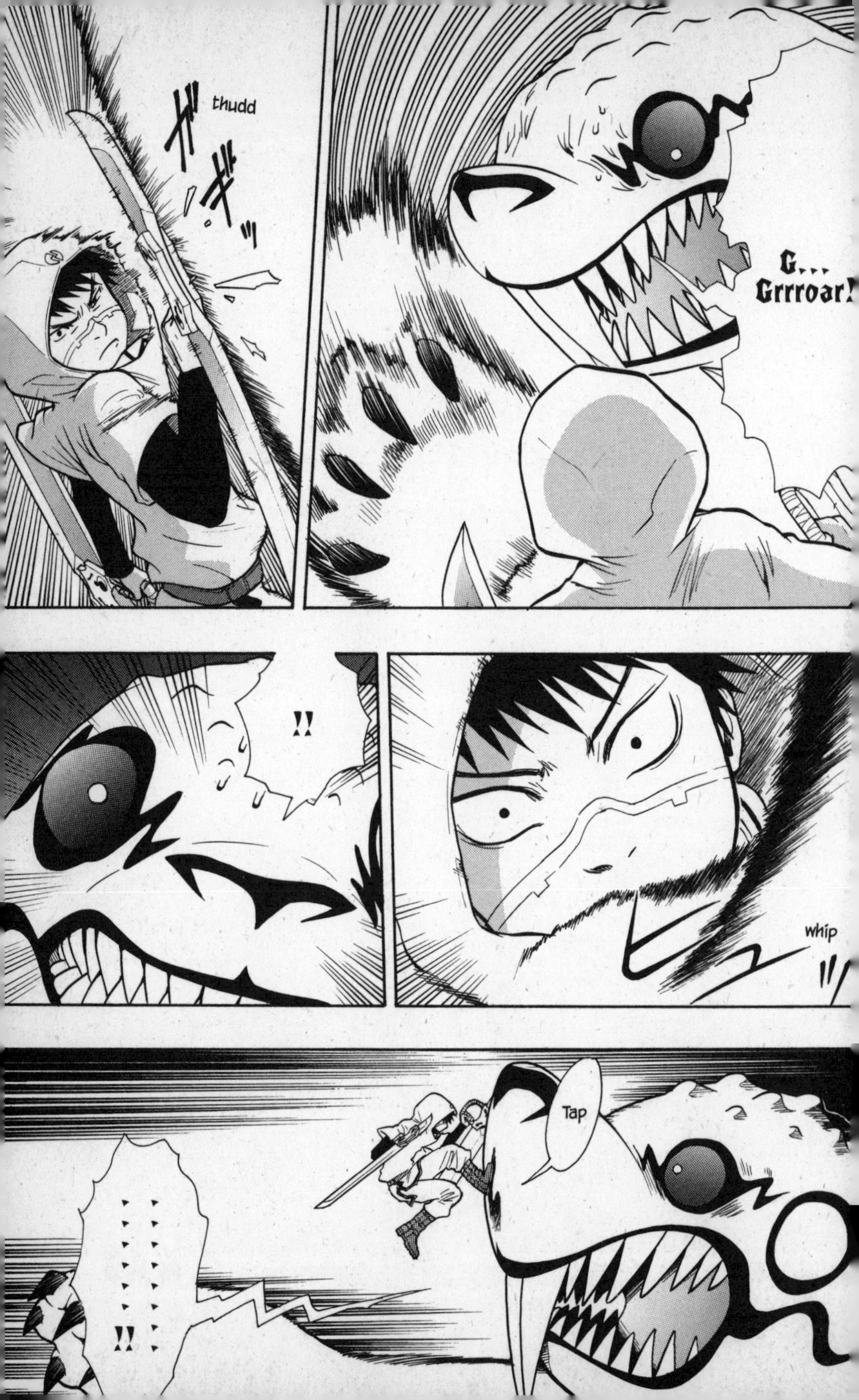
G... Grrroar!
thudd
!!
whip
Tap
......
!!

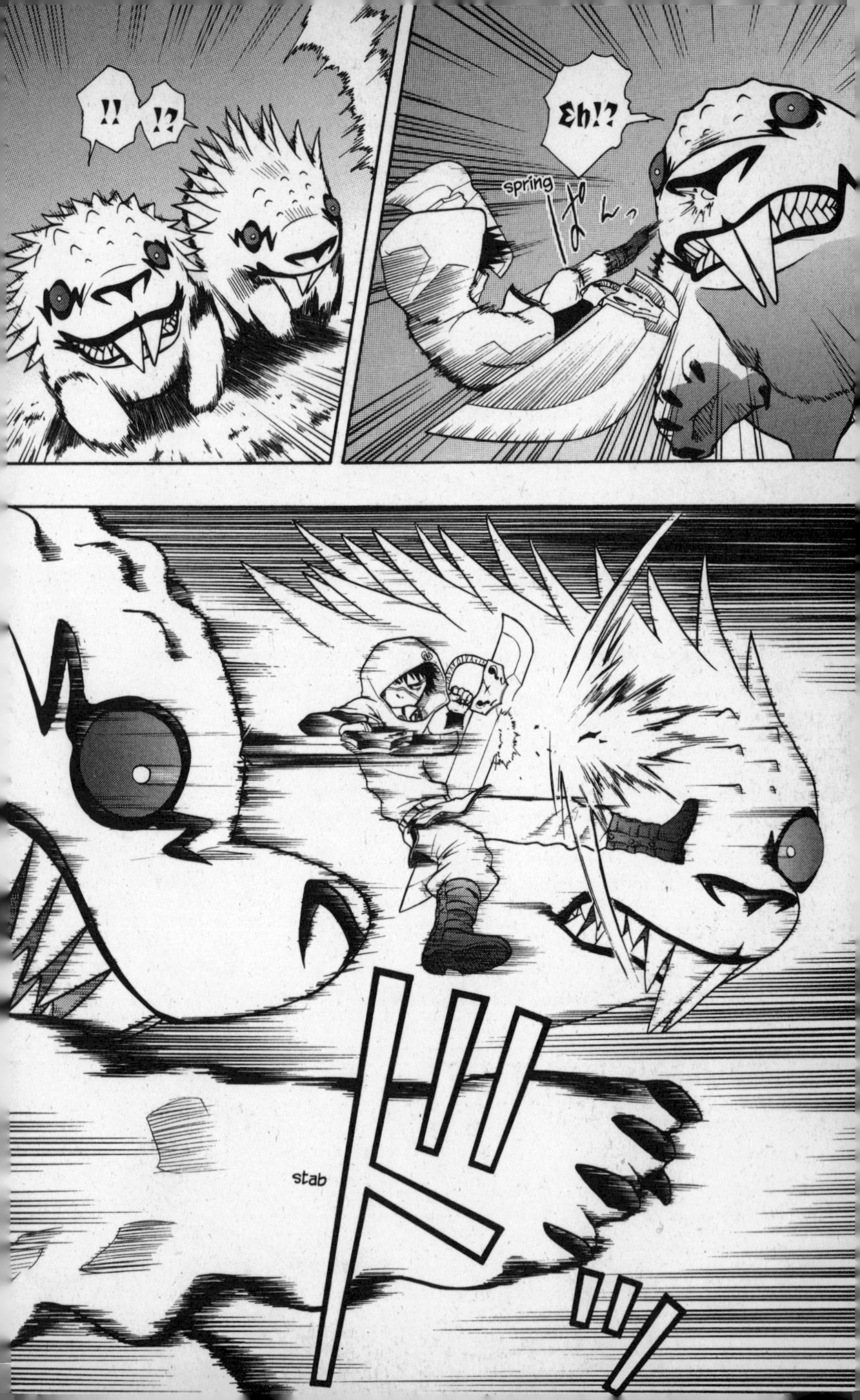
Eh!?
spring
ぽんっ
!?
!!
stab

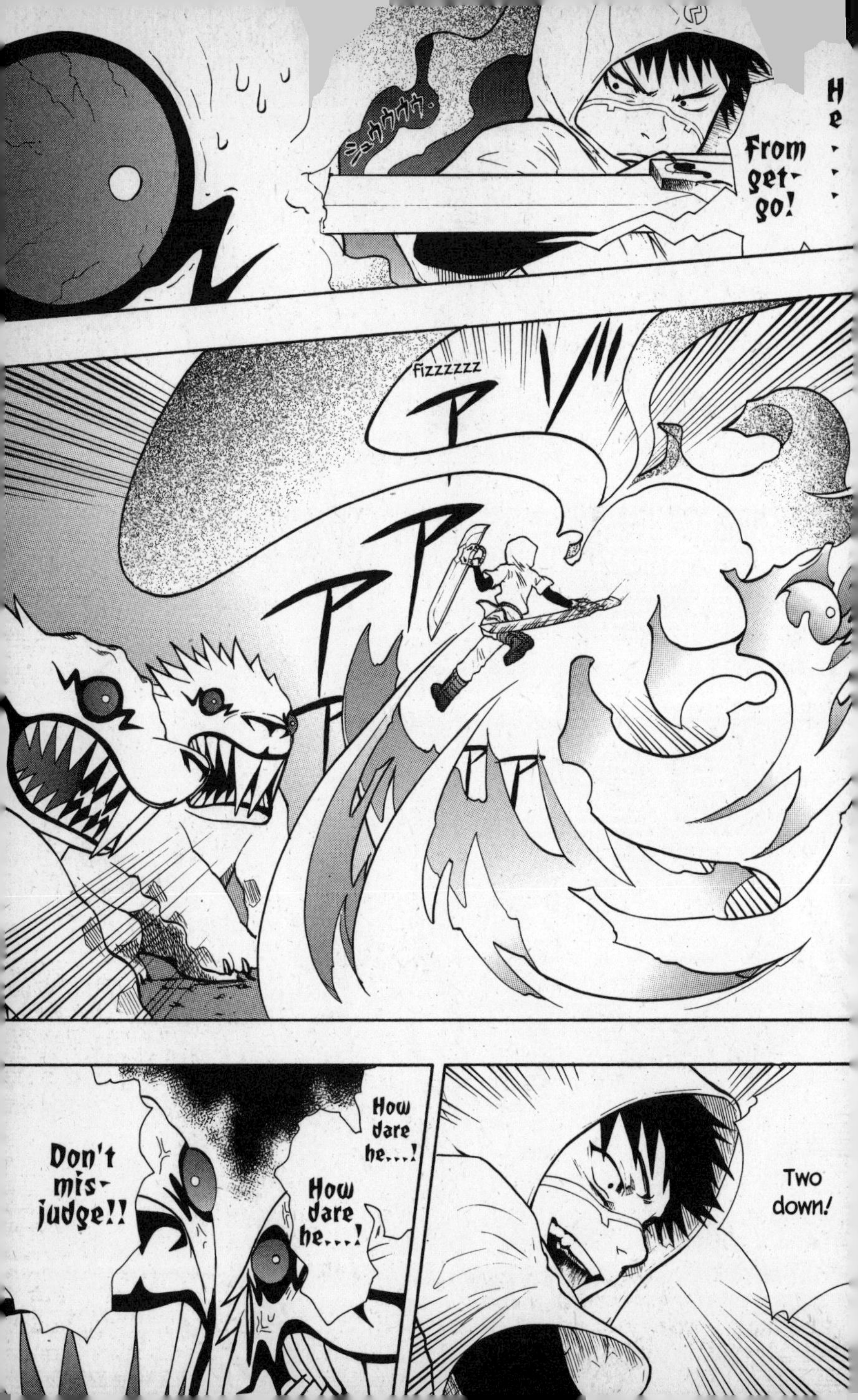

He...
From get-go!
シュウウウウ。
Fizzzzzz
Two down!
How dare he...!
How dare he...!
Don't mis-judge!!

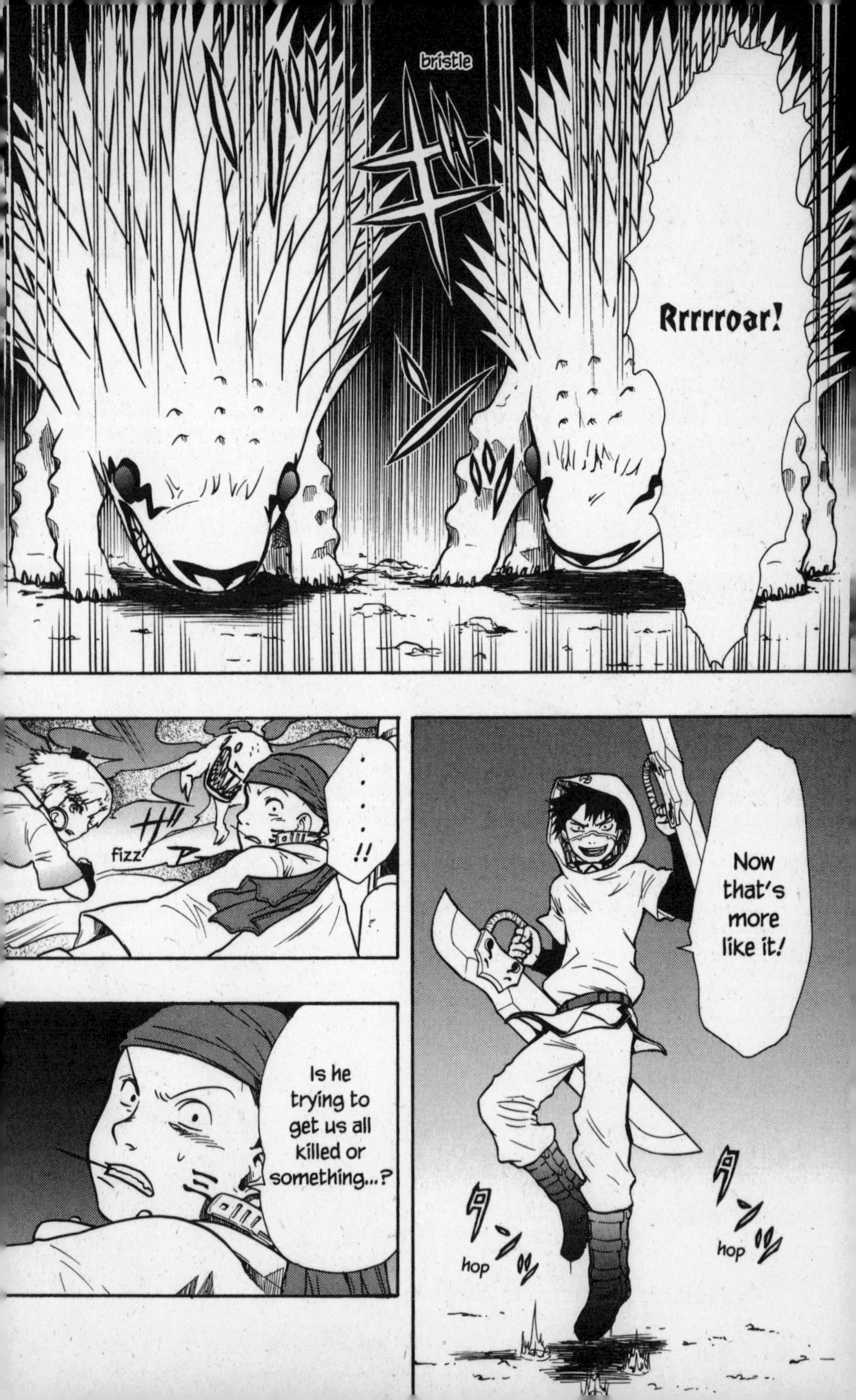
bristle
Rrrrroar!
Now that's more like it!
hop
hop
fizz
. . . . . !!
Is he trying to get us all killed or something...?

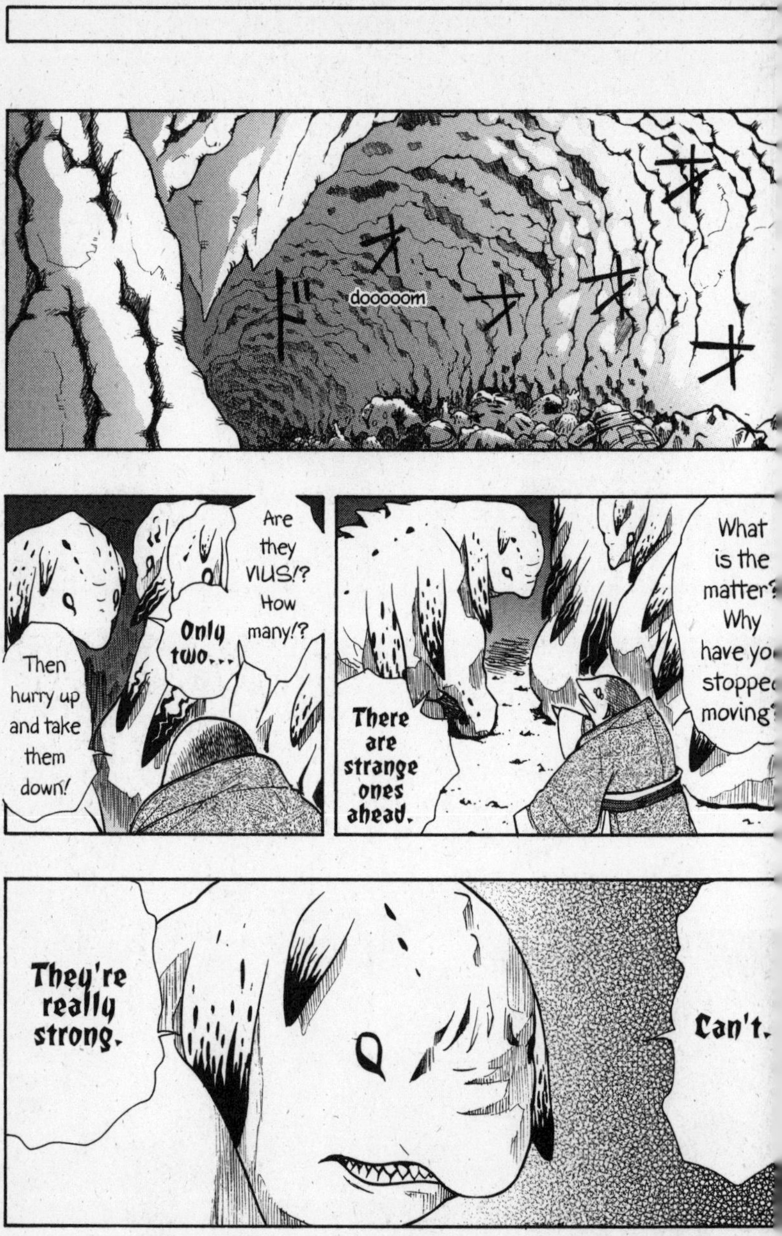
doooooom
What is the matter? Why have yo stoppe moving?
There are strange ones ahead.
Are they VIUS!? How many!?
Only two...
Then hurry up and take them down!
Can't.
They're really strong.

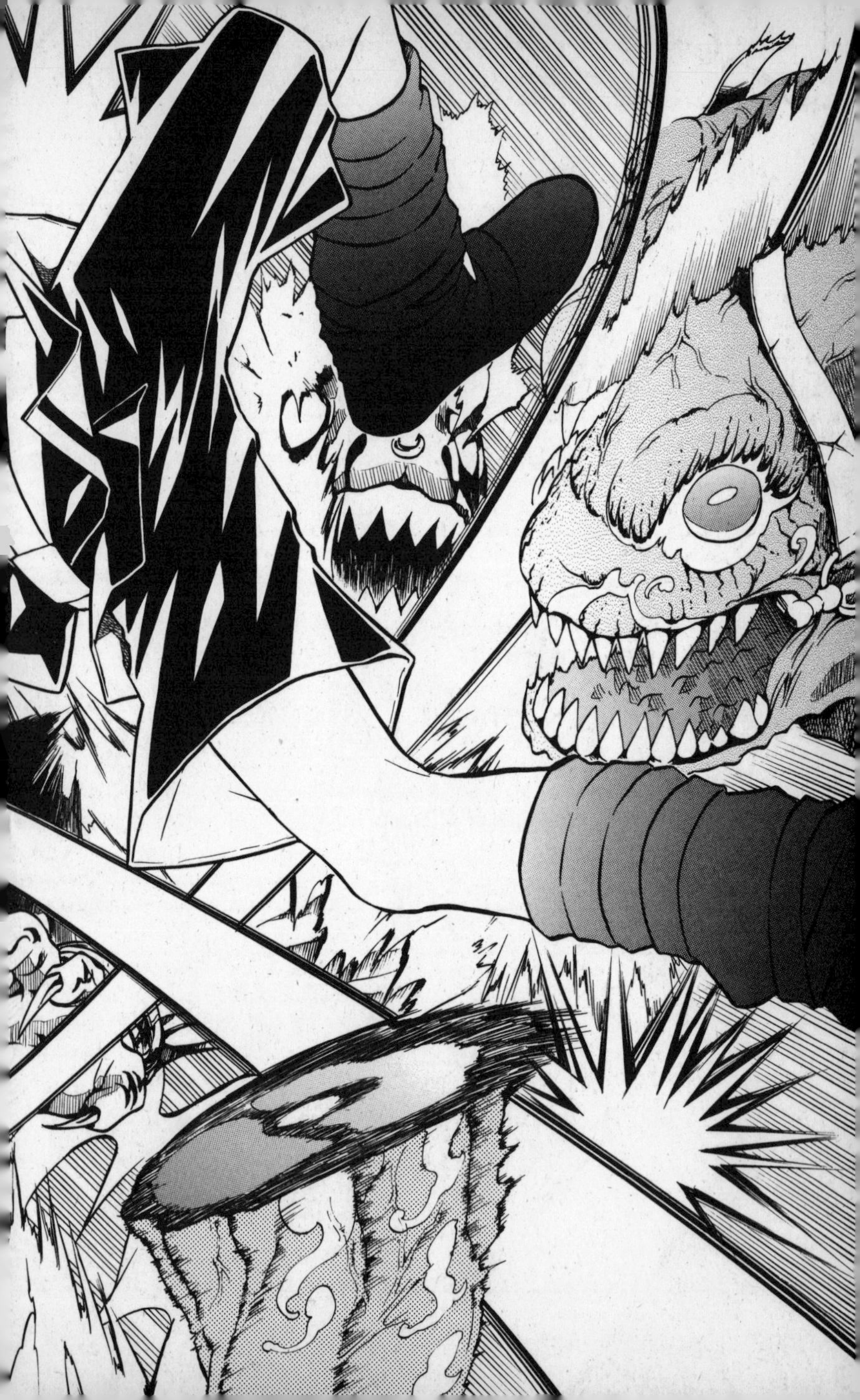

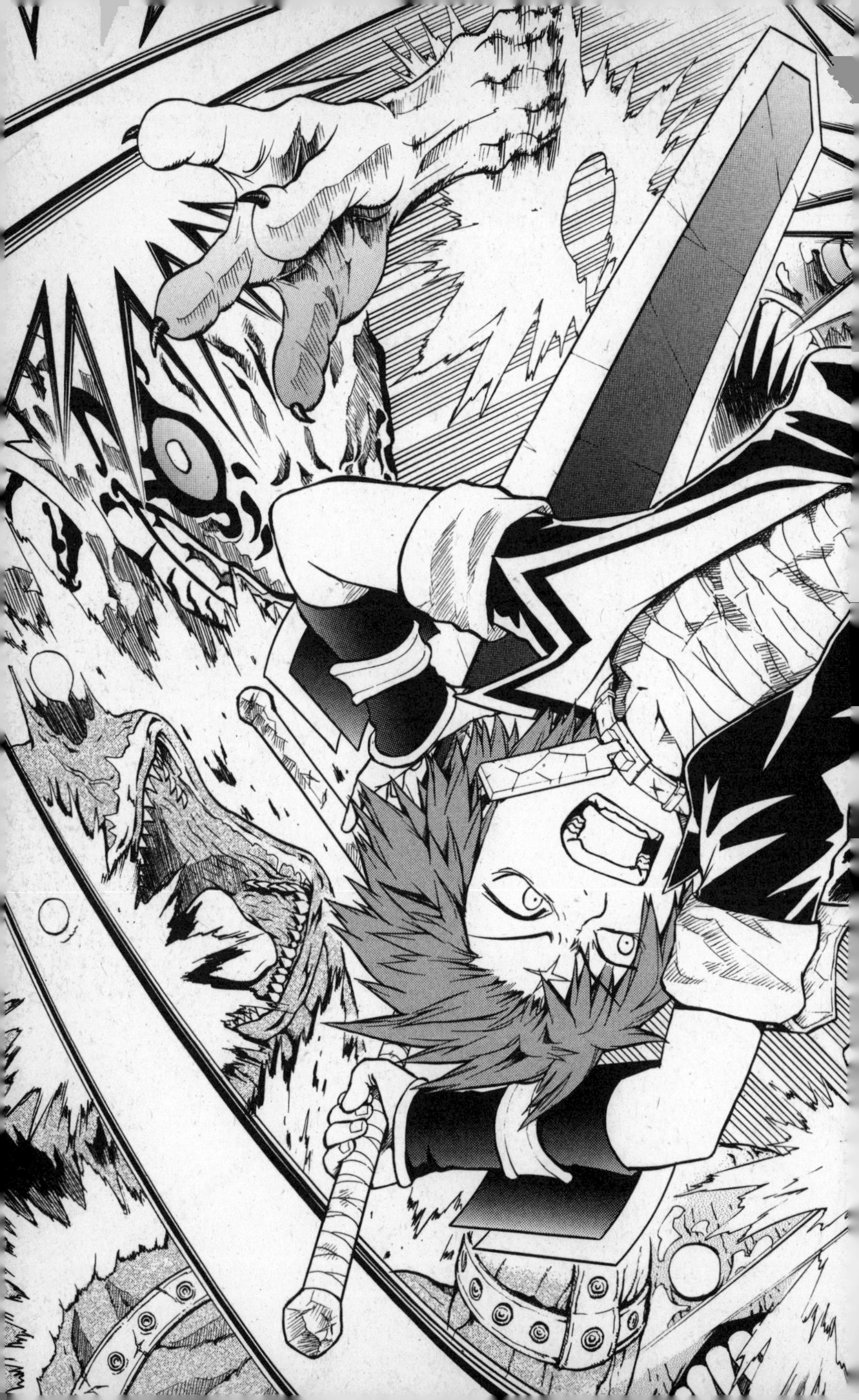

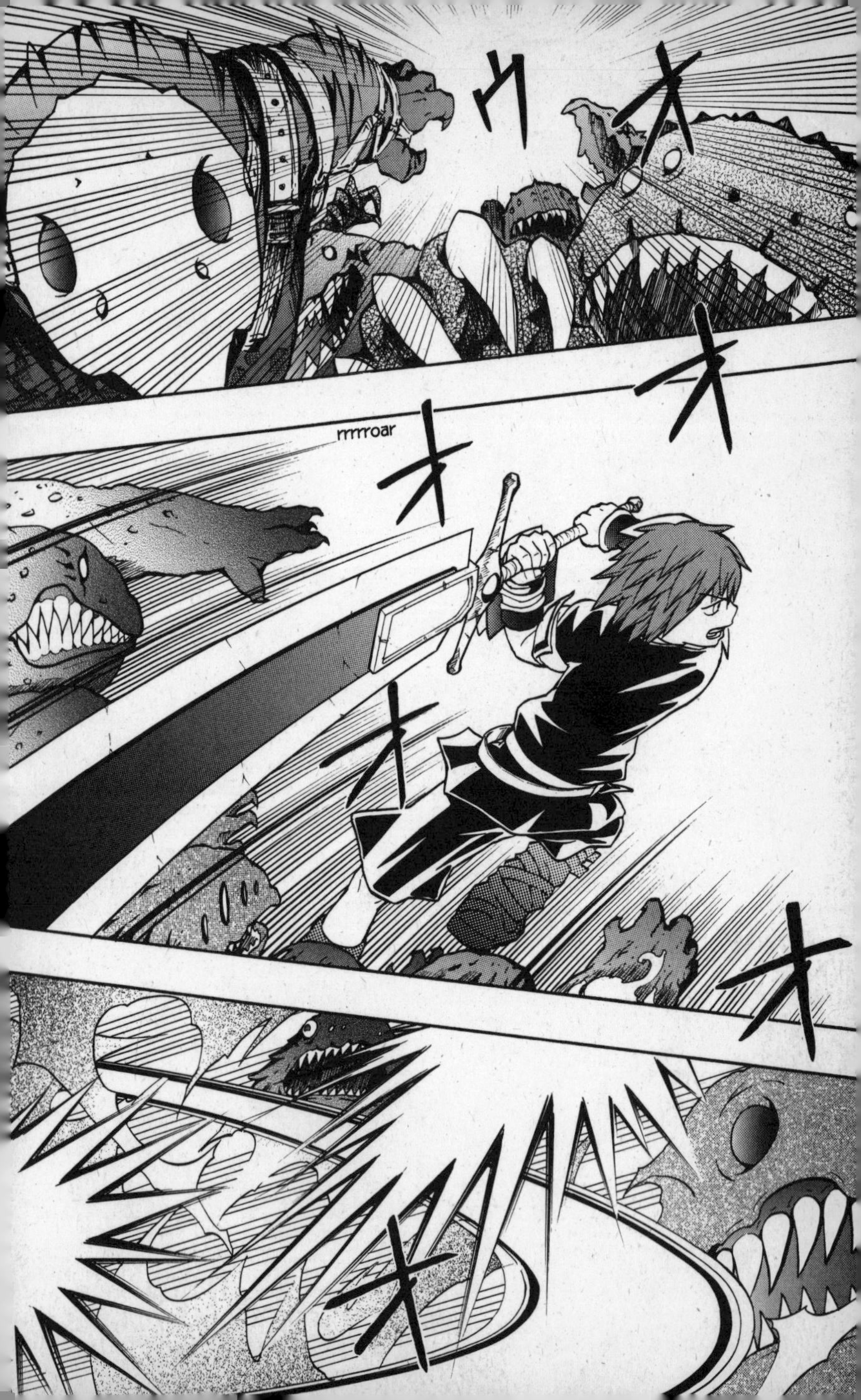
ウオオオオオオ
rrrrroar

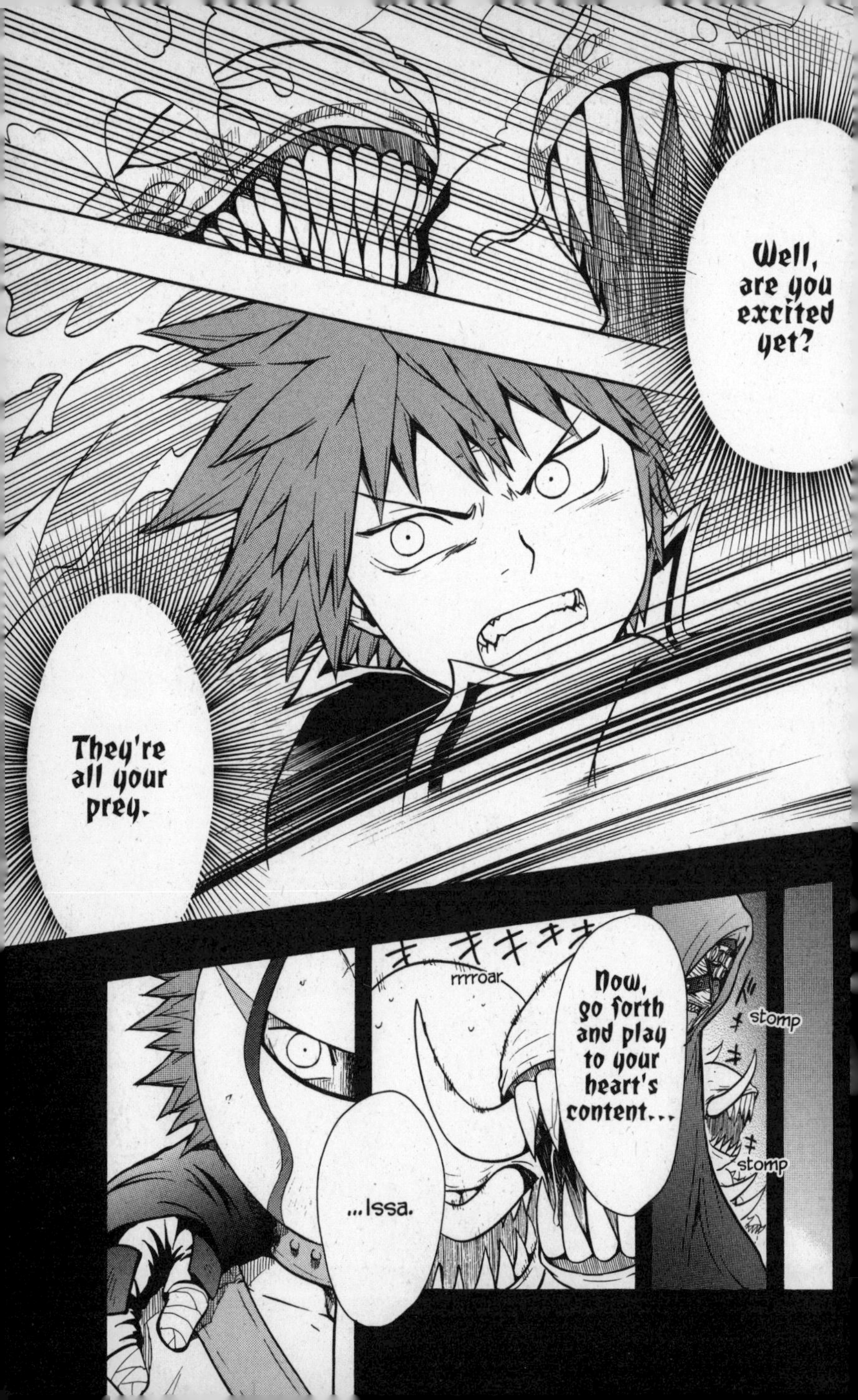
Well, are you excited yet?
They're all your prey.
stomp
stomp
Now, go forth and play to your heart's content...
rrrroar
...Issa.

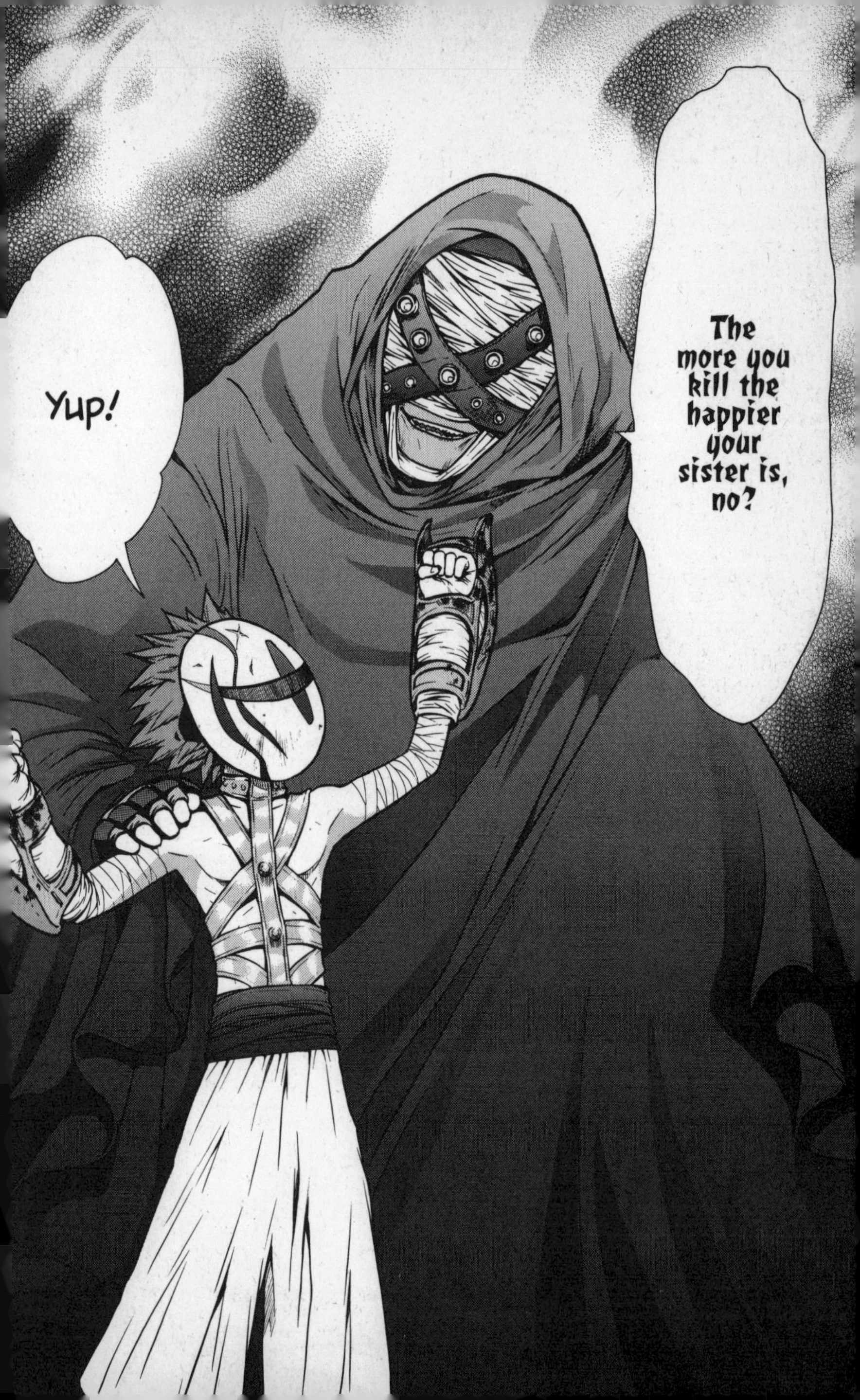

The more you kill the happier your sister is, no?
Yup!

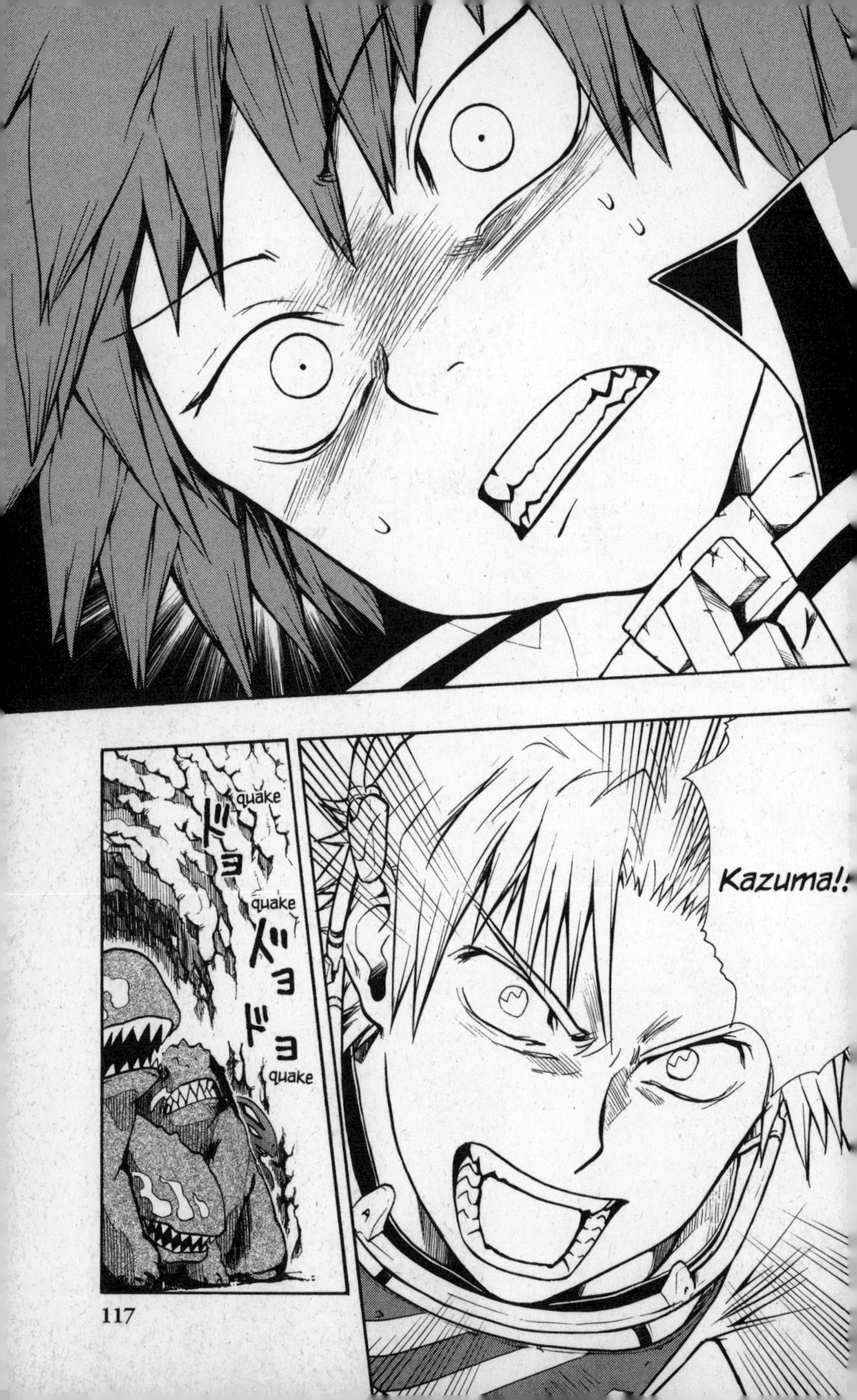
Kazuma!!
ドョ
quake
ドョ
quake
ドョ
quake

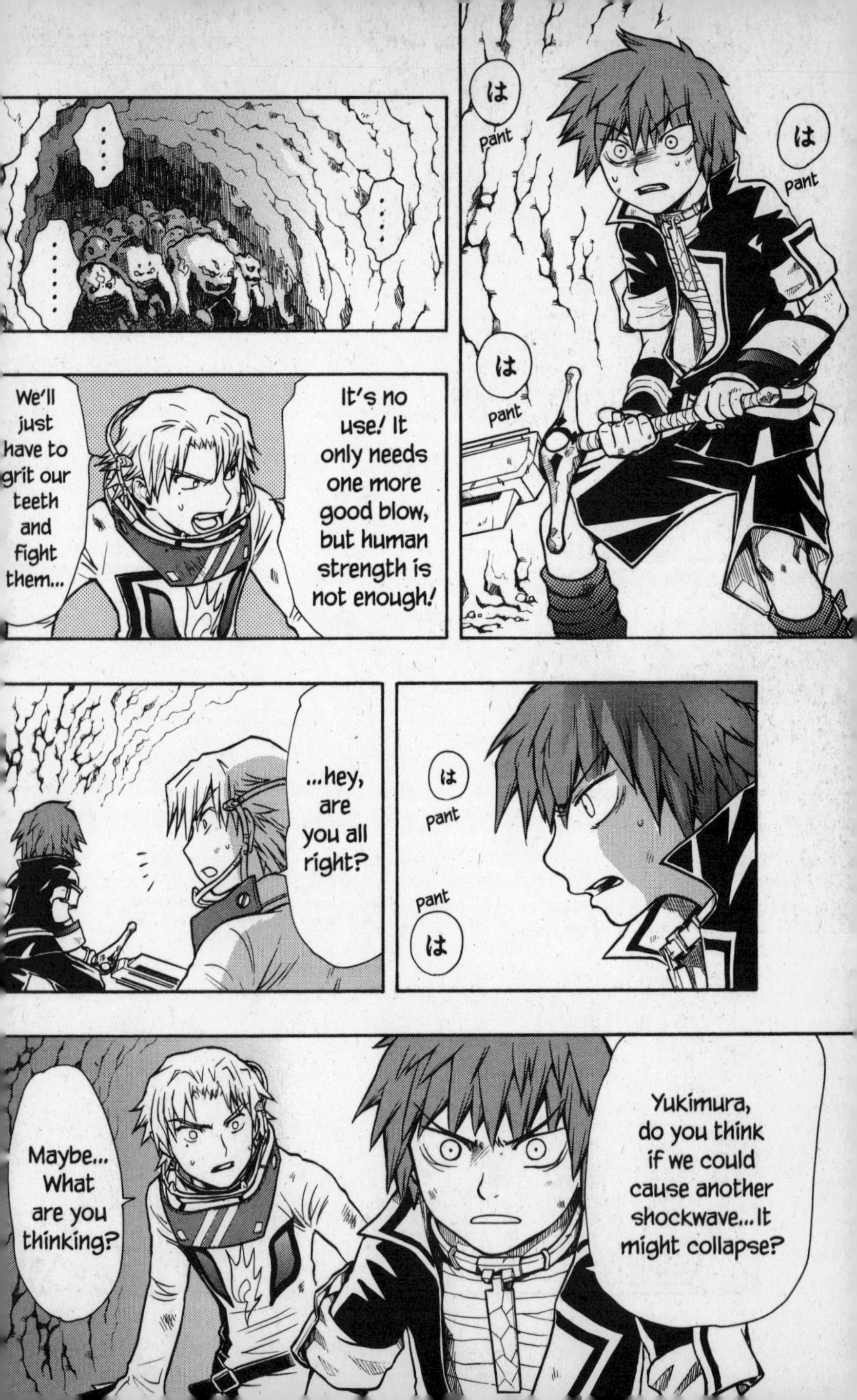

は
pant
は
pant
は
pant
.....
.....
.....
It's no use! It only needs one more good blow, but human strength is not enough!
We'll just have to grit our teeth and fight them...
は
pant
pant
は
...hey, are you all right?
Yukimura, do you think if we could cause another shockwave...It might collapse?
Maybe... What are you thinking?

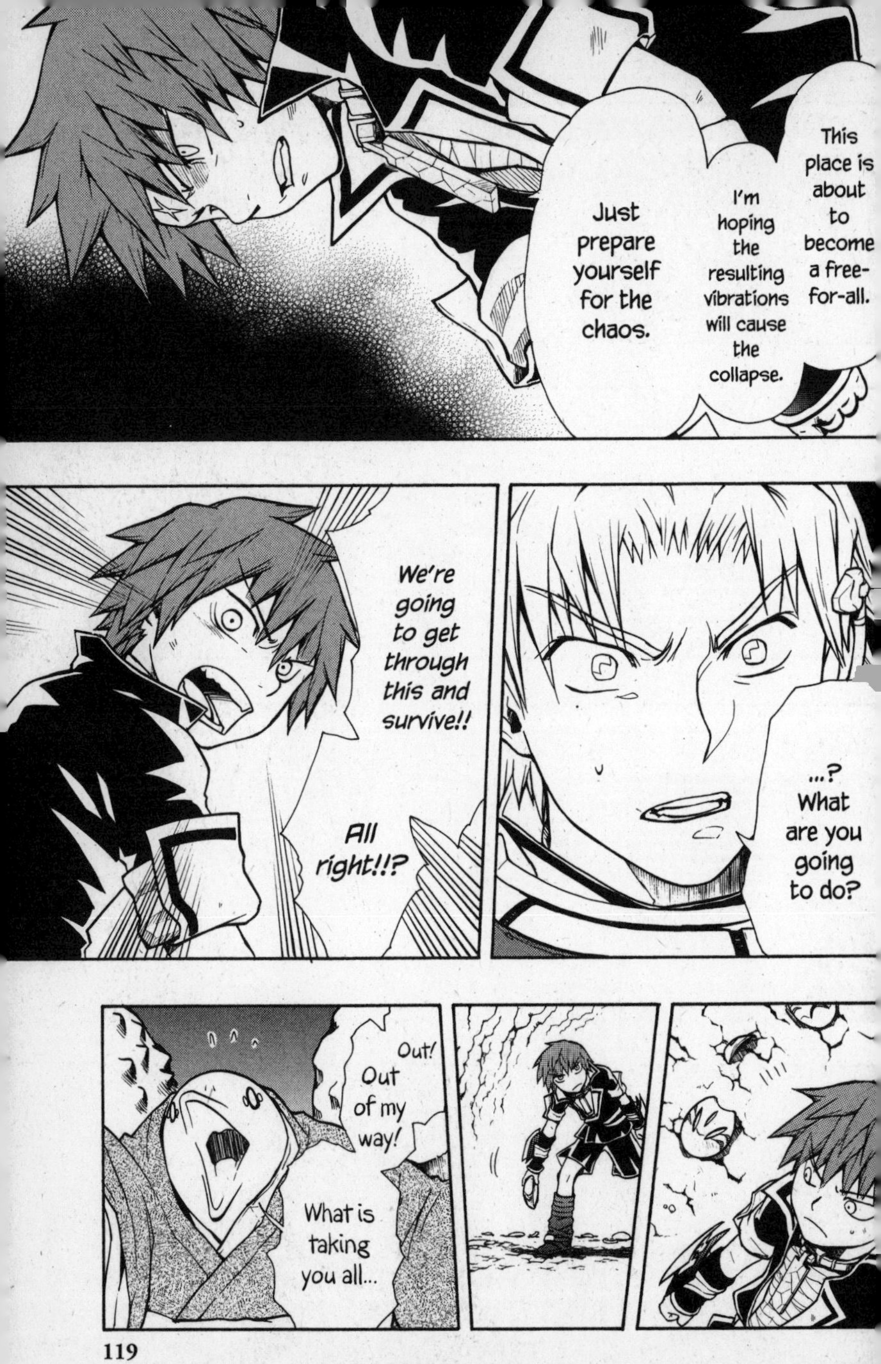
This place is about to become a free-for-all.
I'm hoping the resulting vibrations will cause the collapse.
Just prepare yourself for the chaos.
...? What are you going to do?
We're going to get through this and survive!!
All right!!?
Out! Out of my way!
What is taking you all...

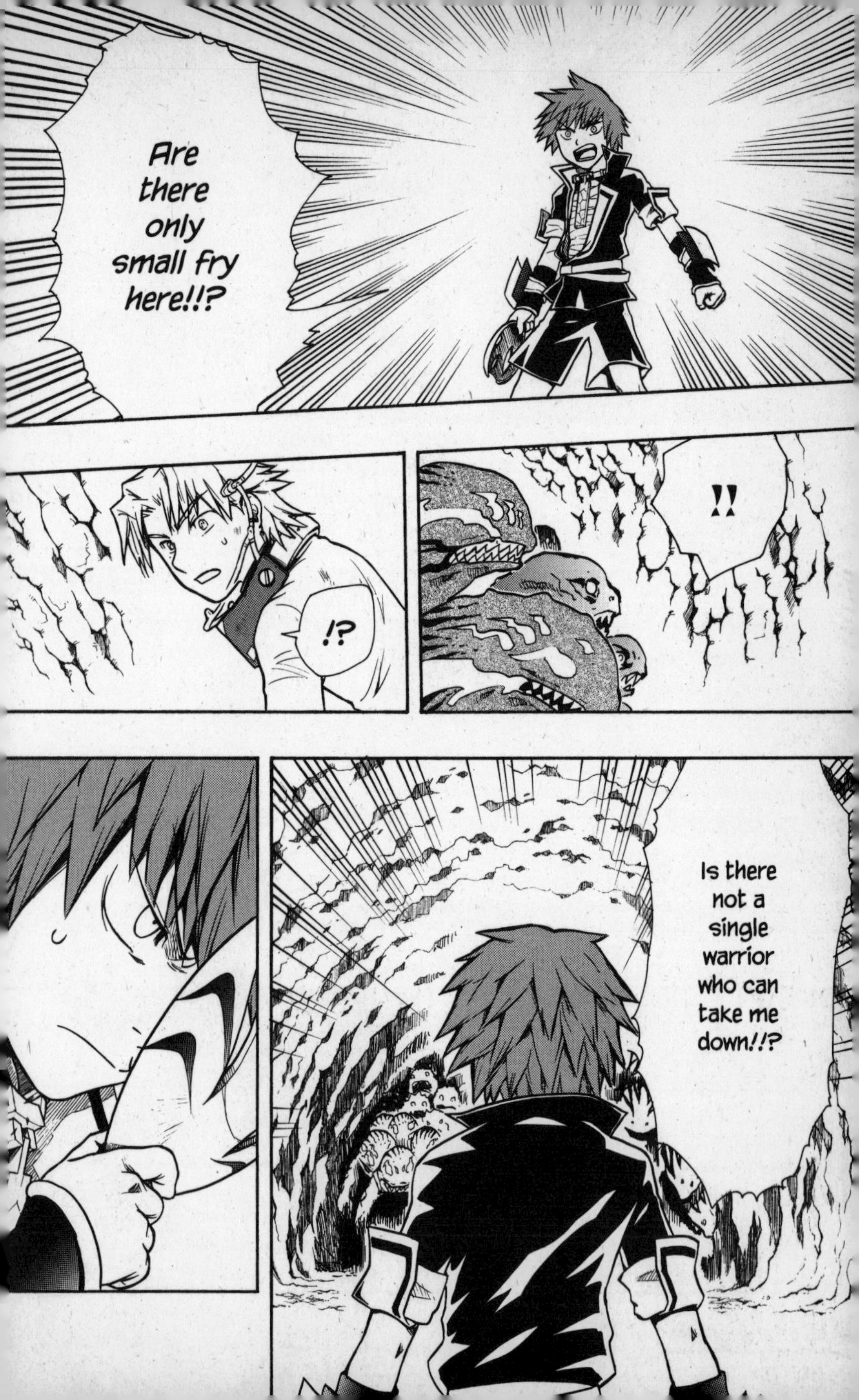
Are there only small fry here!!?
!!
!?
Is there not a single warrior who can take me down!!?

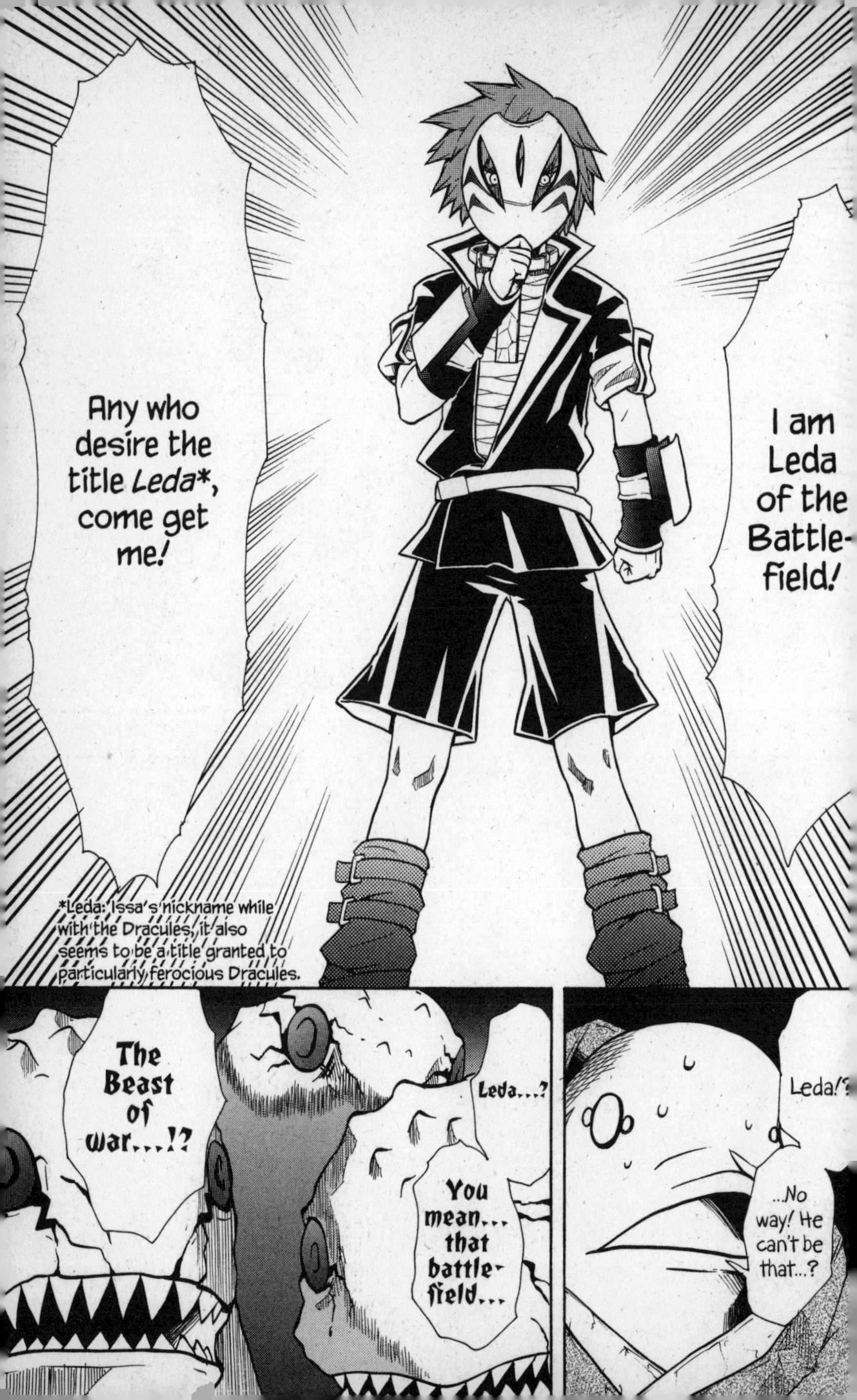
I am Leda of the Battlefield!
Any who desire the title *Leda**, come get me!
*Leda: Issa's nickname while with the Dracules, it also seems to be a title granted to particularly ferocious Dracules.
Leda!?
...No way! He can't be that...?
Leda...?
You mean... that battlefield...
The Beast of war...!?

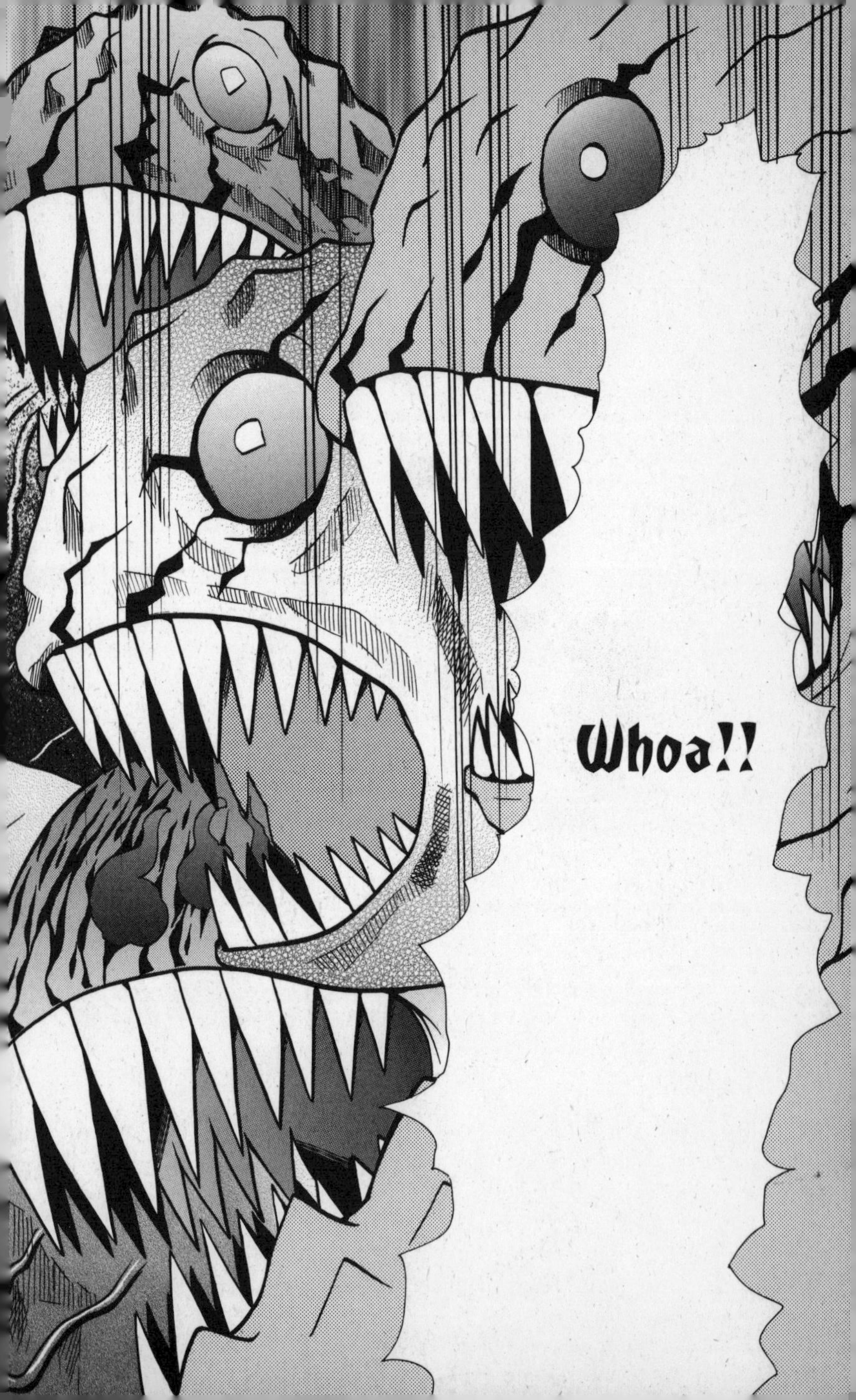
Whoa!!

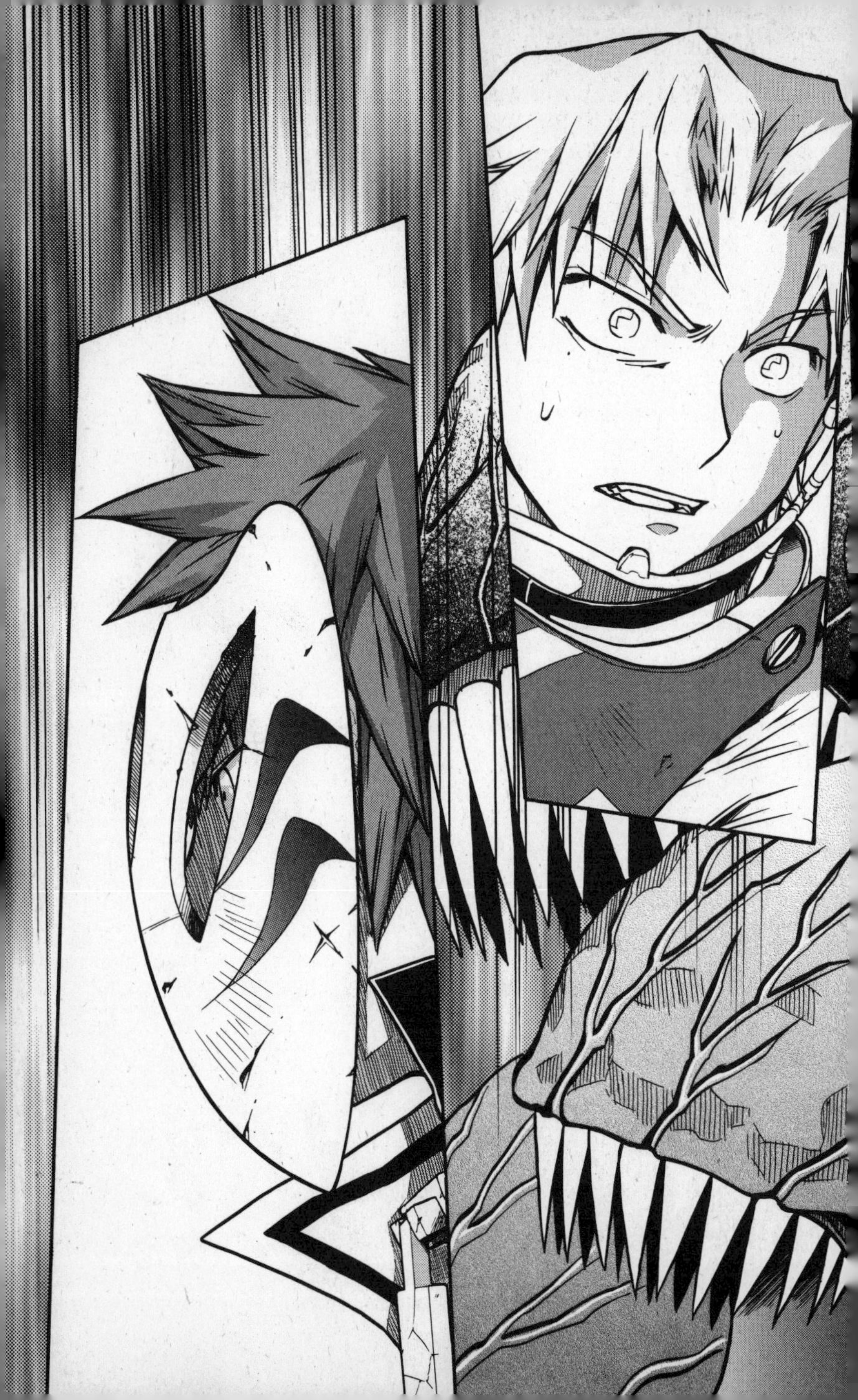

Samurai Principles

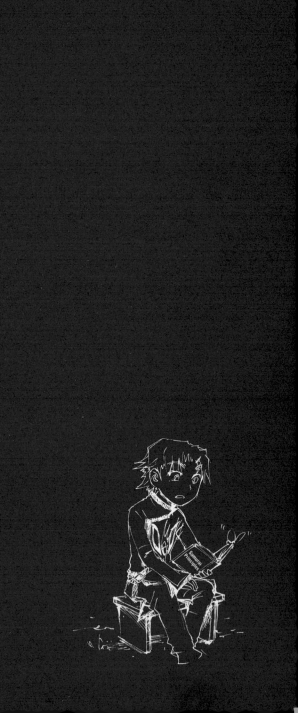

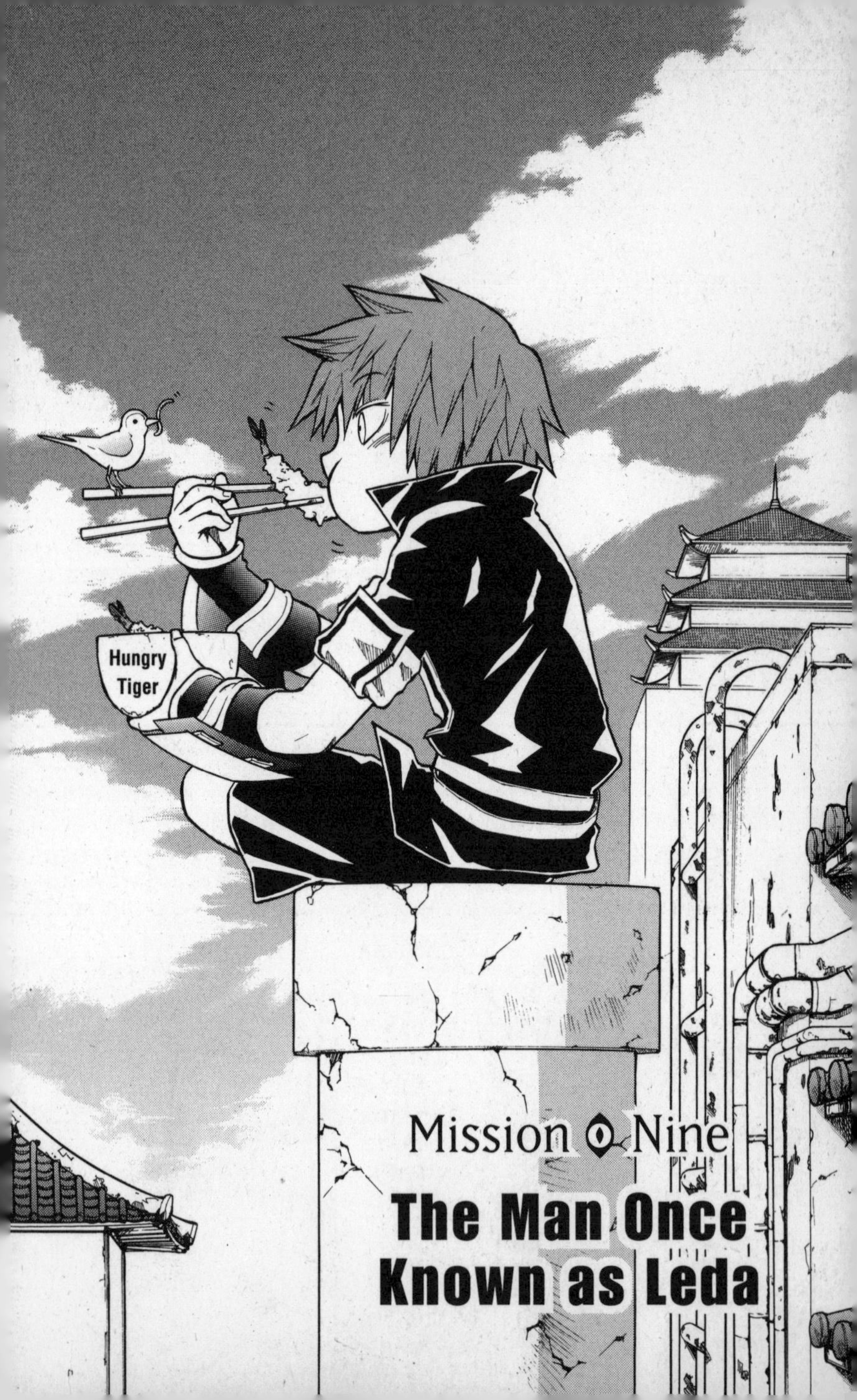
Hungry
Tiger

Mission Nine

The Man Once Known as Leda

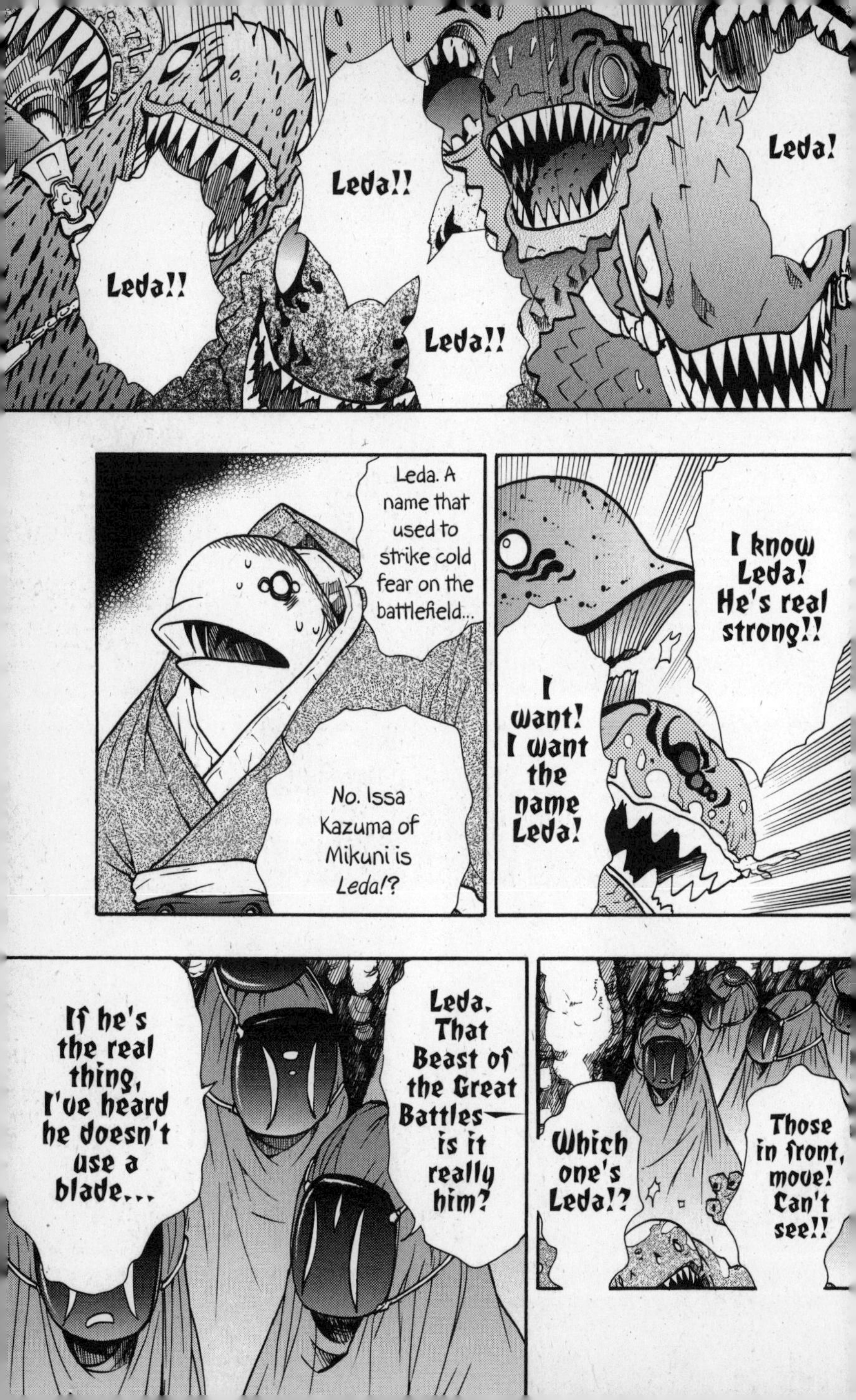
Leda!
Leda!!
Leda!!
Leda!!
I know Leda! He's real strong!!
I want! I want the name Leda!
Leda. A name that used to strike cold fear on the battlefield...
No. Issa Kazuma of Mikuni is Leda!?
Those in front, move! Can't see!!
Which one's Leda!?
Leda. That Beast of the Great Battles— is it really him?
If he's the real thing, I've heard he doesn't use a blade...

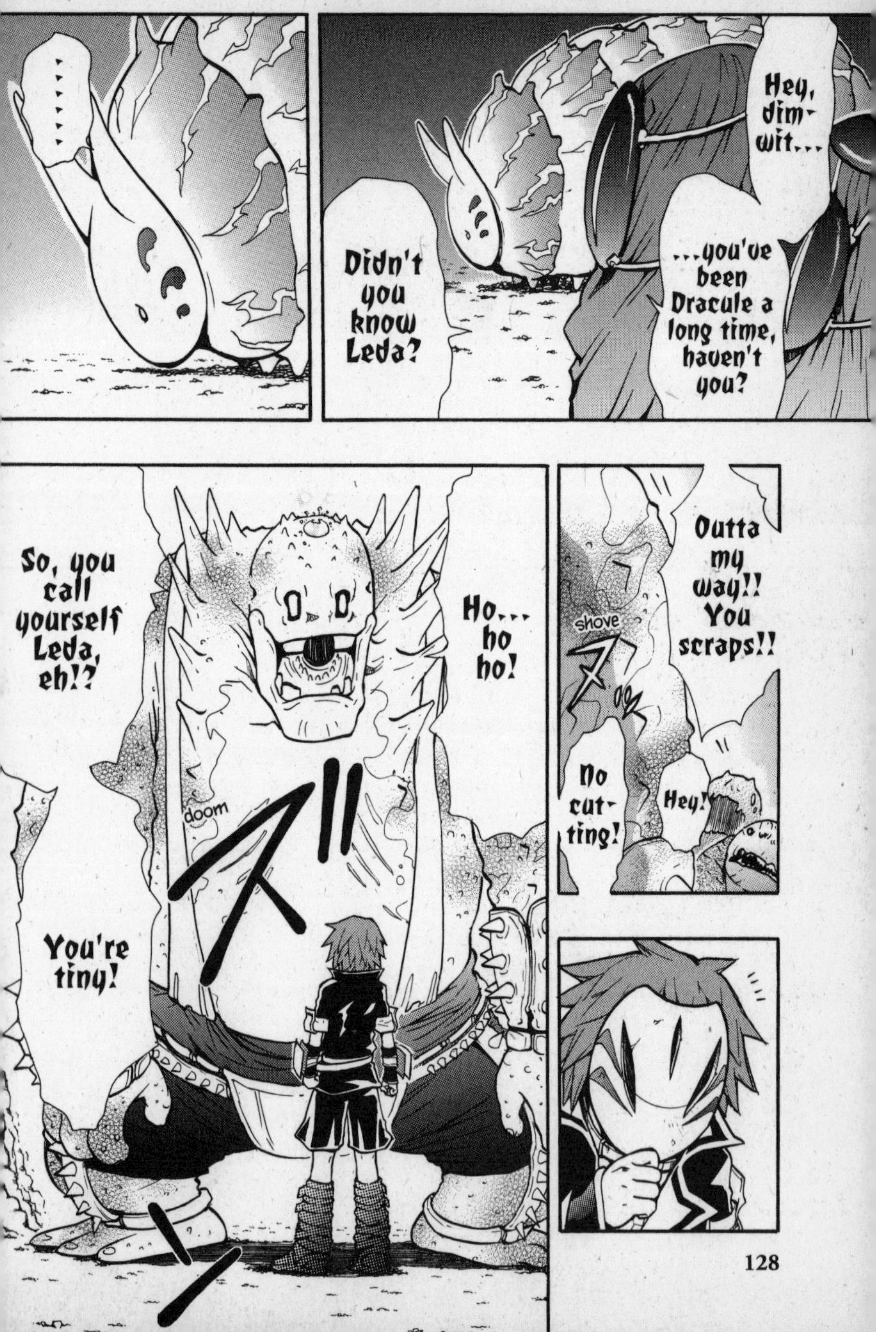
Hey, dimwit...
...you've been Dracule a long time, haven't you?
Didn't you know Leda?
......
Outta my way!! You scraps!!
shove
Hey!
No cutting!
Ho... ho ho!
So, you call yourself Leda, eh!?
doom
You're tiny!

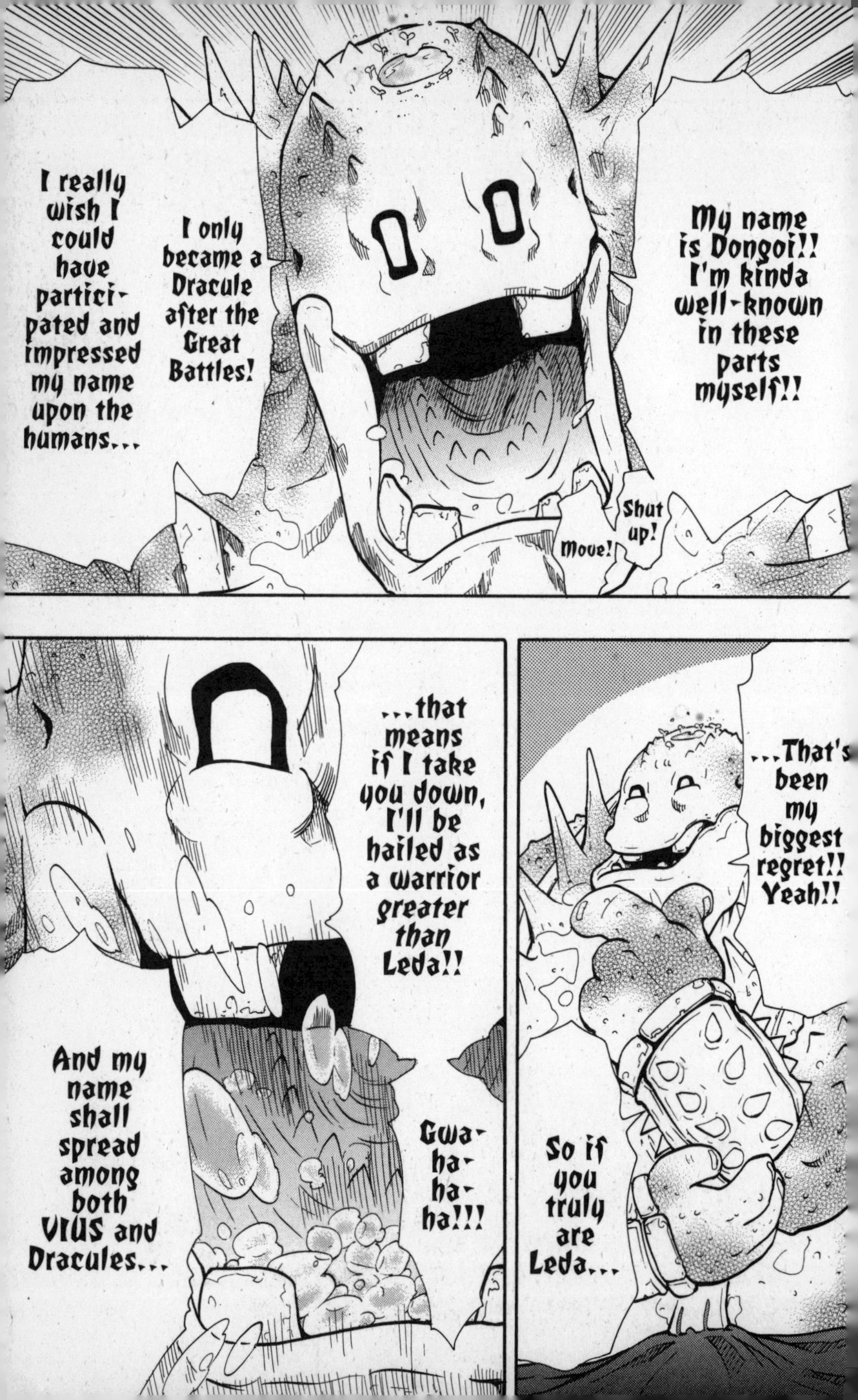
My name is Dongoi!! I'm kinda well-known in these parts myself!!
Shut up!
Move!
I only became a Dracule after the Great Battles!
I really wish I could have partici-pated and impressed my name upon the humans...
...That's been my biggest regret!! Yeah!!
So if you truly are Leda...
...that means if I take you down, I'll be hailed as a warrior greater than Leda!!
Gwa-ha-ha-ha!!!
And my name shall spread among both VIUS and Dracules...

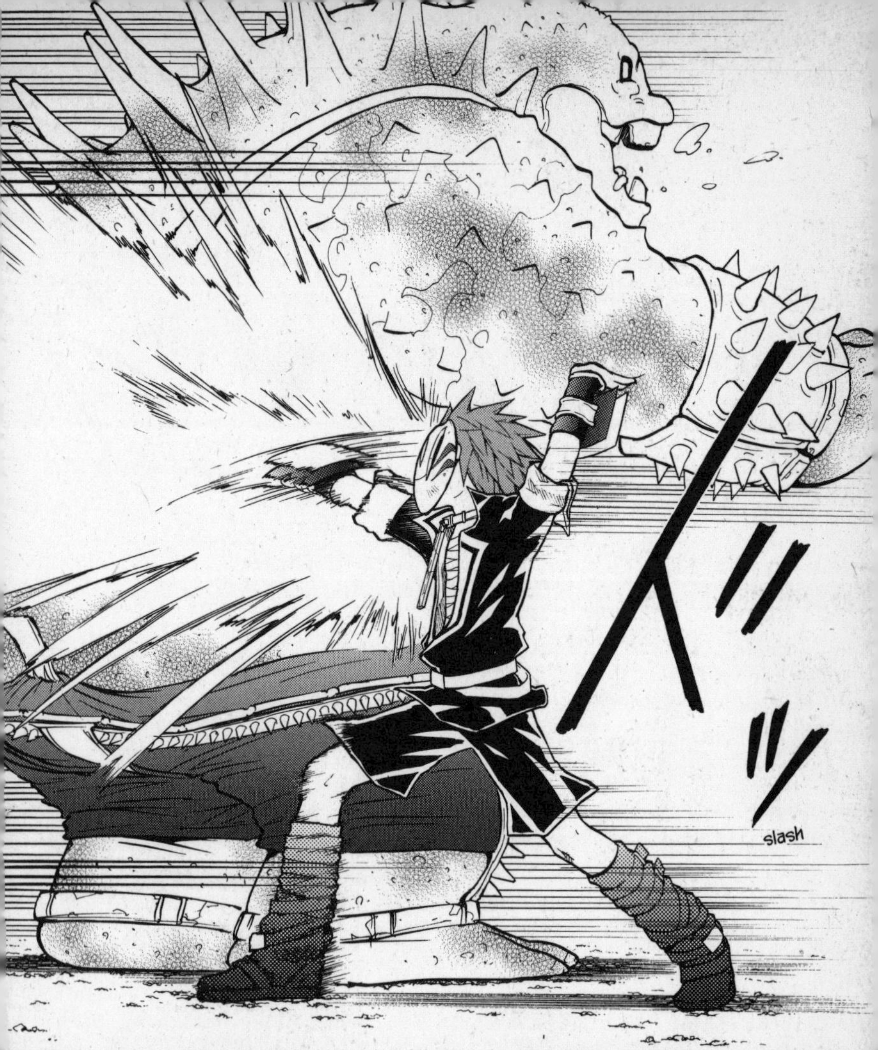
slash

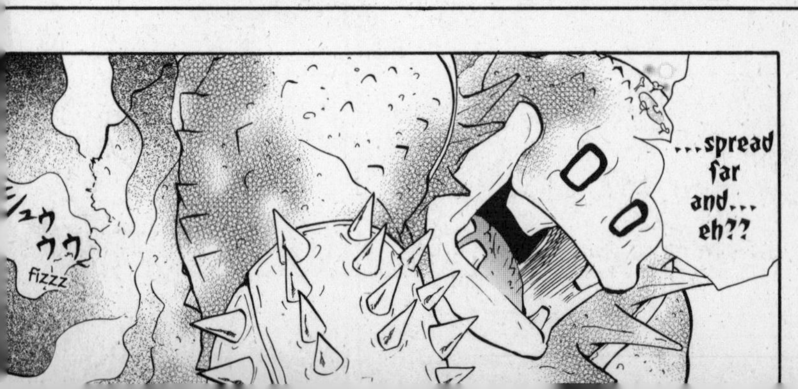
...spread far and... eh??
Fizzz

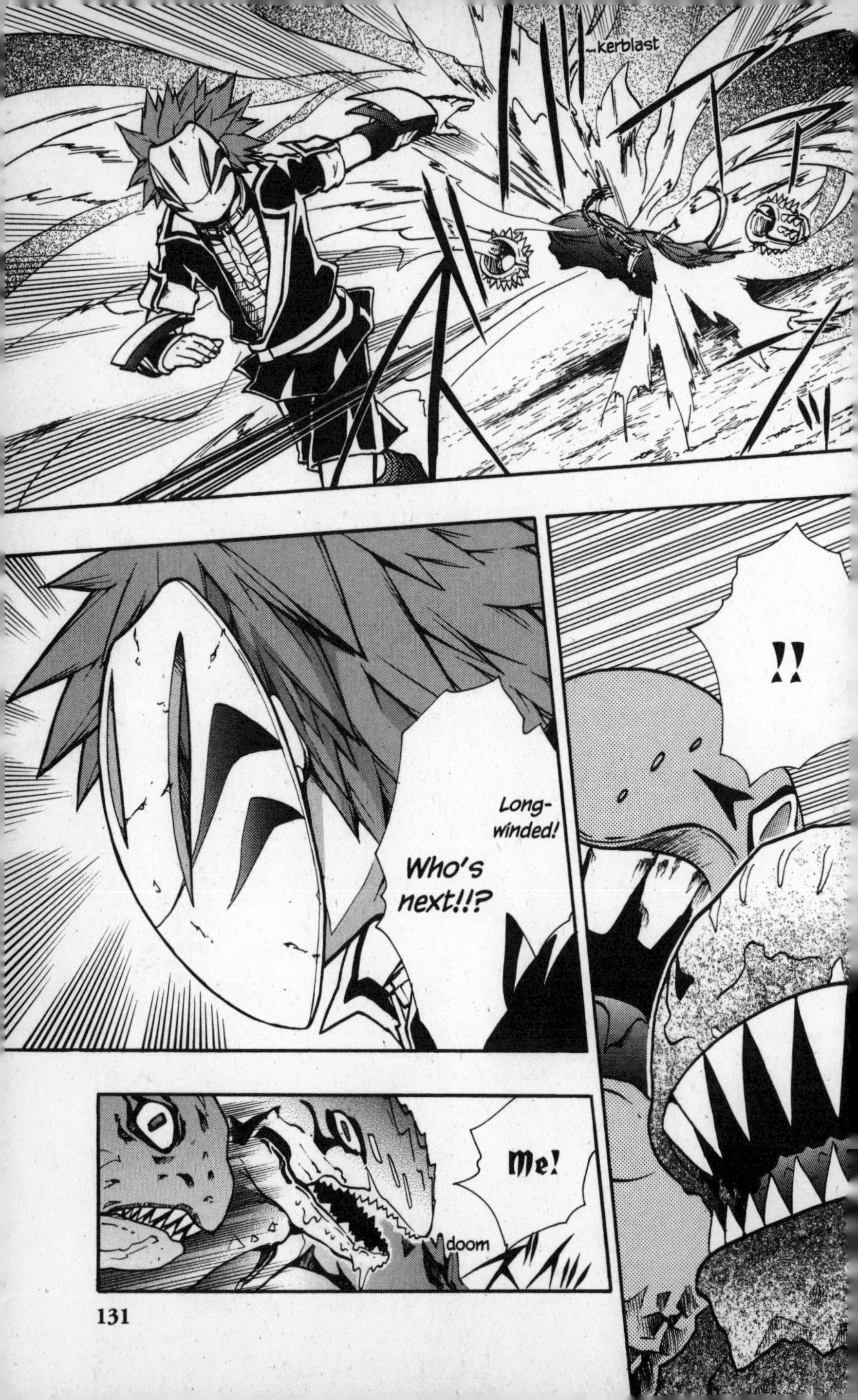
~kerblast
!!
Long-winded!
Who's next!!?
Me!
doom

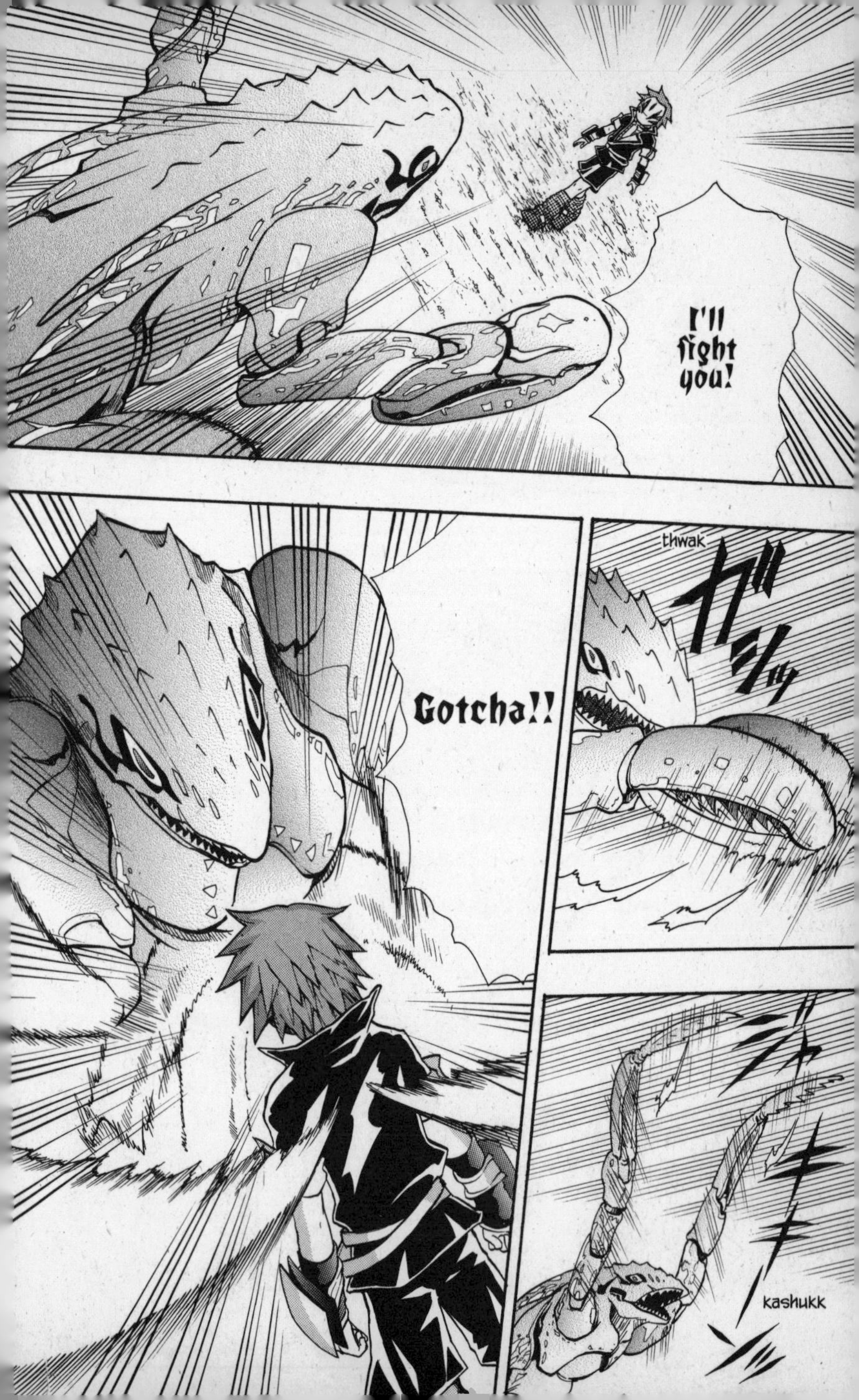
I'll fight you!
thwak
kashukk
Gotcha!!

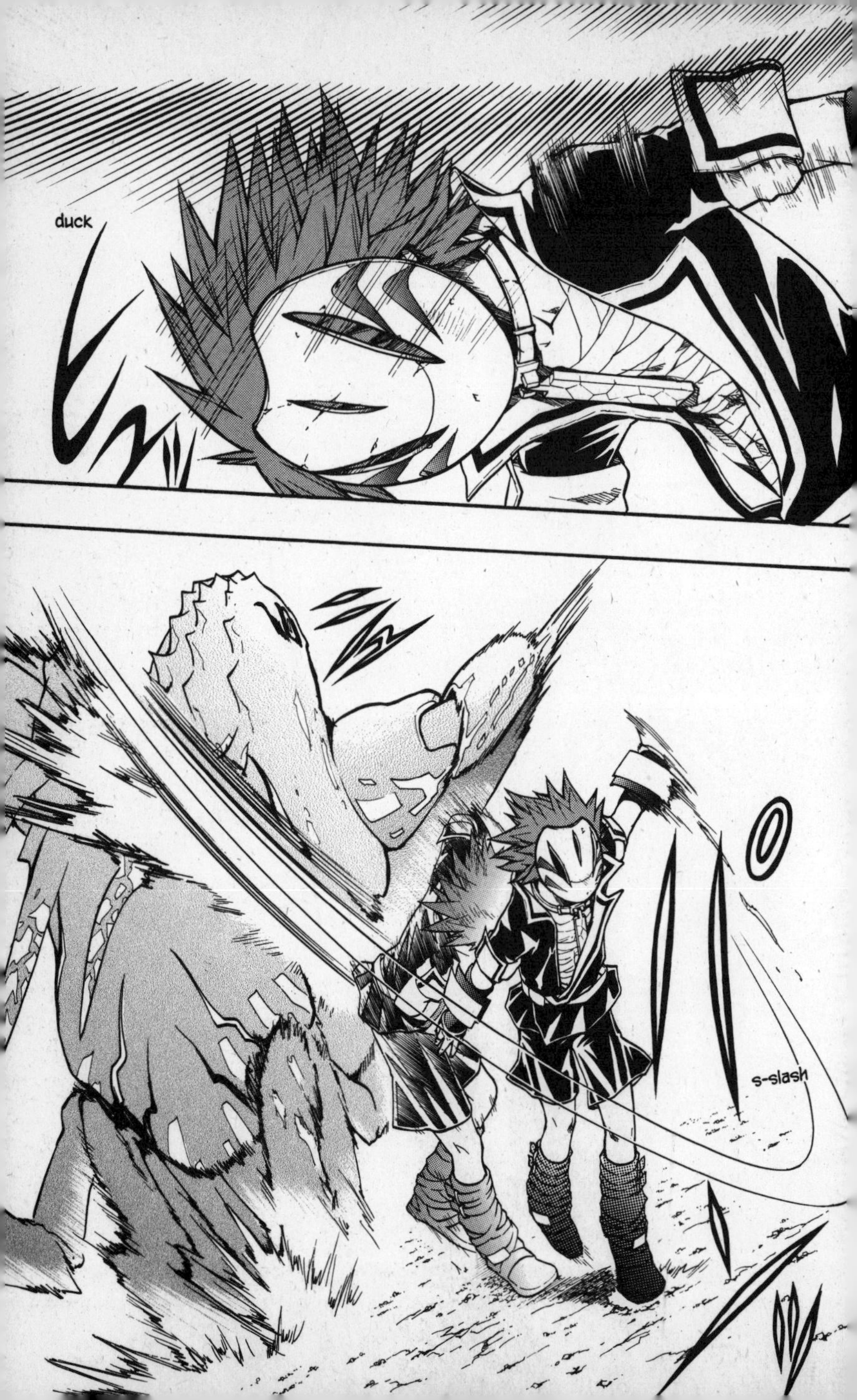
duck
s-slash

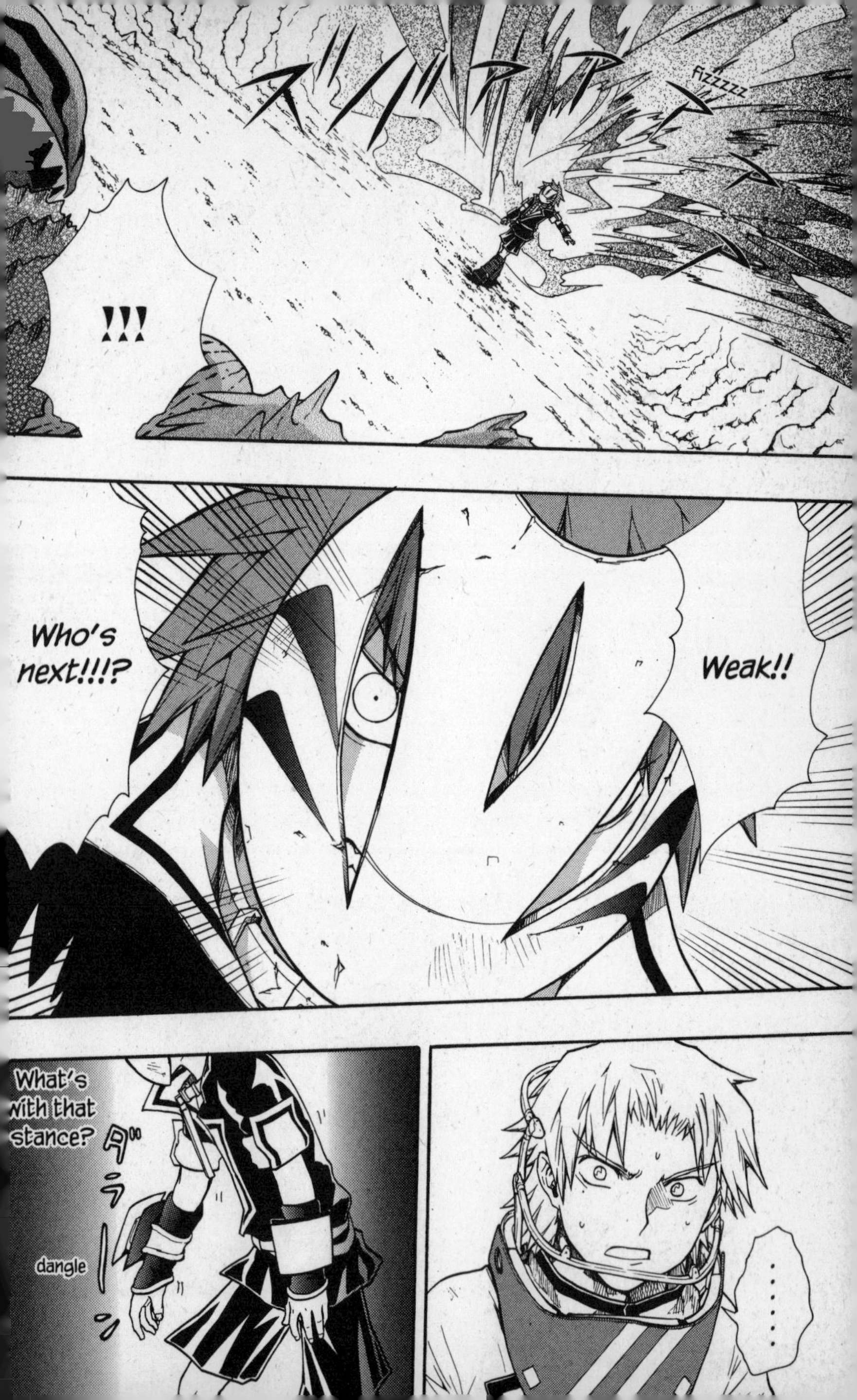
Fizzzzz
!!!
Weak!!
Who's next!!!?
......
What's with that stance?
dangle

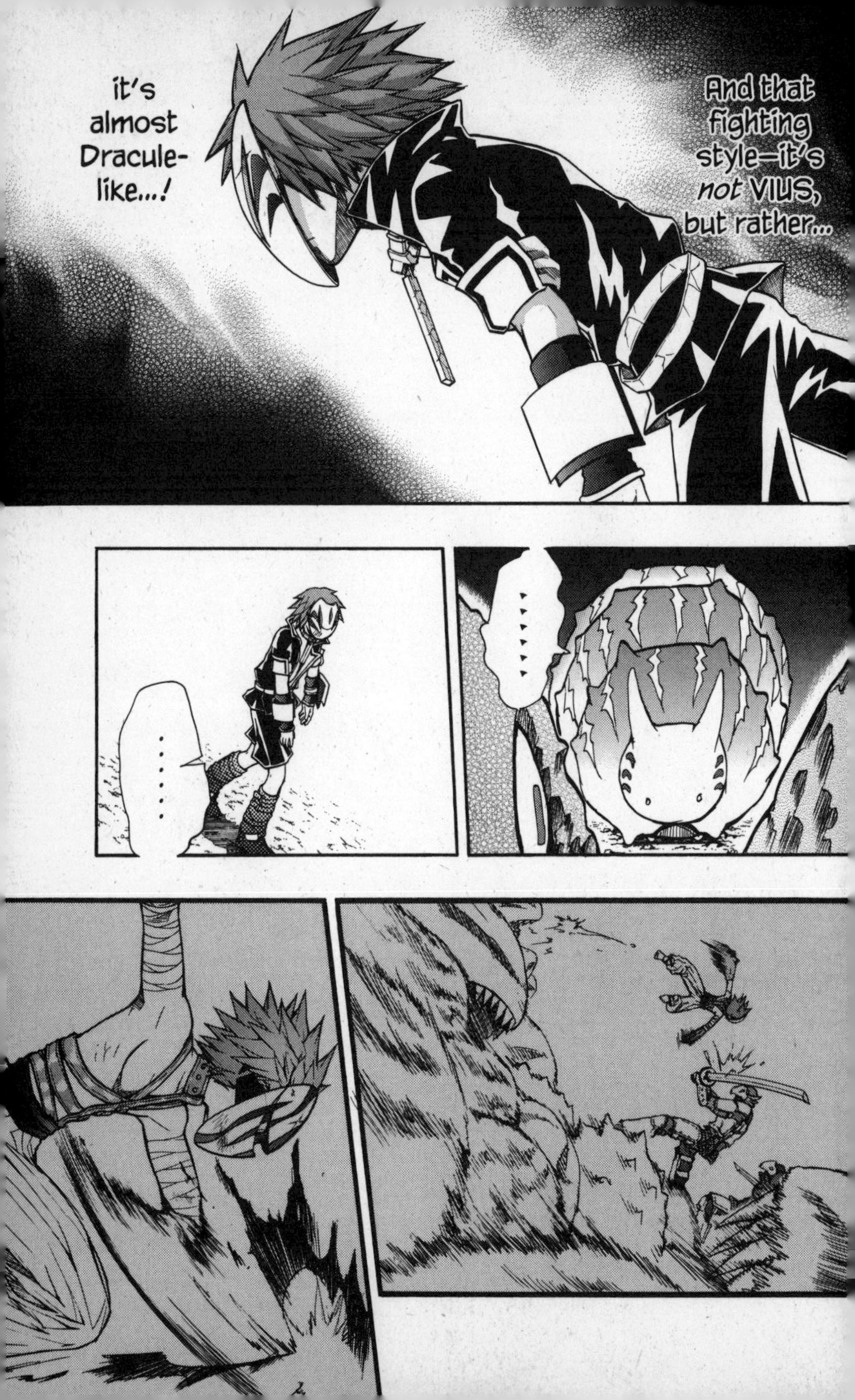
And that fighting style—it's *not* VIUS, but rather...
it's almost Dracule-like...!
......
......

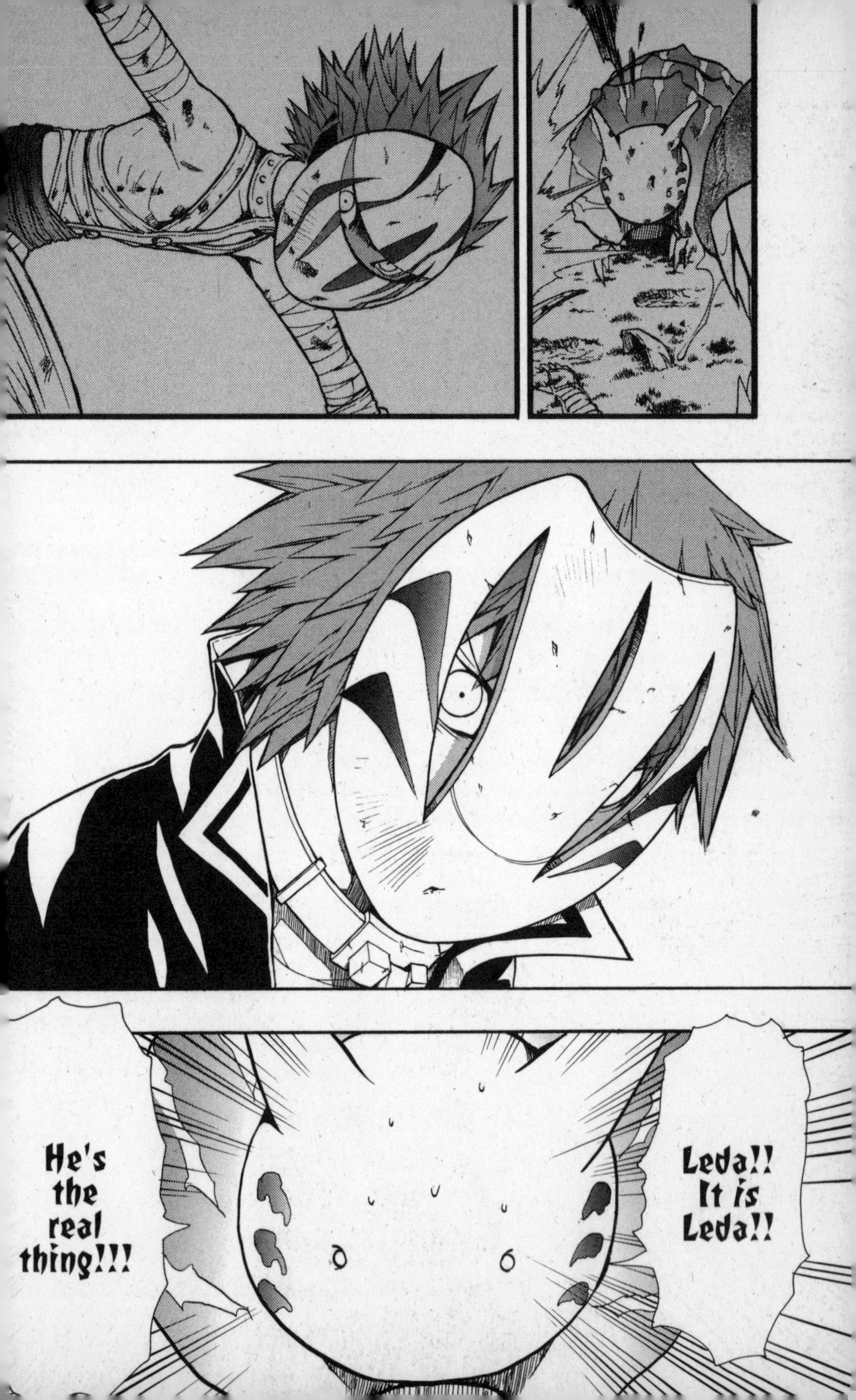
Leda!! It is Leda!!
He's the real thing!!!

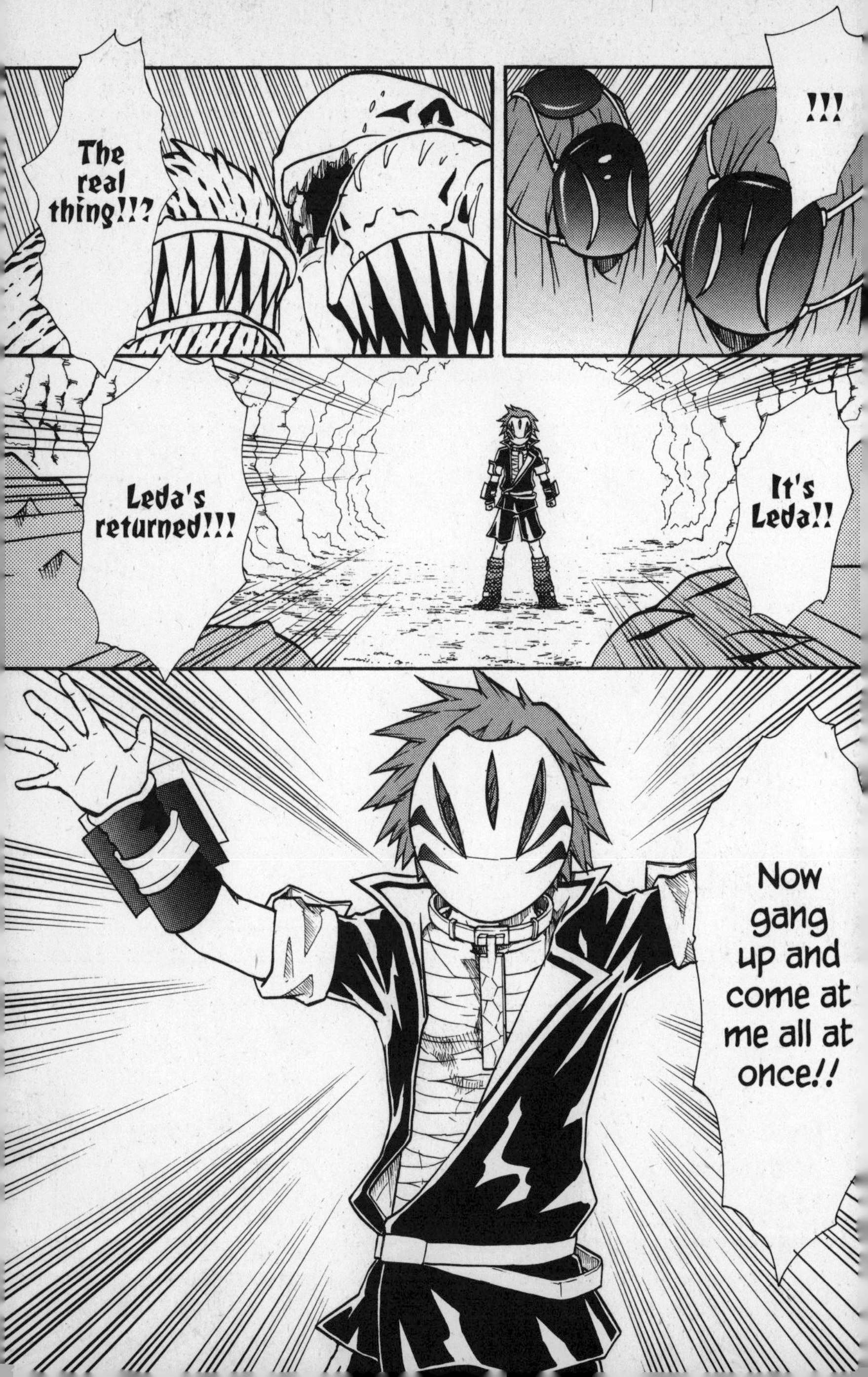
!!!
The real thing!!?
It's Leda!!
Leda's returned!!!
Now gang up and come at me all at once!!

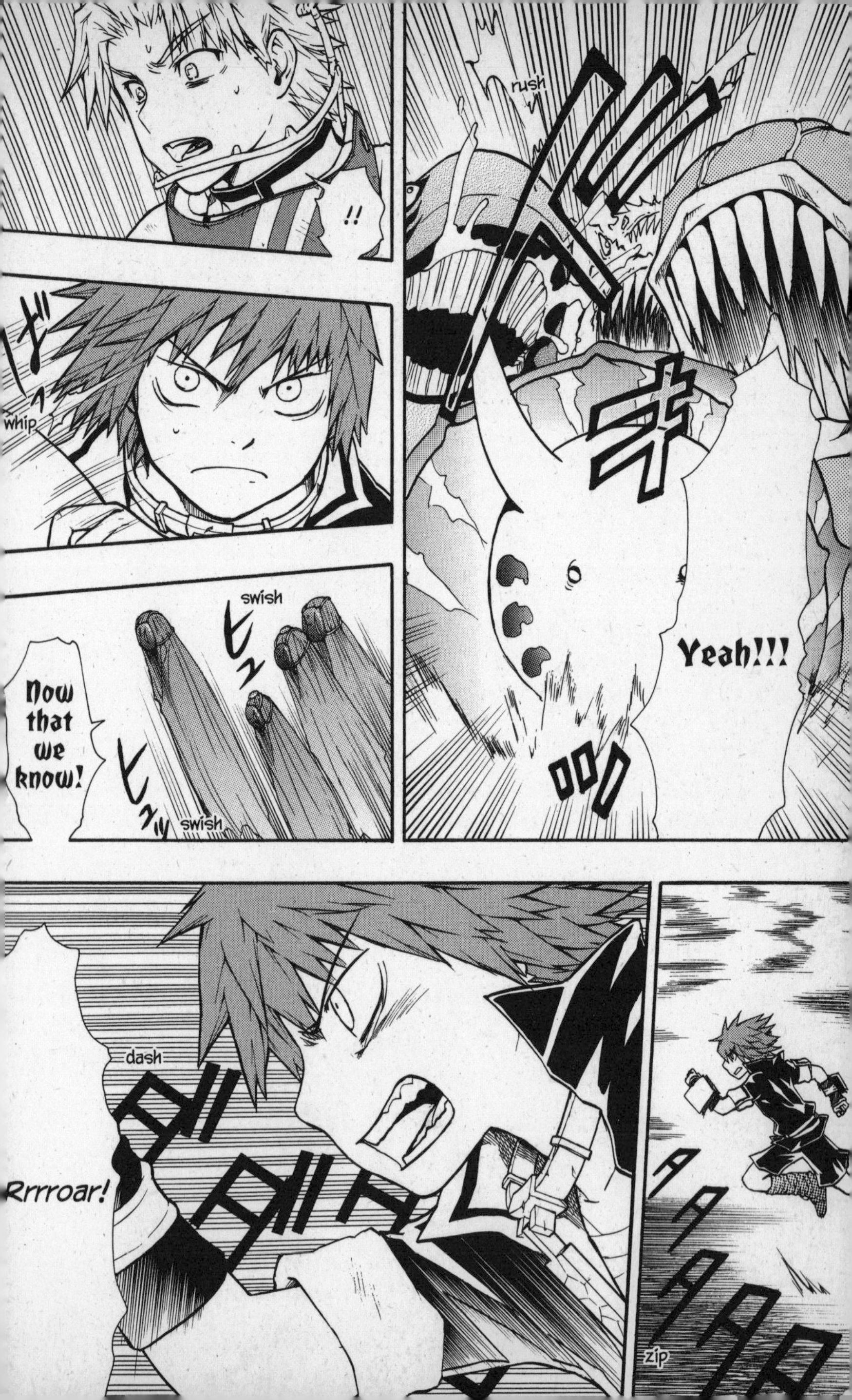
rush
Yeah!!!
!!
whip
swish
Now that we know!
swish
zip
dash
Rrrroar!

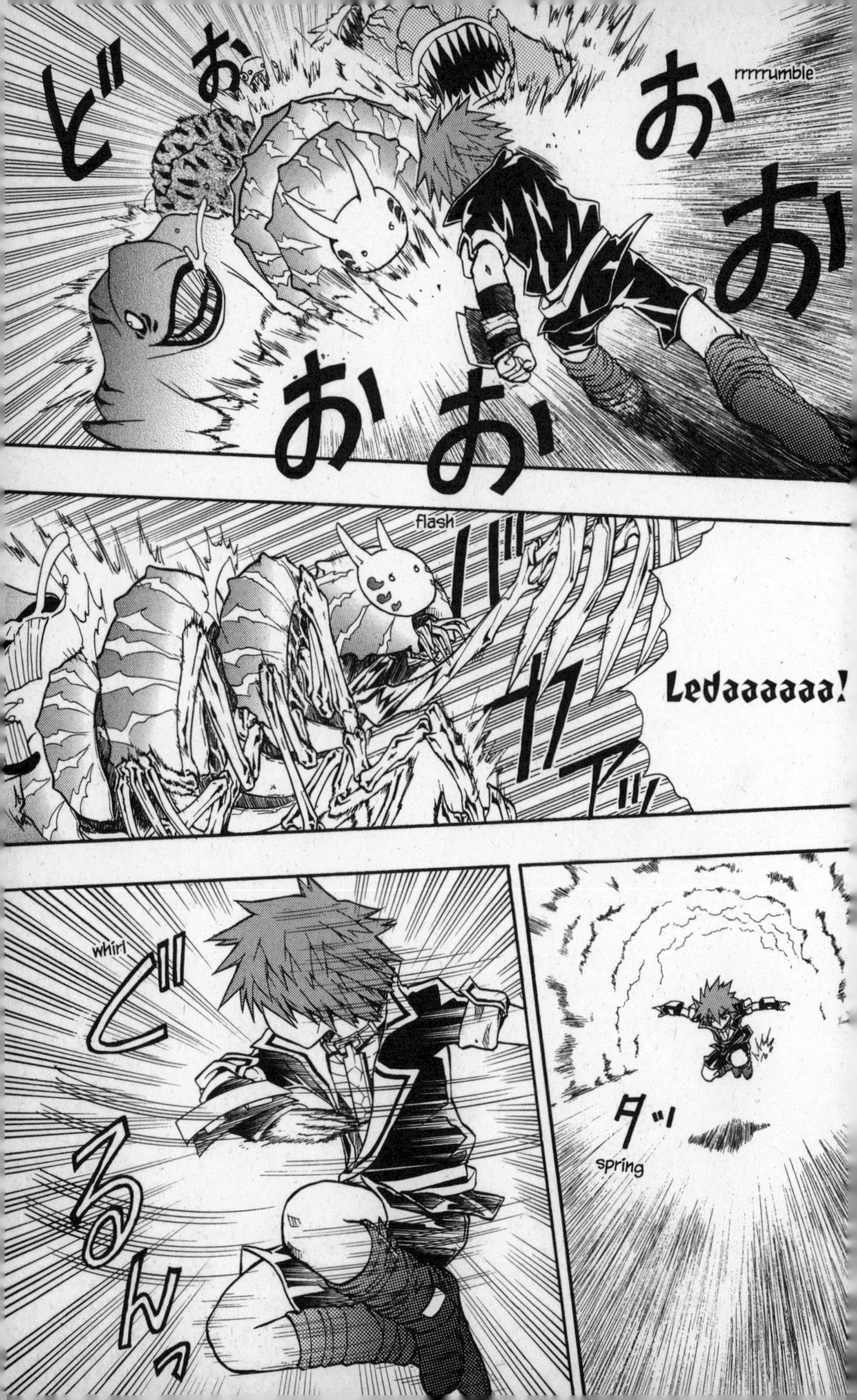
どおおおおお
rrrrrumble
flash
Ledaaaaaaa!
タッ
spring
ぐるんっ
whirl

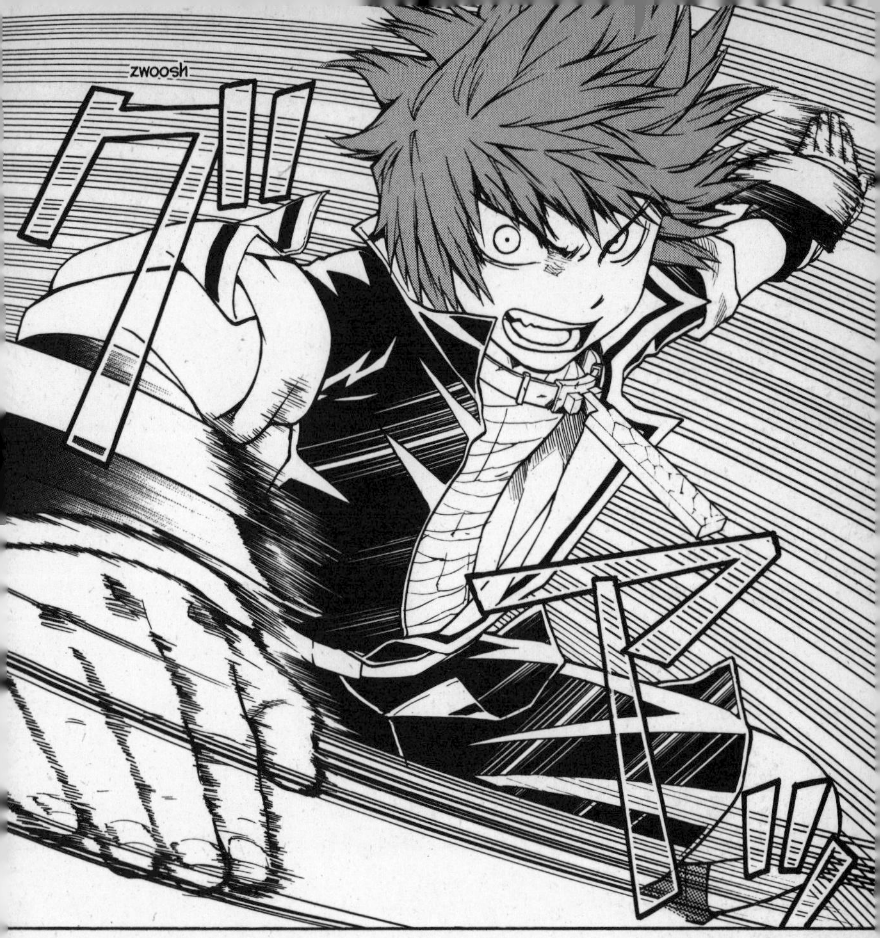
zwoosh
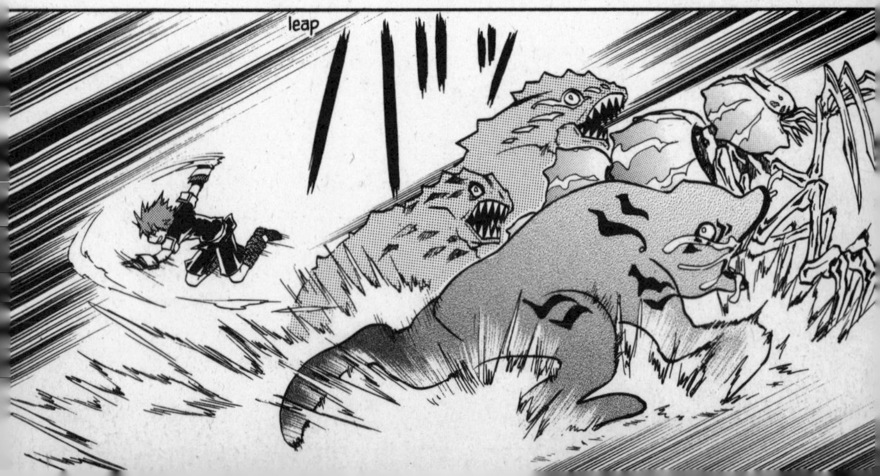
leap

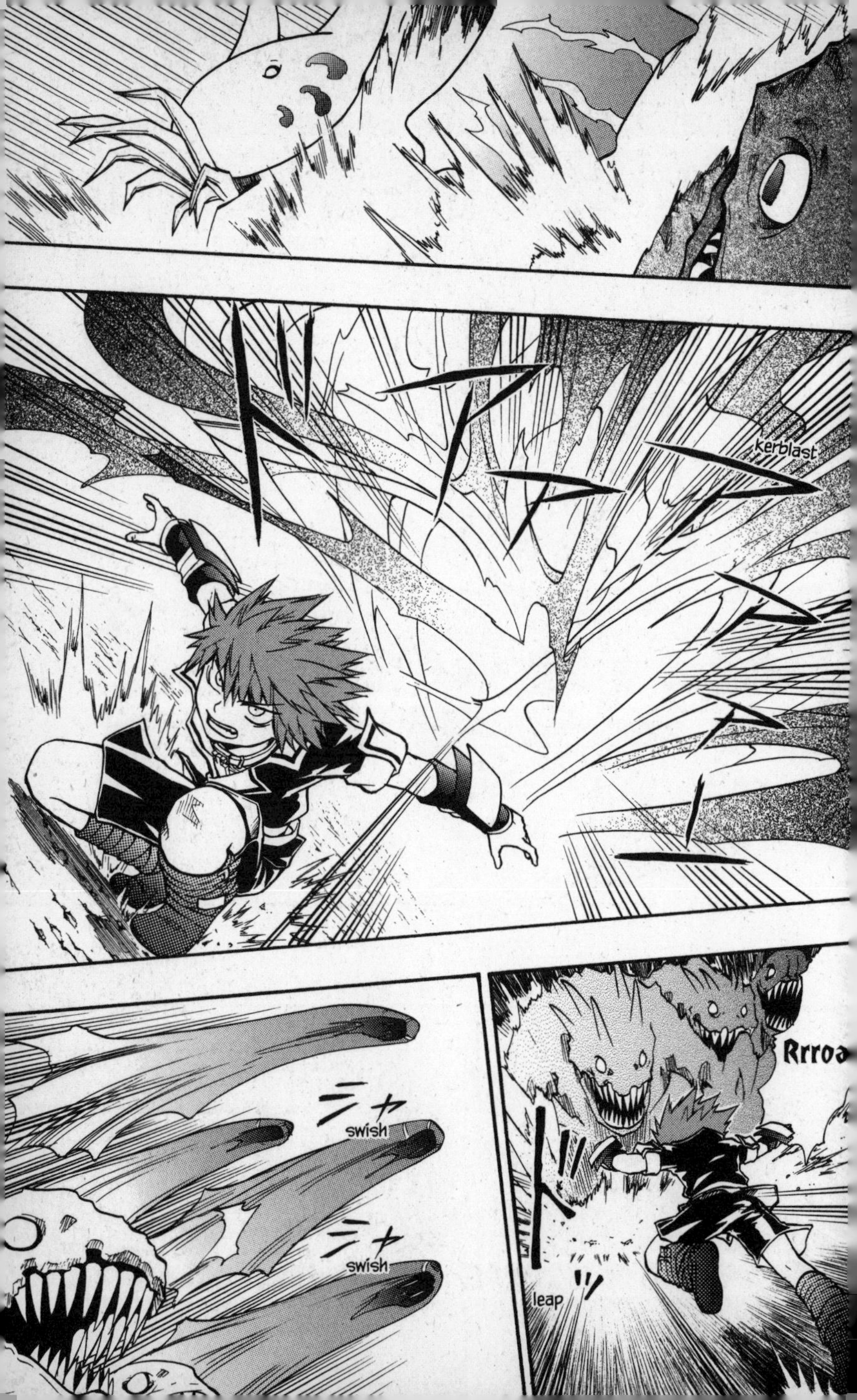
kerblast
Rrroa
leap
シャ
swish
シャ
swish

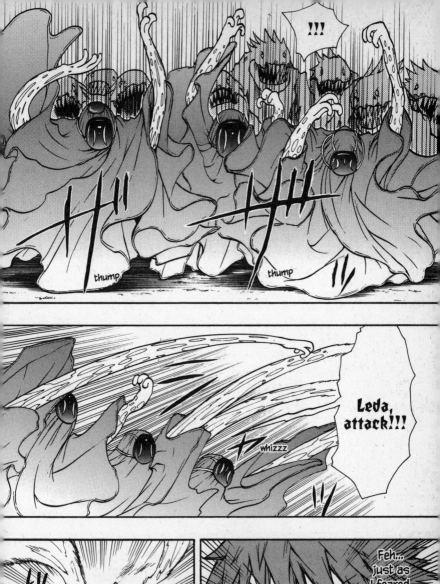

!!!

thump

thump

Leda, attack!!!

whizzz

swoop

Feh... just as I feared, there were some Level 3s mixed in.

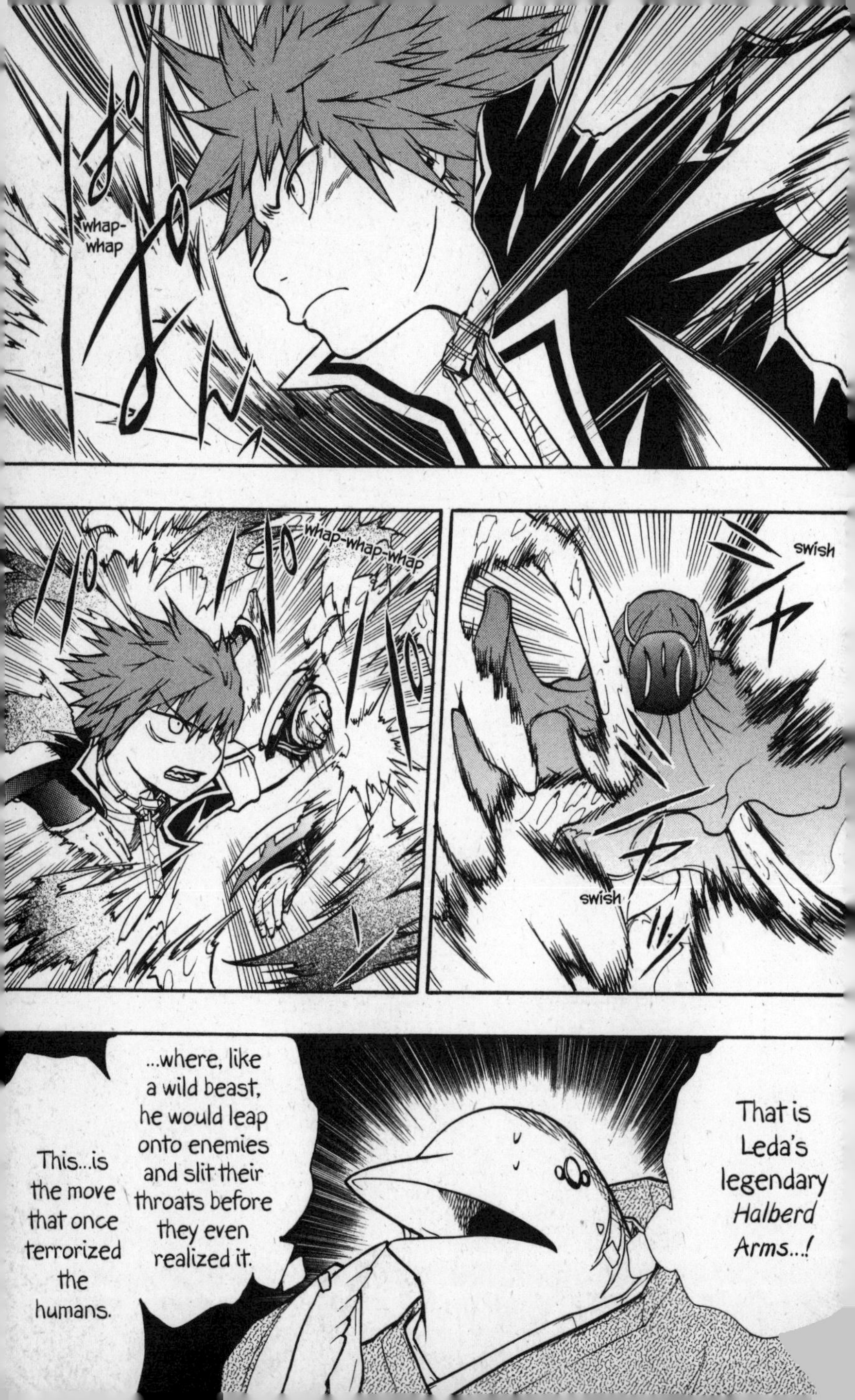
whap-whap
swish
swish
whap-whap-whap
That is Leda's legendary *Halberd Arms*...!
...where, like a wild beast, he would leap onto enemies and slit their throats before they even realized it.
This...is the move that once terrorized the humans.

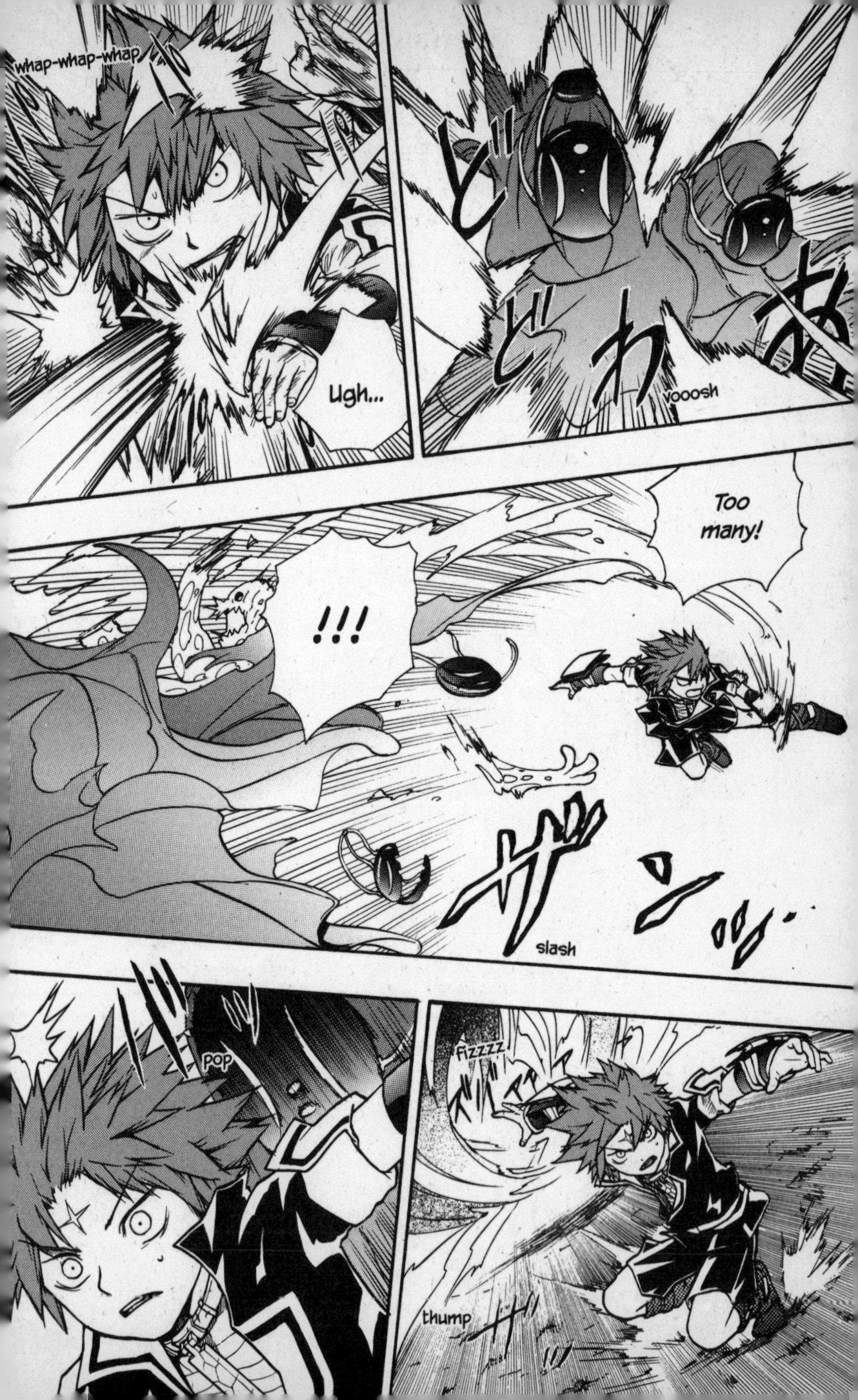
vooosh
whap-whap-whap
Ugh...
Too many!
!!!
slash
Fizzzz
thump
pop

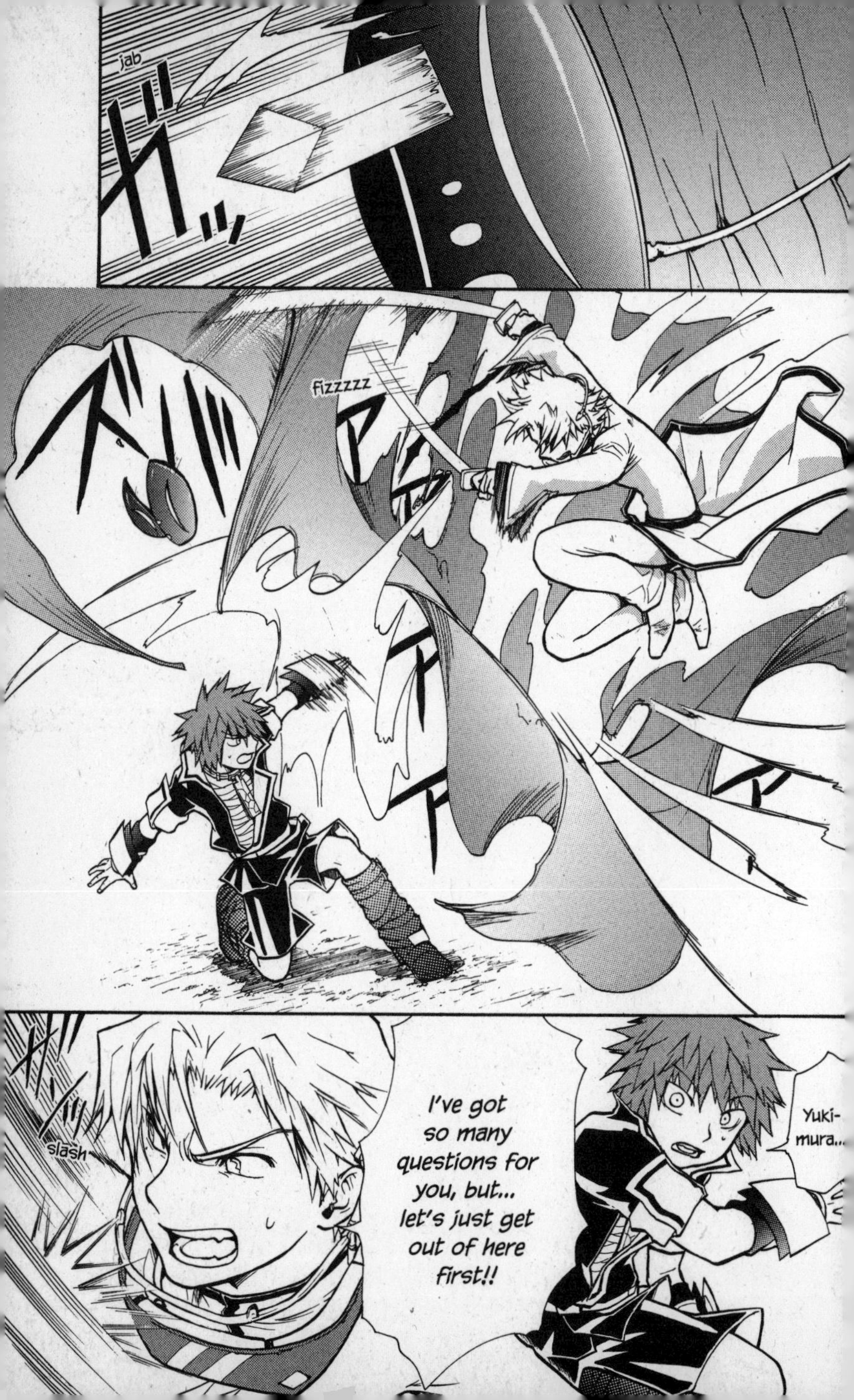

jab
fizzzzz
Yuki-mura...
I've got so many questions for you, but... let's just get out of here first!!
slash

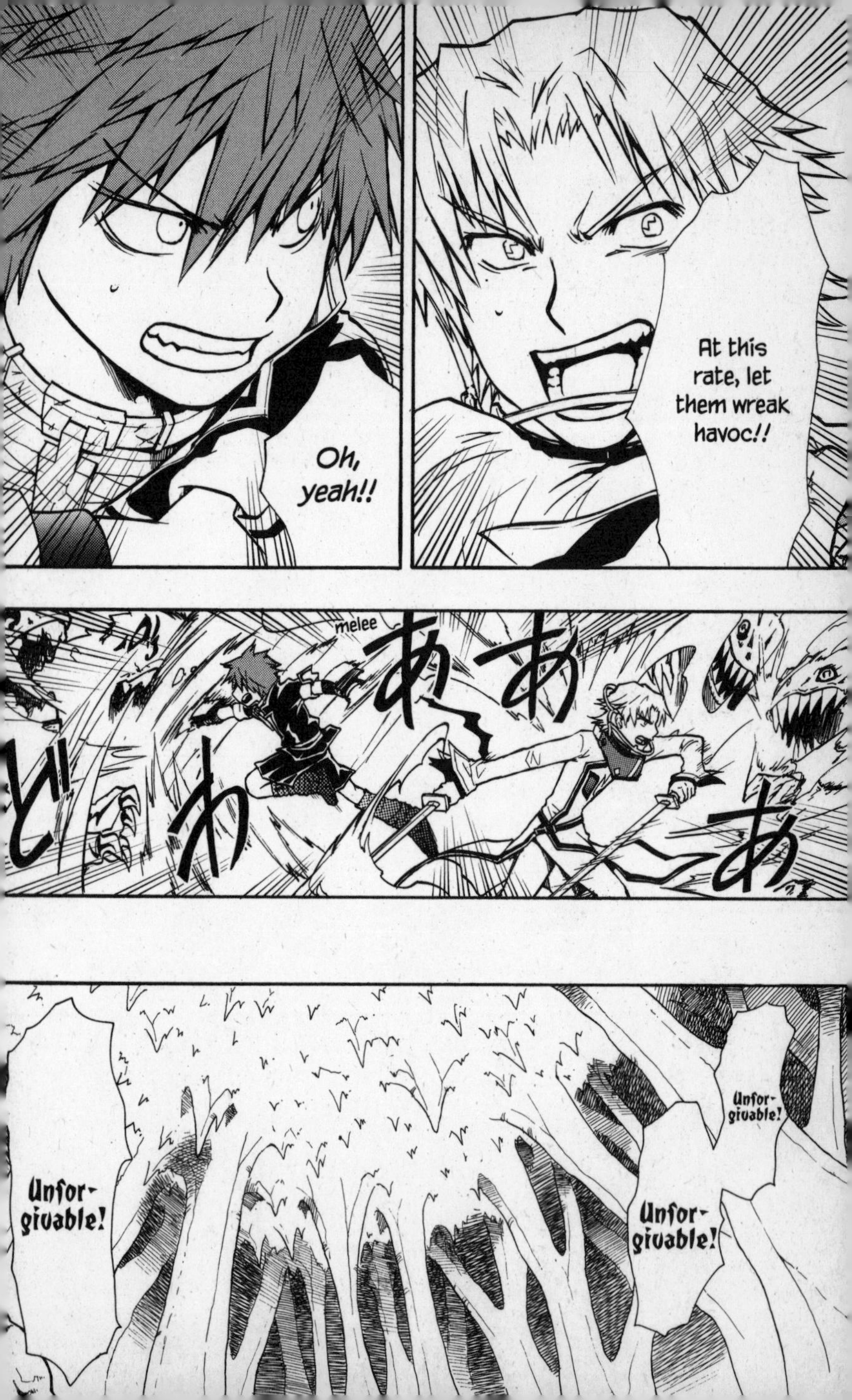
At this rate, let them wreak havoc!!
Oh, yeah!!
melee
どわああああ
Unfor-givable!
Unfor-givable!
Unfor-givable!

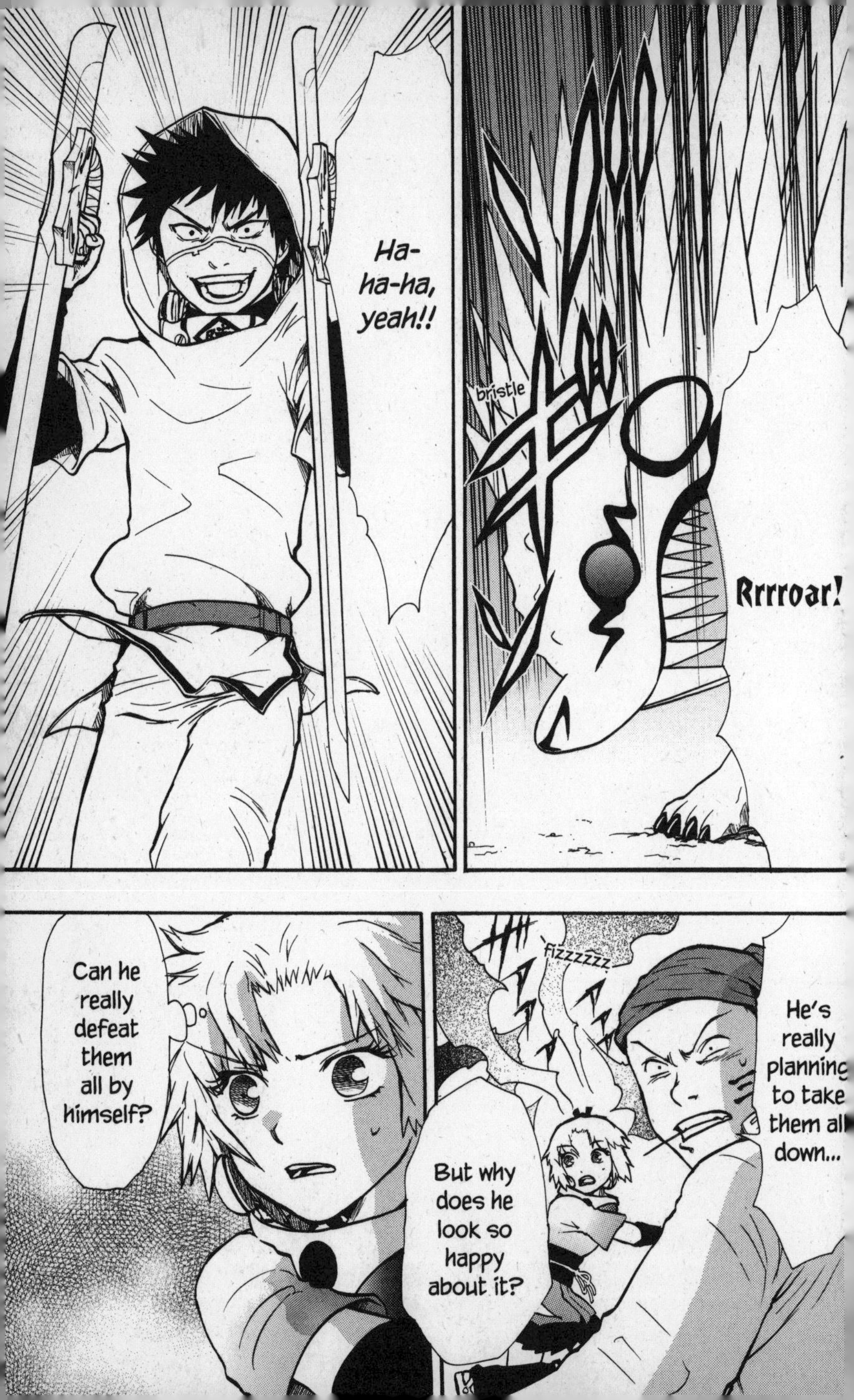
bristle
Rrrroar!
Ha-ha-ha, yeah!!
fizzzzzz
He's really planning to take them all down...
But why does he look so happy about it?
Can he really defeat them all by himself?

launch

Kill!!!!

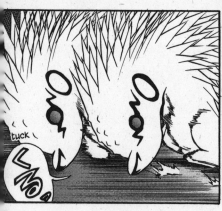
tuck

Come!

zwirl

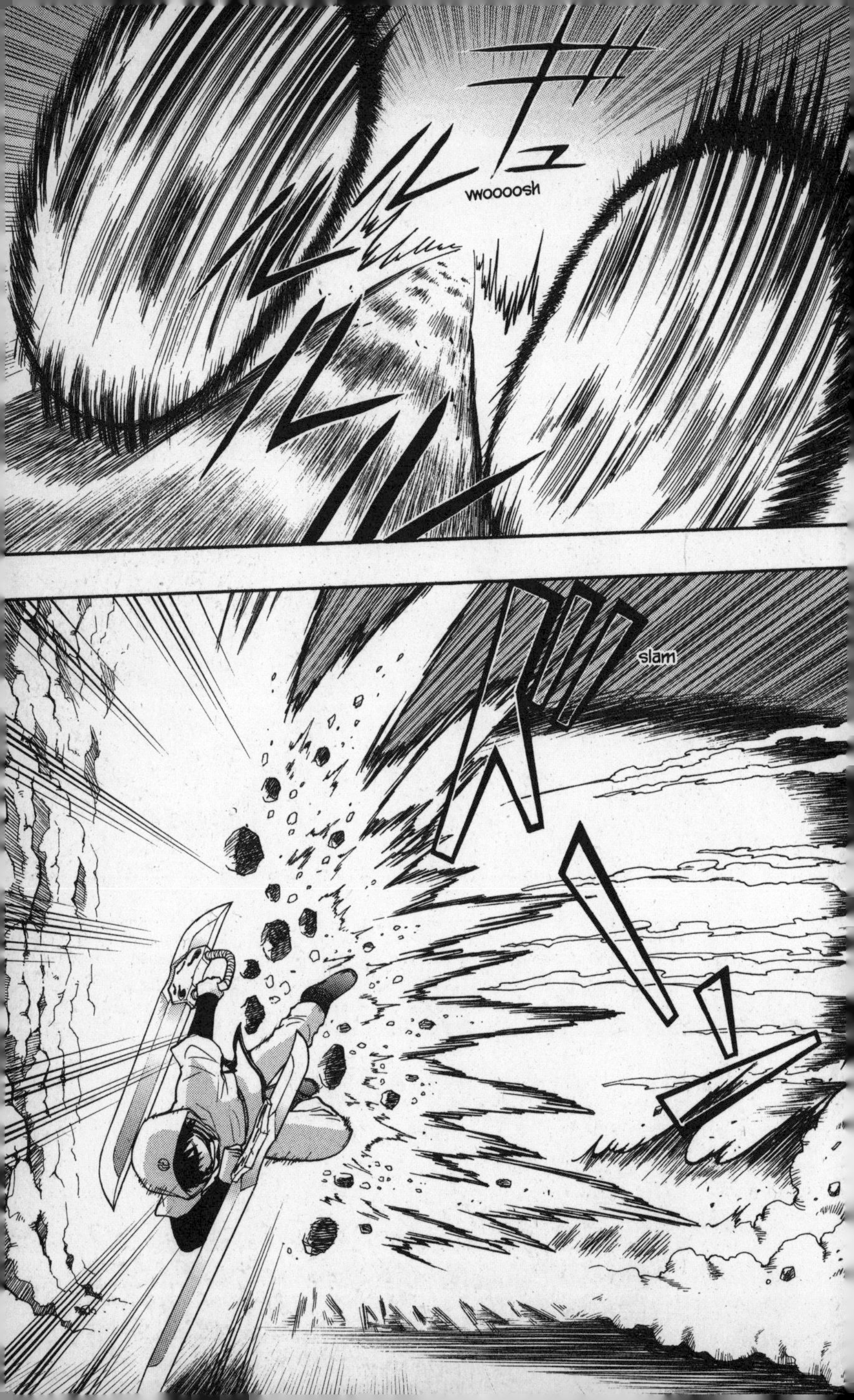
vwoooosh
slam

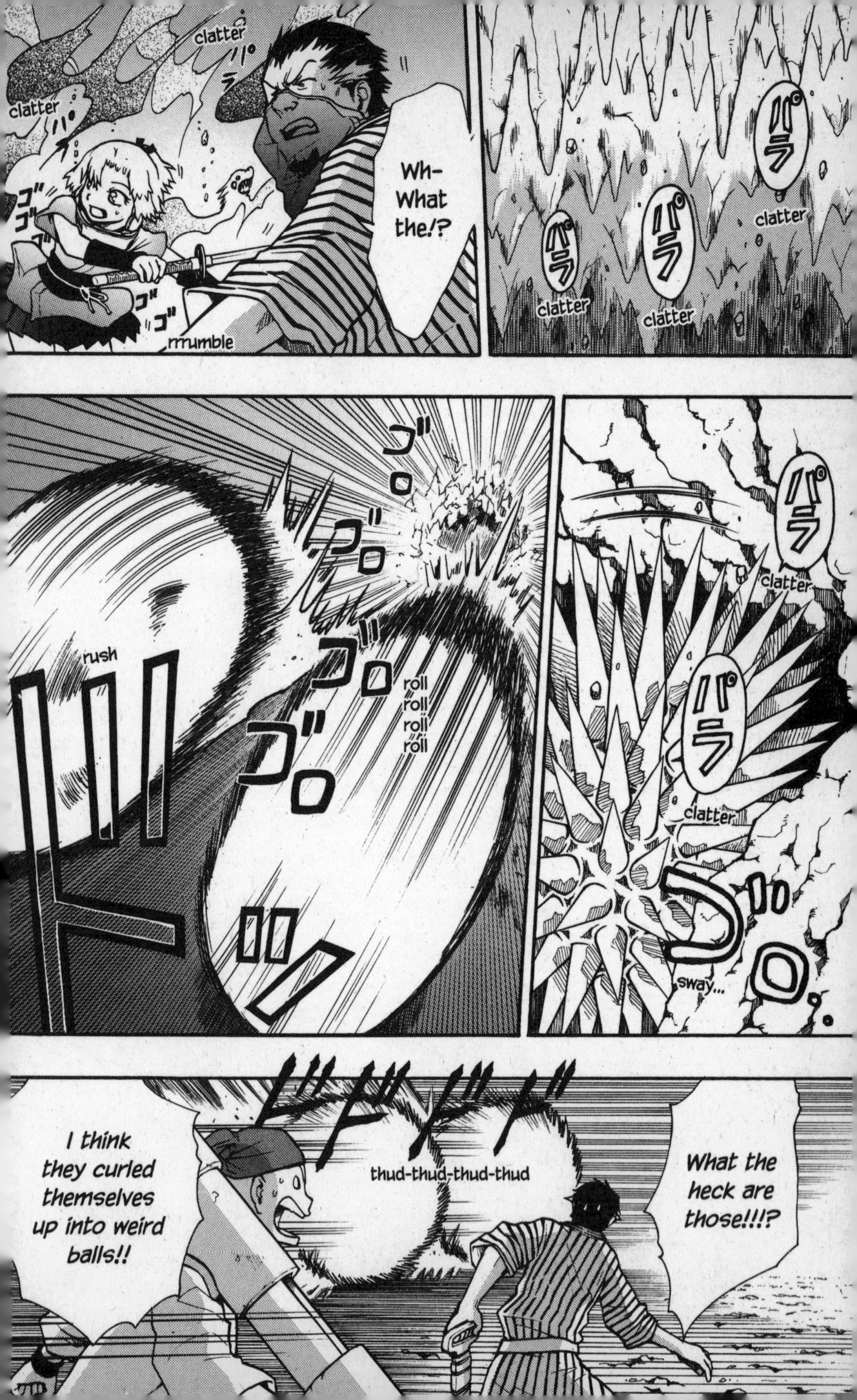
パラ
clatter
パラ
パラ
clatter
clatter
clatter
パラ
Wh- What the!?
clatter
パラ
ゴゴゴ
ゴゴ
rrrumble
パラ
clatter
パラ
clatter
sway...
ゴロ
ゴロ
ゴロ
ゴロ
roll
roll
roll
roll
rush
What the heck are those!!!?
ドドドド
thud-thud-thud-thud
I think they curled themselves up into weird balls!!

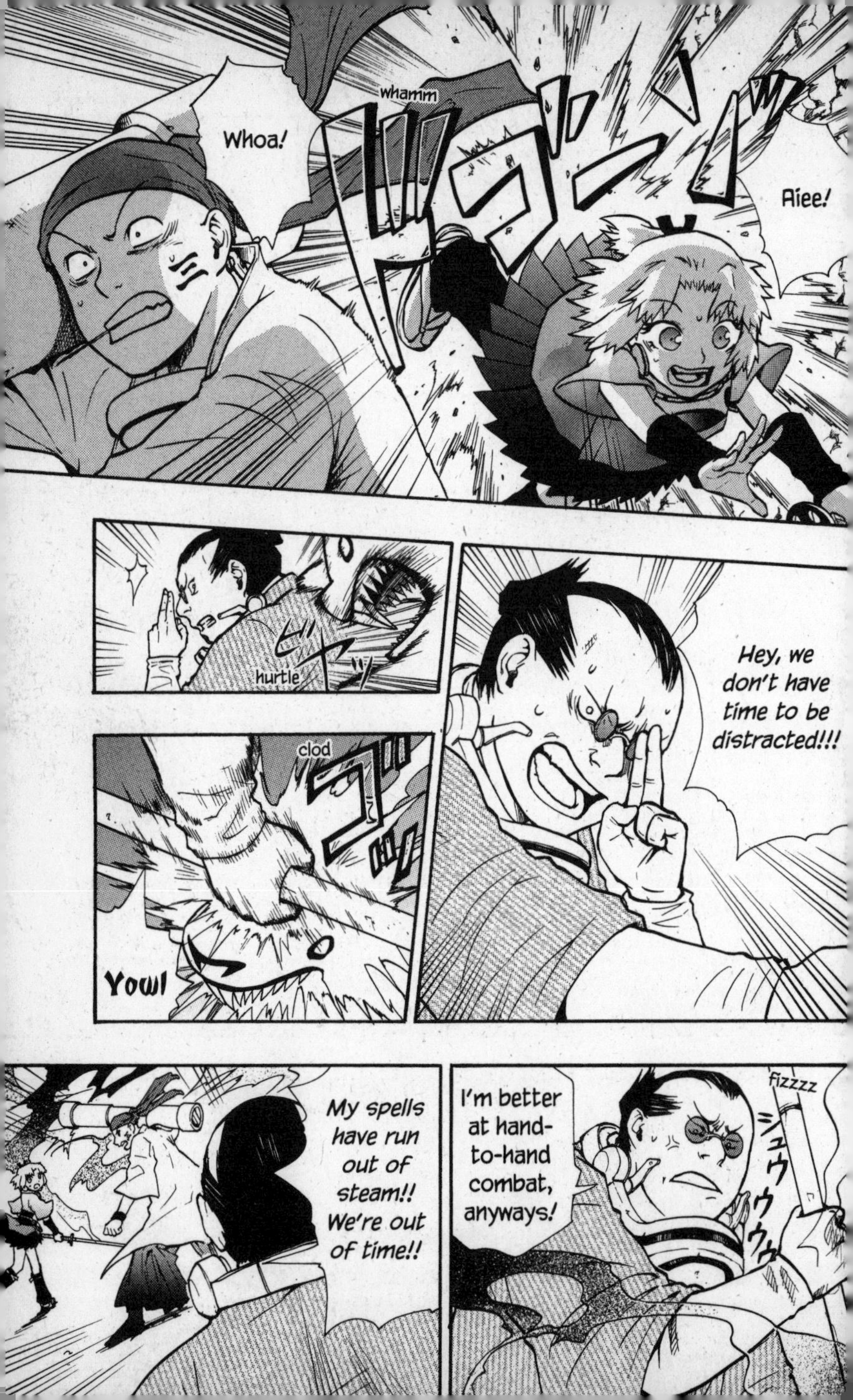
whamm
Aiee!
Whoa!
Hey, we don't have time to be distracted!!!
hurtle
clod
Yow!
fizzzz
I'm better at hand-to-hand combat, anyways!
My spells have run out of steam!! We're out of time!!

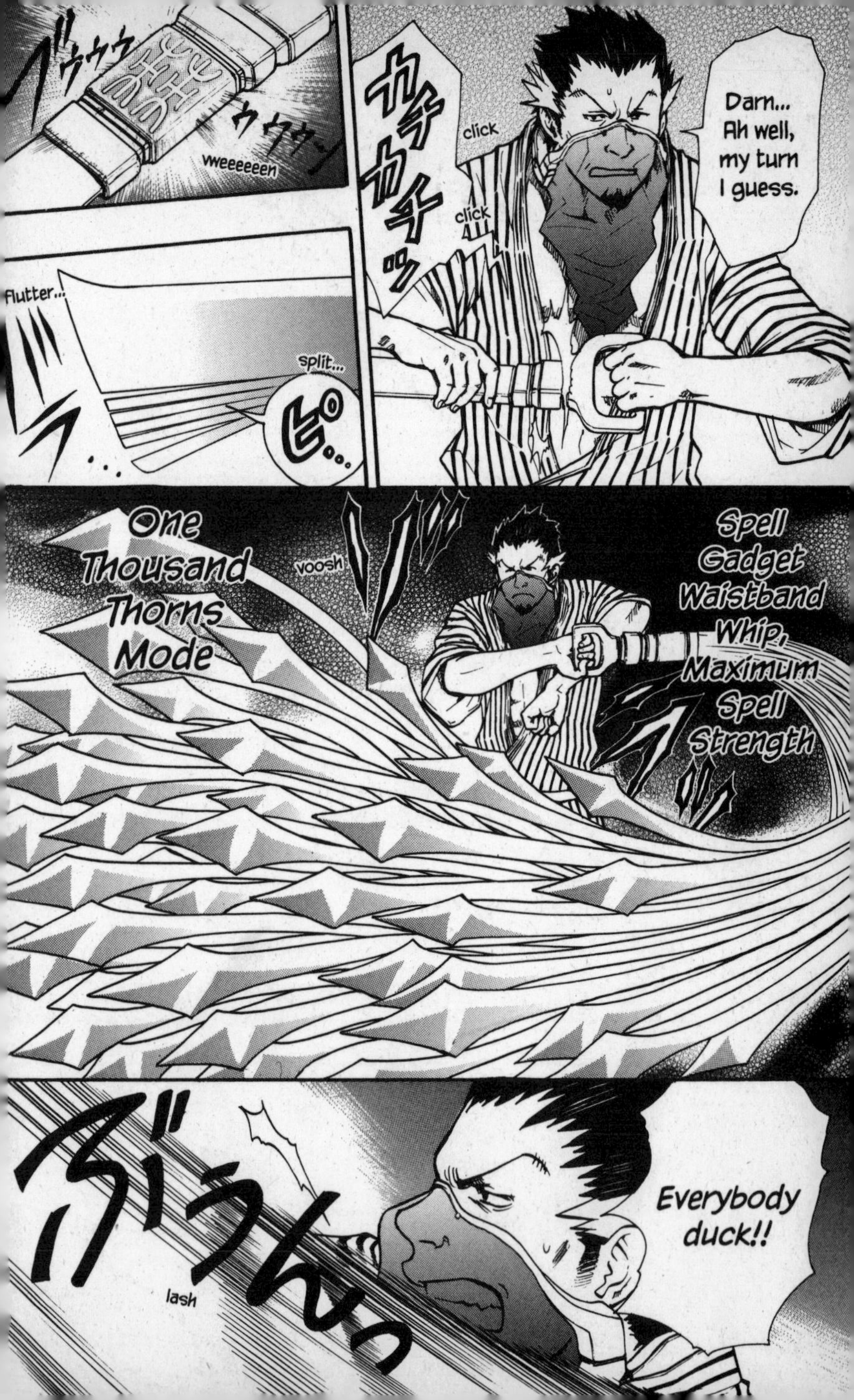

Darn... Ah well, my turn I guess.
click
click
vweeeeeen
flutter...
split...
Spell Gadget Waistband Whip, Maximum Spell Strength
voosh
One Thousand Thorns Mode
Everybody duck!!
lash

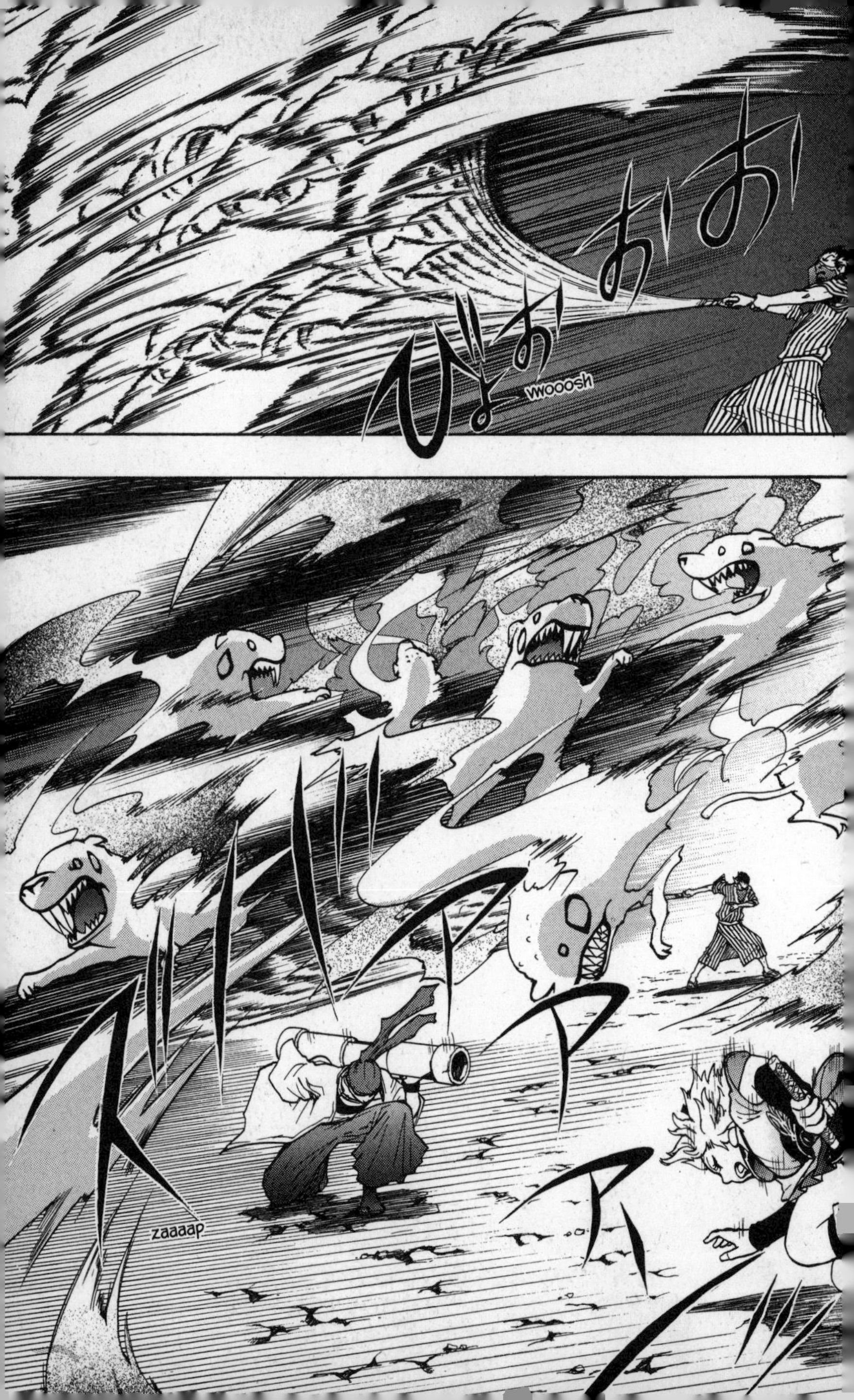
びょおおお
vwooosh
zaaaap

Fizzzz

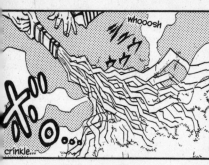

whooosh

afoo

crinkle...

sizzle

That took care of a bunch of them!!

Me too...!

swing

Darn...I raised the spell strength too high, so it's kaput.

crouch

Oh well!

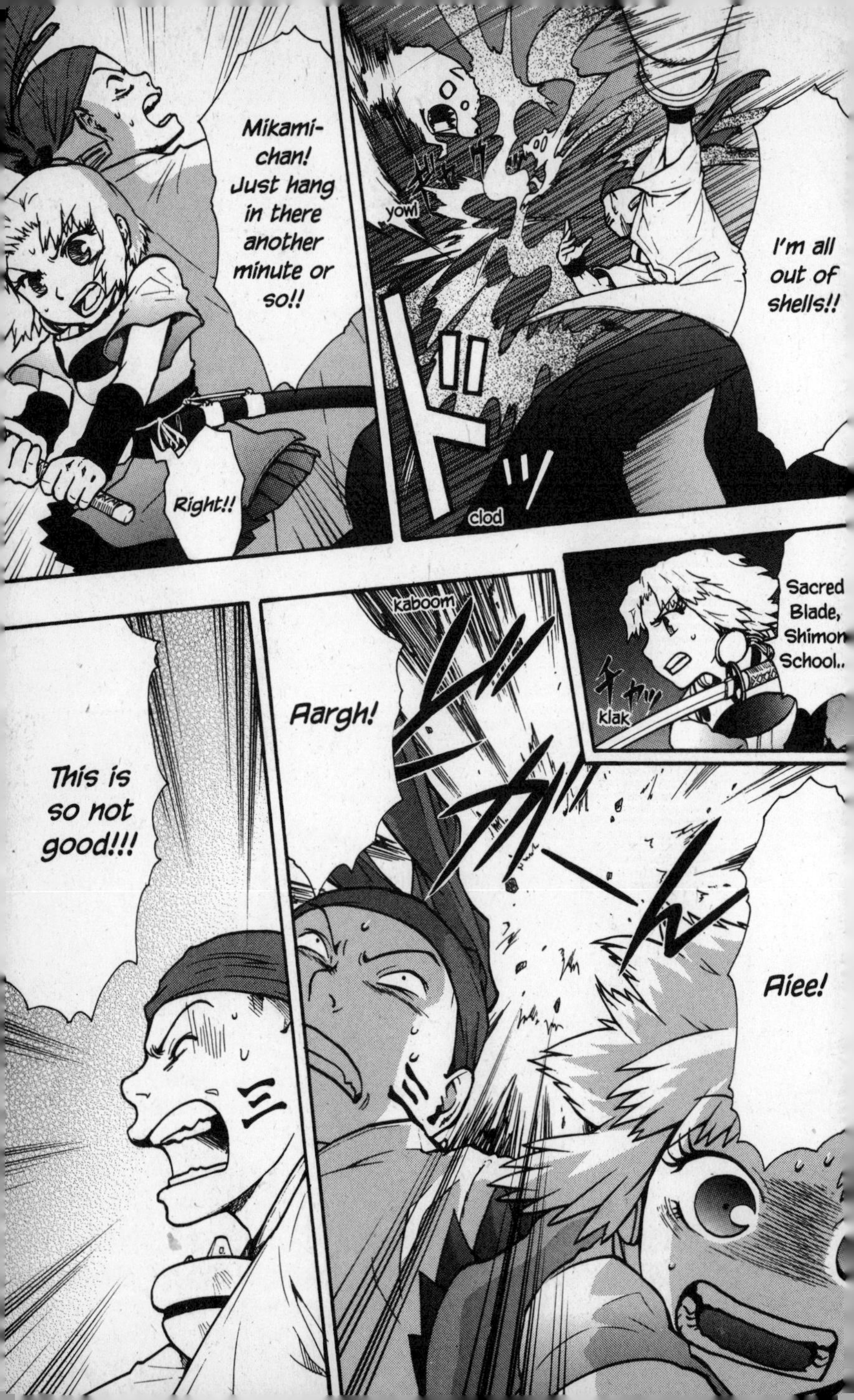
I'm all out of shells!!
yowl
clod
Mikami-chan! Just hang in there another minute or so!!
Right!!
Sacred Blade, Shimon School..
klak
kaboom
Aargh!
Aiee!
This is so not good!!!

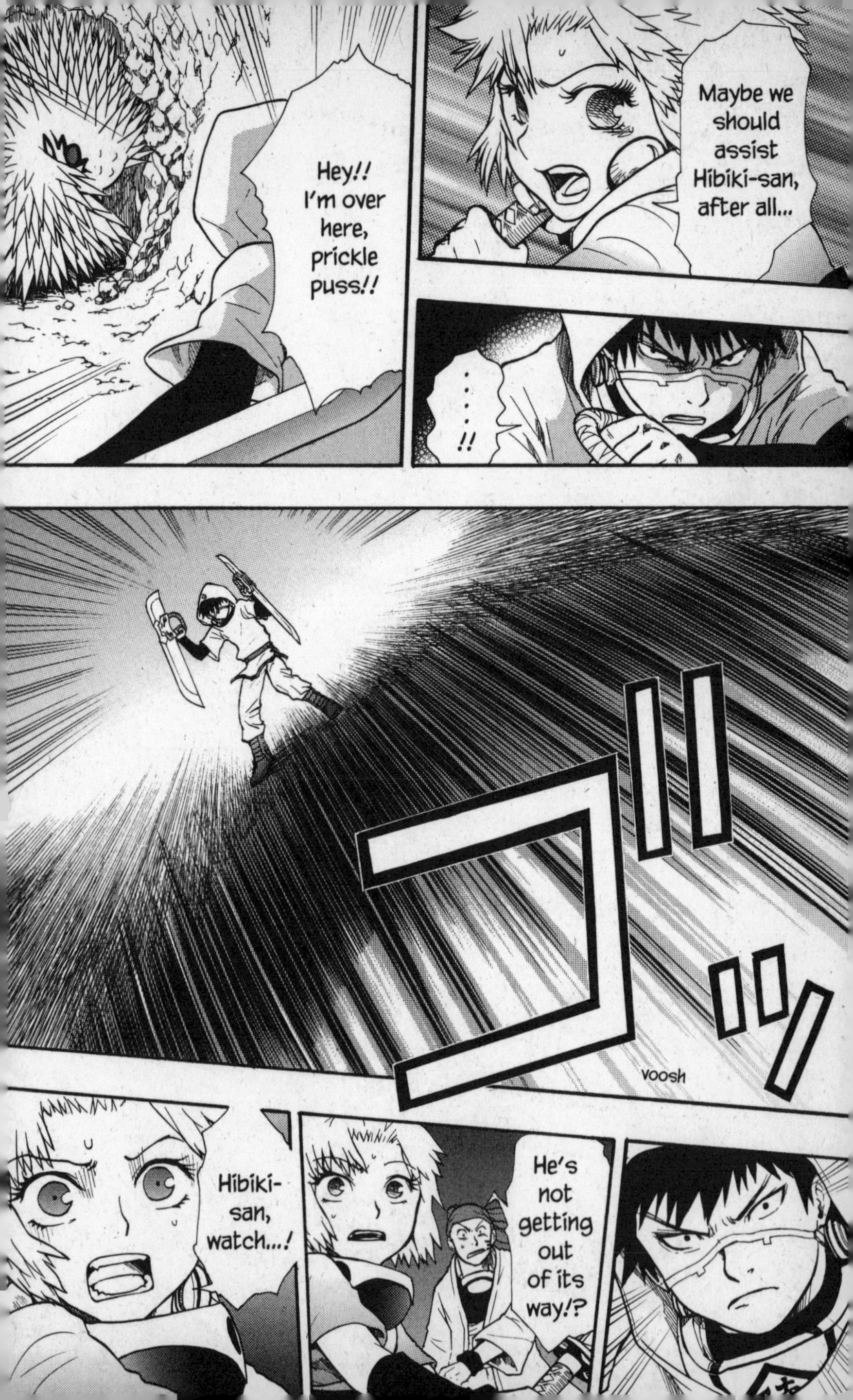

Maybe we should assist Hibiki-san, after all...
......!!
Hey!! I'm over here, prickle puss!!
ゴッ
voosh
He's not getting out of its way!?
Hibiki-san, watch...!

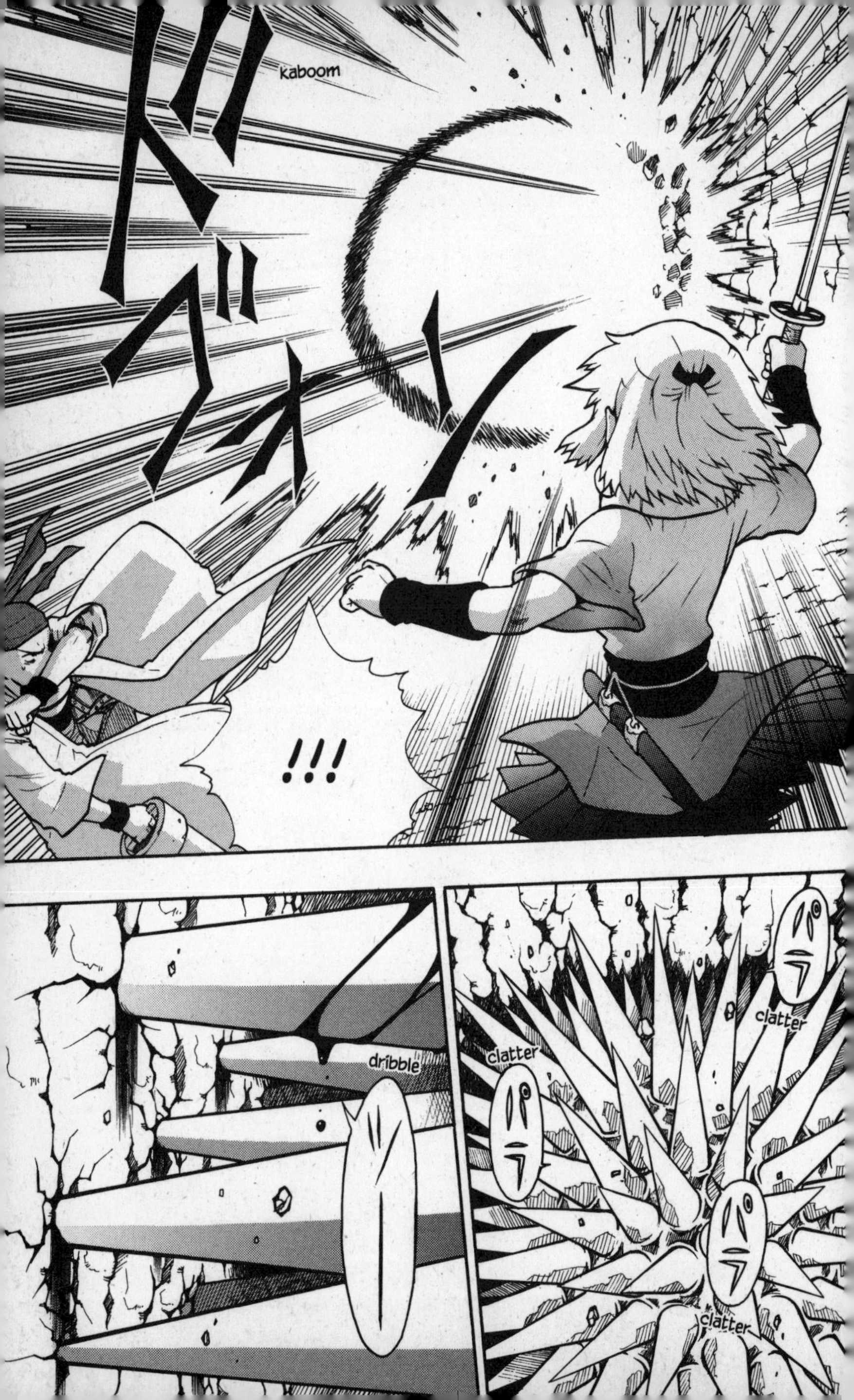
ドゴォーン
kaboom
!!!
clatter
clatter
clatter
dribble

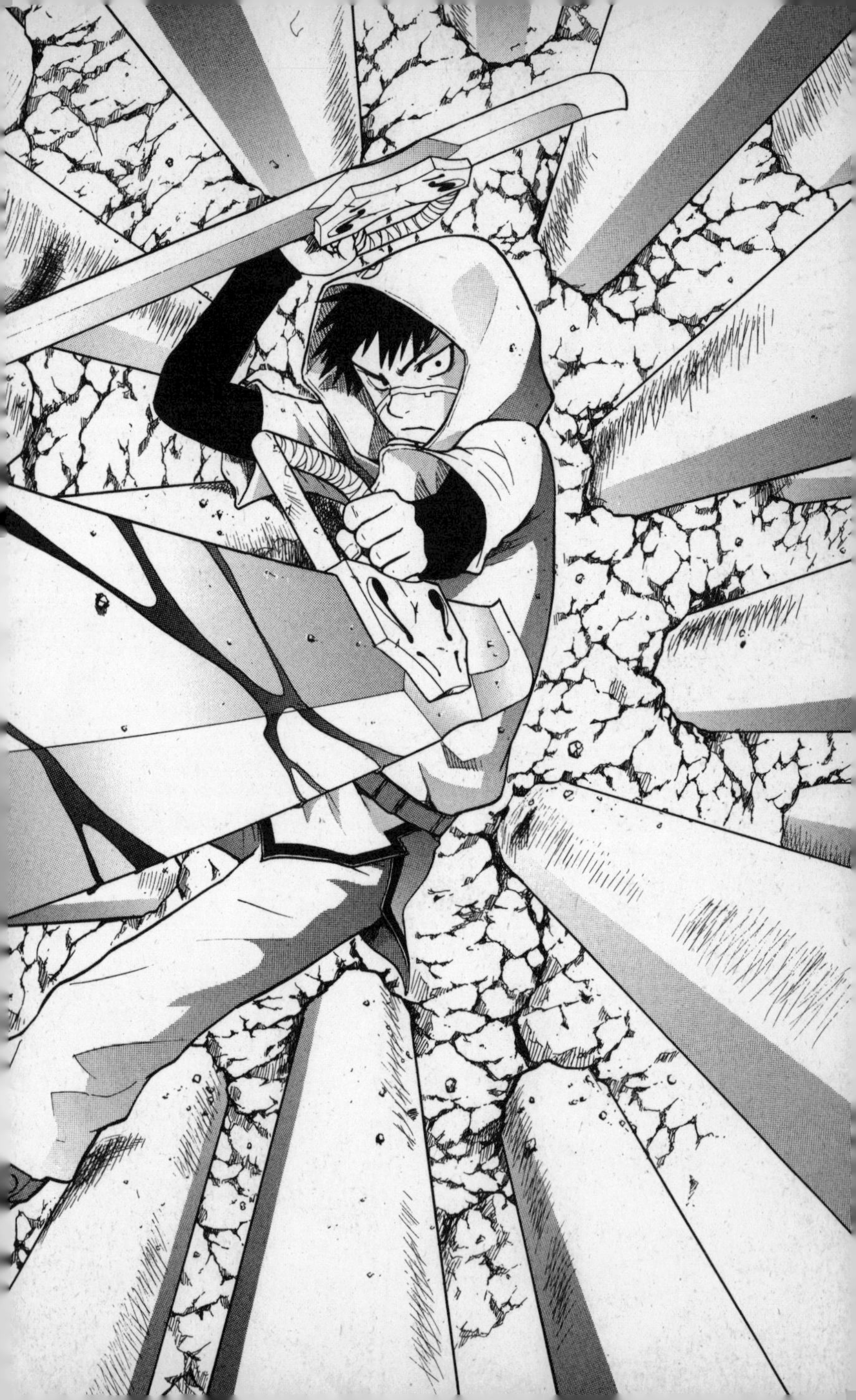

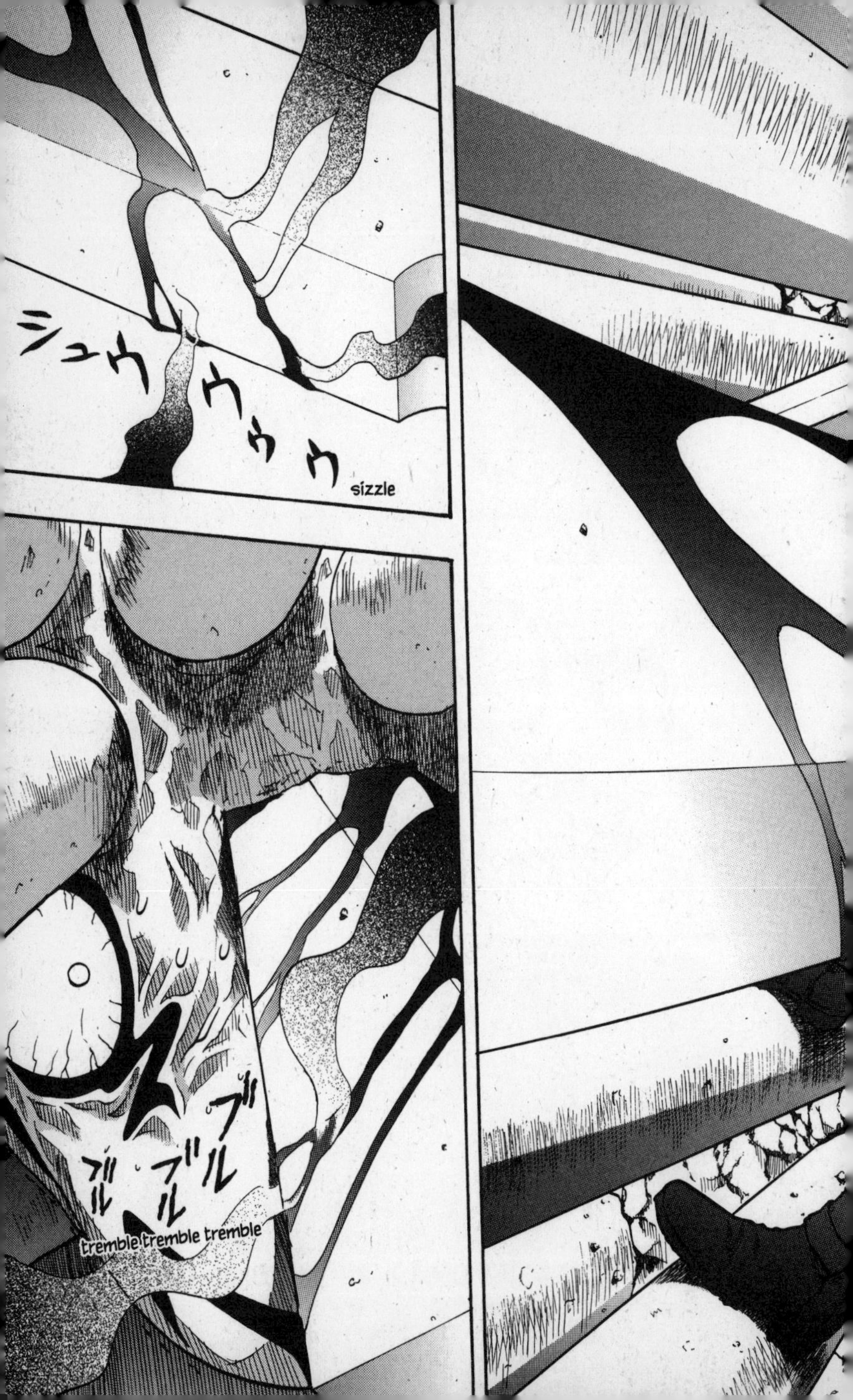
シュウウウウ
sizzle
ブルブルブル
tremble tremble tremble

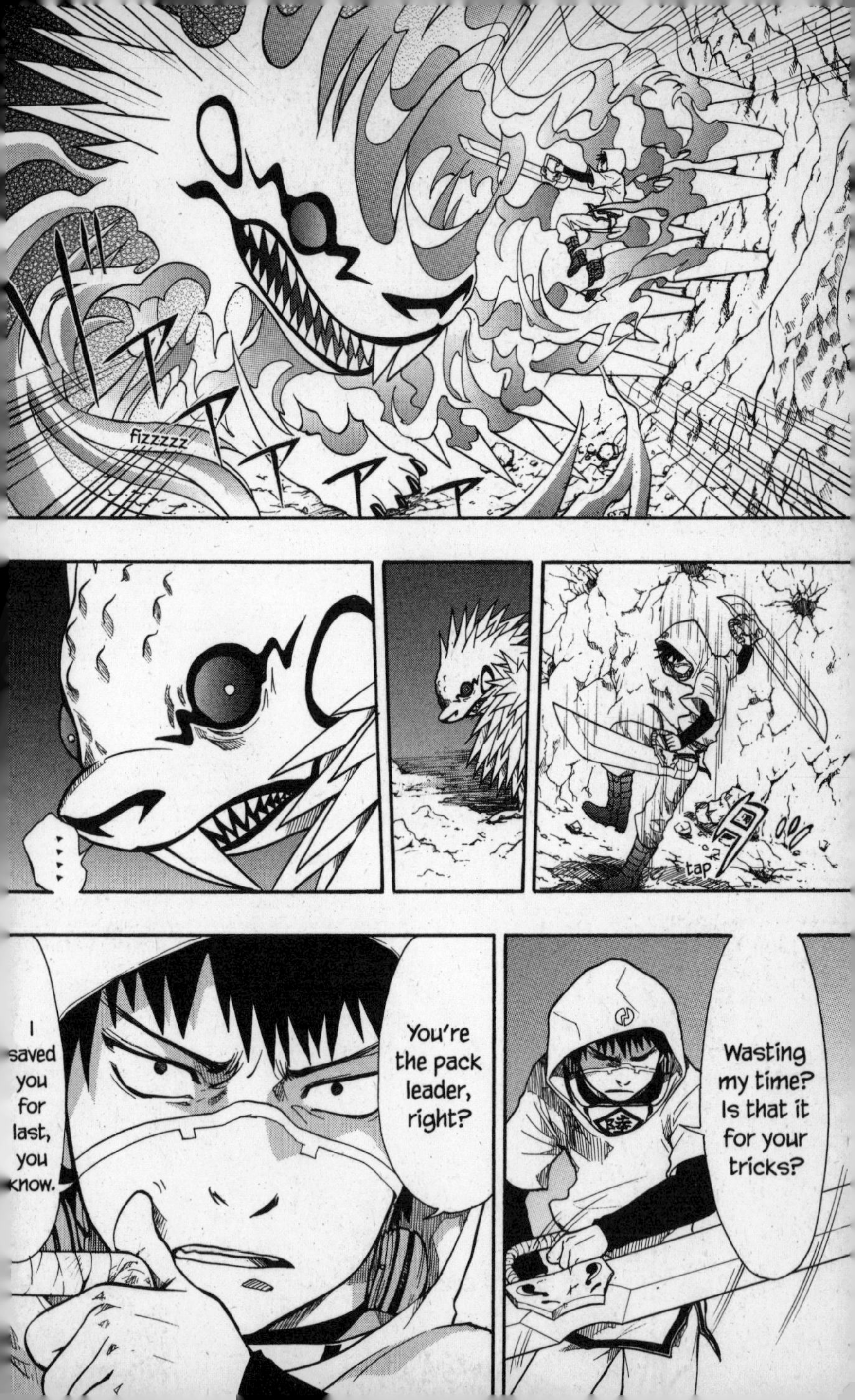
fizzzzz
tap
Wasting my time? Is that it for your tricks?
You're the pack leader, right?
I saved you for last, you know.

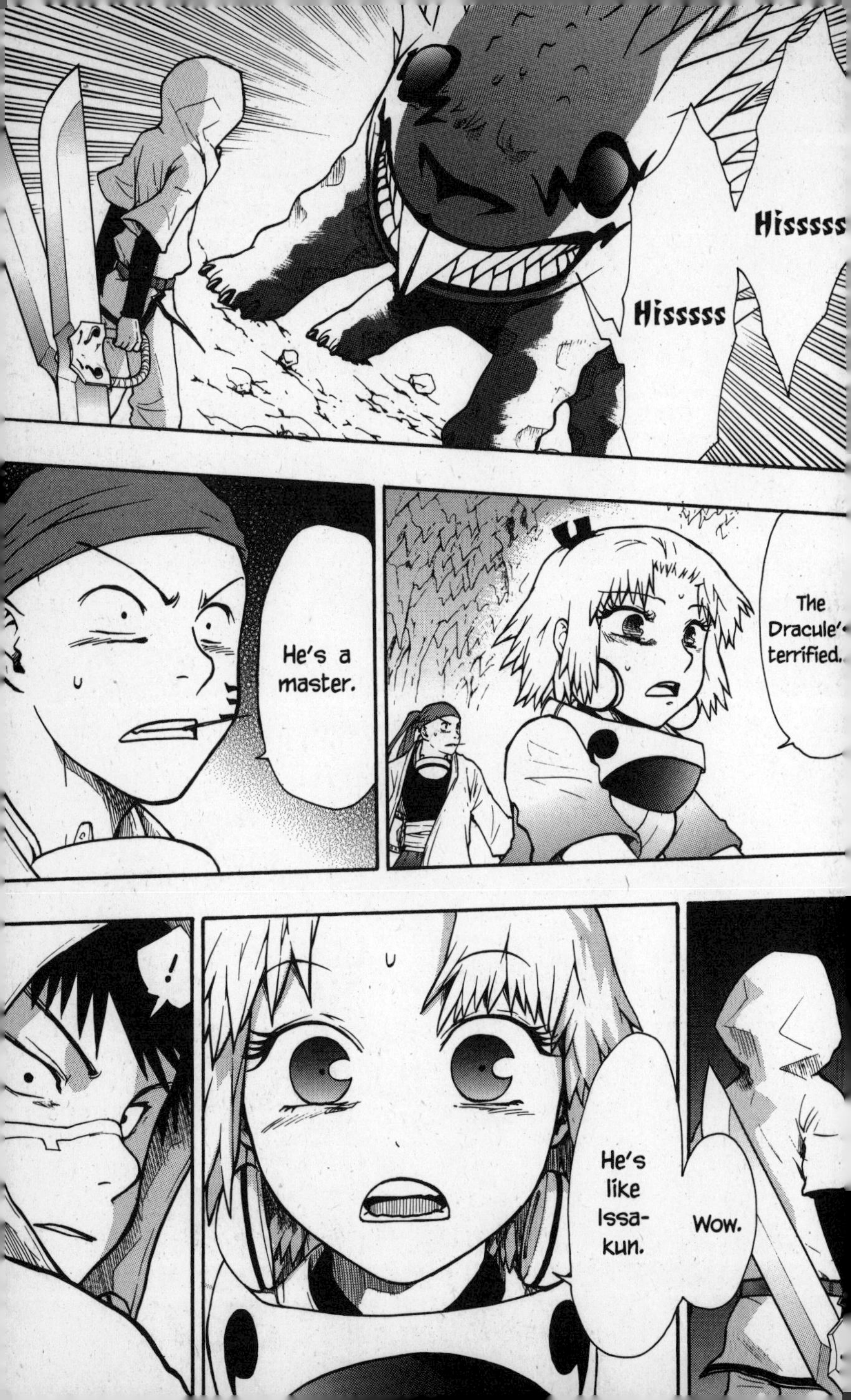

Hisssss
Hisssss
The Dracule' terrified.
He's a master.
Wow.
He's like Issa-kun.
!

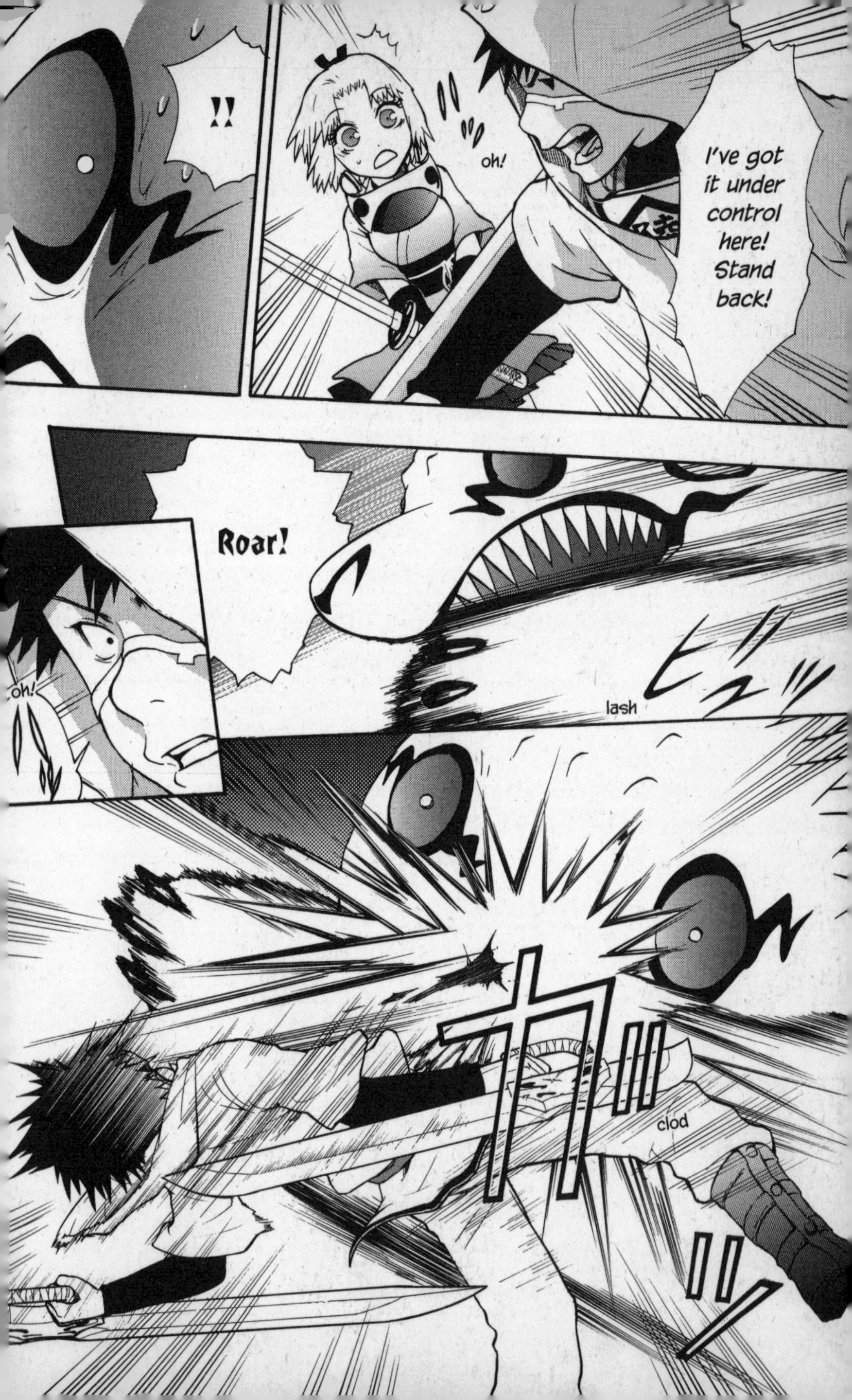
I've got it under control here! Stand back!
oh!
!!
Roar!
lash
oh!
clod

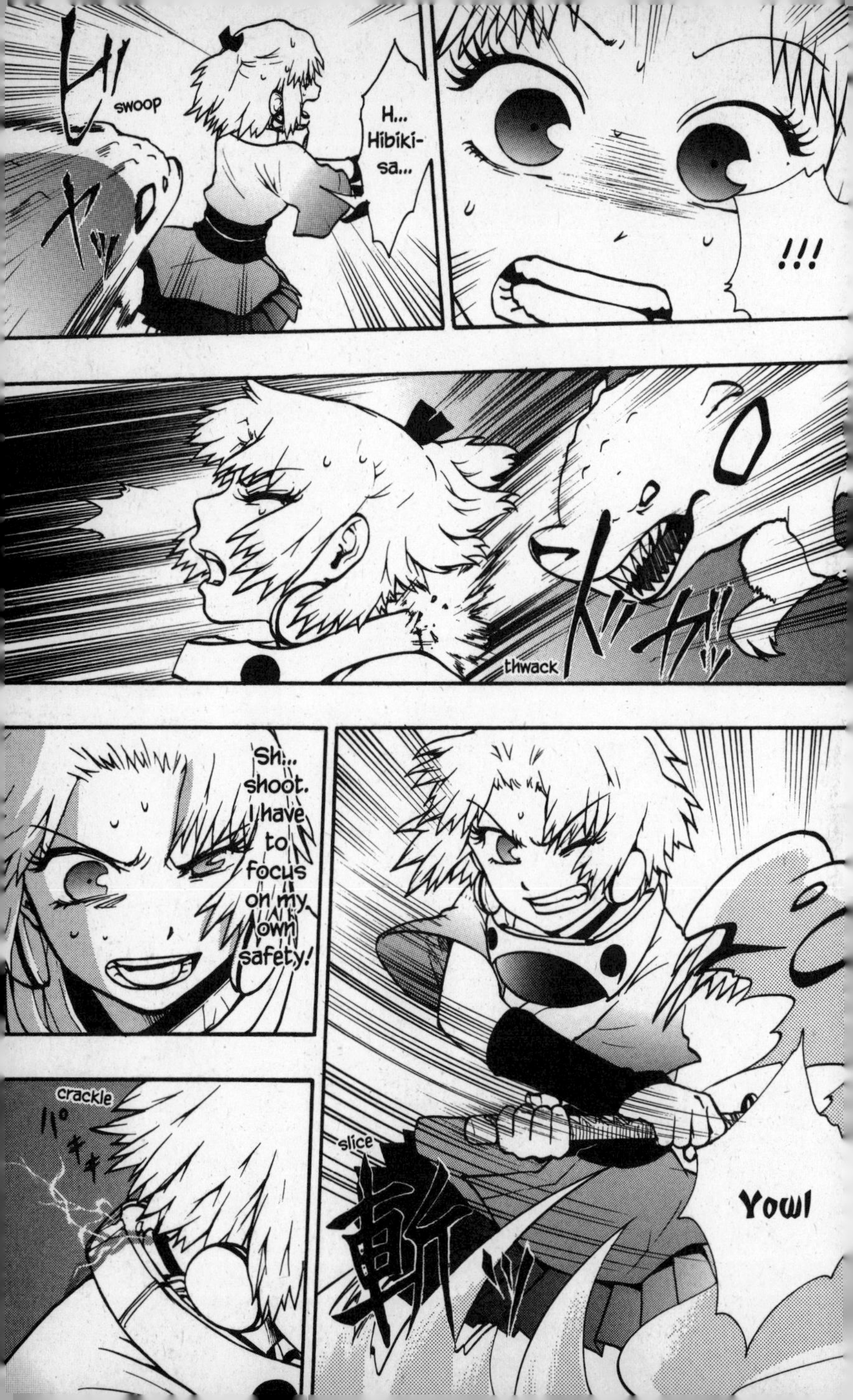
!!!
H... Hibiki-sa...
swoop
thwack
slice
Yow!
Sh... shoot. I have to focus on my own safety!
crackle

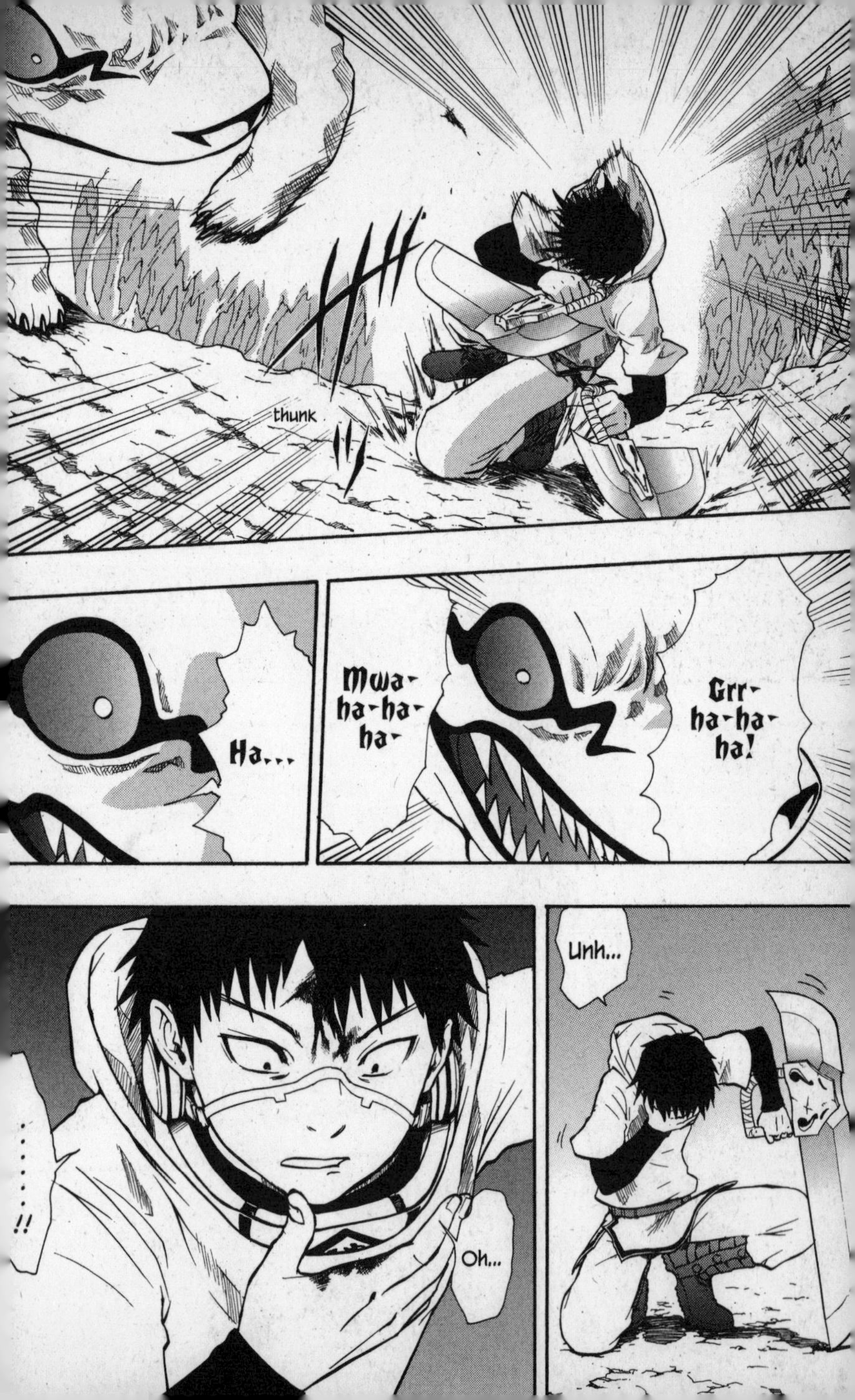
thunk
Grr-ha-ha-ha!
Mwa-ha-ha-ha-
Ha...
Unh...
Oh...
......!!

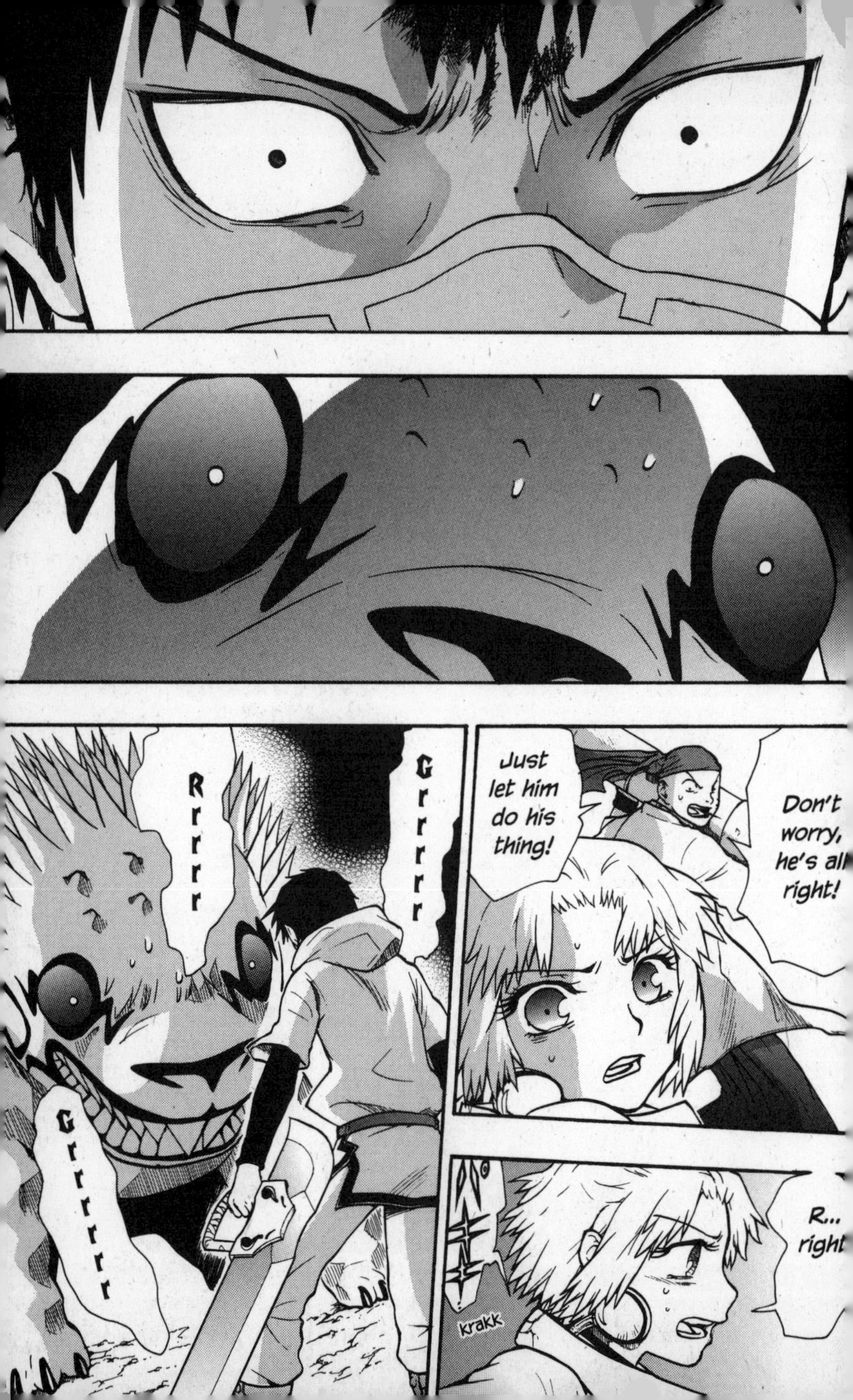
Don't worry, he's all right!
Just let him do his thing!
R... right
krakk
Grrrrr
Rrrrr
Grrrrrr

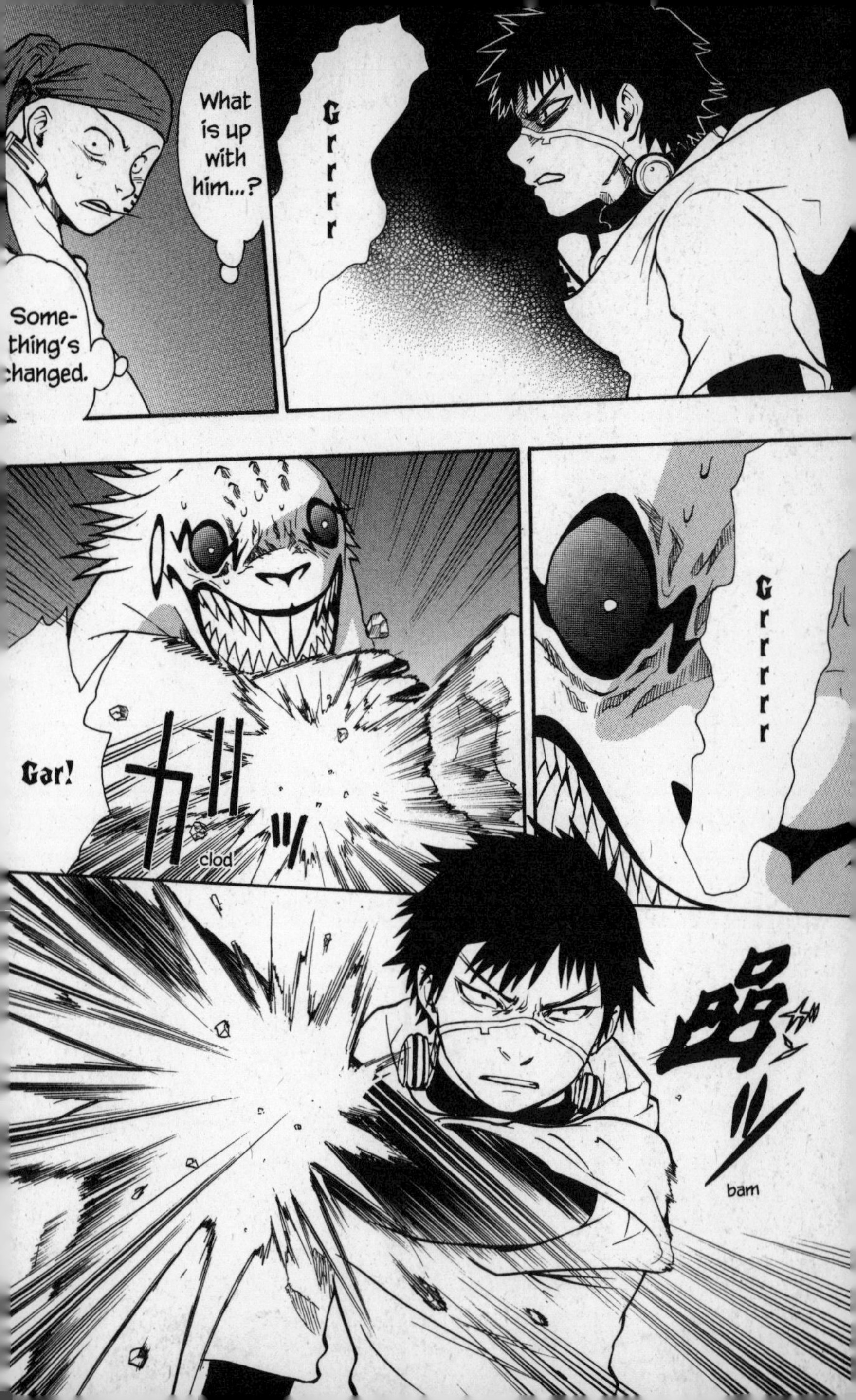

Grrrr
What is up with him...?
Something's changed.
Grrrrr
Gar!
カッ
clod
bam

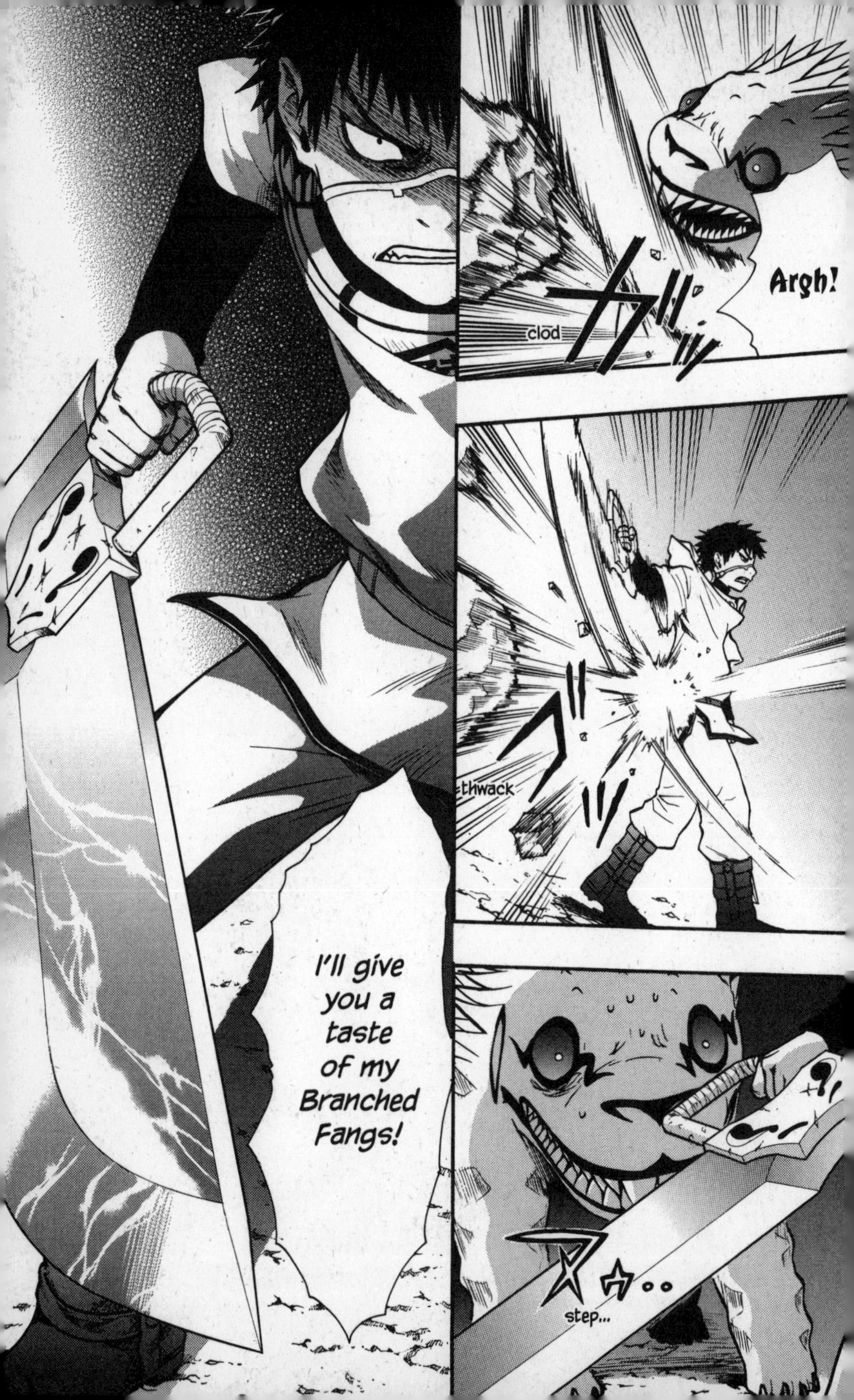
Argh!
clod
thwack
step...
I'll give you a taste of my Branched Fangs!

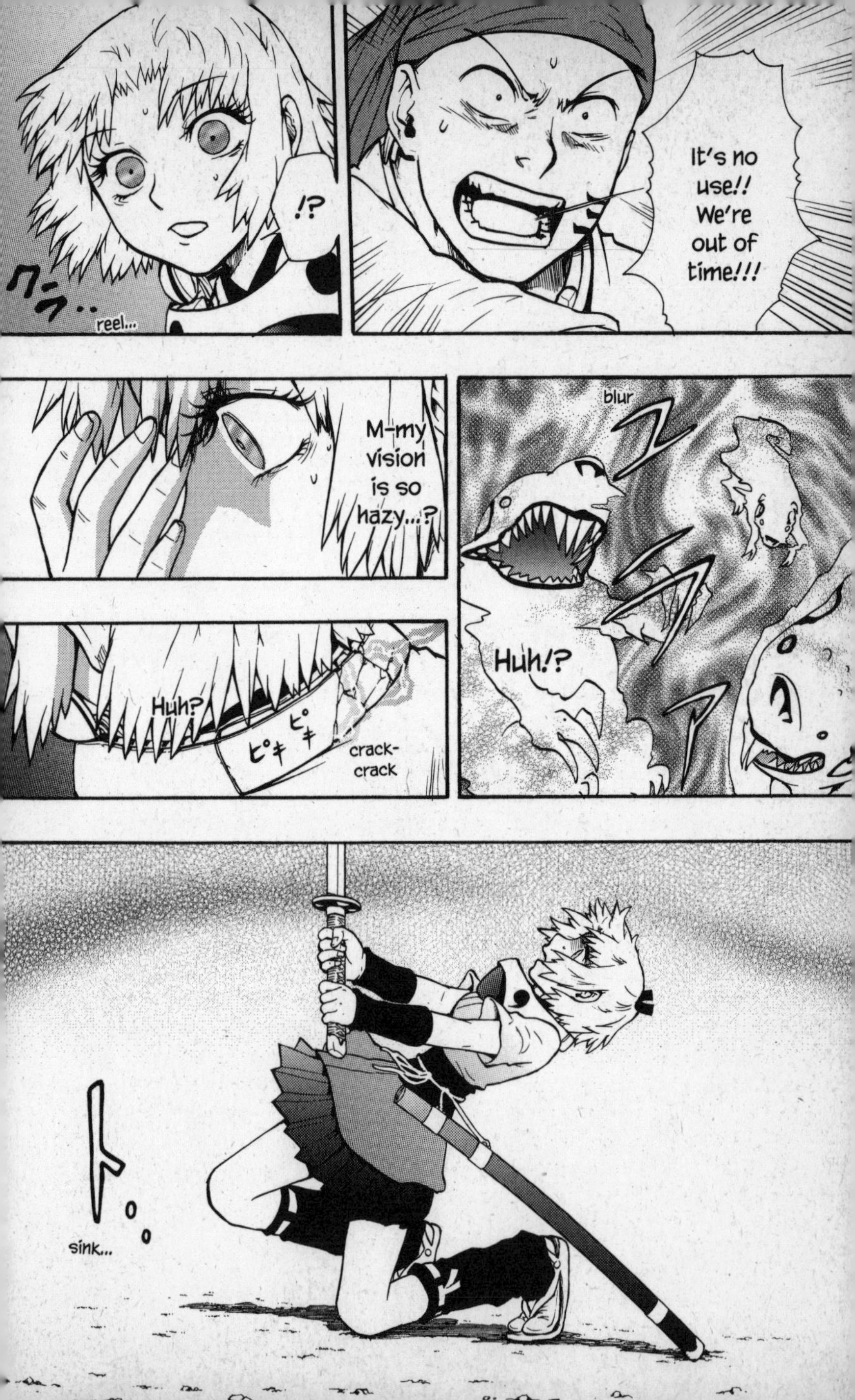
It's no use!! We're out of time!!!
!?
reel...
blur
Huh!?
M-my vision is so hazy...?
Huh?
ピキ ピキ
crack-crack
sink...

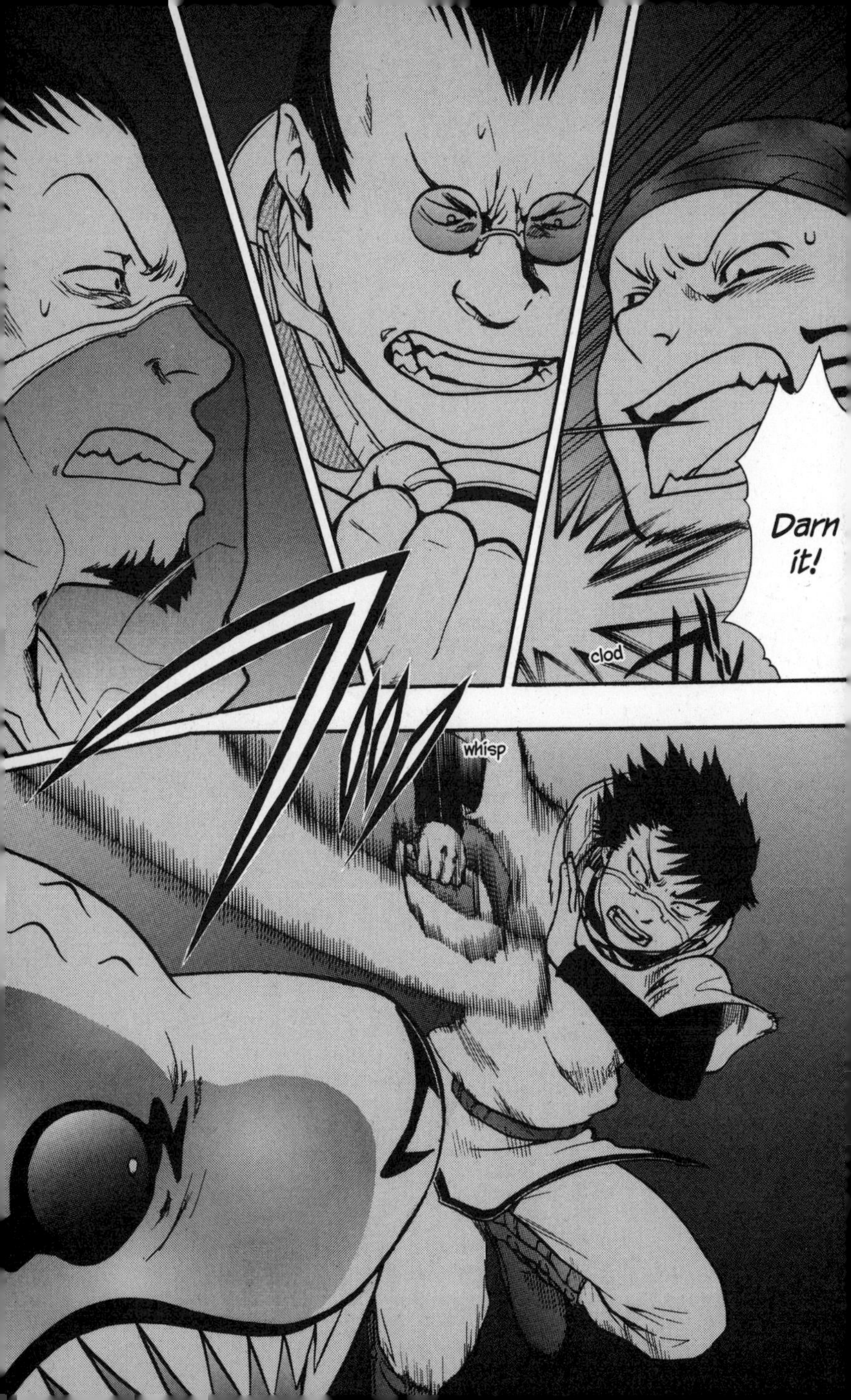
Darn it!
clod
whisp

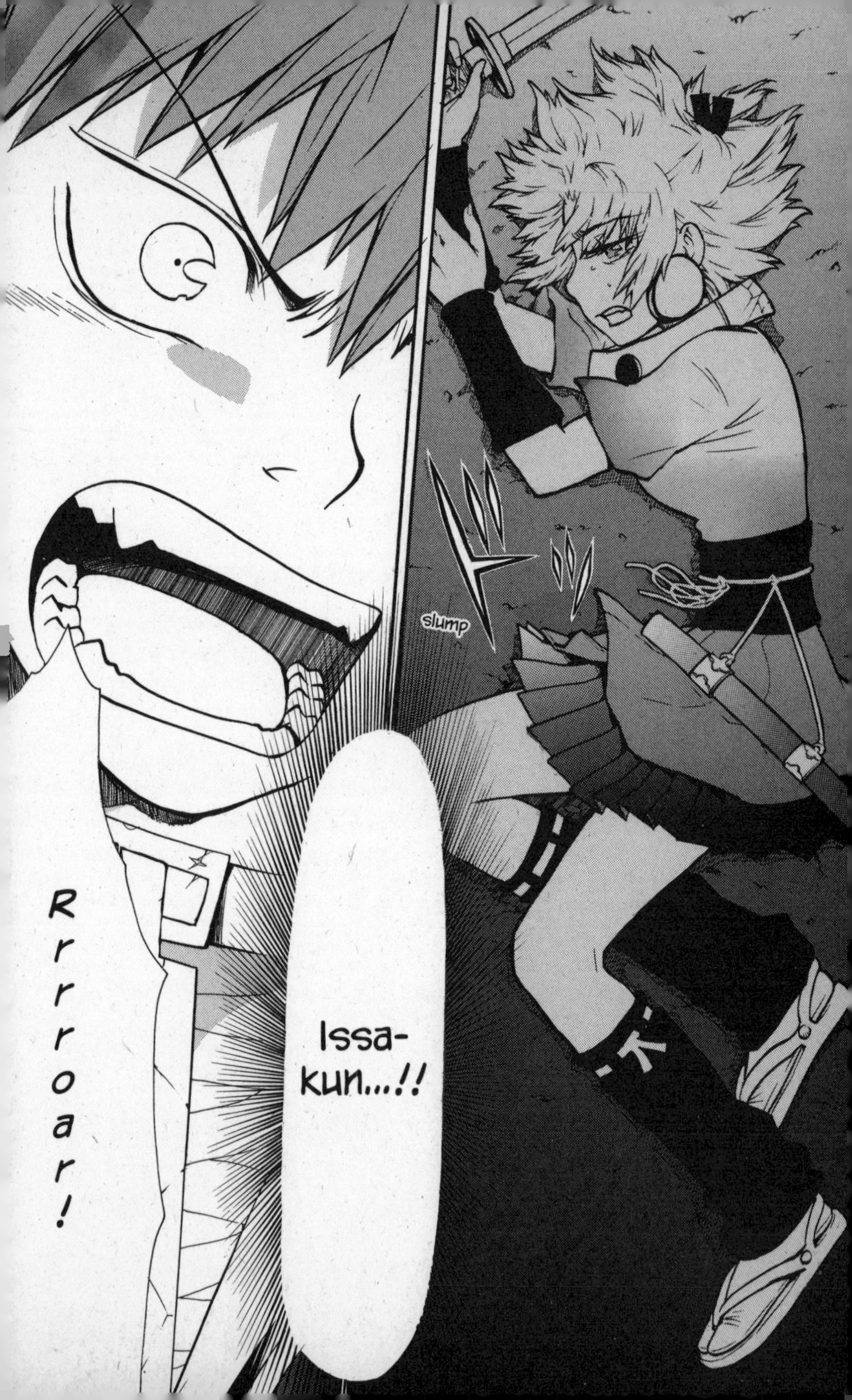
slump
Issa-kun...!!
Rrrroar!

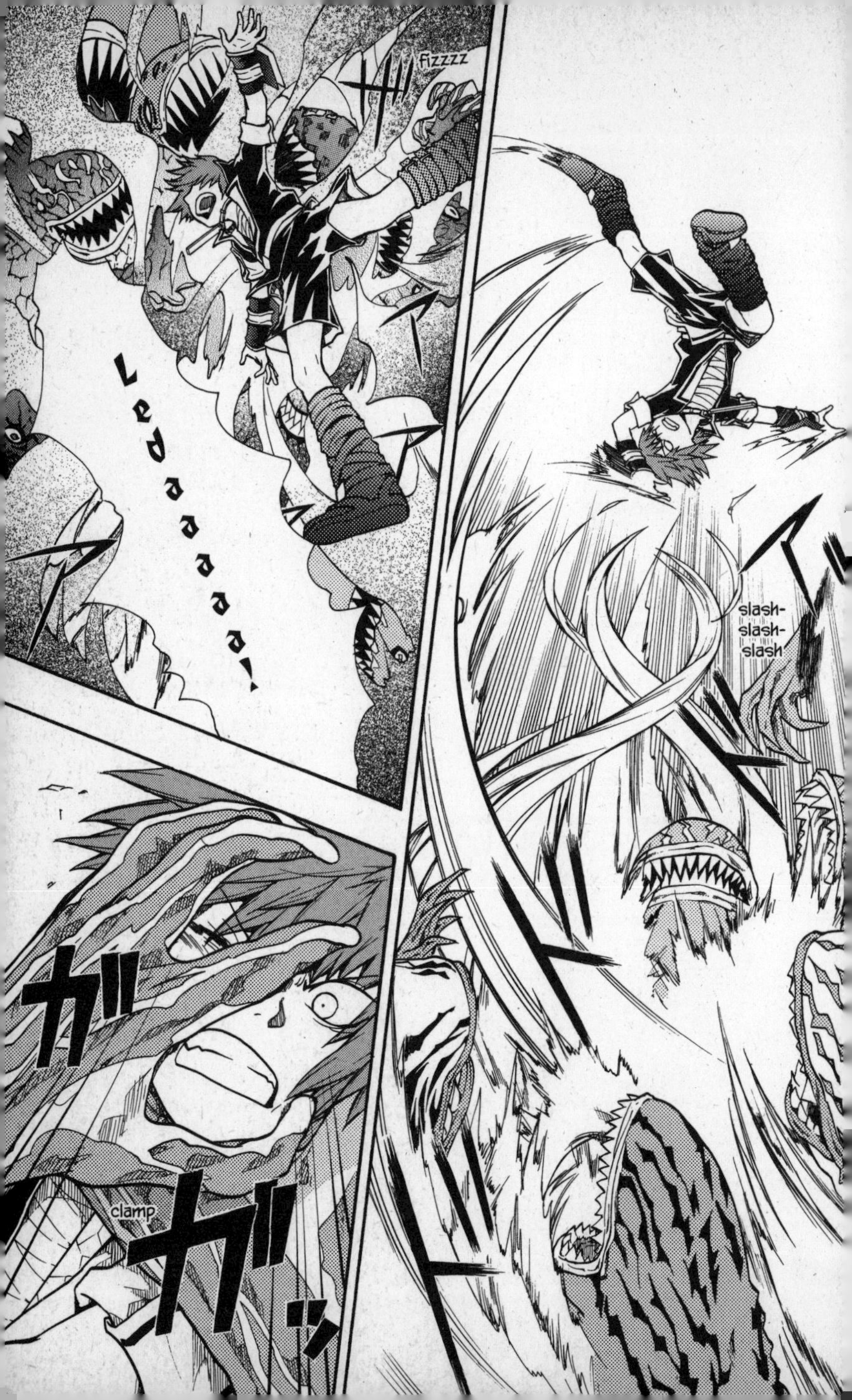
slash-slash-slash
fizzzz
Ledaaaaa!
ガ
ガッ
clamp

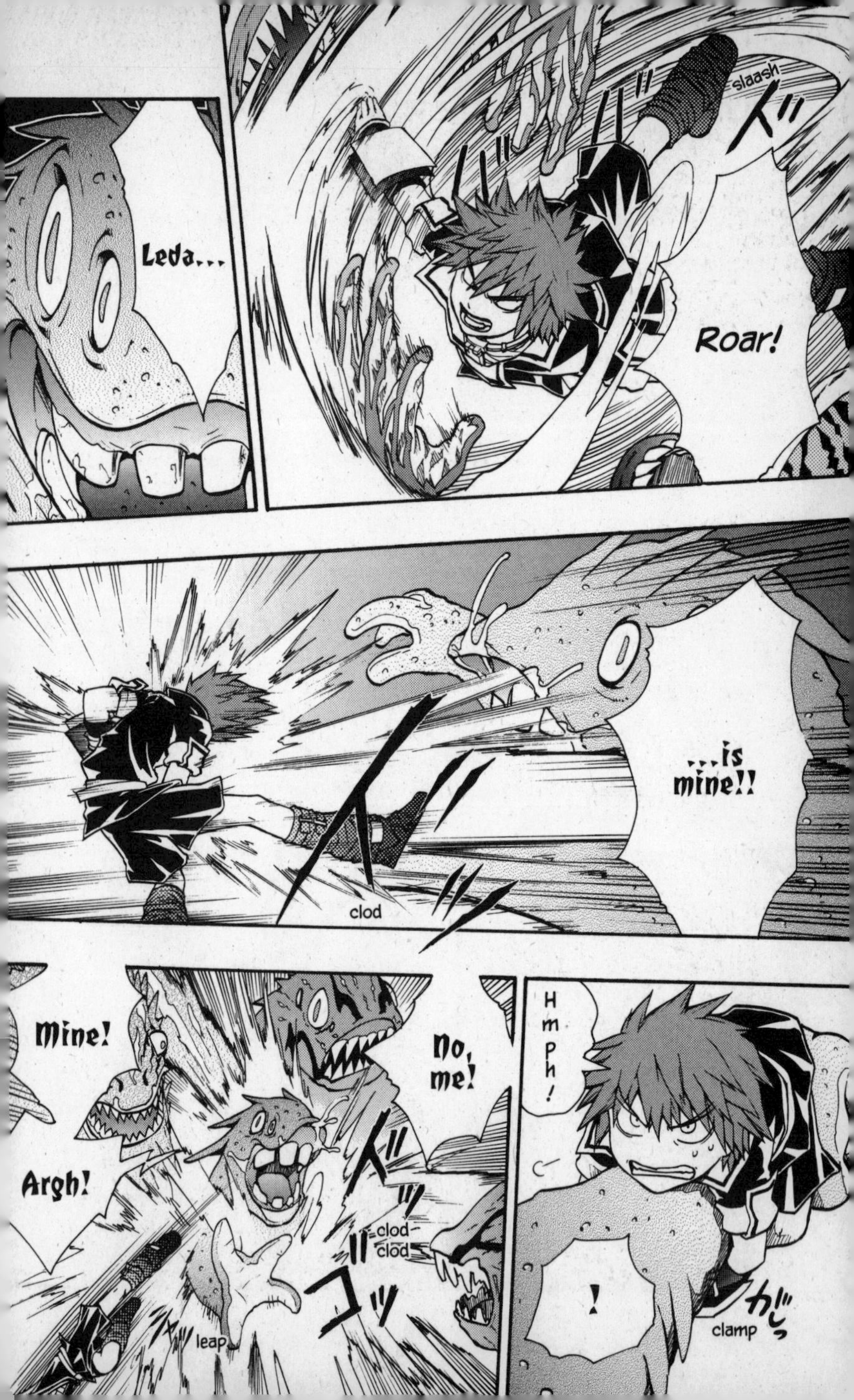
slaash
Roar!
Leda...
...is
mine!!
clod
Hmph!
!
clamp
No,
me!
Mine!
Argh!
clod
clod
leap

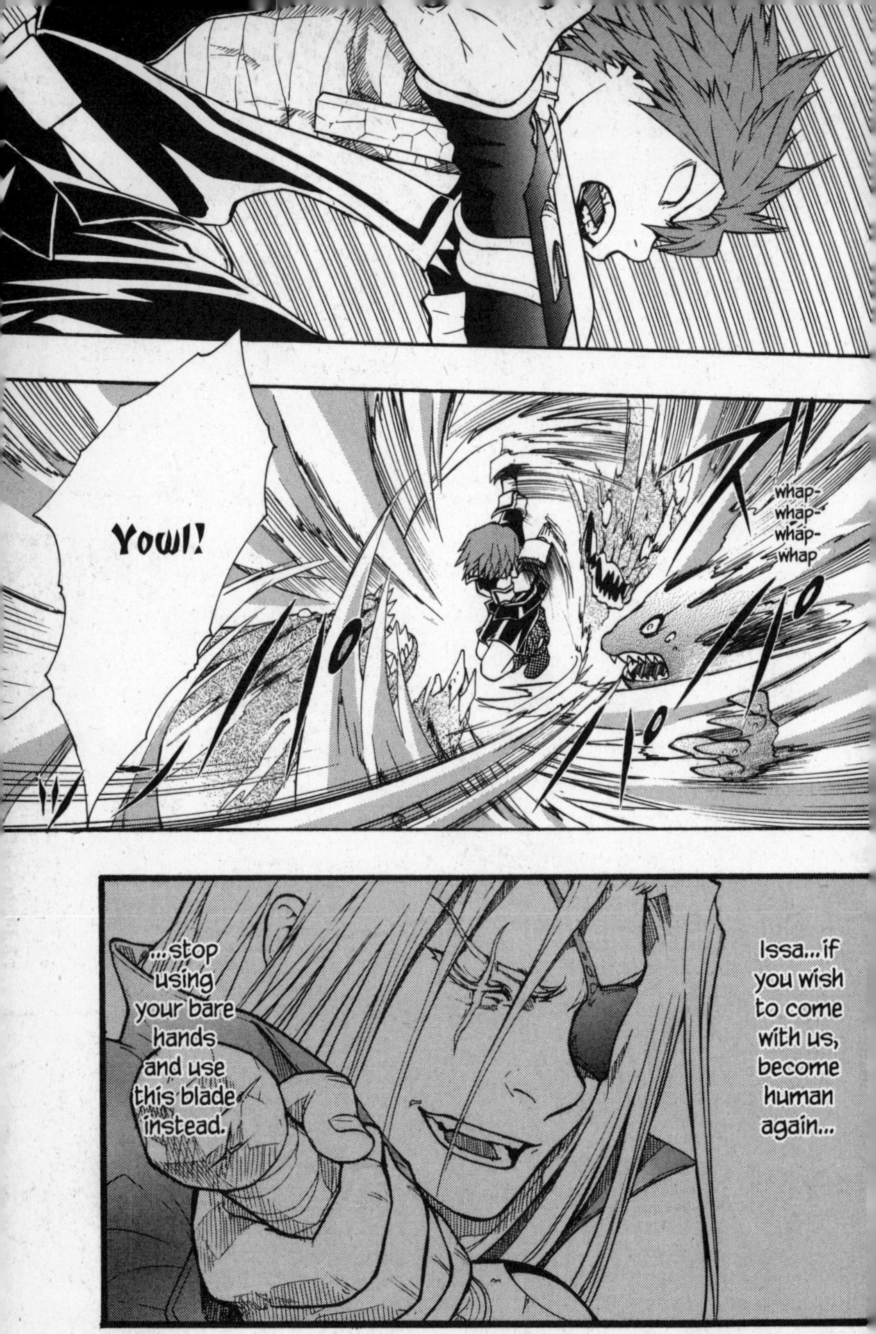
whap-whap-whap-whap
Yowl!
Issa...if you wish to come with us, become human again...
...stop using your bare hands and use this blade instead.

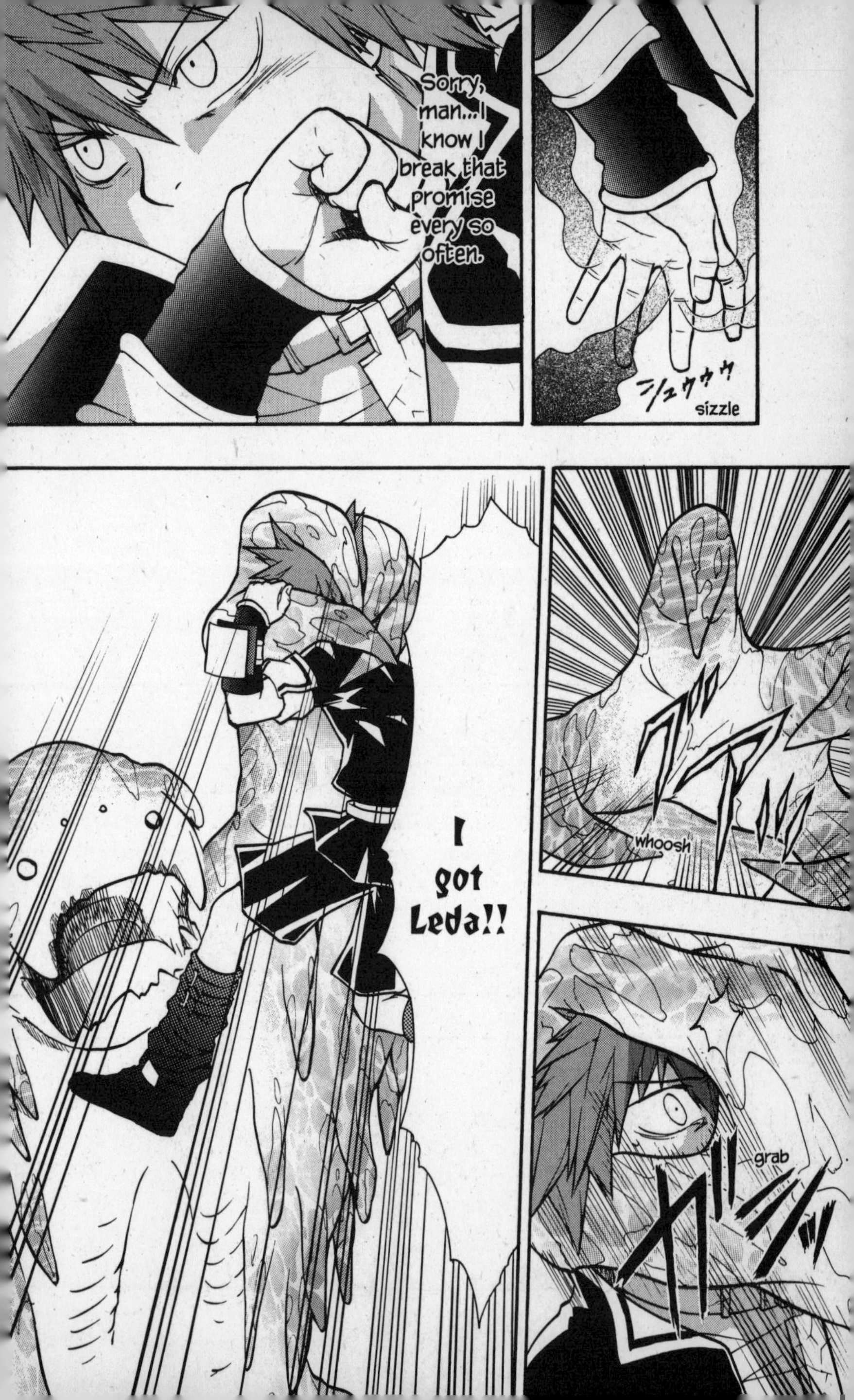
シュウウウ
sizzle
Sorry, man...I know I break that promise every so often.
whoosh
grab
I got Leda!!

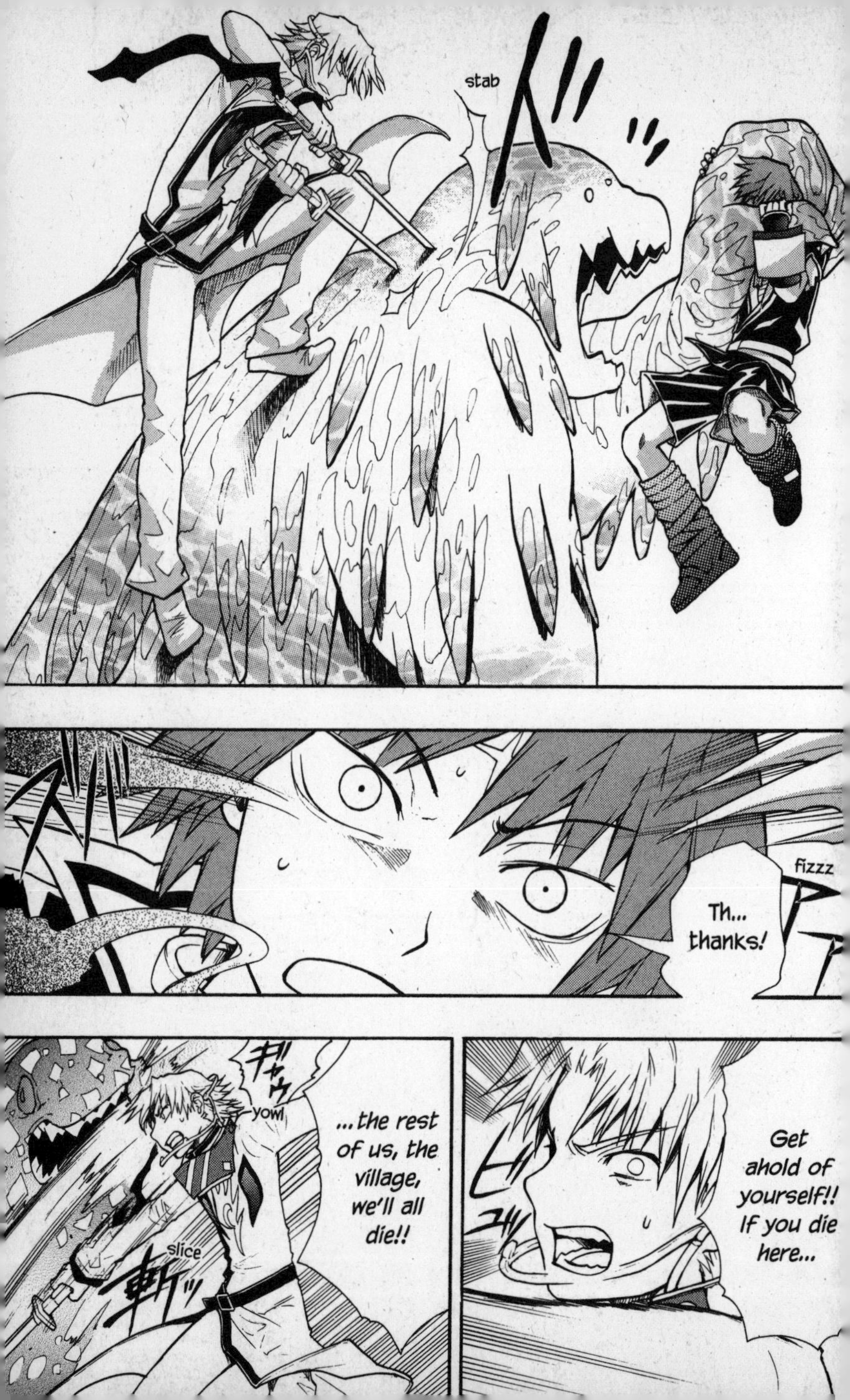
stab
fizzz
Th... thanks!
Get ahold of yourself!! If you die here...
yowl
...the rest of us, the village, we'll all die!!
slice

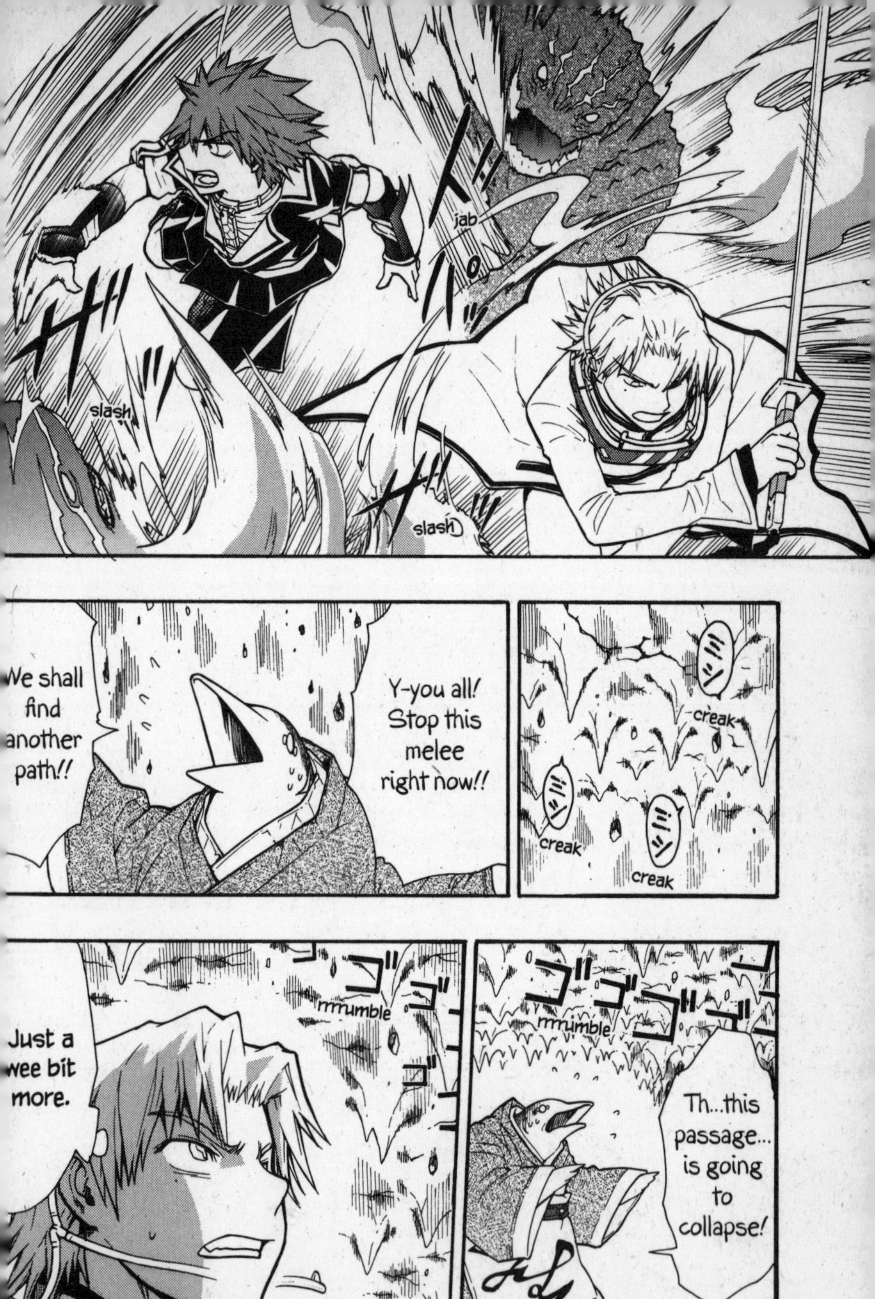
jab
slash
slash
creak
creak
creak
Y-you all! Stop this melee right now!!
We shall find another path!!
rrrumble
Th...this passage... is going to collapse!
rrrumble
Just a wee bit more.

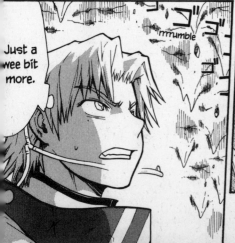

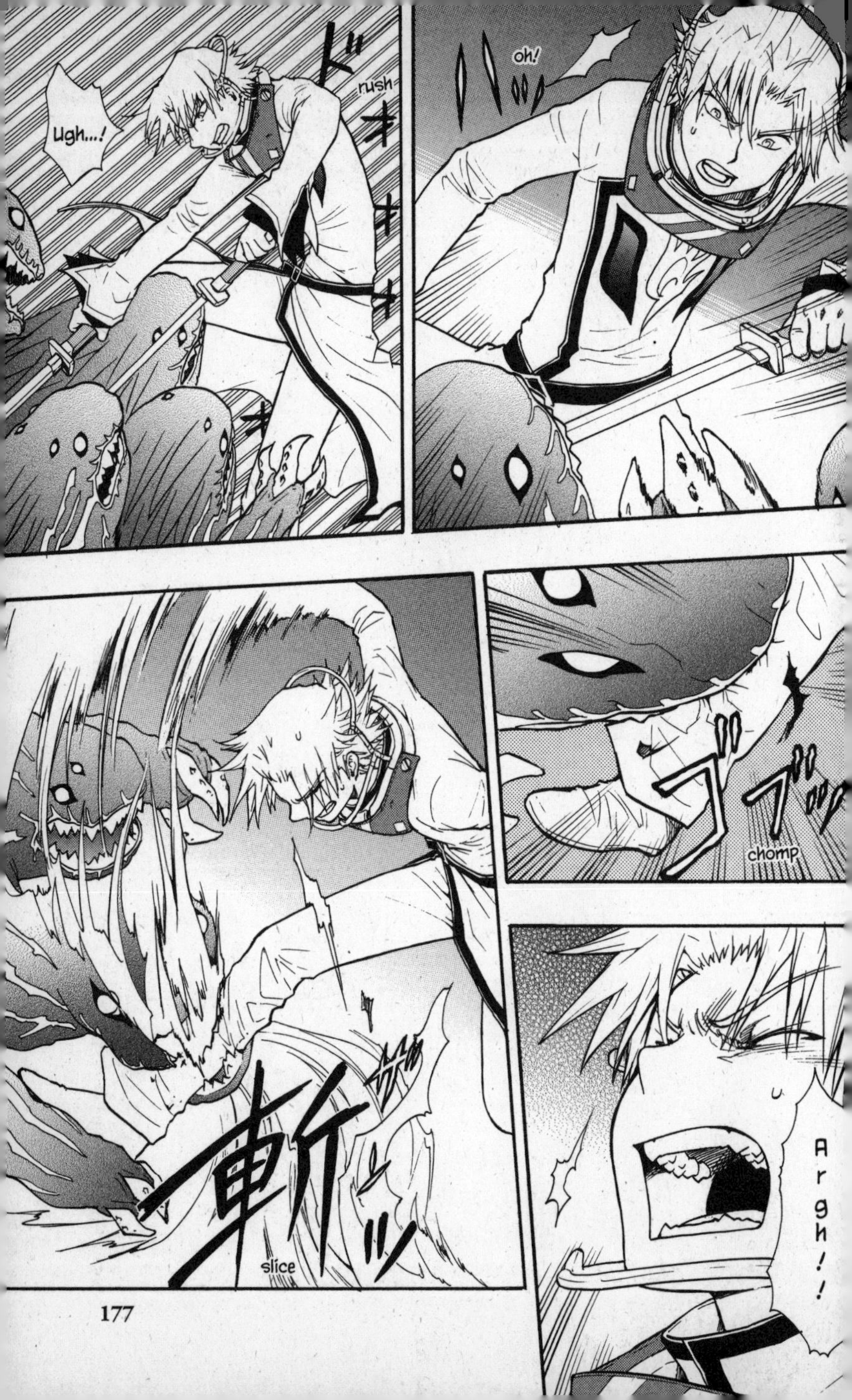
oh!
rush
Ugh...!
chomp
Argh!!
slice

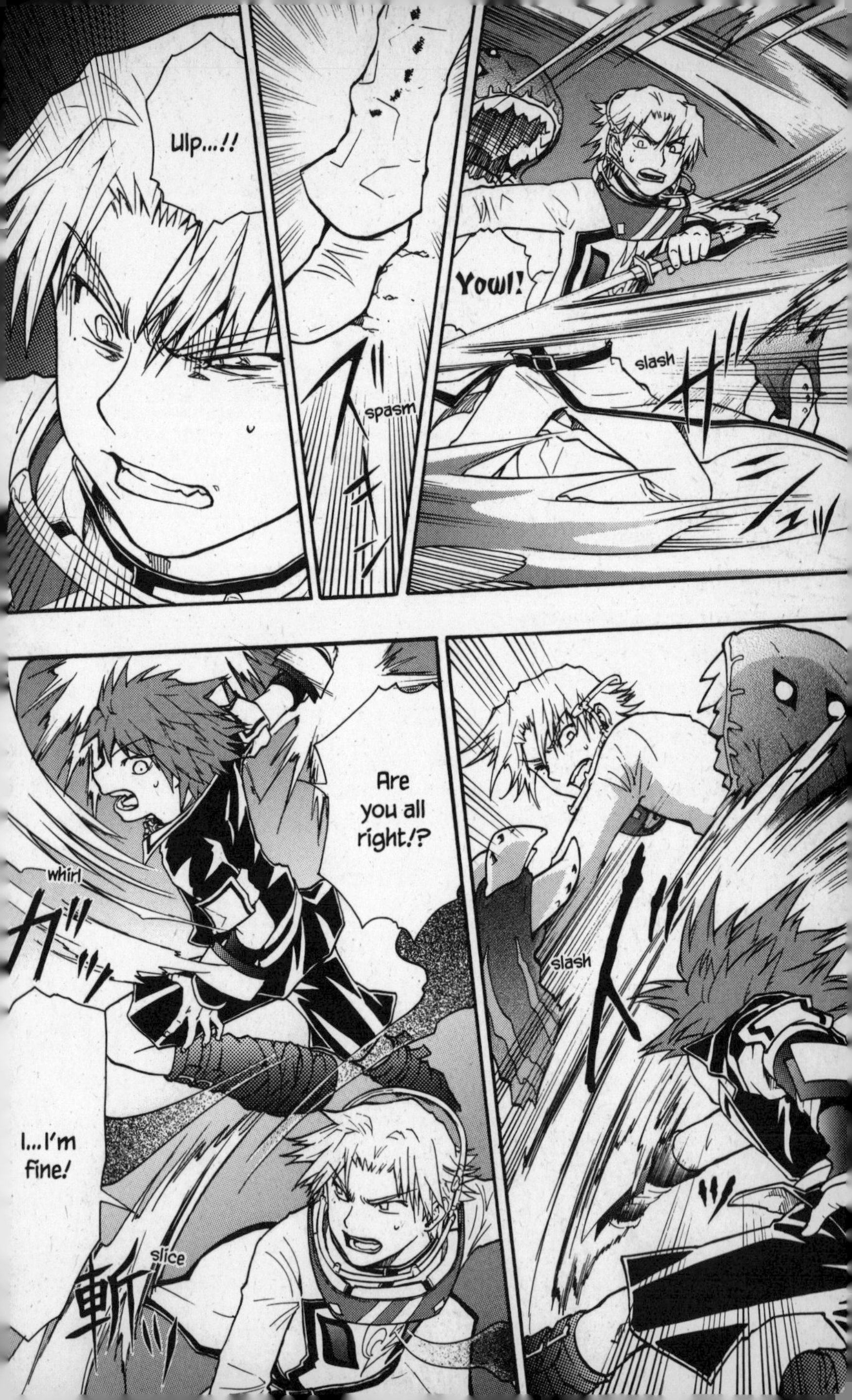
Yowl!
slash
spasm
Ulp...!!
slash
Are you all right!?
whirl
I...I'm fine!
slice

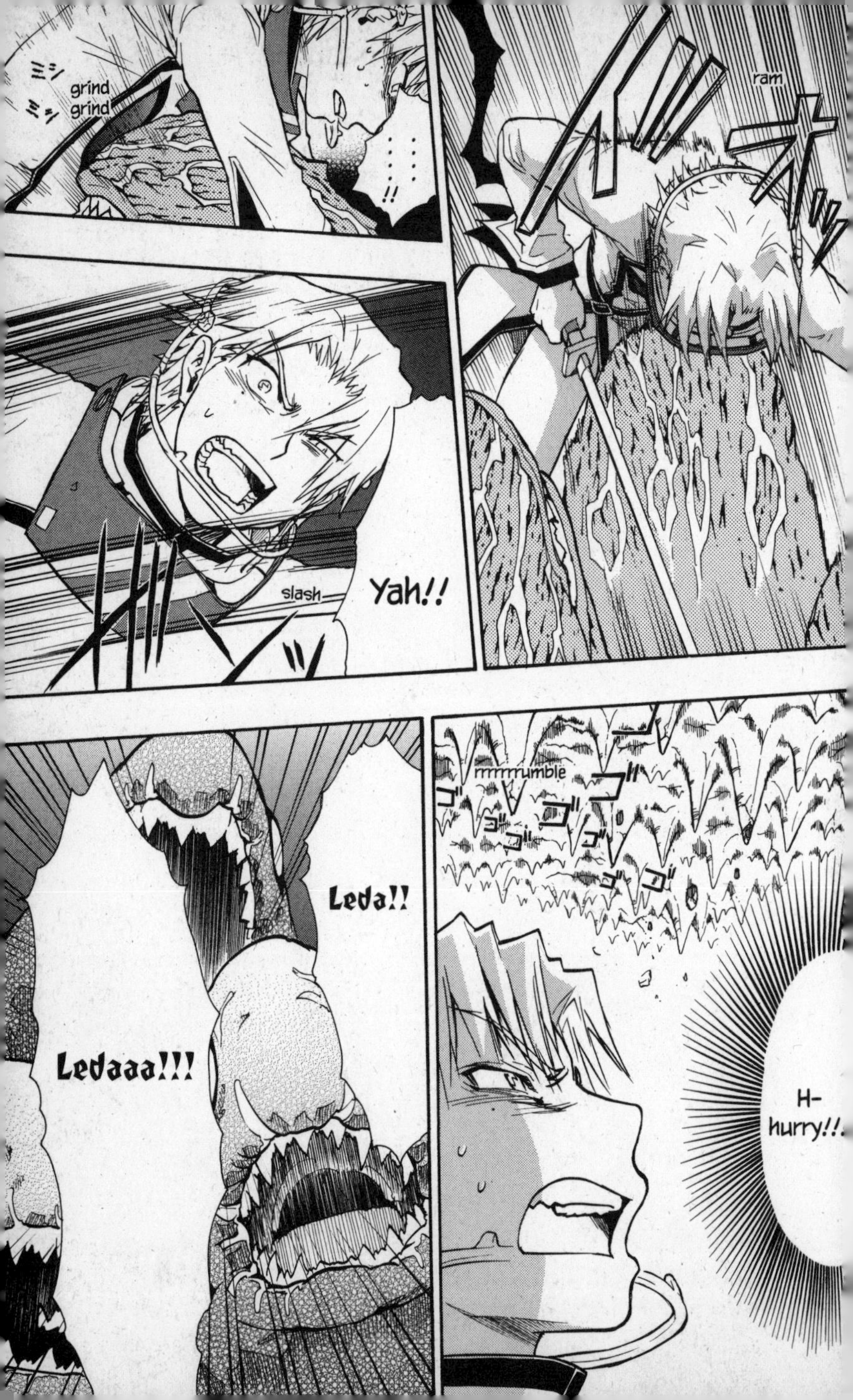

ram
ミシ
ミシ
grind
grind
!!
slash
Yah!!
rrrrrrrumble
H-
hurry!!
Leda!!
Ledaaa!!!

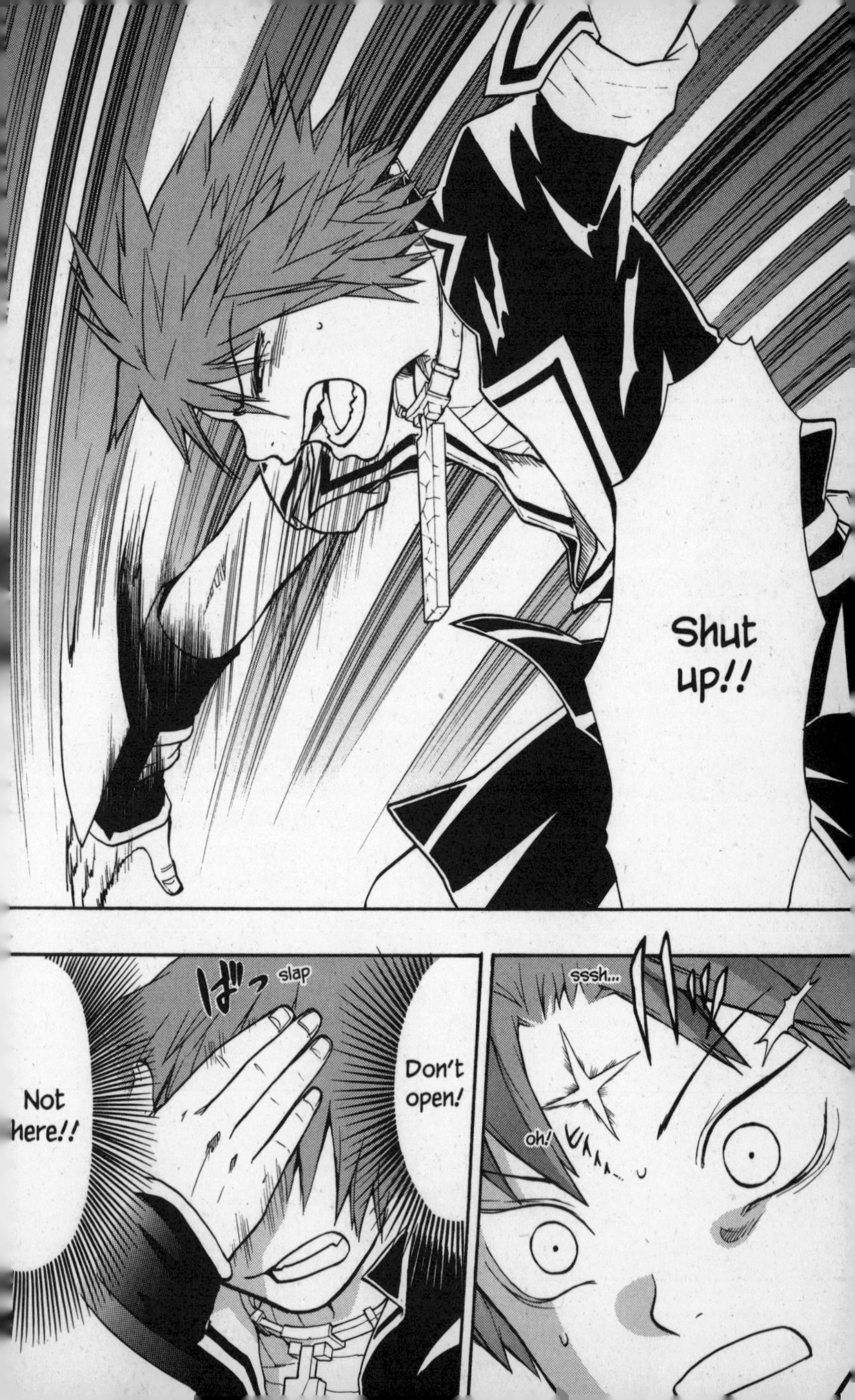
Shut up!!
sssh...
oh!
ばっ
slap
Don't open!
Not here!!

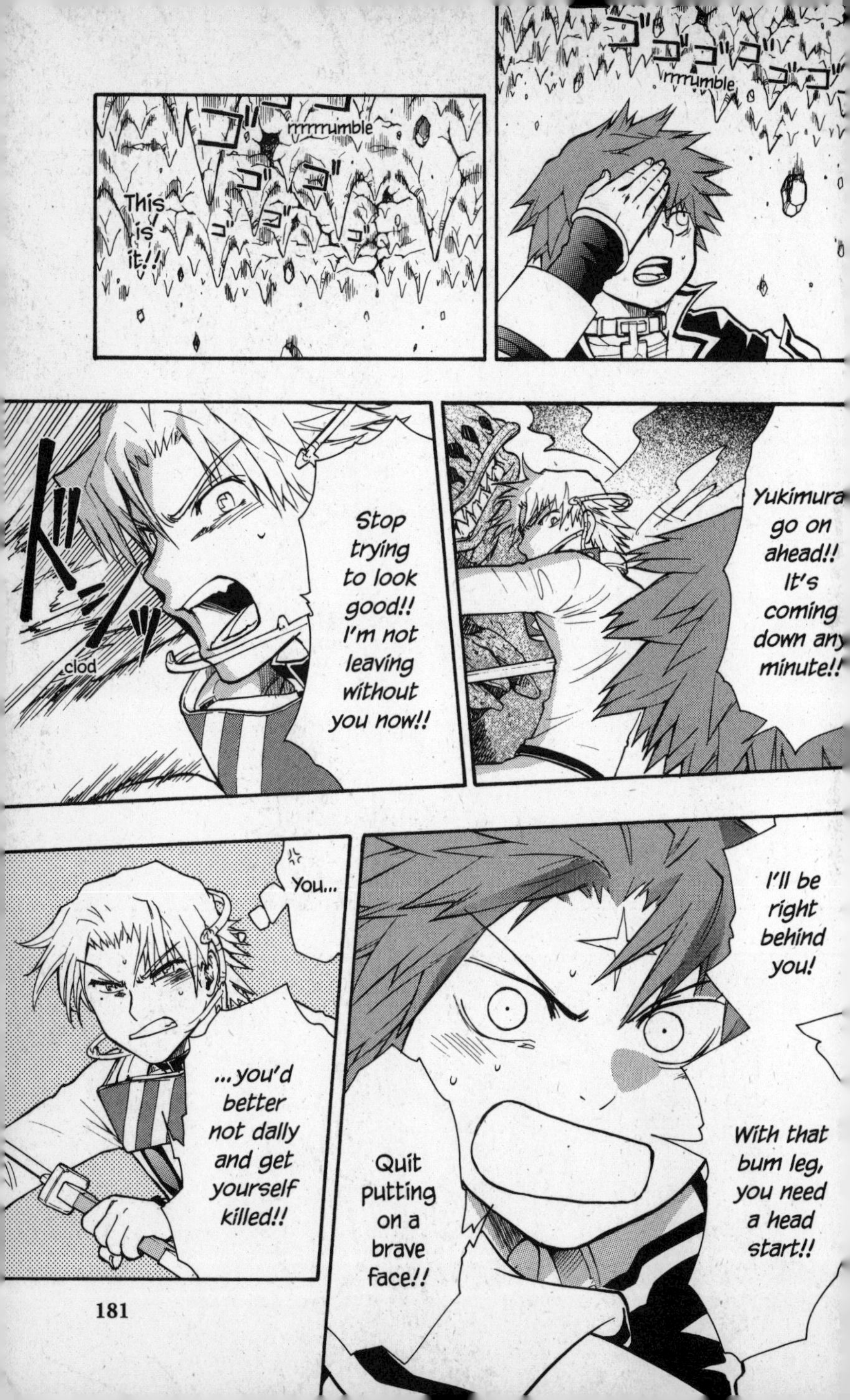
rrrrumble
rrrrrumble
This is it!!
Yukimura go on ahead!! It's coming down any minute!!
Stop trying to look good!! I'm not leaving without you now!!
clod
I'll be right behind you!
With that bum leg, you need a head start!!
Quit putting on a brave face!!
You...
...you'd better not dally and get yourself killed!!

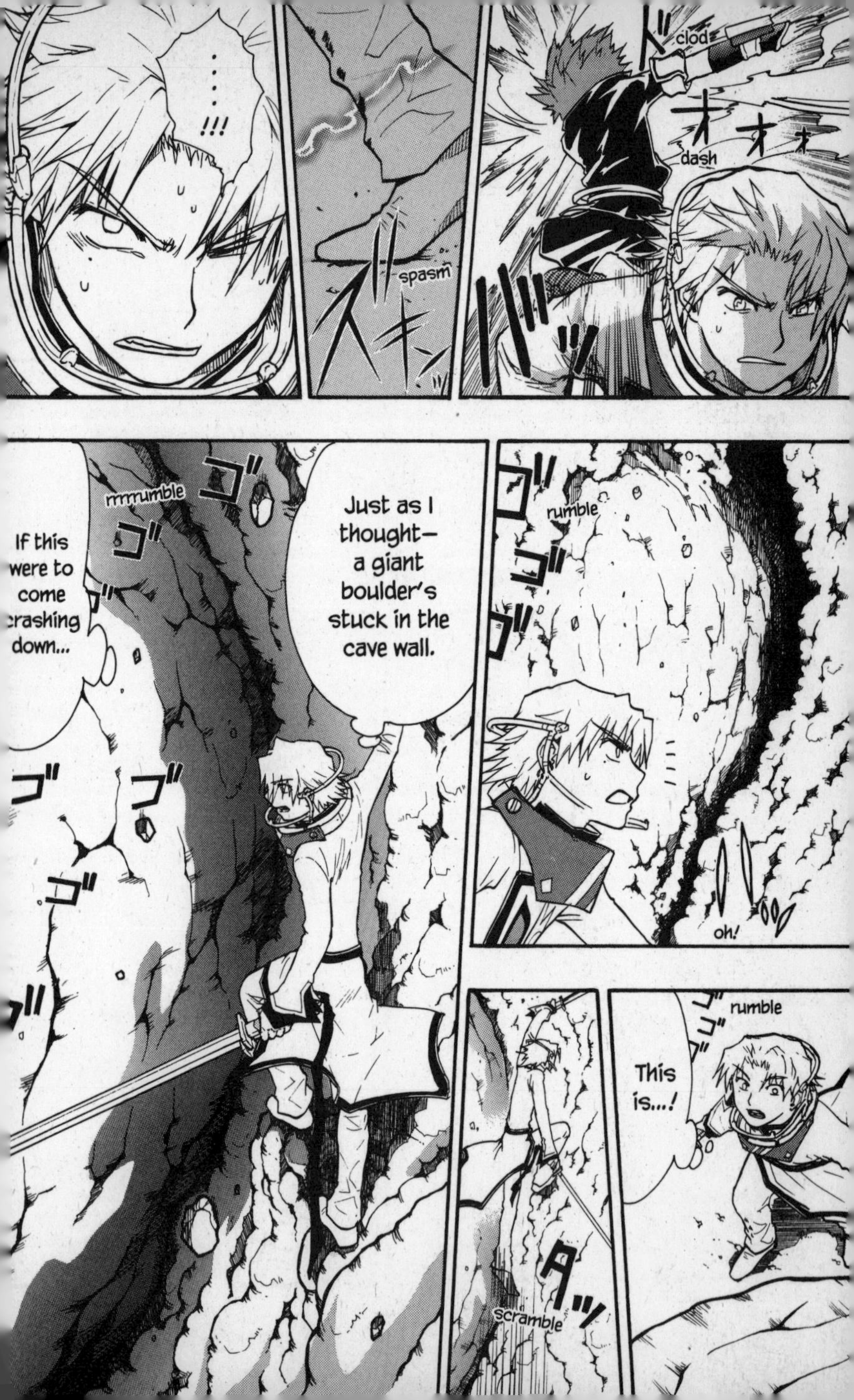
clod
dash
spasm
...
!!!
rumble
oh!
rumble
This is...!
scramble
rrrrrumble
Just as I thought— a giant boulder's stuck in the cave wall.
If this were to come crashing down...

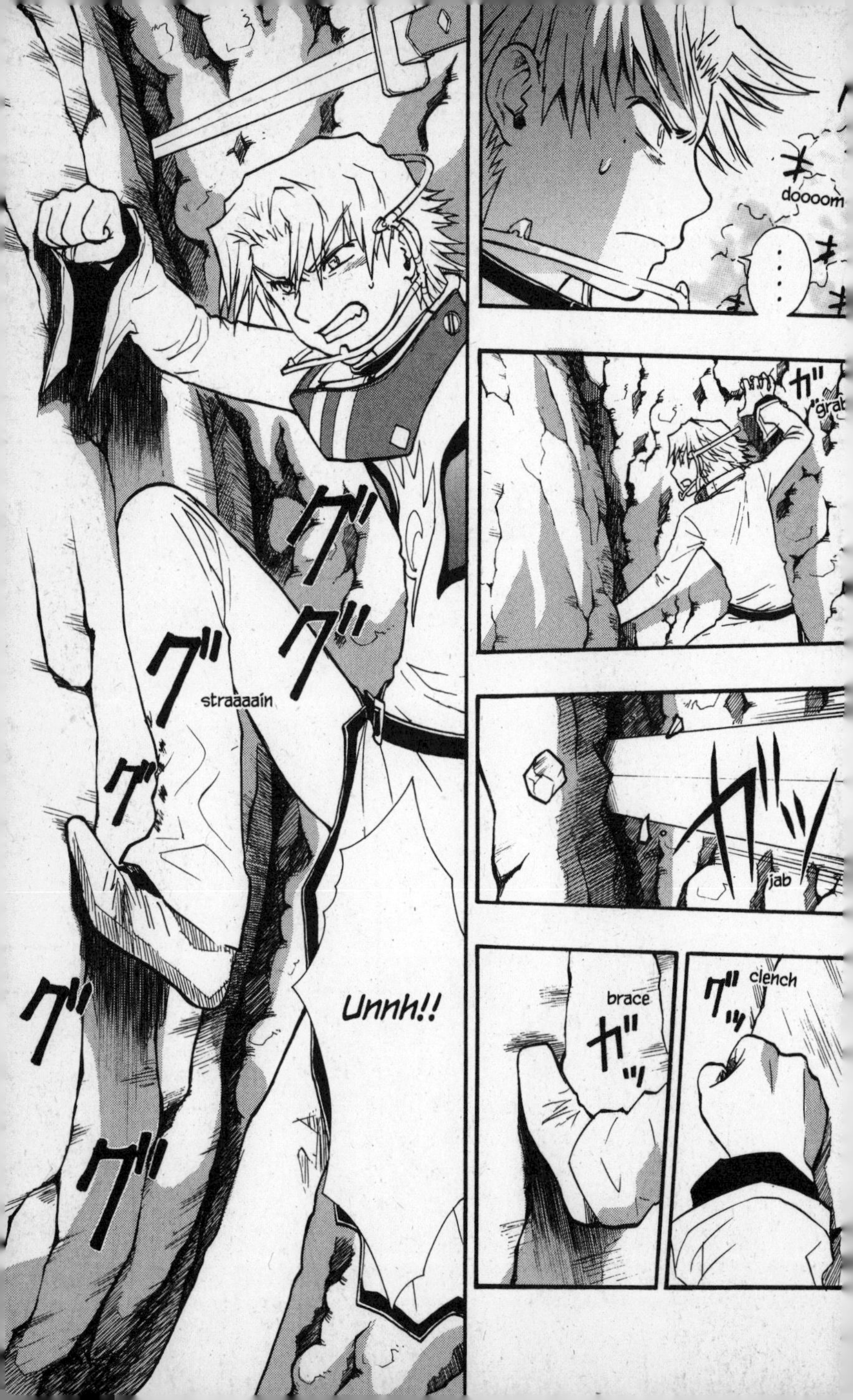
doooom
. . . . .
ガ
grab
ガッ
jab
グッ
clench
ガッ
brace
グ
straaaain
Unnh!!

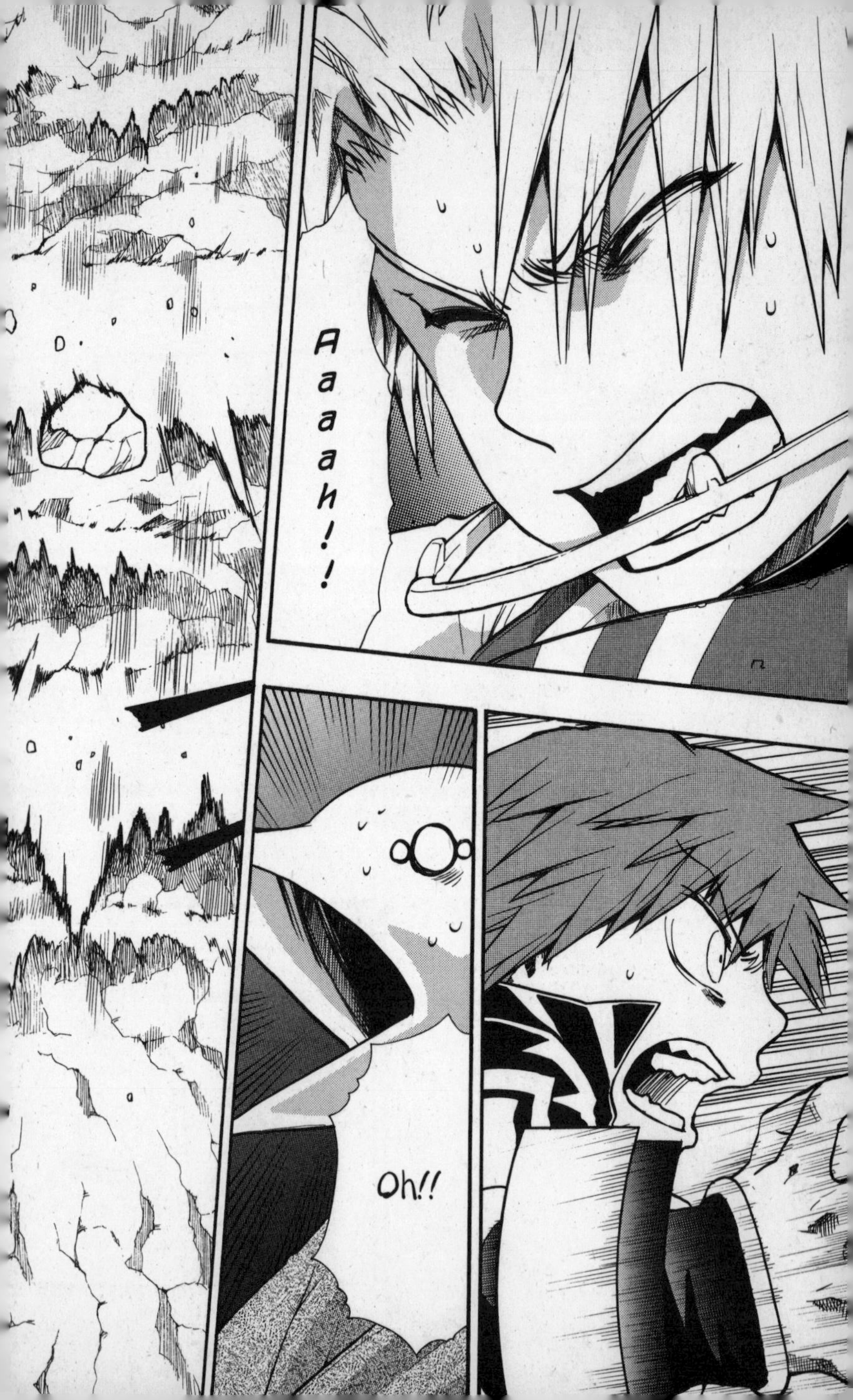
Aaaah!!
Oh!!

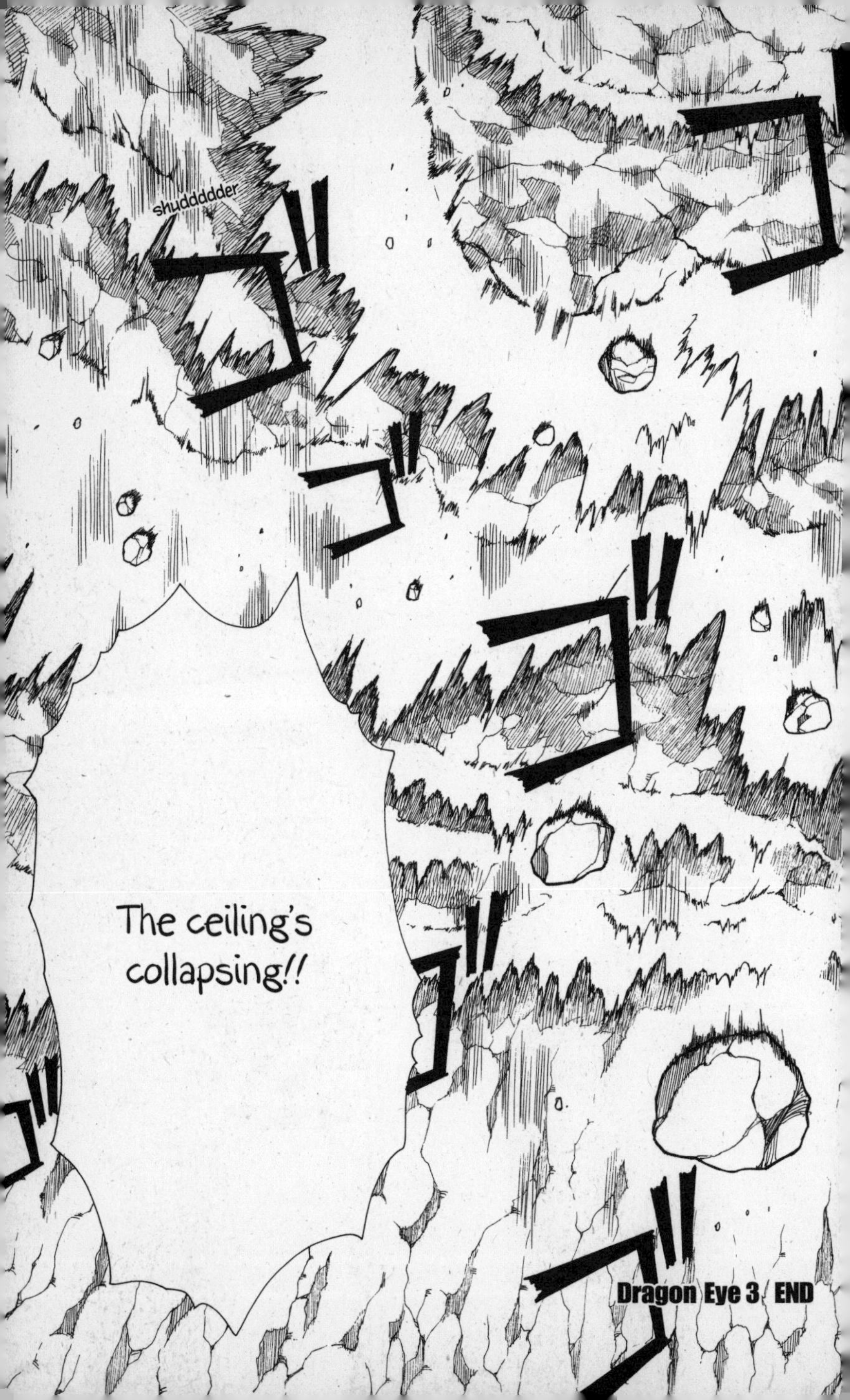
shuddddder
The ceiling's collapsing!!
Dragon Eye 3 END

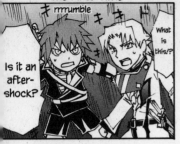

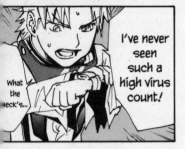

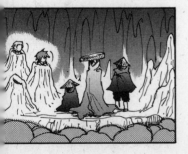

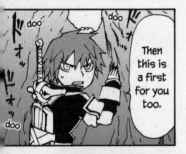

Dragon Eye

4-Panel Strip Extras

Shoot!!
I'm outta time!!

I was originally planning
different extras, but...
Oh my.
4-panel strips again.
But they're extras, so it's OK,
right!?
Please buy Volume 4 too!

Fujiyama

Staff
Uemura Erika
Ueda Satomi

Thanks
Bibii
Dantani Ai

The First Time

What is this!?
rrrumble
Is it an after-shock?
I've never seen such a high virus count!
What the
eck's...
doo
Then this is a first for you too.
doo
doo

Be mine

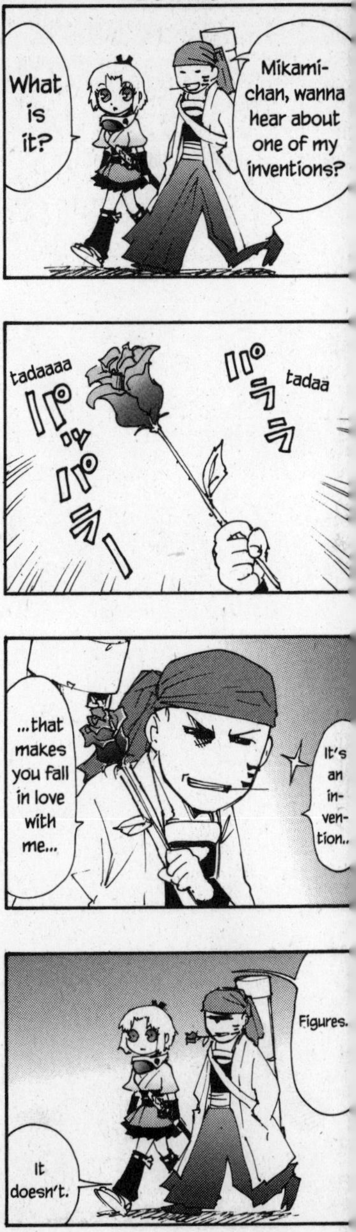
Mikami-chan, wanna hear about one of my inventions?
What is it?
tadaa
tadaaaa
It's an invention..
...that makes you fall in love with me...
Figures.
It doesn't.

Your bad

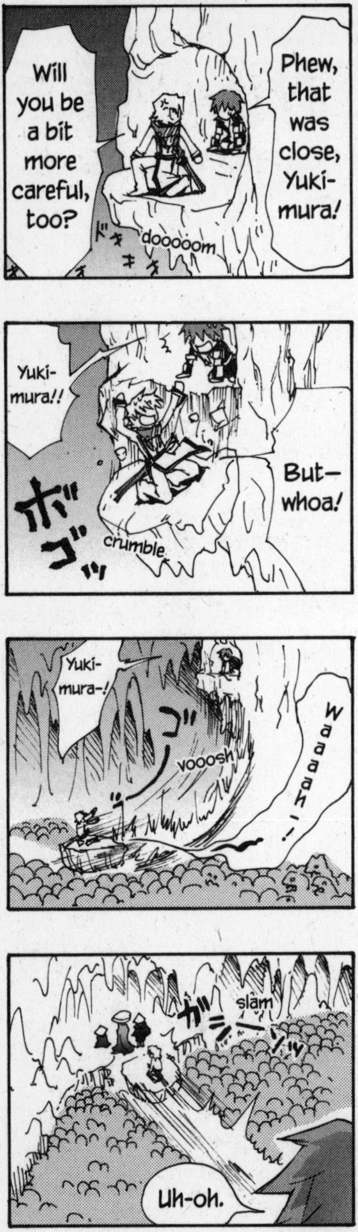
Phew, that was close, Yuki-mura!
Will you be a bit more careful, too?
dooooom
But— whoa!
Yuki-mura!!
crumble
Waaaah—!
vooosh
Yuki-mura-!
slam
Uh-oh.

This time for sure

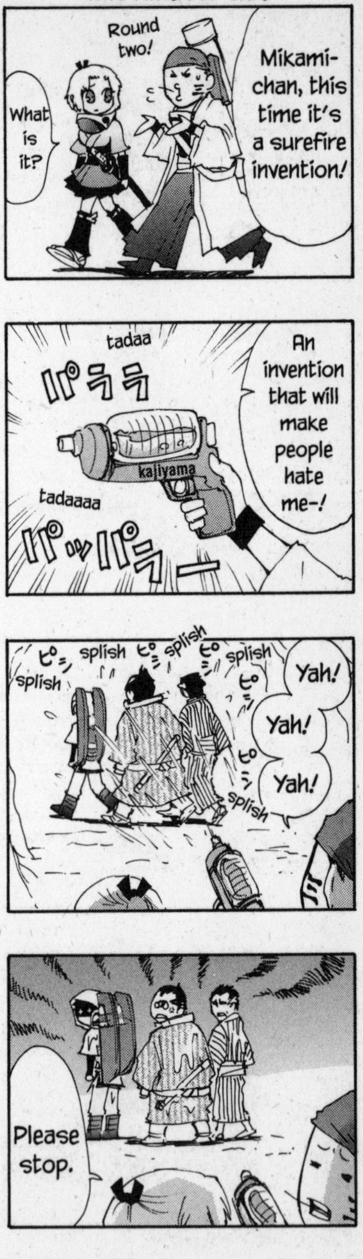

Mikami-chan, this time it's a surefire invention!
Round two!
What is it?
An invention that will make people hate me-!
tadaa
パララ
kajiyama
tadaaaa
パッパラー
Yah!
Yah!
Yah!
splish
splish
splish
splish
splish
Please stop.

Redirection

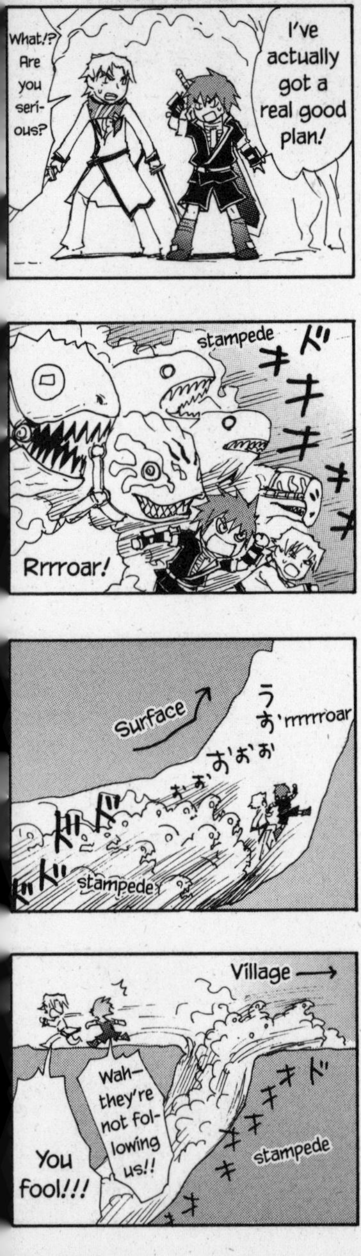

I've actually got a real good plan!
What!? Are you seri-ous?
stampede
Rrrroar!
Surface
rrrrrroar
stampede
Village
Wah— they're not fol-lowing us!!
stampede
You fool!!!

It worked!

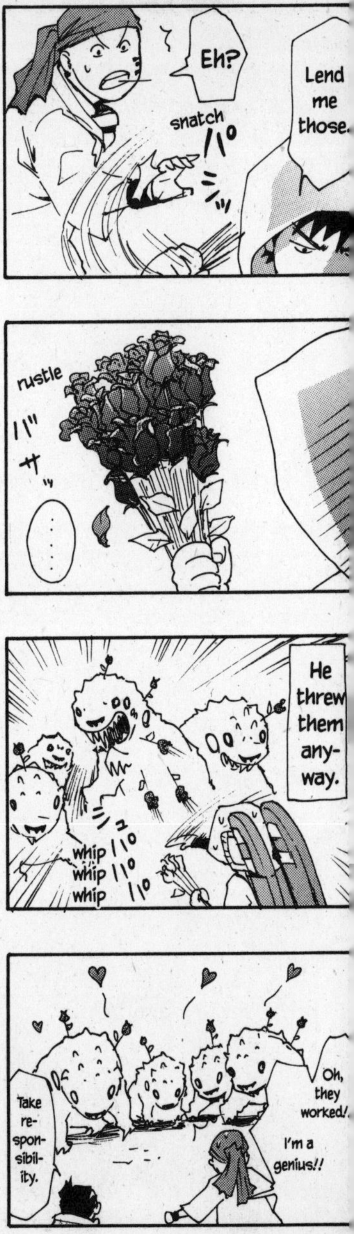
Lend me those.
Eh?
snatch
rustle
......
He threw them any-way.
whip
whip
whip
Oh, they worked!
I'm a genius!!
Take re-spon-sibil-ity.

The duo, afterwards

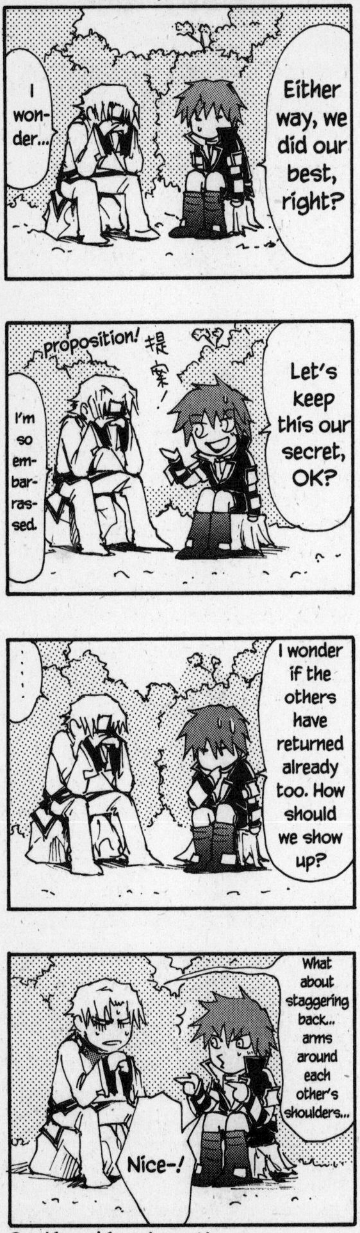
Either way, we did our best, right?
I won-der...
Let's keep this our secret, OK?
提案!
proposition!
I'm so em-bar-ras-sed.
I wonder if the others have returned already too. How should we show up?
....
What about staggering back... arms around each other's shoulders...
Nice-!

Continued in volume 4

TRANSLATION NOTES

Japanese is a tricky language for most Westerners, and translation is often more art than science. For your edification and reading pleasure, here are notes on some of the places where we could have gone in a different direction in our translation of the work, or where a Japanese cultural reference is used.

San, cover

This is an older way of writing the numeral three.

Troop designation symbols, various pages

Most VIUS members wear their troop designations somewhere on their uniforms, and equipment and objects sometimes bear stamps as well. For example, on page 7.1 Leila's banner has both the Mikuni shield and the character for zero.

Flag, page 7

The flag Issa carries on page 7 reads "clear skies."

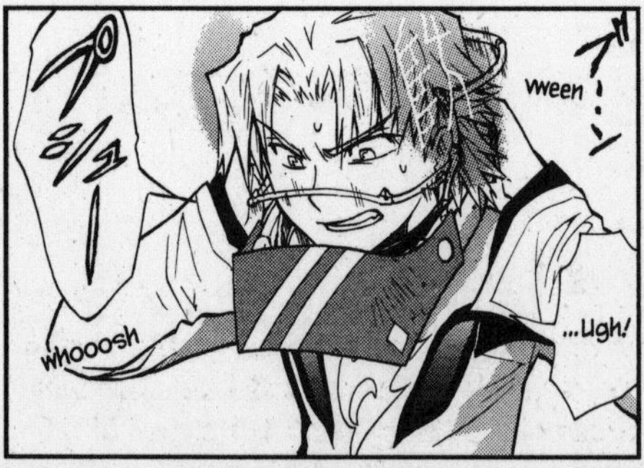

vween
...Ugh!
whooosh

Anti-virus masks, page 12

A part of the standard equipment pack issued to all VIUS members, the mask displays a character meaning "ward" when activated.

Tonkotsu, page 53

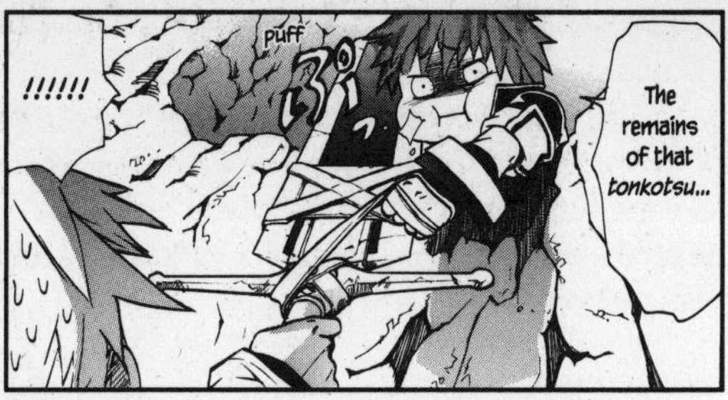
The remains of that *tonkotsu*...
puff
!!!!!!

Tonkotsu, or "pork bone," both describes a type and flavor of ramen broth as well as literally what goes into making it. Supposedly originating from the Hakata area of Fukuoka City in Kyûshû, it is best when the pork bones, onions, and garlic have been stewed for many hours. Ramen noodles are added to the strained soup, which are then typically topped with sliced pork, dried seaweed, chopped scallions, and pickled ginger and bamboo shoots.

One bowl of rice a day, page 62

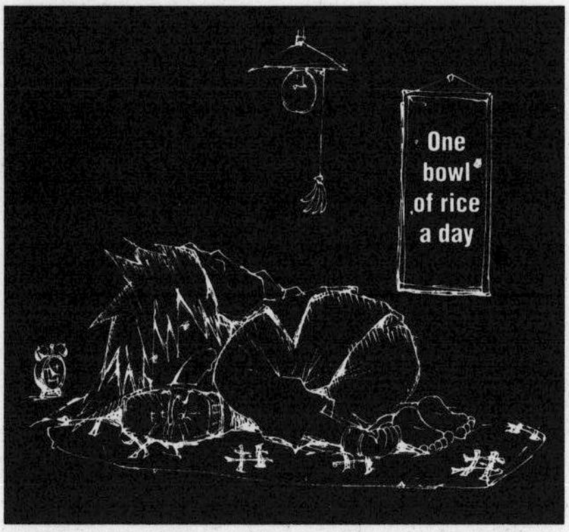
One bowl of rice a day

The original phrase, *Ichinichi Ichizen*, literally translates into "One good deed a day." Here, however, the fourth *kanji* is replaced by another, visually similar character, turning the phrase into "One bowl of rice a day." In addition, a character meaning "rice bowl dish" appears all over Issa's sleeping cushion.

VIUS helmets, page 63

The *samurai*-style helmets worn by the VIUS display a character meaning "victory."

Yama/Eight Mâras [八魔], page 76

The eight enemies or destroyers of *bodhisattvas* in Buddhism, representing the obstacles to achieving nirvana. They are: death, uncontrolled emotions, conditioned existence or incorrect view of self, being stuck in the bliss of meditation, impermanence, joylessness, impersonality, and impurity.

Leda of the Battlefield, page 121

Issa's nickname while with the Dracules, the term means "Ogre Child." Abbreviated, Leda also seems to imply a title granted to particularly ferocious Dracules.

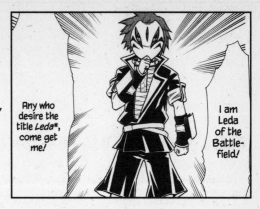

I am Leda of the Battle-field!
Any who desire the title *Leda**, come get me!

Donburi/Rice Bowl, Page 126

Along with ramen, one of Issa's favorite foods. Here, he is eating *tendon*, or a tempura rice bowl, which consists of deep-fried battered shrimp and vegetables laid out over a generous serving of rice, then drenched with the fish broth-based tempura sauce.

Sacred Blade, Shimon School, page 155

A school of martial arts founded by Leila's pre-VIUS mentor, Master Shimon. Practitioners flow so gracefully and effortlessly through complex moves that they appear to be sword-dancing.

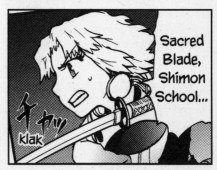

Sacred Blade, Shimon School...
Klak

PREVIEW OF VOLUME 4 OF *DRAGON EYE*

We're pleased to present you a preview from Volume 4.
Please check our website (www.delreymanga.com) to see when
this volume will be available in English. For now you'll have to
make do with Japanese!

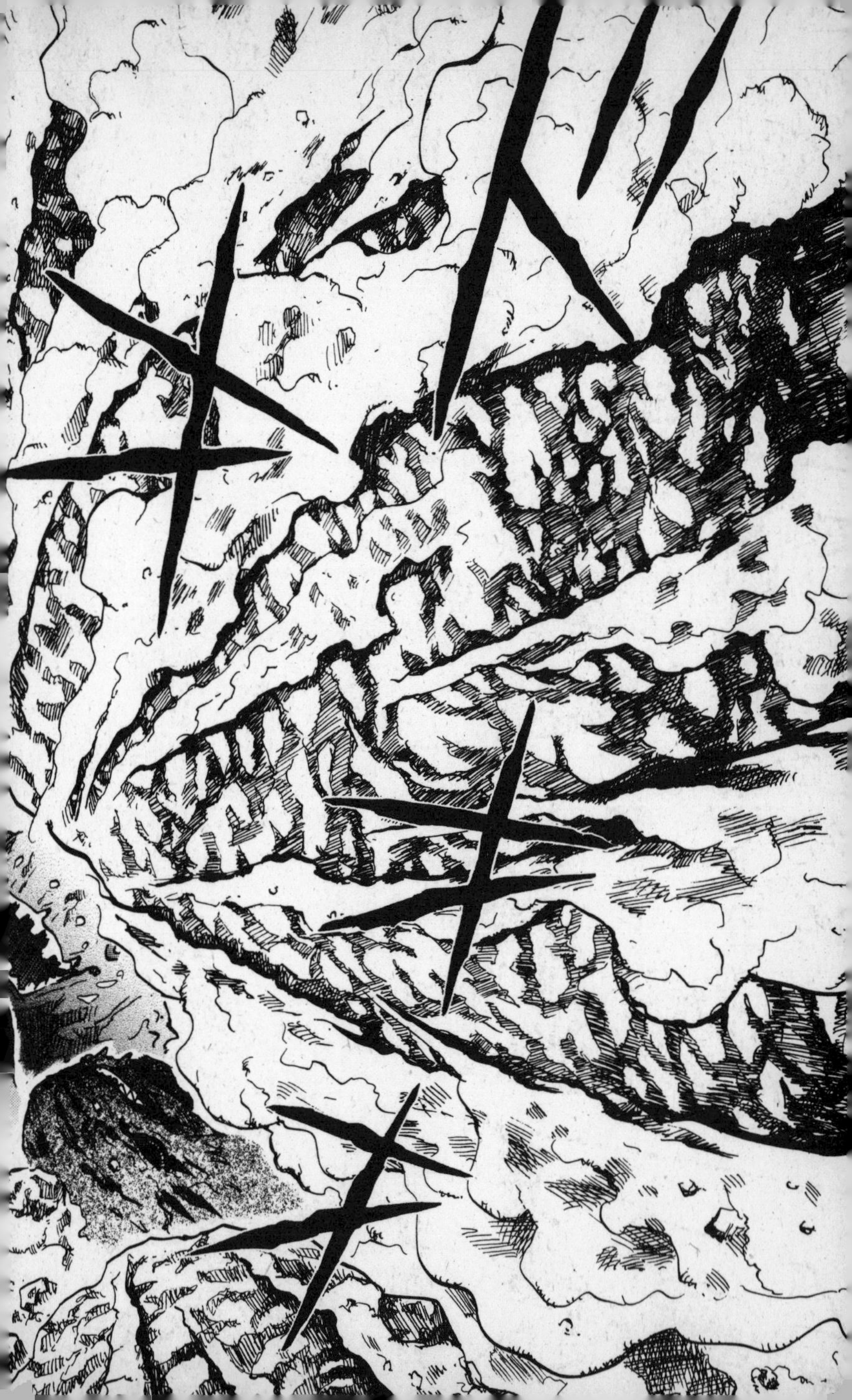

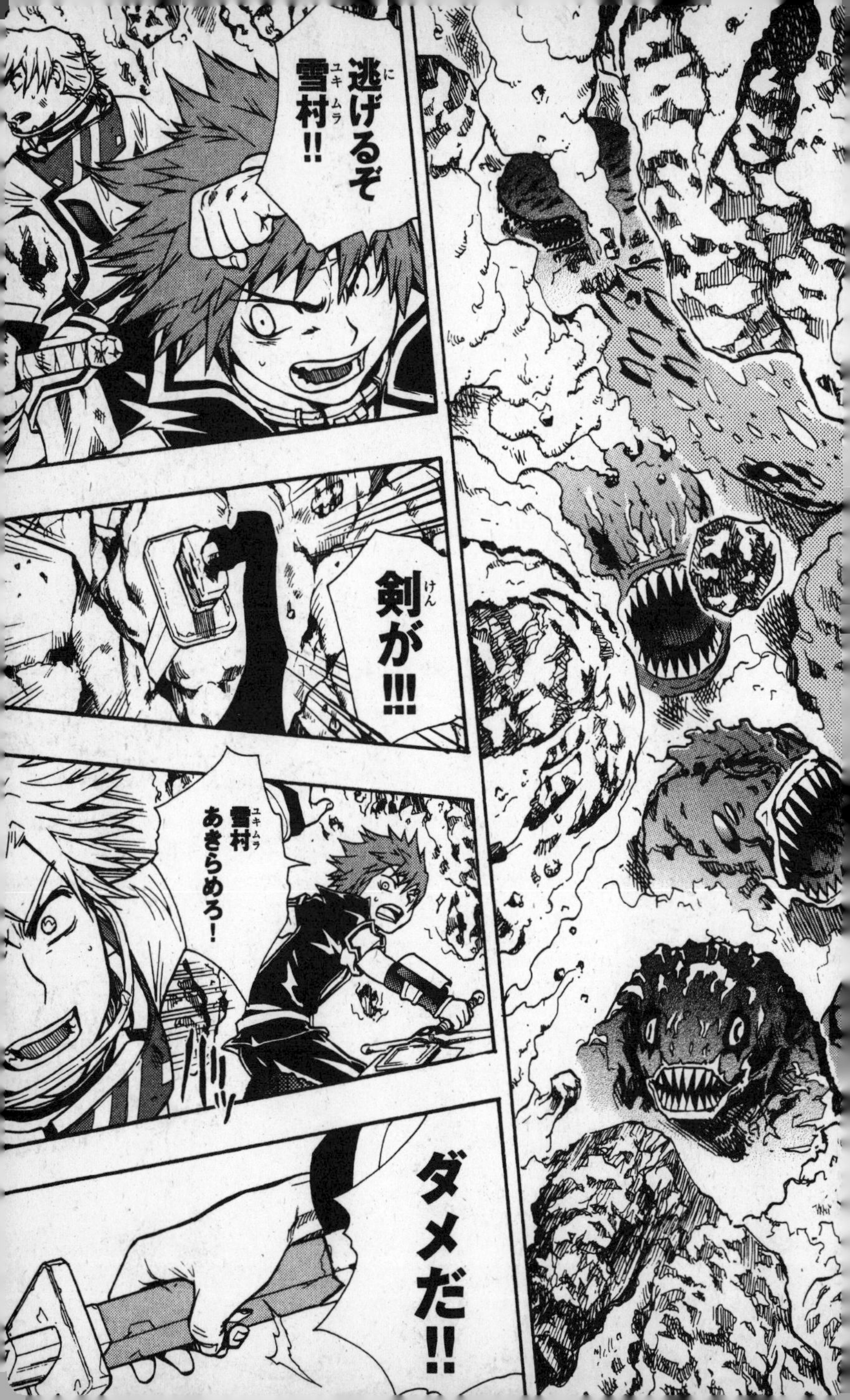
逃げるぞ雪村!!
剣が!!!
雪村あきらめろ!
ダメだ!!

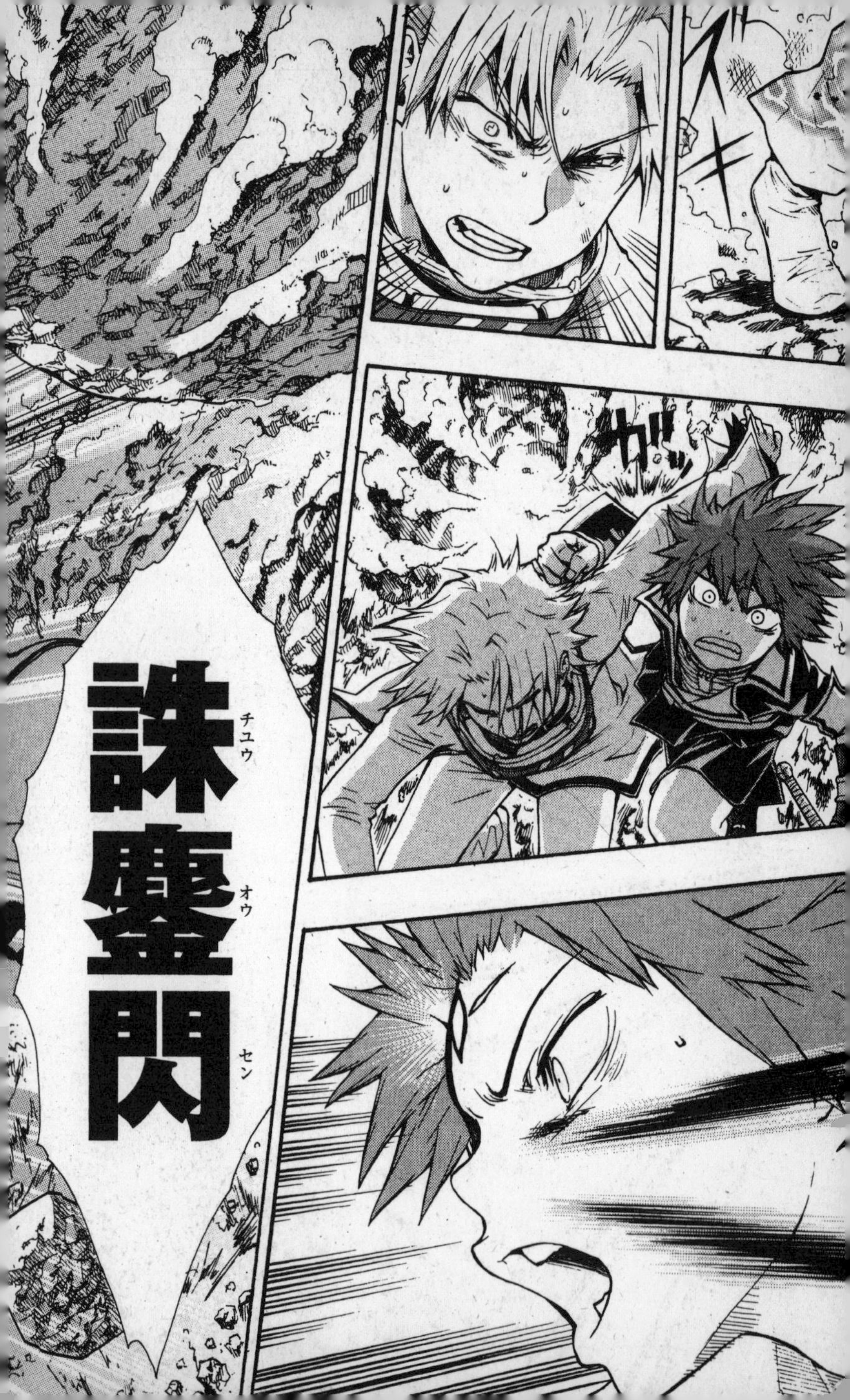

ガッ
誅鏖閃

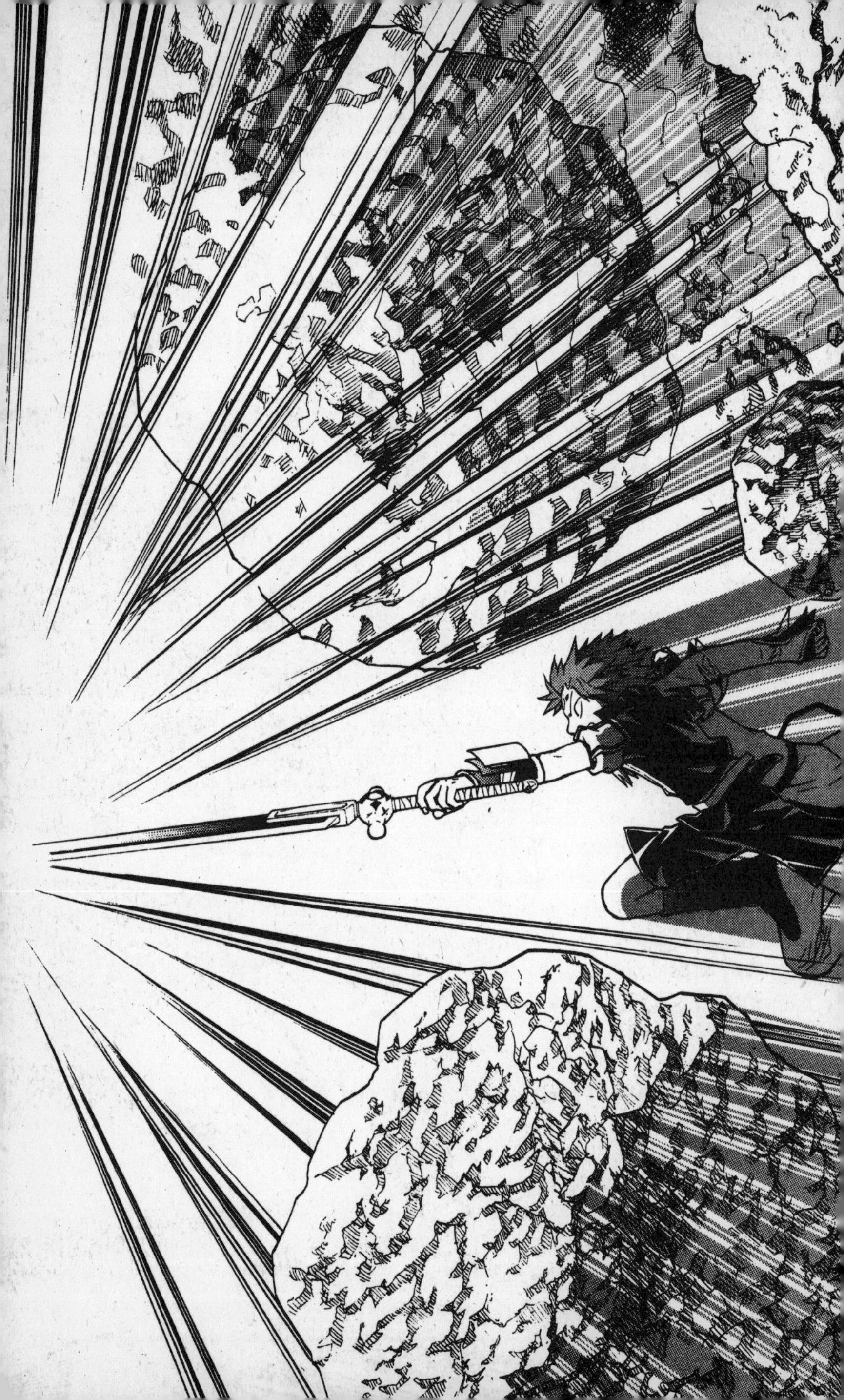

BY AKIRA SEGAMI

MISSION IMPOSSIBLE

The young ninja Kagetora has been given a great honor—to serve a renowned family of skilled martial artists. But on arrival, he's handed a challenging assignment: teach the heir to the dynasty, the charming but clumsy Yuki, the deft moves of self-defense and combat.

Yuki's inability to master the martial arts is not what makes this job so difficult for Kagetora. No, it is Yuki herself. Someday she will lead her family dojo, and for a ninja like Kagetora to fall in love with his master is a betrayal of his duty, the ultimate dishonor, and strictly forbidden. Can Kagetora help Yuki overcome her ungainly nature . . . or will he be overcome by his growing feelings?

Ages: 13+

Special extras in each volume! Read them all!

VISIT WWW.DELREYMANGA.COM TO:
- Read sample pages
- View release date calendars for upcoming volumes
- Sign up for Del Rey's free manga e-newsletter
- Find out the latest about new Del Rey Manga series

RESERVoir CHRoNiCLE

TSUBASA

BY CLAMP

Sakura is the princess of Clow. Syaoran is her childhood friend, and leader of the archaeological dig that cost him his father. Fans of Cardcaptor Sakura will recognize the names and the faces, but these aren't the people you know. This is an alternate reality where everything is familiar and strange at the same time.

Sakura has a mysterious power, a power that no one understands, a power that can change the world. On the day she goes to the dig to declare her love for Syaoran, a mysterious symbol is uncovered that will have vast repercussions for Sakura and Syaoran. It marks the beginning of a quest that will take Syaoran and his friends through worlds that will be familiar to any CLAMP fan, as our heroes encounter places and characters from X, Chobits, Magic Knight Rayearth, xxxHOLiC, and many more! But all that matters to Syaoran is his goal: saving Sakura.

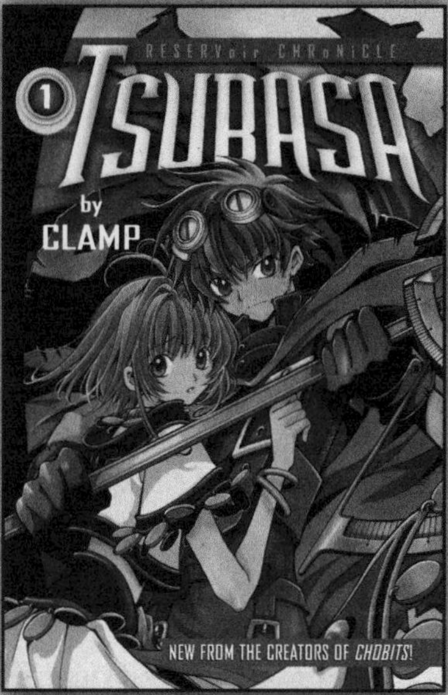
RESERVoir CHRoNiCLE
1
TSUBASA
by
CLAMP
NEW FROM THE CREATORS OF *CHOBITS*!

Ages: 13 +

Special extras in each volume! Read them all!

DEL REY

VISIT WWW.DELREYMANGA.COM TO:
- View release date calendars for upcoming volumes
- Sign up for Del Rey's free manga e-newsletter
- Find out the latest about new Del Rey Manga series

MICHIYO KIKUTA

BOY CRAZY

Junior high schooler Nina is ready to fall in love. She's looking for a boy who's cute and sweet—and strong enough to support her when the chips are down. But what happens when Nina's dream comes true . . . twice? One day, two cute boys literally fall from the sky. They're both wizards who've come to the Human World to take the Magic Exam. The boys' success on this test depends on protecting Nina from evil, so now Nina has a pair of cute magical boys chasing her everywhere! One of these wizards just might be the boy of her dreams . . . but which one?

Special extras in each volume! Read them all!

School Rumble

BY JIN KOBAYASHI

SUBTLETY IS FOR WIMPS!

She . . . is a second-year high school student with a single all-consuming question: Will the boy she likes ever really notice her?

He . . . is the school's most notorious juvenile delinquent, and he's suddenly come to a shocking realization: He's got a huge crush, and now he must tell her how he feels.

Life-changing obsessions, colossal foul-ups, grand schemes, deep-seated anxieties, and raging hormones—School Rumble portrays high school as it really is: over-the-top comedy!

Ages: 16 +

Special extras in each volume! Read them all!

VISIT WWW.DELREYMANGA.COM TO:
- Read sample pages
- View release date calendars for upcoming volumes
- Sign up for Del Rey's free manga e-newsletter
- Find out the latest about new Del Rey Manga series

TOMARE!

[STOP!]

You

way!

Manga is a completely different
type of reading experience.

To start at the beginning,
go to the end!

That's right! Authentic manga is read the traditional Japanese way—
from right to left. Exactly the opposite of how American books are
read. It's easy to follow: Just go to the other end of the book, and read
each page—and each panel—from right side to left side, starting at
the top right. Now you're experiencing manga as it was meant to be!